IN REMEMBRANCE OF THE SAINTS

TRANSLATIONS FROM THE ASIAN CLASSICS

TRANSLATIONS FROM THE ASIAN CLASSICS

IN REMEMBRANCE OF THE SAINTS

The Rise and Fall of an Inner Asian Sufi Dynasty

MUḤAMMAD ṢADIQ KASHGHARI

TRANSLATED BY DAVID BROPHY

Columbia University Press

New York

This publication was made possible in part by an award from the James P. Geiss and Margaret Y. Hsu Foundation.

Columbia University Press
Publishers Since 1893
New York   Chichester, West Sussex
cup.columbia.edu

Library of Congress Cataloging-in-Publication Data
Names: Kāshgharī, Muḥammad Ṣadiq, active 1780, author. |
Brophy, David John, translator.
Title: In remembrance of the saints : the rise and fall of an Inner Asian Sufi dynasty / Muḥammad Ṣadiq Kashghari ; Translated by David Brophy.
Other titles: Tazkira-yi ʻazīzān. English
Description: New York City : Columbia University Press, 2020. |
Series: Translations from the Asian classics |
Includes bibliographical references and index.
Identifiers: LCCN 2020028800 (print) | LCCN 2020028801 (ebook) |
ISBN 9780231198189 (hardback) | ISBN 9780231198196 (trade paperback) |
ISBN 9780231552523 (ebook)
Subjects: LCSH: Sufis—Xinjiang Uygur Zizhiqu (China)—Biography. |
Sufism—Xinjiang Uygur Zizhiqu (China)—History. | Naqshabandīyah—Asia, Central—History. | Xinjiang Uygur Zizhiqu (China)—History.
Classification: LCC BP189.7.N35 K4513 2020 (print) | LCC BP189.7.N35 (ebook) |
DDC 297.4/8—dc23
LC record available at https://lccn.loc.gov/2020028800
LC ebook record available at https://lccn.loc.gov/2020028801

Cover image: Section of a genealogical scroll of the
Naqshbandi Sufis of Xinjiang, circa 1800.
Cover design: Milenda Nan Ok Lee

CONTENTS

Acknowledgments *vii*

Introduction *ix*

In Remembrance of the Saints 1

Abbreviations *227*

Notes *229*

Bibliography *251*

Index *259*

ACKNOWLEDGMENTS

This translation is the product of a long, on-again off-again, engagement with Kashghari's work, and various friends and colleagues have helped along the way. I first began dabbling with *In Remembrance of the Saints* some fifteen years ago, when I was thinking about writing a dissertation on eighteenth-century Xinjiang. In the end, I set that topic aside, but this text remained with me. I was able to make a start on it thanks to the late Joseph Fletcher, who acquired copies of various manuscripts from European libraries for the collection of Harvard's Widener Library. Bodleian MS Turk. d. 20, which I eventually took as my base text for this translation, was among them. Back then I had the great pleasure of reading sections with Wheeler Thackston, who took enough interest in it to convince me it was worth translating in full. Since then, his exemplary generosity has given me the encouragement and energy to continue the work.

Along the way I've been able to examine manuscripts of *In Remembrance of the Saints* in the Bodleian and British Libraries, the Institute of Oriental Manuscripts in Saint Petersburg, the Jarring Collection in Lund, the Toyo Bunko in Tokyo, and most recently, at the Al-Beruni Institute of Oriental Studies in Tashkent. I want to thank the staff of all these institutions for facilitating my visits and allowing me to make copies when necessary—the Bodleian in particular for providing figure 0.3. Writing as I am from Covid quarantine in Sydney, I must also make mention of the ongoing digitization projects at Lund, and the Staatsbibliothek in Berlin, which have made

Kashghari's work accessible to far-flung scholars such as myself. The great confinement of 2020 has made academics everywhere acutely aware of the value of such initiatives, and we pray they continue to receive the support they need.

After a long hiatus, I was able to return to this translation and complete it with the generous support of the Australian Research Council's *Discovery Early Career Researcher Award* for my project "Empire and Religion in Early Modern Inner Asia" (DE170100330). I want to thank Christine Dunbar at Columbia University Press who gave enthusiastic support to the book, and her colleagues who contributed to its editing and production. For sharing sources, offering improvements to the translation, and responding to various historical and linguistic inquiries, I'd like to thank Eric Schluessel, Onuma Takahiro, Christopher Atwood, Morimoto Kazuo, Dan Sheffield, Rian Thum, and Najam Haider. Ying Qian has provided love and companionship throughout.

Sadly, this translation is being published at a time when the study of works such as Kashghari's is all but impossible inside China. Many Uyghur philologists, translators, and scholars of religion have vanished into Xinjiang's internment camps, and for all we know, some of them may well be languishing in prison. Of course, I'll be glad if this book contributes in some small way to raising the profile of the culture and language of the Uyghurs, though I don't pretend that this will do anything to change the dire situation they currently face. It's been a long time since I've felt it was safe to communicate with colleagues and friends in Xinjiang, but I'd like to acknowledge and pay my respects to the Uyghur language teachers who first set me on this path during my studies at Xinjiang University in 2002–2003. I can only hope that we can meet again one day in better times.

INTRODUCTION

In the middle of the eighteenth century, the Qianlong emperor of the Qing dynasty seized on an opportunity to do something that had long eluded his predecessors: eliminate the Manchu empire's chief rival for control of Inner Asia, the Junghar Mongols. It was, in his view, the crowning achievement of his long reign, the highlight of a sustained period of imperial expansion that contemporaries saw as a flourishing age comparable to the height of the Han and Tang dynasties. In carrying out this campaign, the Qing not only established its uncontested rule across the Mongolian steppe but also made its decisive entry into Islamic Inner Asia. While the Junghars had occupied a domain of pastoral nomadism to the north of the Tianshan Mountains (today's Jungharia), to the south of that mountain range the Tarim Basin was home to an oasis society of Turkic-speaking Muslims, centered politically on the trading centers of Kashgar and Yarkand. Because these lands and their inhabitants had previously been loose vassals of the Junghars, the Qing now claimed them as their own. From that time until the present, with only brief interruptions, the Tarim Basin has remained subject to Beijing's rule. Today it forms part of the Xinjiang Uyghur Autonomous Region, the vast northwestern territory of the People's Republic of China.[1]

Here Qing officials found a society in which families of "khojas," or Sufi shaykhs, not only were revered as religious figures but also held political authority. A century earlier, the reigning Chaghatayid dynasty, descended

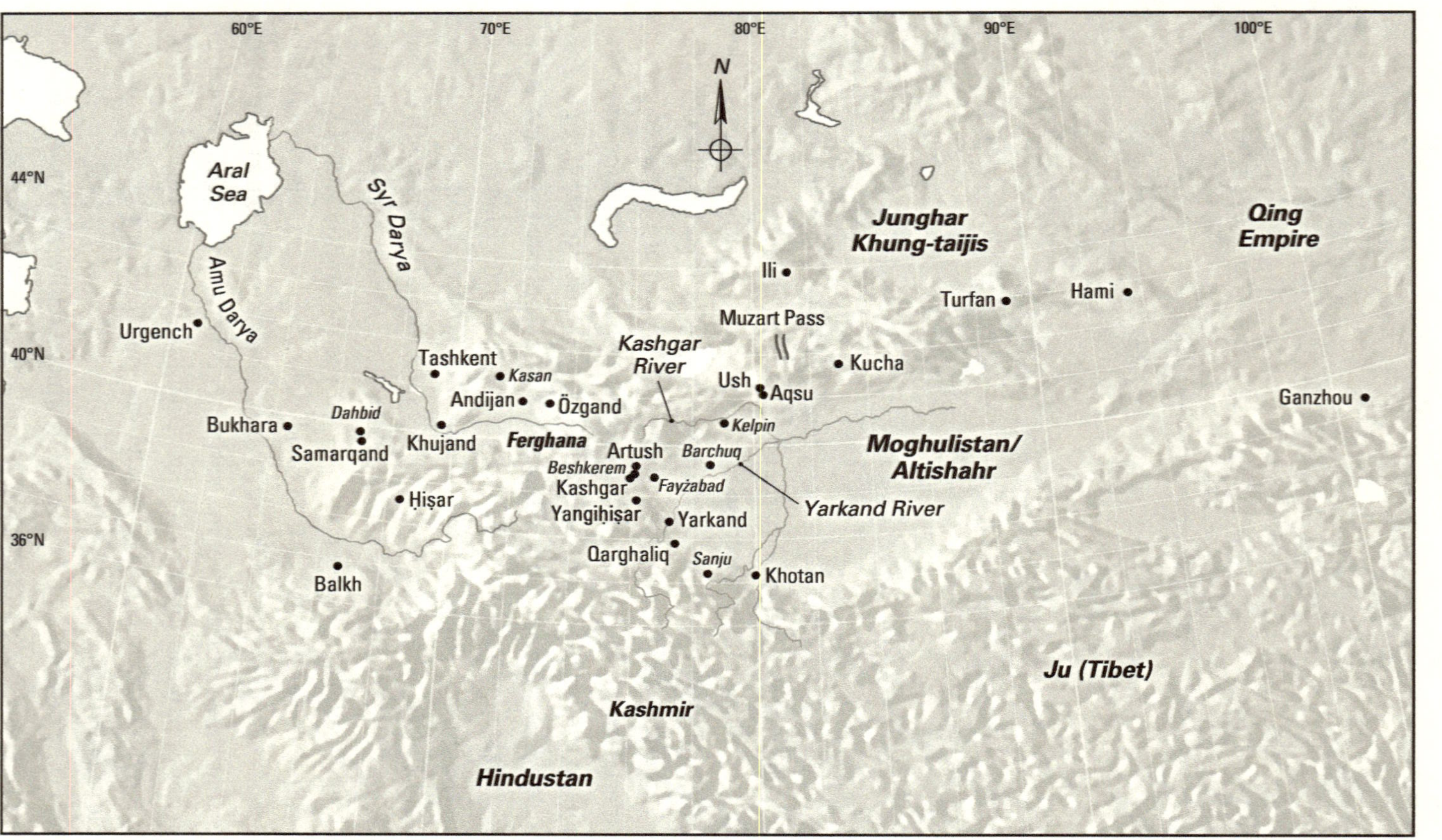

FIGURE 0.1 Map: China and Inner Asia in the eighteenth century.

from the line of Chinggis Khan, had gone into decline, and these khojas had emerged as the key intermediaries between the oasis communities of the Tarim Basin and the Junghars to the north. In their teachings, they were affiliated to the Naqshbandiyya, a Sufi brotherhood that took its name from Baha al-Din Naqshband, a fourteenth-century Bukharan saint. By bloodline, they belonged to the family of a holy man from Samarqand, Makhdum-i Aʿẓam, who died in 1542.[2] Because of this affiliation, they became known collectively as the Makhdumzadas, or "sons of the Makhdum." In the Tarim Basin, the status of the Makhdumzadas had been further embellished by the articulation of a claim to *sayyid* ancestry, a claim that rested on legends linking Makhdum-i Aʿẓam to the family of the Prophet Muḥammad via his son-in-law Ali. Their sanctity thus embodied both a chain of master-disciple transmission and an inherited saintly charisma. Put simply, they were a Sufi dynasty.

Since the late sixteenth century, two branches of the Makhdumzada family had vied among themselves, and with rival Sufi lineages, for influence in the Tarim Basin—first for the patronage of the Chaghatayid khans, then as power holders in their own right (see figure 0.2). The first of these was the line of Khoja Isḥaq Vali (d. 1599), who was born to a woman said to trace her descent from the Qarakhanid dynasty of the eleventh-century—a prestigious association in the Tarim Basin. In the seventeenth century, this family was joined by a rival line of Makhdumzadas from Bukhara, in the form of Khoja Muḥammad Yusuf and his son Hidayatullah, a figure better known as Khoja Afaq (d. 1694). The first of the two parties became known as the Isḥaqiyya, the second as the Afaqiyya. In Sufi fashion, they drew disciples to themselves and installed loyal deputies across the oasis archipelago. They became rich from pious endowments (*waqf*) dedicated to the support of their familial shrines: the Isḥaqiyya's in Yarkand and the Afaqiyya's in Kashgar. They built up large followings, drawn from all sections of local society and extending far beyond their immediate circles of Sufi initiates (sources describe them as *jamāʿa*, or "communities"). Combining this urban support with the military backing of nomadic groups like the Kirghiz or the Junghars, the khojas became formidable political actors, and a deep rivalry between the two lineages came to define local politics.[3]

Qing officials had little knowledge of all this when, in 1755, they met a pair of great-grandchildren of Khoja Afaq, who had grown up in Junghar captivity in the Ili Valley: Khoja Burhan al-Din and Khoja Jahan. Persuaded

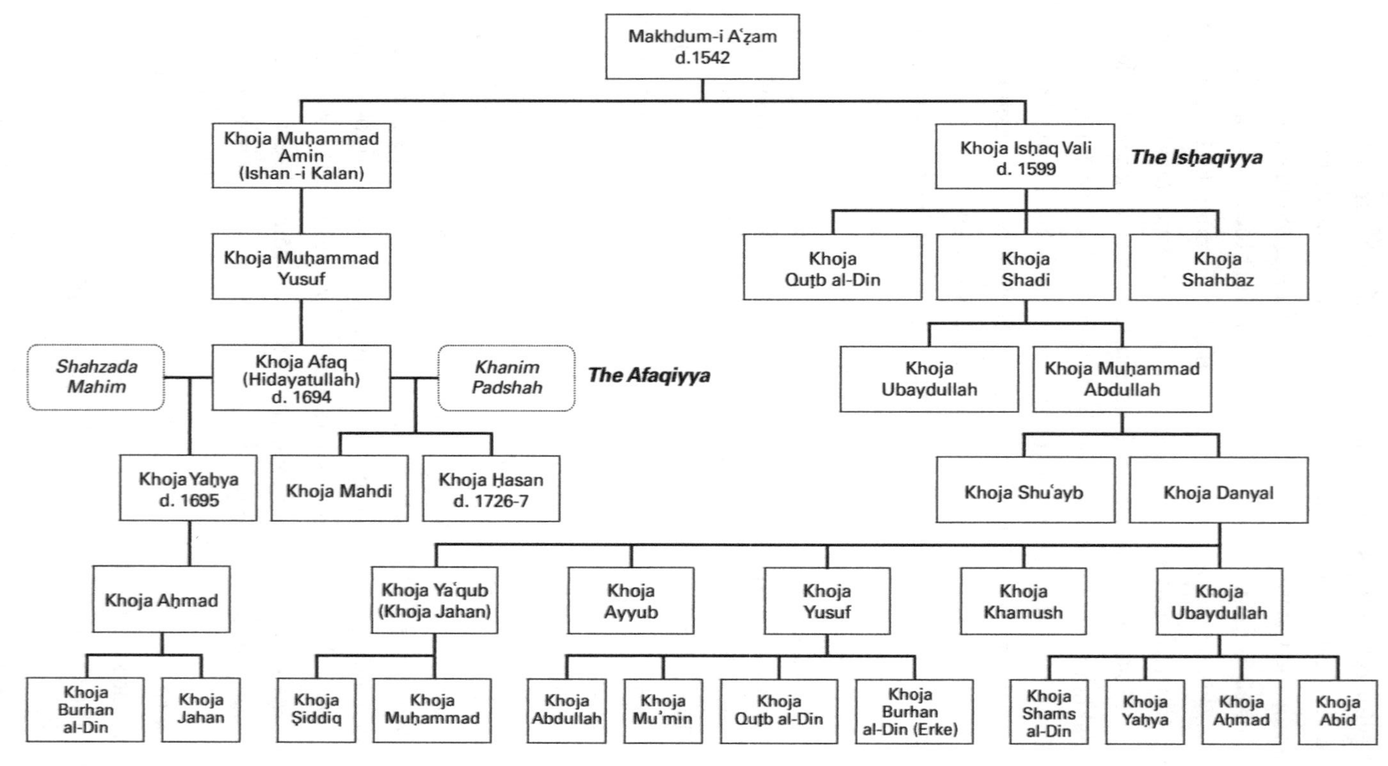

FIGURE 0.2 Family tree of the Makhdumzada Khojas.

that they would make reliable clients through which to rule the Tarim Basin, they dispatched them south with a Muslim and Mongolian army ten thousand strong. At the same time, in Kashgar and Yarkand, members of the Isḥaqiyya were taking advantage of the chaos in Jungharia to make a bid for independent rule themselves. The Qing expansion into what is now Xinjiang thus took the form of a showdown between rival Sufi factions. The Isḥaqiyya mobilized to repel their Qing-aligned cousins but failed, and were killed almost to a man. The Afaqiyya were victorious, but their victory was to be short-lived.

The Qing conquest of Jungharia was a stop-start affair that ultimately required four separate campaigns from 1755 to 1759. At key moments, putative allies among the Junghar Mongol aristocracy rebelled in last-ditch efforts to retain their independence—men like Amursana, who remains a folk hero in Western Mongolia to this day. Against this constantly shifting backdrop, the Afaqiyya khojas reigning in Kashgar and Yarkand likewise broke with their Qing patrons and tried to fortify themselves against reprisals from Beijing. In 1759, they fell victim to the fourth, final Qing invasion of the northwest and fled to Badakhshan, where they were captured and executed. When the dust had settled on the tumultuous half-decade, the cataclysm had wiped out both leading families of the Makhdumzada khojas.

As a consequence of this game of deadly musical chairs, in consolidating their rule in Xinjiang, Qing officials often relied on people whose loyalties lay with the first party to be deposed—the Isḥaqiyya—and who had sought revenge for their demise by siding with the final Qing invasion. These were members of prominent families of begs, aristocrats who descended from the tribal elite of the Chaghatayid period and who held high office in oasis administrations. In the 1780s, with the divisive events surrounding the transition to Qing rule still well within living memory, one of these begs commissioned a local scholar, Muḥammad Ṣadiq Kashghari, to write an account of the Makhdumzadas and their downfall in the local literary language, Chaghatay (classical Uyghur). Judging from the number of surviving manuscript copies, Kashghari's *In Remembrance of the Saints* was the most popular and widely circulating effort to retell this story. It ranks as the most important original Chaghatay composition to emerge from eighteenth-century Xinjiang, and deserves to be considered a late classic of Inner Asia's Turkic literary tradition.

In Remembrance of the Saints is a complex work with many themes. It is, in the first place, a saga of martyrdom and loss, and a sense of impending doom pervades the text. Kashghari expresses mourning for a fleeting, and highly idealized, episode of Islamic rule in the Tarim Basin, which some scholars have referred to as the "khoja period" of the early eighteenth century. Despite enjoying the imprimatur of a high-ranking beg who had sided with Qing rule, it is nevertheless a story that glorifies resistance to non-Muslim rule, the confrontation between believers and nonbelievers, and the virtues of holy war. For most of the narrative, the infidel enemy is the Junghars, or Qalmaqs as they were known to Muslims, but the incoming Qing dynasty also looms large toward its conclusion. Alongside the religious divide, the text also depicts a deep fault line between nomadic and sedentary society in the Tarim Basin. The non-Muslim Qalmaqs are far from the only enemy ravaging this oasis community. Kashghari's work evinces deep hostility toward the Kirghiz, who are depicted as false friends whose profession of Islam is only skin deep. *In Remembrance of the Saints* is thus a tale of woe that summons up an image of a Tarim Basin Muslim community embattled from all sides—an image that has resonated in the centuries since its composition. In one of the many verses in which the author airs his sorrows and regrets, he asks himself: "Say, Ṣadiq, is there any hope of salvation at a time like this? Facing the onslaught of the Chinese, Qalmaq, Kirghiz, and Kazakh." Since it was first written, Kashghari's *In Remembrance of the Saints* has held the interest of Uyghurs and outsiders alike, both for its literary quality, and as a reflection on the fate of Xinjiang within the Qing empire from a local, Islamic point of view.

SUFISM AND THE INNER ASIAN HAGIOGRAPHIC TRADITION

As its title informs us, *In Remembrance of the Saints* (*Taẕkira-i Azizan*) is a *taẕkira*, a word meaning "memorial" or "remembrance." In Kashghari's day, this was the standard term for a Sufi hagiography in the Tarim Basin. Sufism, an esoteric interpretation of the Islamic tradition, was elaborated and transmitted by miracle-working mystics considered especially close to God. Not only in life but also in death, these "friends of God" (*avliyāʾ*) were believed to act as intermediaries between ordinary believers and the divine. To commemorate these mystics and preserve examples of their wisdom and ethics, the first Arabic-language compilations of Sufi lives came to be written around 1100. The genre of Sufi hagiography soon became popular in Persophone Central Asia, reflecting both the spread of mystical practice there and Sufism's wider cultural resonance as part of courtly and literary culture. In the twelfth and thirteenth centuries, traditions of Sufi teaching differentiated themselves into more organized brotherhoods, literally "paths" (*ṭuruq*). Hagiographies of individual Sufi shaykhs and their immediate circle, drawing on anecdotes (*naql*) transmitted within the community of disciples, emerged alongside the traditional collective form. These maintained a focus on miracle working and the conversion of nonbelievers, but also presented vignettes of a saint's engagements with worldly authority and the wider community.

By the eighteenth century, the term *tazkira* therefore had a range of meanings in the Tarim Basin. Popular early works, such as Farid al-Din Aṭṭar's thirteenth-century *Tazkirat al-Awliya* or those of Timurid author Abd al-Raḥman Jami, were an established part of the literary landscape, both in their Persian originals and, from the eighteenth century onward, in Chaghatay translation. Sufi brotherhoods, along with local saintly families whose "path" organization was less formalized, wrote and transmitted *tazkira* texts describing the exploits of their founding figures, as well as their offspring and trainees. Alongside these, a third corpus of *tazkiras* were associated with specific local shrines and their occupants, many of them legendary warrior saints credited with the Islamization of the region. These include figures such as Satuq Bughra Khan of the Qarakhanid dynasty (whose shrine lies outside Artush) and the shrine of the martyred imams on the edge of the Khotan oasis. Some of these shrine-centered narratives originated in more literary, Persian works which were then vernacularized into Chaghatay, or rewritten in more epic-style verse form, to heighten their emotive impact and facilitate their use in shrine visitation.[4]

In Remembrance of the Saints was one of the last original *tazkiras* to be written in Xinjiang and can be thought of as a late evolution of the genre. In its first half, it conforms to the template of Sufi hagiography as an explication of familial charisma. The *ʿazīzān* ("dear ones") of the title, which I have translated as "saints," refers to the dominant branch of the Naqshbandiyya, the lineage known as the Khojagan ("the khojas").[5] This sense is reflected in the title of a short recension of Kashghari's work, *In Remembrance of the*

Khojagan (*Tazkira-i Khojagan*), by which many manuscripts are known. More specifically, the term *ʿazīzān* refers to Khoja Isḥaq Vali and his line, who were the object of devotion of Kashghari's patron, Mirza Usman. In his dedication, Kashghari explains that Usman's family had been long-standing well-wishers of the Isḥaqiyya, and elsewhere we learn that they had intermarried with them. The text begins by devoting significant space to both Makhdum-i Aʿẓam and his son Isḥaq Vali, for which Kashghari draws on earlier Persian hagiographies. These anecdotes establish a key premise of his work: the role of the Isḥaqiyya as spiritual guides to the Chaghatayid dynasty. This pairing of spiritual and worldly authority is disrupted through the intervention of Khoja Afaq and the Junghars, which sets the scene for the rise of the chief hero of the work, Isḥaq Vali's heir Khoja Yaʿqub, or Khoja Jahan (also known by his pen name Arshi). Here again, alternative titles of the work are revealing, with at least three manuscripts designated as the *In Remembrance of (Khoja) Jahan* (*Tazkira-i Jahan* or *Tazkirat al-Jahan*). Kashghari describes Khoja Jahan's period of rule in the 1730s and 1740s in the most glowing terms and cites his poetry at key points. In one of the most important scenes of the entire work, Khoja Jahan is depicted reciting a lengthy poem that prophesies the terrible events to come—not only the downfall of his own family but also the eventual second Qing invasion, which wiped out his Afaqiyya enemies (see section 14). In this way, Khoja Jahan becomes the crux around which the entire work turns.

Throughout his work, Kashghari retains an essentially hagiographic view of events as the working out of of divine will, but there is a noticeable shift in style as his narrative turns to more recent history. Kashghari confirms the status of figures such as Khoja Jahan as the *quṭb*, or "pole," a position that signifies preeminence among all the world's saints at any given time, and which is demonstrated here on the basis of dream visions. He is also at pains to validate the Isḥaqiyya's claim to the *sayyid* bloodline, and dedicates much of section 13 to this point. The khojas are able to intercede with God in the interests of the Muslim community, and they display an uncanny ability to predict the future. But Kashghari does not attribute to these more recent figures the same kind of miracle-working capacities that feature in accounts of Makhdum-i Aʿẓam and Isḥaq Vali. At the end of the work, the khojas have no magic with which to stave off the oncoming Qing invasion, and they can only instruct their disciples to resign themselves to fate and the inscrutable purpose of divine will (*tavakkul*).

Indeed, while Khoja Jahan's status as a holy man is never questioned, at times Kashghari gives voice to criticism of his fatalistic resignation in the face of the enemy. This subtle critique is a sign that Kashghari's work served purposes others than simply glorifying this saintly family. The second half of *In Remembrance of the Saints* is for the most part mundane in tone, shifting from the style of collective hagiography to a fast-moving account of political intrigues and military engagements. In these parts of the work, various beg families join the Isḥaqiyya khojas as the protagonists of the story, and the realities of elite politics come to the fore. Many of these sections of *In Remembrance of the Saints* are designated as either "stories" (*qiṣṣa*) or "sagas" (*dāstān*), calling to mind the epic genre and its interest in the rise and fall of dynasties. Likewise, the mixed style of prose and verse is more reminiscent of Islamic historiography than hagiography, with the author using his own poetic compositions to voice his feelings toward the events he describes. Although the narrative unfortunately lacks the precise dates we might expect from a chronicle, Kashghari tries to impart a sense of historical authenticity to his work by citing correspondence between the actors. While these letters are almost certainly the author's own invention, he was no doubt drawing to some extent on the firsthand testimony of participants in these events.

This blurring of generic boundaries reflects the unusual circumstances surrounding the composition of *In Remembrance of the Saints*, commissioned by a beg and written by an author whose own spiritual comittments are left vague. A standard *taẕkira* would usually conclude by continuing the chain of spiritual transmission down to the author's day. We know that there were in fact disciples of the Isḥaqiyya who carried on this tradition into the nineteenth century. Yet Kashghari only hints at this, in one of the concluding scenes, where he describes the escape from Yarkand of three sons of deputies (*khulafā*) of the Isḥaqiyya saints.[6] Althoughly deeply reverential toward the Isḥaqiyya bloodline, therefore, the stance of *In Remembrance of the Saints* toward any surviving Isḥaqiyya network is ambiguous at best. Kashghari's primary task was to commemorate the past and describe the downfall of this Sufi family. In his concluding *sāqīnāma* (a genre of long-form verse addressed to the *sāqī*, or cupbearer), he expresses his hope that those devoted to the Isḥaqiyya khojas will sustain their memory by reciting his work.[7] Reflecting this function as a recited text, many sections of the *In Remembrance of the Saints* are introduced by a formula such as "one must listen" (*ešitmäk keräk*). But Kashghari was clearly less interested in advertising the existence of this tradition's direct inheritors in the present. *In Remembrance of the Saints* is thus in many ways not a conventional *tazkira* at all.

Kashghari's strange silence on the survival of the Isḥaqiyya may reflect a hesitancy to advance his narrative into the more politically sensitive Qing period. It may also reflect his views on the nature of spiritual succession. *In Remembrance of the Saints* shows how well entrenched the principle of hereditary transmission of sainthood was in the Tarim Basin. Those who, in Kashghari's day, kept the Isḥaqiyya alive by reverting to a master-disciple form of shaykh succession may simply not have been deemed worthy of the same reverence. Yet there may be political factors at work here too. In Qing Xinjiang, the Sufi brotherhoods were stripped of the political authority they had previously enjoyed and a new regime put in place that consciously excluded the Makhdumzada *sayyid* families and officially denied a political role to the region's Islamic scholars (the *akhunds*). The begs of Qing Xinjiang were among the chief beneficiaries of policies such as these, which singled them out as the exclusive local intermediaries of Qing rule. As much as people like Kashghari's patrons may have wished to advertise their piety toward the departed khojas, therefore, they probably would have had little interest in promoting a rival, spiritual source of authority alongside their own. If this interpretation is correct, then we see that Kashghari's work, for all its value as a source for the events it describes, may equally provide insights into the political climate of Qing Xinjiang in which it was written.

KASHGHARI AND HIS PATRONS

Muḥammad Ṣadiq Kashghari served the first and second generations of the Qing dynasty's newly created Muslim elite, who held hereditary aristocratic titles while governing oasis cities such as Kashgar and Yarkand. He was one of the most accomplished local literati of Qing Xinjiang, but unfortunately little is known of his life. The only possible source to come to light so far is a *waqf* deed dating to 1252/1836, which registers the donation of a copy of

Jalal al-Din Rumi's classic Sufi work, the *Masnavi*, to a shrine in the village of Opal, south of Kashgar.[8] The benefactor here is one Mulla Ṣadiq, son of Shah Aʿla Akhund, who held the title of *aʿlam* (chief jurisprudent) and was serving as a judge (*qażi*) in Kashgar. The document also says that Mulla Ṣadiq had reached the ripe age of one hundred and four. If the document is authentic and "Mulla Ṣadiq" is indeed Muḥammad Ṣadiq Kashghari, as some believe, this would place his birth in the early 1730s.[9] Uyghur-language studies state that he received his education in Kashgar, and also taught in its madrasas. He was certainly a capable translator from Persian, and *In Remembrance of the Saints* shows his familiarity with the higher registers of the Chaghatay literary tradition—e.g., Timurid authors such as Alisher Navaʾi—as well as Indo-Persian poetry.

To the extent that a chronology can be established for Kashghari's literary output, *In Remembrance of the Saints* seems to have been his earliest work, although it was not as early as received wisdom would have it. The date of composition commonly given for *In Remembrance of the Saints* is 1182/1768–69, which occurs in some manuscripts of its short recension.[10] A second date of 1771 is given in a description of an Ürümchi manuscript that I have been unable to examine.[11] However, both of these dates conflict with an obvious fact about the work's origins. Kashghari wrote *In Remembrance of the Saints* at the behest of his patron Mirza Usman, who is described in the work's dedication as the governor (*ḥākim beg*) of Kashgar. Usman was not appointed to this position until 1778, and he died in 1788 while on visit to Beijing, placing the work somewhere within this ten-year-long tenure as governor. A second patron mentioned in the dedication is Usman's mother, Raḥima Aghacha, who died in the middle of 1784.[12] While Kashghari describes Usman's father Hadi as "the late," he speaks of Raḥima as if she is still alive, and we can therefore narrow down the approximate date of the text to the early 1780s. This dating is supported by certain parenthetic phrases occurring elsewhere—e.g., describing a certain Mirza Danyal as "father of the *current* deputy governor of Kashgar, Mirza Ḥaydar." I have been unable to ascertain when exactly Mirza Ḥaydar was appointed to this position, but he held it into the late 1780s.[13]

Apart from *In Remembrance of the Saints*, much of Kashghari's surviving oeuvre consists of translations. After his service with Usman, he found employment with a second prominent beg family. Kashghari wrote two works for Yunus Taji Beg, who was the grandson of Emin Khoja of Turfan, a leading figure in the Qing conquest of Xinjiang. The first of these was a translation of sections of Abu Jaʿfar al-Ṭabari's *History of the Prophets and Kings*, probably made from a Persian version of this Arabic-language classic. While the title of his translation, the *Tajnama*, can be read in Persian as the "Book of the Crown," it is in fact a pun on his patron Yunus's aristocratic rank of prince, or *tājī*, the local Turkic rendering of the Mongolian title *tayiǰi*.[14] Kashghari's second commission from Yunus was a translation of Mirza Ḥaydar's history of the Chaghatayids of Yarkand, the *Tarikh-i Rashidi*. Here too he refers to him by the title "prince."[15] This allows a rough dating of these texts, because Prince Yunus was promoted from *tayiǰi* to the higher rank of *junwang* in 1811. We can conclude, therefore, that these translations were finished prior to that date, most likely in the first decade of the nineteenth century. Kashghari may also be the author of a second translation from Ṭabari, this time commissioned by Us̱man's son Mirza Muḥammad Ḥasan, who governed Yarkand from 1811 to 1824. Although anonymous, the dedication of this translation copies language directly from the dedication of the *In Remembrance of the Saints*.[16] If this identification is correct, this would give us a picture of Kashgar's career spanning the 1780s until possibly as late as the 1820s.

Apart from these more or less datable works, Kashghari is also the author of the *Zubdat al-Masaʾil wa-l-Aqaʾid*, a handbook of religious precepts and law deriving from a range of Arabic and Persian sources, and a work of ethics entitled *Adab al-Ṣaliḥin*.[17] The two works were often copied and published as one, and both would prove popular. According to Mahmud Qutluqov, for example, in the early twentieth century the khan of Khiva had them copied and introduced as textbooks in madrasas within his domains.[18] Both works were also printed in lithograph editions, and an Istanbul lithograph of Kashghari's *Adab al-Ṣaliḥin* attracted the interest of the Russian colonial official Nil Sergeevich Lykoshin, who in 1900 published a Russian translation as a guide to the ethics of the Orient.[19] As Paolo Sartori discusses, some manuscripts (as well as the lithographs) of these works include the same preface as *In Remembrance of the Saints*, naming Us̱man as the patron, but this preface may not reflect the original inspiration for their composition. Kashghari is also credited with a verse account of the shrine of the Seven Sleepers in the oasis of Tuyuq outside Turfan. No attribution of authorship can be found in the published manuscript of this work, although both Yusupbek Mukhlisov and the editors of a modern Uyghur version name Kashghari as the author.[20] It is certainly possible that Kashghari wrote such a work: the family of Emin Khoja, who patronized him in the second half of his writing life, were originally from Turfan and associated themselves with the shrine of the Seven Sleepers.[21] Finally, Kashghari is identified as the author of an untitled work of supplications (*munājāt*).[22]

Hadi and his son Us̱man, who commissioned *In Remembrance of the Saints*, hailed from the oasis of Kucha, on the northwestern edge of the Tarim Basin. An early twentieth-century source tells us that the family claimed descent from Amir Khudaydad, one of the powerful mirzas of the Dughlat tribe of Mongols, who were granted the territory of Kashgar and the southern Tarim Basin by Chinggis Khan's second son, Chagadai.[23] The salience of this genealogy seems to have diminished by the Qing period and is not mentioned in Kashghari's dedication, although he still refers to his patrons by their hereditary title of mirza. They were living in Ili at the time of the initial Qing invasion in 1755 and immediately submitted. They then provided their advice and resources to the Qing military in Jungharia, before accompanying the 1759 expedition south into the Tarim Basin. They were, as mentioned, devotees of the Isḥaqiyya, and expressed its reverence for the line of Isḥaq Vali in various ways apart from *In Remembrance of the Saints*. A copy of two *waqf* documents, for example, dating to 1804 and issued by Us̱man's son Muḥammad Ḥasan, confirm the property of a *khanqah* (Sufi lodge) in Aqsu established by Isḥaq Vali. These serve as evidence of Us̱man's family's ongoing interest in the welfare of this Sufi community into the nineteenth century.[24] A second example of this association may be seen in one of the very few Qing-era additions to the Golden (Altunluq) Shrine in Yarkand: the tomb of Muḥammad Ḥasan (d. 1824), who was buried there alongside the Isḥaqiyya khojas.[25]

Despite the obvious Isḥaqiyya loyalties of *In Remembrance of the Saints*, the precise factional affiliation of the text has caused a degree of confusion among scholars. This arises from a second set of terms that describe the schism within the Tarim Basin Naqshbandiyya: a division into Black Mountain and White Mountain parties (or in Chinese, "Black Hat" and "White Hat"). On the assumption that Isḥaqiyya is synonymous with Black Mountain and Afaqiyya with White Mountain, most have identified Kashghari's work as a Black Mountain text. Yet at the same time, the text is mostly respectful toward the eponymous founder of the Afaqiyya, Khoja Afaq, and particularly so toward his son Khoja Ḥasan. This seeming contradiction can be dispelled once we recognize that the Black/White Mountain terminology arose only in the Qing period, and reflected a political divide that was consolidated in the 1750s. Importantly, the division was not simply into Isḥaqiyya versus Afaqiyya. As Kashghari describes it, the Isḥaqiyya were aided in their resistance by disciples of Khoja Afaq's son Ḥasan, who returned to Kashgar from exile in regions to the west. The civil war of the 1750s therefore pitted the Isḥaqiyya and one branch of the Afaqiyya against a rival branch of the Afaqiyya, led by the Junghar captive Khoja Burhan al-Din. The Black Mountain party refers to the first group, and came to incorporate other sections of the Naqshbandiyya who sided with the Qing invasion, while the term White Mountain should be reserved exclusively for Khoja Burhan al-Din and his sons, who resisted the Qing and remained a thorn in the dynasty's side well into the nineteenth century.

It is correct, therefore, to identify *In Remembrance of the Saints* as a Black Mountain text, as long as we recognize that this term represents a Qing-period reconfiguration of Sufi factional divisions, involving a partial mitigation of the earlier rivalry between the Isḥaqiyya and Afaqiyya. In this sense, we can see Kashghari's work as seeking not so much to inflame as to reconcile the contradictions of a period of severe inter-elite conflict. As a polemic, therefore, *In Remembrance of the Saints* directs its fire not against the Afaqiyya in its entirety, but exclusively toward the White Mountain Khoja Burhan al-Din, who led the initial Qing invasion of 1755 to dethrone the Isḥaqiyya. At the same time, it is notable that one version of the long recension, represented by a minority of texts, adopts a more hostile stance toward Khoja Afaq and the entire Afaqiyya, suggesting that not everyone was happy with Kashghari's handling of this issue. Khoja Afaq's status as either villain or hero remains a hotly debated point among Uyghurs to this day.[26]

For Kashghari, this was not simply a case of setting the historical record straight. White Mountain loyalties continued to run strong in parts of the Tarim Basin, particularly in Kashgar itself, and *In Remembrance of the Saints* was therefore a direct challenge to a rival, possibly more widely held, view that vindicated Khoja Burhan al-Din's actions.[27] In the work's final *sāqīnāma*, Kashghari directly attacks those in his community who were still loyal to the White Mountain family: "There are many in this time / Vulgar, heretical, and vile troublemakers / Who take law-breaking as their friend / And remain faithful to their sinful heroes."

Naturally, those begs who sided with the White Mountain khojas also play the role of villain in Kashghari's narrative. Some of these men in turn broke with Khoja Burhan al-Din before his rebellion against the Qing, and became influential Qing aristocrats in their own right. Chief among these was Khojasi Beg, whom Khoja Burhan al-Din appointed as governor of the Khotan oasis before the two fell out. Because of their questionable political history, both Khojasi and the Junghar appointed governor of Kashgar, Khosh Kifäk Beg, lived out their lives in luxurious captivity in the Qing capital of Beijing, while remaining in contact with Tarim Basin society. Tellingly, both men died in 1781, around the time that Kashghari must have set to work on *In Remembrance of the Saints*. We might speculate that their passing from the scene may have given Isḥaqiyya loyalists like Us̱man an opportunity to establish their own hegemonic narrative of the conflict of the 1750s. Khojasi is singled out here for particular opprobrium, depicted as the chief architect of Khoja Burhan al-Din's disastrous assault on Kashgar and Yarkand.

The decade of the 1780s was also the point at which the Afaqiyya rebel Khoja Burhan al-Din's sole surviving son, Khoja Sarimsaq, made his way back toward Xinjiang from a period of exile in Afghanistan and Transoxiana. From the neighboring regions of Shahrisabz and Ura Tepe, he sought to reestablish contact with the White Mountain network in the Tarim Basin. Therefore, while memory of who had been on which side during the confrontation of the late 1750s was starting to fade by this time, the question was beginning to take on renewed political significance. Particularly toward its conclusion, *In Remembrance of the Saints* displays a keen interest in determining who took which side, and Kashghari provides lists of begs and Sufis in attendance at the respective Isḥaqiyya and White Mountain courts.

These tensions sat at the center of a major political controversy that erupted during Us̱man's tenure as governor of Kashgar, when letters from Sarimsaq were discovered circulating in outlying regions of the oasis in 1784. The ensuing scandal exacerbated a second line of conflict in Kashgar society, between the sedentary oasis population and the Kirghiz nomads of Kashgar's surrounds. Among those exposed in the Sarimsaq scandal was Ḥakim Mirza of the Qipchaq tribe of Kirghiz, who was governor of

Tashmaliq, southwest of Kashgar. He is described in *In Remembrance of the Saints* as a key military ally of Khoja Burhan al-Din. Clearly, then, he did have compromising associations with the White Mountain faction. Yet in response to these accusations, Ḥakim fought back with a counterdenunciation of U̱sman, arguing that the governor was sheltering family members of close associates of the White Mountain khojas.[28] It was only thanks to the testimony of multiple colleagues that the Qianlong emperor was convinced that these accusations were false and U̱sman was able to survive. The incident demonstrates how the events and political alignments depicted in *In Remembrance of the Saints* were of much more than simply historical interest. The deep hostility that its author displays toward the Kirghiz, whom he holds responsible for much of the instability plaguing the Tarim Basin in the first half of the eighteenth century, may have also had something to do with the politics of Kashghari's day.

RECEPTION AND STUDY

Scholars have long recognized the value of *In Remembrance of the Saints* as a rare local source from the first decades of Qing rule in Xinjiang, and references to it feature in most accounts of the so-called khoja period and the region's incorporation into the Qing empire.[29] Manuscripts of the work, in both its long and short recensions, were collected by various visitors to Xinjiang in the nineteenth and early twentieth centuries and now form part of collections in Great Britain (the British and Bodleian libraries), Sweden (the Jarring collection in Lund), France (the Institute de France), Russia (the Institute of Oriental Manuscripts in Saint Petersburg), and Uzbekistan (the Al-Biruni Institute of Oriental Studies in Tashkent). Texts in Xinjiang are less well known, although an edition in modern Uyghur script, which was compiled on the basis of three manuscripts held at the Office of Ancient Texts in Ürümchi, was published in Kashgar in 1988.

In Remembrance of the Saints was first drawn on for its historical value in the middle of the nineteenth century by a Russian agent in Kashgar, Chokan Valikhanov, who summarised its account of the rivalry between the Afaqiyya and Isḥaqiyya branches of the Nashbandiyya for his historical description of the Tarim Basin.[30] Following Valikhanov, Sir Douglas Forsyth's diplomatic mission to Kashgar in the 1870s acquired more than one copy of the work, and Henry Bellew incorporated some of its information into a "History of Kashgar" that he contributed to the mission's report in 1875.[31] The following year, a precis was published in the Indian newspaper *The Pioneer*, under the title "Fall of the Mussulman Dominion in Kashgharia."[32] At the time, the independent emirate of Yaʿqub Beg had wrested control of the Tarim Basin from the Qing. For British Indian officials who were speculating as to future of the region, *In Remembrance of the Saints* was of interest for its depiction of the social conditions that preceded the first Qing conquest of the region. Because the level of intercommunal Sufi rivalry had diminished, the anonymous author of *The Pioneer*'s precis predicted that a Qing reconquest of Xinjiang was unlikely. On this score, he was soon to be proven wrong.

One of the members of the Forsyth mission, Robert Shaw, left behind his own brief summary of the short recension at his death, and also prepared a draft edition of the original Arabic-script text, for which he relied primarily on a manuscript now kept in the British Library (Or. 5338). In 1897 the British Indian official Ney Elias edited and published Shaw's translation, adding his own introduction. Although highly abbreviated, Shaw's English version remains to this day one of the most widely cited forms of Kashghari's work.[33] A Chinese translation of Shaw's work was published in 1980 and has recently become publicly available in a reprint series.[34]

In 1905, the German Orientalist Martin Hartmann, recently returned from a trip to Xinjiang, published an abridged translation of the long recension of *In Remembrance of the Saints*, using as his base text one of two manuscripts that he acquired during his stay in Kashgar and eventually sold to the Staatsbibliothek in Berlin (Ms. or. fol. 3292).[35] Hartmann's work is a better guide to the text than Shaw's and includes valuable annotations, but it is not a full translation. He entirely excluded Kashghari's lengthy discourse on Sufi doctrine (section 13), excised all poetry, and abbreviated much of the prose narrative, particularly at points when the author puts speeches in the mouths of his protagonists or quotes from what purport to be original letters and decrees.

Scholars in the Soviet Union, while often dismissive of the value of hagiographic works, nevertheless made considerable use of *In Remembrance of the Saints*. Salakhetdinova's 1959 study focused on the work's value as a source for the history of the Kirghiz, and provided a Russian translation of sections of the work corresponding here to section 11 and parts of sections 17 and 19.[36] Others who took an interest in Kashghari's work included Maḥmud Qutluqov, who wrote the only monograph dedicated to the life and works of its author, and I. Saidullaev.[37] In 2006, Aitjan Nurmanova published a Kazakh version of the work, a rendering that varies between direct transcription and Kazakh translation, depending on how well Kashghari's Chaghatay prose fits the standards of modern Kazakh.[38] The work contains a valuable introduction reviewing scholarship on Muḥammad Ṣadiq Kashghari and his work, though the text itself contains minimal critical apparatus and provides no alternative readings from other manuscripts.

The most scholarly treatment of the text to date is Sawada Minoru's Japanese translation of the short recension of Kashghari's work (*In Remembrance of the Khojagan*), which was published in serial form from 2014 to 2018.[39] For his base text, Sawada relies on Saint Petersburg D126, a neatly written early twentieth-century manuscript, and he provides extensive references to alternative readings from a range of manuscripts of the same family of texts.

THE TEXT

As previously mentioned, the *In Remembrance of the Saints* survives in more than twenty known manuscript copies. Digital copies of the text are now available on the websites of the Staatsbibliothek (https://digital.staatsbibliothek-berlin.de/) and Jarring collections (http://www.alvin-portal.org/). Nurmanova's translation contains a facsimile of the Saint Petersburg manuscript D191, while a Chinese publication series includes a copy of unknown provenance.[40] Meanwhile, manuscripts of the work continue to circulate in private hands in China.[41] Unfortunately, in the repressive political climate of contemporary Xinjiang, it is dangerous for Uyghurs to acknowledge ownership of such texts, rendering them effectively off limits to scholars.

Scholars have long been aware of the division among versions of Kashghari's work into long and short recensions, one entitled *In Remembrance of the Saints*, the other *In Remembrance of the Khojagan*. Through an analysis of variant accounts of the exile of Khoja Afaq (section 8), Sawada Minoru has extended this binary classification into a tripartite one, identifying two different families of texts within the long recension. We therefore have three groups of texts: Group A, accounting for the majority of the manuscripts of the long recension; Group B, corresponding to the *Khojagan* family of manuscripts; and Group C, representing a variant text of the long recension.

It is not possible to describe with any confidence the course of editing that led to such variation among the texts in a relatively short span of time. Nor can we be sure whether it was Kashghari or someone else who was responsible for the reediting of his work. Nevertheless, a comparison of the texts has led me to conclude that the Group A text most probably represents the earliest version of the work, and it is this text I have decided to translate. The Group B text in some locations improves on the level of historical detail found in the long *In Remembrance of the Saints*, including, for example, a better description of the Junghar civil war. (I have made note of these additions in annotations to my translation.) It strikes me that these details probably represent additions to the original composition. Apart from this distinction, Group B omits much of the doctrinal discussion contained in *In Remembrance of the Saints* (section 13), as well as its hagiographic account of Khoja Jahan (section 14). It also excises a lot of the poetry, including two of the *sāqināmas*.

This chief difference between Group A and Group C lies in their treatment of the Isḥaqiyya-Afaqiyya rivalry. As Sawada has discussed, Group C's account of Khoja Afaq is briefer and slightly more polemical than Group A's. Consistent with his findings, we can also note that in introducing Isḥaq Vali (section 5), Group C texts state that Isḥaq Vali received his license to instruct in the Sufi path (*ruḫṣat-i iršād*) directly from his father, Makhdum-i Aʿẓam, whereas Group A conforms to the orthodox narrative of transmission via Mawlana Luṭfullah Chusti. On this basis, I would hypothesize that the Group C text is the work of an editor interested in heightening the pro-Isḥaqiyya slant of Kashghari's original text, most likely someone other than Kashghari himself. Consistent with this, Group C texts tend to show more vitriol in denouncing the various begs who sided with the White Mountain branch of the Afaqiyya against the Isḥaqi khojas.

The base manuscript for this translation is Bodleian Library MS Turk. d. 20.[42] For the sake of comparison, from Group A I have also made use of Bodleian Library MS Ind. Inst. Turk 10, IVR D191, and IVAN RUz 45 (which carries the alternative title *Durr al-Maẓhar*).[43] From Group C I have consulted Bodleian Library MS Ind. Inst. Turk. 3 and Staatsbibliothek Ms. or. fol. 3292.[44]

Where appropriate, significant variations across the family of Group A texts, and between this group and Groups B and C, are indicated in the endnotes. The task of cross-referencing has been made easier by the existence of Sawada's translation of a Group B text (referred to as TKSawada) and Hartmann's of a Group C text (TAHartmann).

NOTE ON THE TRANSLATION

My translation adheres closely to Bodleian Library MS Turk. d. 20, for which folio references are provided. Kashghari subdivided his work into sections of various length, with most divisions announced with a formula beginning with a phrase such as "One must listen . . ." (*eshitmäk keräk*). These quasi-headings are not applied with consistency throughout the work, however, and scholars have cut the text into a varying number of sections. The division here into fifty sections is my own, therefore, as are the titles I give to them.

The multilingual nature of the text is reflected in the choice of font for the English translation. All Turkic (i.e., Chaghatay) text is represented in standard font. Persian is given in *italics*, while Arabic is in SMALL CAPITALS.

In my use of diacritics for personal names and book titles, I mostly follow the recommendations of the *International Journal of Middle East Studies*, but I have omitted initial *ʿayn*. For the spelling of Mongolian names and terminology, I rely on Christopher Atwood's *Encyclopedia of Mongolia and the Mongol Empire*. Translation of Quranic quotations follows *The Study Quran*, edited by Seyyed Hossein Nasr and colleagues, with chapter and verse references given in-text. I have relied on Reynold A. Nicholson's translation of Rumi's *Mas̲navi-i Maʿnavi* and Peter Avery's rendition of Ḥafiẓ's divan.[45]

IN REMEMBRANCE OF THE SAINTS

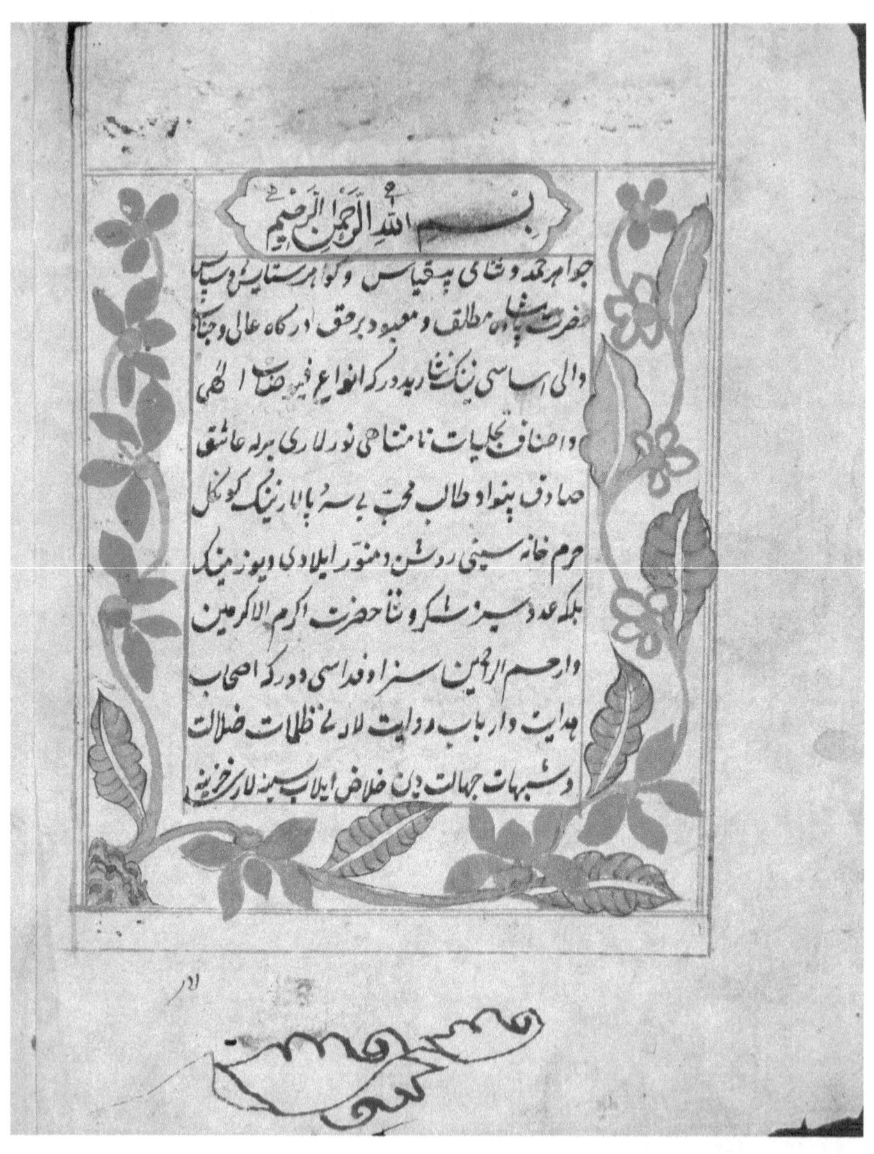
بسم الله الرحمن الرحیم
جواهر حمد و ثنای بی قیاس و گواهر ستایش و سپاس
حضرت پادشاه مطلق و معبود برحق درگاه عالی و جناب
والی اساسی نینک نثاری بیدورکه انواع فیض الهی
و اصناف تجلیات نامتناهی نورلاری بیرله عاشق
صادق بینوا و طالب محب بی سر و پالارینینک کونکل
حرم خانه سینی روشن و منور ایلادی و یوزینینک
بلکه عدد بی حد شکر و ثنا حضرت اکرم الاکرمین
و ارحم الراحمین سزاوار داسی دورکه اصحاب
هدایت و ارباب درایت لارنی ظلمات ضلالت
و شبهات جهالت دین خلاص ایلاب سینه لاری خزینه

FIGURE 0.3 The opening folio of Bodleian Library MS Turk. d. 20.

IN REMEMBRANCE OF THE SAINTS

1. PREFACE

/1b/ IN THE NAME OF GOD, THE MOST MERCIFUL AND MOST COMPASSIONATE

Jewels of praise and countless exultations, and gems of tribute and thanks to the supreme Lord are an appropriate offering to the lofty court of His authoritative majesty, He who by various graces and heavenly illuminations lit up and brightened the hearts of His forlorn and listless devotees and pupils. And a hundred thousand—indeed limitless—encomiums are due to the Most Merciful of the Merciful and the Most Compassionate of the Compassionate, who freed those who offer guidance and narrate traditions from the darkness of disorientation and the errors of ignorance, and decorated their breasts /2a/ with the light of faith and Islam. With the command of WHAT OF ONE WHOSE BREAST GOD HAS EXPANDED FOR SUBMISSION, SUCH THAT HE FOLLOWS A LIGHT FROM HIS LORD? [39:22], he bestowed high office on the ranks of the religious scholars and wise men, and distinguished them from the rest of humanity and all living things as THOSE WHO HAVE BEEN GIVEN KNOWLEDGE [58:11]. And also to a Generous one, who ennobled and gave high status to the theologian gnostics and those who divulge incomparable secrets, and made the diploma of WE HAVE INDEED HONORED THE CHILDREN OF ADAM [17:70] into a crown of honor for their heads. And to a King, whose heavenly mysteries elicited an admission of deficiency and incomprehension from the sharp wits and eloquent tongues of humanity's intellects. As it is said, TONGUES GREW TIRED IN DESCRIBING YOUR QUALITIES / AND MINDS WENT WEAK AT COMPREHENDING YOU. And to a Sublime one, whose eternal science confounds even an accomplished mind when approaching its boundaries; an Abiding one, whose everlasting grace the tongue of a rational human soul falls mute in describing; a Mighty one, within whose power it is to link the nine pavilions of the heavens without any columns and set them in motion through His full wisdom; and to a Creator, who has the capacity to bring the four mutually contradictory elements into harmony, and out of them fashion a template for the image of humankind. TRULY WE /2b/ CREATED MAN IN THE MOST BEAUTIFUL STATURE [95:4].

> Which of his acts of creation should I describe? Which of his capacities?
> I admit I am at a loss, I see no choice but to abridge my account.

> THE INABILITY TO COMPREHEND THE COMPREHENSION IS COMPREHENSION.[1]

Likewise, let there be gifts of praise and countless pious invocations to the Master of the Universe and the Pinnacle of Creation, i.e. Muḥammad Muṣṭafa, as an offering before his blessed shrine and as alms for his fragrant tomb. His bright rays of prophecy obliterated and annihilated the darkness of heresy with the light of guidance, and with a flash of his saintly glimmer he privileged certain men of insight, either by consensus of the community or by inheritance, gave them a share of his own rank and station, and ennobled them as intimates to the court of his inestimable essence. There are good grounds to call him the foremost of the saints and the paragon of the pious, and to recognize him as the seal on the registry of creation's secrets, and as the index to the drafts of prophecy. He is proof and witness to the truth of the hadith I WAS A PROPHET WHEN ADAM WAS BETWEEN WATER AND CLAY, and I AM THE MASTER OF THE HUMANITY is applicable in respect to his virtue and perfection. IF NOT FOR YOU, I WOULD NOT HAVE CREATED THE HEAVENS is a hadith that confirms his propensity for greatness, and the verse AND WE SENT THEE NOT, SAVE AS

A MERCY UNTO THE WORLDS [21:107] is evident proof of his noble being's capacity for mercy.

I am tarnished with sin, intercede for me, O Apostle of God,
I am alone and helpless, show me favor, O Apostle of God.
Bowing my head in shame, I am drowning in my sins,
Show mercy and take pity on me, O Apostle of God.

And finally, a hundred thousand gifts of greetings and blessings be upon his ennobled children and magnificent wives, as well as his honorable companions /3a/ and respected devotees, each one of whom is a star at the zenith of dominion and a celestial body in the constellation of grandeur, such that the hadith MY COMPANIONS ARE LIKE THE STARS. WHICHEVER OF THEM YOU FOLLOW YOU WILL BE LED ARIGHT is in their honor, and MY COMPANIONS ARE LIKE THE ARK OF NOAH, HE WHO CLINGS TO IT IS SAVED BUT HE WHO IS LEFT BEHIND IS DROWNED is also in reference to them. Happy is he, therefore, who emulates their humility and preserves himself from the penalties for deviation and ignorance, and thereby enters the ranks of the redeemed. And unlucky and miserable is he who exhibits opposition to that prince's companions and, in his skewed faith, commits distortions and errors. He will succumb to disgrace in this life and the next. GOD PRESERVE US FROM THIS!

2. DEDICATION

Now, before the pure gaze of the world's intellects and men of accomplishment, and the luminary comprehension of this age's learned and educated, the most meek and humble Muḥammad Ṣadiq Kashghari hereby submits that the amir of the amirs and patron of the people, sun in the sky of justice and pearl of the ocean of authority, the noble and high-born administrator of the state, his honor the plenipotentiary governor of Kashgar Mirza Us̱man Beg[2] (GOD GRANT PERPETUITY TO HIS KINGDOM AND HIS GLORY!), was the dearly beloved son of that radiant star of the sultanic sphere and shining gem in the caliphal crown, a man whose writ as governor ran throughout Yarkand, and who was greatly revered by the scholarly elite, /3b/ i.e. the late Mirza Hadi Beg (MAY GOD ILLUMINATE HIS TOMB WITH THE

LIGHTS OF PARADISE AND ABSOLUTION!).[3] Since this illustrious amir came to occupy the throne of the Kashgar sultanate, with the benefit of his justice and rectitude this province of Kashgar, which is a beautiful city in the clime of Moghulistan, and an awe-inspiring fortress among the provinces of Turkistan, and which is the residence of saints and the native land of versifiers and philosophers, has attained such prosperity that the wicked schemes of tyrants, traitors, and evildoers found the environs inhospitable, and they went to share the nest of the Anqa bird in the realm of nonexistence.[4] Scholars and wise men encouraged science and learning, and by promoting the Prophet's Holy Law and propagating the Islamic faith, they made this place an ornament of the world. The common folk received more than they asked for in their petitions for justice, and with their minds thus set at rest, they were constantly praying and giving thanks for such a glorious amir. The poor and oppressed praised his fairness and equity, and their hearts were filled with a desire to see his glory and honor increase. With chastisement and reckoning, he taught a lesson to those unjust brigands who cruelly misappropriate the property of the people, and by distinguishing the scholars and wise men from the ignorant, and differentiating the just and righteous from the miserly, he assigned everyone to an appropriate station. He did away with any remaining injustices and illicit innovations /4a/ that had accumulated down the ages and restored all rights to those who were due them. No claim was left unsatisfied, and no ruling was made outside of the shariʿa of Muḥammad. For this reason, therefore, it is incumbent on all to recite prayers of well-wishing for this just amir, and to give accounts of his virtues.

Lord, make his life everlasting in this world,
Raise him up and multiply his fame and fortune a hundredfold.
With the Huma Bird in the sky of honor shading him like a parasol,[5]
And a crown of justice on his head like Nushirvan.
Give him victory, and drive a crowd of calamities toward his enemy,
Any difficulties he meets with, solve them for him straightaway.
Grant him clarity of mind, a good nature, and an eloquent tongue,
Let the land of Turan submit to him, as well as Iran.
Thanks to him there was such peace and security among the people,
The world flourished with his grace and favor.
Those who laid the foundations of injustice fled in all directions,

Disgraced and destitute, they were lost in the desert of annihilation.
May his goal be realized, his dictate obeyed, and his life prosperous,
Say "answer my prayers!" O Ṣadiq, to the Merciful One.

This justice-professing amir also had a kind mother, Raḥima Aghacha,[6] who was a blooming rose of loyalty and generosity, host of the assembly of kindness, a beautiful bride behind the veil of chastity, and a wise administrator of the sanctuary of purity. She was as noble-minded as Aʾisha with the qualities of Maryam and Zulaykha, and in modesty and piety she was the exemplary woman of her age. Pure in nature and appearance, she would honor the bonds of kinship with all of her relatives and show them solicitude. She was also mindful of the scholars and men of learning throughout the kingdom. /4b/ She took pity on various groups of people who were left lonely and needy, including the sayyids, and exhibited much generosity toward them. From her blessed visage, a light shone forth which gave a hint of the sun of fortune, or the moonlight of honor. For some who were gifted with insight, it was obvious that Kashgar's prosperous state of affairs was due to her noble presence, and dependent on her supplications and entreaties. Recognizing the worth of both this perfect amir and his benevolent mother, they would accord them the utmost respect, and without displaying any immaturity or arrogance, they would kiss the ground before them like disciples.

It is said that the fathers and forefathers of this pair were loyal devotees of the sultan of truth-seekers and proof of the monotheists, the miracle-working Khoja Isḥaq Vali, along with his sons. During their youth and in the prime of their life, there lived such saintly men as Khoja Jahan, who was a key to the treasures of gnosis and a discloser of signs of divine favor, chief of the truth-seekers and pole of the gnostics, and heir to the Prophet and the apostles, as well as Khoja Yusuf, who was the king of the clime of sayyid-hood, sultan of the city of integrity, perfect and beyond compare in comprehension and wisdom, and a shining sun of intellect and insight. Oftentimes they would tell stories about the strange events and uncommon hardships that these saints had endured, and in recounting their tribulations, and recalling the blessings and mercies that they received from them, they would pronounce benedictions for their spirits and dedicate recitations from the Quran to them. All the time they would say: "If only someone had the initiative to pen an account of these saints, /5a/ and make a written record of the weighty events that befell them."

At this time, they were patronizing this meek and lowly servant and showing me favor well beyond my due. It occurred to my deficient mind that there might be some service I could offer them as recompense for one in a thousand of their favors toward me, but such was the extent of their magnanimity that it seemed impossible. Then suddenly one day they turned to this humble slave and declared: "If you could accomplish this task and create a memorial of these events, it would leave a lasting mark on the page of the world until Judgment Day. Those who follow us will say blessings for these saints, and will heed the lesson that this mortal realm never keeps faith with anyone: since it inflicted such cruelty on these heirs of the Prophet, they will ask, what might it do to someone else? Let this work also serve as an everlasting reminder of our name, so that we will remain the beneficiaries of well-wishing until the end of time." At this request, this talentless servant looked within and was unable to detect the requisite ability, but at the same time felt unable to refuse the commission. I had no choice but to cast divinations, look for signs and omens, seek assistance from the spirits of the saints and the Khojagan, and make a start. Binding the belt of submission tight around my waist and observing the injunction to OBEY GOD AND OBEY THE MESSENGER AND THOSE IN AUTHORITY AMONG YOU [4:59], I set out toward my goal.

It is my sincere wish that if I have made any errors in this *In Remembrance of the Saints*, either in the phrasing or in the sequence of the narrative, then, for ease of understanding, my virtuous and gifted readers /5b/ will take up the eraser of forgiveness, remove the error, and correct it with appropriate words, and that they will remember this poor man of limited capacity with their blessings. May these not go to waste in God's eyes! My hope is that the verse TRULY GOD NEGLECTS NOT THE REWARD OF THE VIRTUOUS [11:115] will prove to be applicable in my case, for GOD IS POSSESSED OF TREMENDOUS BOUNTY [2:105].

3. ON MAKHDUM-I AʿẒAM

Now, let it be known that wherever an anguished soul has emitted a sigh of divine love along the noble Path, then without doubt he was affiliated to a chain of transmission leading back through several intermediaries to His

Holiness Makhdum-i Aʿẓam. His rain of limitless mercy drenched every locale, and he spread his generous bounty everywhere.[7]

Makhdum-i Aʿẓam once said:

God's grace and favor toward my feeble young self was so evident that every day and every hour I had a sense of progressive awakening all by myself. No one had the capacity to compete with me—they would be bested straightaway. God's first blessing came once when my father had put me to work in the fields. In the evening I went to collect hay to feed the cows, but I was so exhausted I fell asleep on the haystack. When I eventually woke up, it occurred to me that if I spent my time doing farmwork while I was young I'd end up illiterate, and I became very worried. "If only I had a copy of the Quran," I sighed, "so that I could occasionally go to school and learn enough to know how to pray." Strengthening my resolve with this thought, I got up and noticed a Quran lying there. I picked it up, and it struck me that the children of the neighbors might have left it behind while they were playing. /6a/ I put it inside my shirt and drove the cows out to pasture. After this I thought to take the Quran to the schoolroom, that maybe its owner could be found. But when I went to the school and showed it to them, everyone said that there was no Quran like it in that classroom, and maybe even the entire district. It then became clear to me that this was a blessing from God Almighty. I busied myself with reading the Quran, and in a short while my learning greatly surpassed that of the other children. I memorized the *Haftyak* of the Quran and then went on to the study of grammar and syntax.[8] I attained sufficient mastery to debate all the higher-level subjects and rose to the top of the class.

There was a holy man by the name of Amir Sayyid Ali, who was the shaykh of a shrine and had the training of a mulla. I studied in his presence with a large group and performed him appropriate service. He in turn showed me considerable favor and said benedictions in my name. He would always say, "In a short time the world will be illuminated by your blessing." Following this he assigned me to work in the melon fields, and on his instructions, I planted melons along the roadside. When they ripened, I would put two melons and two cups of melon juice on the wall, and I would tell everyone who came along the road to drink the two cups of juice and take the two melons home. Every few days, Amir Sayyid Ali /6b/ would come past with all of his students, and I would offer them the best melons.

The venerable sayyid would pray for me and say, "God has created this blessed young man so that for generations to come, bold and noble individuals will come into existence."

I was in a state of complete listlessness and helplessness, when suddenly one night an ecstasy took hold of me and made me lose my senses.

> You've sent me witless by revealing your face,
> Congratulations, you've put on quite a show.

From that moment on, I was consumed with anxiety and distress. I had no stamina or composure. By night I would frequent the holy shrines and beat my anguished head against the tombs. I cried and wept but couldn't find any remedy for this affliction. Anyone who saw me would assume that I was mad. I told the venerable sayyid about the burning pain that had arisen within me and asked him what could be done. He told me that the remedy was patience.

> Be patient, for PATIENCE IS THE KEY TO HAPPINESS,
> With patience you'll reach your goal safe and sound.

This painful yearning rendered me so infirm that I would run in all directions in a distraught state. Then out of the blue I heard word that a holy man had arrived at a certain place. Upon learning of this, I immediately ran into his presence and explained my condition to him. "This pain of yours is the pain of seeking," he told me. "Such a pain can be remedied in the service of His Grace Mawlana Muḥammad Qażi, who was one of the favorite deputies of His Grace Khoja Naṣir al-Din Ubaydullah Aḥrar.[9] At the present time, /7a/ God's workshop is in his hands. He has recently ennobled Tashkent with his presence." On hearing this news, I felt within me a love and attraction toward that saint.

> *If there is a sudden attraction, then have no doubt,*
> *We will embrace it, for it is pulling you toward me.*

Following this I set off from Kasan into his service. On the night I spent at the Kendir Pass, a beautiful saint in a colorful outfit appeared to me in a dream.[10] He handed me a decorated musical instrument and told me to play, which I did. While I was still pondering this dream, I made my way to Tashkent and alighted in a dervish lodge. I set my books down, and since it was Friday I went out for the communal prayers. As I looked around the crowd, my eyes suddenly fell on the same handsome man whom I had seen in my dream. I recognized him as soon I saw him and obtained the honor of kissing his feet.

> Don't ever get up from bowing at this threshold, Arshi,
> Anyone who was ever in love made recourse to the court of the beloved.[11]

With motherly kindness, His Grace took me aside and comforted me, and led me by the hand to his residence. "What goal has brought you here?" he inquired.

I told him, "A pain arose in my heart, for which I couldn't find any cure."

His Grace said, "This pain is the coin of the realm in this life and the next. It's the medium of exchange in this mortal world and the afterlife." He also told me, "I'm a mulla, and I have a group who studies with me. You should join the class too."

"Master," I replied, "I don't have any capacity for classroom study."

His Grace insisted: "Whatever I say, the best thing to do is simply to accept."

"Well then," I said, "by God I accept."

He said kindly, "You should study the treatises of His Holiness Khoja Ubaydullah Aḥrar." So I set about reading these treatises.

I had taken three classes, when I felt myself flagging considerably. His Grace perceived my condition and summoned me to ask how I was getting along.

/7b/ "I find myself greatly distressed," I told him.

"Then you should stop reading these treatises," His Grace said, and so I did. From that point on, His Grace gave up his teaching. He explained to his students, "A high-flying falcon has arrived and wants to take me as his shaykh. Training him is my obligation; would you excuse me?"

Earlier, when Khoja Ubaydullah Aḥrar came back from attending on Mawlana Yaʿqub Charkhi, he built a cottage in which to converse with his close companions. In constructing it, he had laid every brick with a pure intention, and with praise and remembrance of God. His Grace Mawlana Muḥammad Qażi now took up residence in that same cottage, swept it clean, and set up a room for ablutions. He appointed my uncle Amir Nur al-Din as cook and put him in charge of the amenities. He intended for me to spend a forty-day retreat in his service, and he paid close attention to me. During the breaking of the fast, he would seat me by his side. With each morsel that I ate, he would say, "Stay conscious, don't eat in ignorance, otherwise you won't be up to the task." At every moment, he would remind me: "Whenever you bite something, say IN THE NAME OF GOD (*bismillah*), and while you're chewing it, say PRAISE BE TO GOD (*al-ḥamdu lillah*)." He was so solicitous, similar to the way that His Holiness Baha al-Din Naqshband is said to have taken care of Khoja Ala al-Din. /8a/ He would have him sit close by his side and never let him out of his sight. "If you're far away from me," he'd say, "I worry that your passions and desires will tear you apart." Because of this, Khoja Ala al-Din achieved great insights in a short space of time.

News reached Samarqand that Mawlana Muḥammadi Qażi had set himself up for a forty-day retreat, and some of His Grace's companions also joined us, including Mawlana Muḥammad Amin and Mawlana Muḥammad Qanuni. A lot of remarkable exchanges took place, and certain signs manifested themselves. Some of the Makhdumzadas are reported to have said that, according to the Path of the Khojagan, one should not hold forty-day retreats, but His Grace explained to me, "The Khojagan are like a composite manuscript, meaning that they combine the paths of all of God's friends with the Naqshbandi Path. At any given time, a path will emerge that is appropriate for that age and its people. Their noble path is not defined by any single path."

Makhdum-i Aʿẓam continues the story:

God Almighty had brought me to fortune, happiness, and correct guidance.[12] But these pious deeds that I was performing—were they things that the Khojagan considered appropriate or not? Would they be satisfied with them? As I was contemplating this, it struck me that I needed to visit the shrines of the Khojagan and do whatever it was that they instructed me. Thus, I headed toward Bukhara.

I had traveled as far the shrine of His Holiness Khoja Jahan [Abd al-Khaliq Ghijduvani], the guide to all humanity.[13] There I meditated on his victorious spirit, /8b/ and from his tomb I heard a voice say: "What you have wrought is the height of achievement in the Khojagan, congratulations!" After that, when I visited the various other shrines of the Khojagan, I heard the same thing. From that time on, whatever I did, it was with the grace of God and the assistance of the holy Khojagan. This was the reason for all the various signs and blessings that occurred, and will occur until Judgment Day, God willing.

Makhdum-i Aʿẓam also said:

The Path of the Holy Khojagan, which is the path of Abu Bakr (MAY GOD BE PLEASED WITH HIM!) was almost blocked and obstructed. God Almighty brought me into existence in order for this path to advance. Praise be to God that with divine grace such progress has been made!

His Grace Mawlana Muḥammad Qażi finished his forty-day retreat and departed for his main residence but left me behind.[14] I was distraught and set off in pursuit of him with tears in my eyes. Every evening, I would arrive at the exact place where His Grace had set off from in the morning, and everyone who saw me in this state took pity on me.

> Happy is he who takes hold of his lover's curls,
> Who calms his nerves and finds composure.

Following this, I set about building a hut in which to hold spiritual retreats. At this point in time, this weakling's spiritual sensitivity (*ḥāl*) was growing by the hour, and I was experiencing strange and astonishing states of being.[15] All the prophets and saints, and all the angels of heaven, manifested themselves before me in friendly guises. Each one of them kindly explained their path, /9a/ but I wasn't interested in any of them. This was primarily a test, and it became obvious to them that I was determined on my own path. They all became my tutors, and were immensely generous to me. I experienced incredible visions and ecstasies: Day and night, I was listless and would cry from infirmity, and sometimes the earth and sky would look as one to me. In my enervated state, I would jump onto the bed of my great teacher with my muddy feet and embrace him, and His Grace would take me aside and comfort me. When I came to my senses, I realized that I been brazen and taken privileges, and I would bow and humbly offer my apologies to him.

On one occasion, when His Grace Mawlana Muḥammad Qażi was traveling to Tashkent, we arrived in Kasan only to learn that my dear father was on his deathbed.[16] His strength of mind had unwittingly drawn me to him. Two days after this, he died. TRULY WE ARE GOD'S, AND UNTO HIM WE RETURN [2:156]. All the local notables came forward to recite prayers and bury him. Then his relatives assembled and busied themselves preparing a feast of pilaf. I told them, "You're wasting your time going to such trouble. Aḥmad the Moghul is coming on a raid with his tribe and will eat up the pilaf."[17] People mocked me for these words. They considered me a lunatic who had lost his mind and poured scorn on me. But at that time, my state of being was such that throughout all the eighteen thousand worlds, from top to bottom, no speck of dust or drop of water was hidden to me. I had insight into all the secrets. /9b/ At midmorning on the next day, they started cooking the pilaf, and sure enough, Aḥmad the Moghul came with a gang of Moghuls and raided the Muslims of the district and ate their food. The people all took themselves into the citadel.

The Moghuls then came and shot at me from all sides, but it had no effect—the arrows broke into shards as if they were striking stone. Witnessing this, the Moghuls were astonished. "He's a wizard," they said. But in the end, these oppressive skeptics won the day. They dragged me by my hands and threw me off a cliff. My back struck a stone platform at the bottom of the cliff and my bones shattered. In my plight, a group of Invisible Beings (*rijāl al-ghayb*) came and carried me to a nearby mill. They rolled me around on the millstone such that my broken bones came back into place. By way of advice and consolation, these Invisible Beings told me some comforting stories, explaining to me the trials that the prophets of old had gone through: "His Holiness Ibrahim was hanged and thrown into the fire," they told me. "They cut Zakariya with a saw, and they killed Jirjis several times and boiled him in a pot." Then they quizzed me: "Why did you reveal the secrets? To disclose God's secrets is a form of unbelief."

When this group disappeared from view, I felt famished. Something on the roof caught my eye, and I saw that there was a loaf of bread up there. I barely had enough strength, but with immense difficulty I climbed the wall, /10a/ took the bread, and ate it. I had never tasted such a delicious piece of bread.

My family and kinsmen had seen from a distance that I had been thrown off the cliff and were certain that I was dead. They decided to send people down to find my body once the enemies had gone, but as much as they searched, they couldn't find me. Then their eyes fell on the mill, and they found me there. "How amazing," they said, "that you could survive a fall from a cliff like that! What's even more astonishing is that when we came to the door of the mill, it sounded as if there was a large crowd here, but now there's no one but you!" When they were about to take me home, I told them to bring a large pot, set it down, and then stand back. They did as I said and then stood to one side. A group of Invisible Beings came and put me in the pot, and then my relatives carried me back to the house.

For some time after this, I was depressed. Whenever the Invisible Beings visited, I would be reassured, but when they left, the pain would return to my body, and I couldn't find peace of mind. Despite the fact that events such as these were occurring, some people still didn't repent of their skepticism and didn't have faith in my capacities, for God had put the cotton of ignorance into their eyes, ears, and heart, and there was no way to guide them. They were DEAF, DUMB, AND BLIND, SO THEY WILL NOT KNOW.[18] GOD PRESERVE US FROM THIS!

> Skeptics won't believe what the gnostics experience,
> The miracles of the saints won't convince unbelievers.

O forlorn dervish! One must recognize Makhdum-i Aʿẓam's greatness and nobility from the fact that the Invisible Beings /10b/ would come and serve him and solve any difficulty that His Holiness encountered. His close servants would even witness this with their own eyes. Sometimes when overcome by ecstasy, His Grace would call out: "Drunkards, where are you? Your spiritual guide and wine seller has come to town. He's flung open the doors to the tavern of divine unity and gnosis. Come, fill up the eyes of your ability on this wine of love, and become eternally drunk!"

Makhdum-i Aʿẓam, who was lord of Arabia and Persia, also said: "My illustrious master, His Holiness Mawlana Muḥammad Qażi, was once struck by an ailment of itchy limbs. He was so afflicted by the pain that one day he told a group of his companions: 'This assembly always goes on about love and the like, but no true devotee has come forth who would be sufficiently moved by my pain to ask God to cure me with a miracle. There's been no sign of this from any of my companions!' When they heard this, a great commotion broke out. 'What cowards,' I said. I sat down among the shoes and focused my concentration on His Holiness. I lifted the affliction from him and took it upon myself. The itchiness was immediately gone from his body, and he made a full recovery. My illustrious master raised his hands in supplication: 'O Lord and God of the two worlds! /11a/ Until Judgment Day, I hope this noble chain of transmission (*nisbat*) never leaves this one's offspring.'"

This request was approved in the court of the Lord, and this affiliation will remain with his family until the end of the world.

There is one other reason why this spiritual lineage will persist through the offspring of Makhdum-i Aʿẓam.[19] Makhdum-i Aʿẓam's ancestor Sayyid Kamal al-Din Majnun was once resident at the shrine of the Prophet in Medina. A sudden seizure took hold of him, and he was filled with a longing. The physicians for this pain were the friends of God, and he set out in search of them, making his way to the province of Ferghana. He rested for a while on the outskirts of the city of Özgand, which was the capital of the Ferghana region. At that time, the province was under the rule of Sulṭan Ilek Mażi, who was among the fully accomplished saints. He hailed from the line of Commander of the Faithful Abu Bakr Ṣiddiq and was one of the Seven Sultans.[20] Before Sayyid Kamal al-Din came to this region, it had been revealed to Sulṭan Ilek Mażi that at a certain time there would arrive in his province a sayyid to whom his daughter had already been betrothed in heaven. He would be identified by the fact that whenever he slept, an angel in the guise of a dragon would appear and give him shelter and protection.

The sultan was in eager anticipation of this, and when the appointed time came, he gave a command to one of his servants: "At such-and-such a place, someone has arrived who fits this description. Observe him respectfully from a distance, and when he wakes up and the dragon disappears, approach him and deliver my greetings. Tell him that the king of this city is summoning him." When this man came, he passed on the king's greetings as instructed.

His Grace Sayyid Kamal al-Din said, "I am a mendicant. I've left home roaming from door to door in search of God's people. I don't have the standing to go and present myself before the king."

The servant conveyed this response to the sultan, who said, /11b/ "Appeal to him again. If he permits it, I would like to visit him myself." The man came and made this request.

The sayyid indulged him and said, "I suppose there is no choice but to meet him. If the sultan wishes to keep the company of dervishes, then as the verse says, OBEY GOD AND OBEY THE MESSENGER AND THOSE IN AUTHORITY AMONG YOU [4:59]. It's best I go." So saying, he set out.

The sultan came out to greet him, and with great reverence, he brought His Grace to his quarters. "I have a daughter," he mentioned, "I'd like her to provide your ablution water."

The sayyid was taken aback. "I left my homeland for an entirely different purpose," he said. "I don't have the capacity for any kind of authority."

The sultan insisted. "In truth, it was disclosed to me in a vision that my daughter was promised to you in heaven." Ultimately, the sayyid had no choice but to comply with this request, and the sultan married his daughter to him in a royal wedding.

It became evident to the sayyid that the sultan had attained perfection, /12a/ so he spent some time in his company, and he too achieved perfection. Some time after this, he felt himself being drawn away, and he returned to Medina with his family. He lived out his life there, and eventually the hour of death approached. At that time, his wife was with child. The venerable sayyid spoke these last words to his family: "I have had a revelation that a son will be born to me, whom they will name Sayyid Burhan al-Din. He will achieve perfection and be the pole (*quṭb*) of the age, and from his line many perfect beings will come forth. The chain of spiritual transmission will not leave them until the dawn of Judgment Day."

After His Grace died, Sayyid Burhan al-Din was born. Sulṭan Ilek Mazi was still alive, and they brought Sayyid Burhan al-Din before him. The sultan lived a little while longer, eventually installing Sayyid Burhan al-Din on his throne and departing the mortal realm for the eternal world. For some time, Sayyid Burhan al-Din occupied the throne of the sultanate and strode the path of justice. Then suddenly a divine ecstasy seized him, and like Sulṭan Ibrahim, he abandoned his throne and crown and went into the service of Musliḥ al-Din Khujandi, who was the pole of that era, and tied the rope of devotion around his neck.[21]

Let us now contemplate the consummate abilities of Sulṭan Sayyid Burhan al-Din.[22] On the very first night, his shaykh was particularly attentive to him: "Lay out seven mattresses for Sulṭan Sayyid in my private quarters" /12b/ he instructed his attendant. When Sayyid Burhan al-Din retired for the night, he felt that the bed was too thick, so he took out three mattresses and slept on four. The curtain of heaven was raised as far as the fourth level, and he gazed on it all with his own eyes. The next morning, he went to attend on the shaykh, who said to him fondly, "My child, if you had done as I told you and not removed the mattresses, then last night you would have seen all seven levels of the heavens."

Sayyid Burhan al-Din spent a while in the service of Musliḥ al-Din Khujandi, perfecting his training. His shaykh would often bless him and tell him that his spiritual legacy would last until Judgment Day. After his shaykh died, he returned to the city of Özgand and guided the people there. He lived his life according to the principle of Muḥammadan poverty, although he had such a ferocity in him that if anyone was at all impolite, or expressed some objection, then the thread of their life would immediately break and they would be annihilated.

A certain holy man was once curious about this: "God's friends are supposed to be merciful and humble, but Sayyid Sulṭan behaves in this way. What could be the reason?"

This man went to see Sayyid Burhan al-Din, but before he could ask his question, he fainted and lost consciousness. Before his eyes there came a vision of a sharp double-edged sword, hanging by a rope from the ceiling of a room. /13a/ Flies were coming from all directions and flinging themselves at the sword, and being cut into two. When he regained consciousness, Sayyid Sulṭan asked him, "O holy man, was this the fault of the sword or of the flies?" The man was extremely embarrassed and expressed his apologies. This was the reason they called him Sayyid Burhan al-Din "the Sword" (*qïlïch*). Up until Makhdum-i Aʿẓam, most of his descendants were miracle-workers and ecstatics, and were the pole of the world.

Makhdum-i Aʿẓam Mawlana Khojagi Aḥmad Kasani (subsequently Dahbidi) was the pole of the poles and a guide to the peoples. He was the shaykh of the shaykhs, chief among THE FOREMOST SHALL BE THE FOREMOST, THEY ARE THE ONES BROUGHT NIGH [56:10–11] and the best of the friends of God (NO FEAR SHALL COME UPON THEM, NOR SHALL THEY GRIEVE [3:170]). He was a compendium of insights and truths, sultan of the saints, and a leader of all humankind. His perfect states of being were known from horizon to horizon, and the signs of his saintliness were familiar throughout the world. No other friend of God has ever achieved the advances that he made in the noble Path of the Khojagan. When every previous guide of the age reached the end, they assigned four deputies to act as guides on the Path, but Makhdum-i Aʿẓam left behind seventy-three deputies, each one of whom occupied the position of exemplary shaykh, guiding the people and explaining the Path. As Makhdum-i Aʿẓam once said of himself: "While some have sent off one or two men mounted on horseback, by God's grace I have dispatched seventy-three elephant riders, each one of whom has promoted the Path in some city or province, strewn the pearls of God's love into the hearts of His servants, /13b/ and guided them with the lights of sainthood along the road to salvation." From the two noble sanctuaries of Mecca and Medina to the frontiers of Cathay and China, the whole world has been illuminated by his sanctity, and his deputies have traveled widely among these cities.

O beloved, the ecstasy of your love gladdened the world,
The joy of your visage made the kingdom of the heart flourish.
Across the world, noble and common obtained your grace,
The people remembered your qualities till Judgment Day.

It is said that in the land of India there was a king by the name of Babur.[23] A monarch called Sulṭan Ibrahim once conceived a hostile conspiracy against him and mobilized a huge army.[24] Babur was a devotee of the Khojagan, and he made recourse to their beneficent spirits. That night, the pole of the poles, His Grace Khoja Ubaydullah Aḥrar, emerged from the invisible realm, and the king requested his assistance. Right then, Makhdum-i Aʿẓam manifested in physical form, and Khoja Aḥrar entrusted King Babur to him. "In all of these affairs, the assistance should come from you," he told him and vanished. The king woke up, and that same day a huge battle took place. Everyone saw with their own eyes Makhdum-i Aʿẓam emerge from the hidden realm with some of his companions and smite the army of the enemy. A great victory was won, and a horde of booty fell entirely into their hands. That day, Babur made offerings of gold ingots and weaponry and sent them to Samarqand through an eminent holy man called Darvish Muḥammad Quzi.

> You came to the rescue of king and pauper alike,
> And by you all difficulties were solved.
> Those who implored you in their hour of need,
> Their affairs found favor thanks to you.
> In an instant you traversed the face of the earth,
> You surveyed India and Iraq with a single look.
> You're a bird of Paradise, you have no fixed abode,
> Other than your nest in the tent of heaven.

With these lines of verse Babur expressed his spiritual devotion to Makhdum-i Aʿẓam:

> /14a/ Although I am not one of the common folk,
> I am devoted to the *ishan* in heart and soul.
> Don't think that kingship and dervishhood are far removed,
> I am king, because I serve the dervishes.

These two couplets were also among those he sent:

> I've wasted my wayward life with greedy airs,
> I'm ashamed at my conduct among the people of God.

Cast a glace in the direction of your forlorn devotee,
And I'll give up mastership to serve the master.[25]

Darvish Muḥammad Quzi arrived and explained the events and offered the king's pledge of allegiance. His Grace accepted it and set down an account of divine secrets and sublime truths in the form of a treatise, to which he gave the title *Baburiyya*, and presented it to him. This treatise is now included in his *Twenty-Four Risalas.*[26]

4. MAKHDUM-I AʿẒAM'S SON ISḤAQ VALI

Whether in Arabia or Persia, Iran, India, or Turan, let it be known that Makhdum-i Aʿẓam had four wives.[27] His first wife was the daughter of Mir Yusuf Sayyid, who was one of the sayyids of Kasan and an uncle of Makhdum-i Aʿẓam. He had four sons and two daughters from this wife. The first son was Khoja Muḥammad Amin, who was known as Ishan-i Kalan. Second was Khoja Dost, then Khoja Baha al-Din, and Khoja Abd al-Khaliq. Khoja Dost, who was a manifestation of divine grace, and Khoja Baha al-Din, the chief of the deputies, rose to positions of leadership and received permission to proselytize while in the service of their illustrious father, /14b/ but Khoja Abd al-Khaliq, the discloser of divine secrets, obtained authorization from his elder brother Ishan-i Kalan.[28]

Another of his wives was Bibi Malika Kasani, who was the daughter of the king of Kasan. With her he had two sons—Khoja Muḥammad and Khoja Sulṭan Ibrahim—and two daughters.

The wife whom they call Bibicha Kashghari belonged the family of His Holiness Sulṭan Satuq Bughra Khan Ghazi.[29] Khoja Isḥaq Vali, the pole of the firmament of miracle-working and center of the circle of sainthood, was born to this wife. When she was pregnant with him, every time she entered the house, Makhdum-i Aʿẓam would spring up and bow. "O wife," he would say, "this bow is not for you, but for your child, for he will shake the chain of the Holy Khojagan and bring about a great advance in their Path. The whole world will be illuminated by the sun of his saintliness. Islam will find strength and unbelief will be vanquished, and there will be perfect men among his offspring."

When Khoja Isḥaq Vali was born, he instructed her, "Be extremely vigilant in raising him, and give him a healthy upbringing. Don't show any negligence or allow any mistake to be made."

The following account comes from /15a/ Khoja Muḥammad Qasim, who was among Makhdum-i Aʿẓam's companions and confidants.[30] He relates:

"One day I was seated in the presence of His Holiness Makhdum-i Aʿẓam, and apart from me there was a large congregation. At that time Khoja Isḥaq Vali was ten years old and was sitting in my lap.

'Uncle,' he said, 'should I separate the shoes of those destined for heaven from the shoes of those destined for hell?'

'Khoja,' I said, 'this isn't the time for stories.'

Later, during a spiritual retreat, I mentioned this episode to Makhdum-i Aʿẓam. 'Give him a piece of bread from the market,' he said. They brought some bread from the market and gave it to him. Then Makhdum-i Aʿẓam instructed him, 'O child, now distinguish the shoes of those destined for heaven and hell.' Khoja Isḥaq Vali bowed his head in contemplation."[31]

Khoja Muḥammad Qasim continues: "Once when he was ten years old, Khoja Isḥaq Vali was still in my care, and I was in attendance on Makhdum-i Aʿẓam. The whole time Makhdum-i Aʿẓam was gazing at Khoja Isḥaq Vali's face and nodding his head. After a while, he looked in my direction and said, 'Khoja Muḥammad Qasim, don't be negligent with this dear child of mine, and don't make any mistake in serving him. God willing, he will conquer the world. The line of the Khojagan will achieve perfection during his lifetime, and it will sprout branches and leaves. Although this is the case with the rest of my children, it is particularly so with this child.' "

Khoja Muḥammad Qasim also says: /15b/ "Once Khoja Isḥaq Vali was sitting on my shoulder when Makhdum-i Aʿẓam emerged from his wives' quarters. With a joyous laugh he embraced Khoja Isḥaq Vali, and kissed his rosy cheeks. He heaped affection on him, then looked at me and said, 'Tonight I saw this child of mine in a dream. He was standing on top of a mountain as tall as the Milky Way in the sky, and was shouting out to the east and west, and a great crowd was responding from both directions. It's apparent now that at the sound of this child's voice, people from East and West will dedicate themselves to him.' "

The most virtuous and noble Akhund Mulla Saʿid, who was a highly accomplished scholar, tells the following story: "I had come to the presence of Khoja Isḥaq Vali to declare my submission, but he did not accept it. I insisted, but he said, 'Mulla, I'm no dervish, you must've mistaken me.' I told him, 'O grace, when I was in the service of Makhdum-i Aʿẓam, he once said to me, "Mulla Saʿid, my child Khoja Isḥaq Vali is a high-flying falcon, God's grace toward him is abundant, and I see strange and wonderful signs in him. The first of these was that on the night he was born, something as bright as the sun came and entered my room, and its light illuminated the world. At dawn, news came that God had miraculously given me a son. When I set eyes on this son, the same bright light shone forth. Since his birth, /16a/ thanks to his blessed coming, darkness and ill fortune have left my house. Whenever I see him, that sun shines in my heart and bestows its brightness." I also told him: 'One day when I was in the company of Makhdum-i Aʿẓam, someone brought a horse as a donation, and Makhdum-i Aʿẓam gave it to you. Ishan-i Kalan came and took it, saying "This horse is more appropriate for me." Makhdum-i Aʿẓam said with annoyance, "If my horse is for him, then the spiritual lineage will belong to you." I was present and witnessed this from Makhdum-i Aʿẓam myself, therefore I recognize you as a saint.' His Grace relented, and I entered into his service and pledged my allegiance to him."[32]

Ḥafiẓ Niẓam, who had committed the Quran to memory and was among His Grace's initiates and intimate companions, tells the following story:[33]

I was attending on the khoja in the village of Isfiduk one day, when he addressed his companions: "Prepare yourselves," he told us, "I've been taken with a desire to visit Balkh." Thus he set off for Balkh with his following.[34] The one and only Mulla Muḥammad Saḥaf, who was among the leading deputies of Makhdum-i Aʿẓam, traveled out to the Amu Darya to welcome him and offered him every hospitality that was required. The entire population of Balkh, from the aristocracy down to the common folk, came out to greet him—all except for Akhund Mulla Khurd, who was also one of Makhdum-i Aʿẓam's prominent deputies, and who did not welcome him. /16b/ "I obtained my full license from Makhdum-i Aʿẓam," he said dismissively, "but Isḥaq Vali only received his permission from Mawlana Luṭfullah Chusti.[35] He might belong to the Makhdum's family, but we're still his senior."

His Grace entered the city of Balkh, but Mulla Khurd still didn't present himself, and the issue became a sore spot for His Grace. After a few days, Pir Muḥammad Khan, who was the king of Balkh, was persuaded by gossipers to say to him: "Mulla Khurd is an elderly man, he lacks the strength to come. If you were to go and pay the old man a visit, it would be an act of generosity and a sign of kindness." Complying with the khan's request, His Grace set off, but when he arrived at his door, the deputy still didn't emerge. The khan turned to His Grace anxiously, worried that he had come at his request but the deputy still wouldn't come out. The khan saw tears falling from his blessed eyes, and he inquired, "O Grace, what is the reason for these tears?"

His Grace replied, "Did you bring me to see him because he was sick, or to mourn for his passing?"

The khan was struck by these words and sent someone in. They came out and announced: "The deputy has died!"[36] A huge commotion broke out, and the khan looked at His Grace again but could not see him. Everyone suspected that Khoja Isḥaq Vali had laid a curse on Mulla Khurd, and some of the deputy's devotees conceived a grudge against him.

A few days after they buried the deputy, the khan's five-year-old son Shah Maḥmud Sulṭan became ill. Three days went by, and His Grace /17a/ went to check on his condition. Some time after this, news was brought to the khan that the sultan had died. He entered his son's room in distress and saw him lying there dead. In anguish, the khan took his dead son into his arms and laid him at Khoja Isḥaq Vali's feet. "O Grace," he said, "you are close to the court of God Almighty. Pray for him, and maybe with your blessing my son will revive!" Once again the malicious disciples of Mulla Khurd egged the khan on: "If the deputy were still alive," they said, "he would meditate and restore him to life."

From the depths of his soul, His Grace beseeched the court of the Lord. "O God," he said, "for the sake of your strength and greatness, do not abandon this helpless soul! Aid to the fallen, and guide to the perplexed, I beseech the Lord, and the pure offspring of the Prophet, who heed the prayers of the downtrodden!" He cried out so much that even the angels in heaven were moved to tears. God Almighty approved his request, and the sultan suddenly sneezed and sat up. In his fit of excitement, the khan sprang up and flailed around like a moth, until His Grace calmed him down. A hubbub went around the city of Balkh that Khoja Isḥaq Vali had brought the dead back to life, and day by day an immense crowd came to pay their respects. It was a scene that would defy description.

There was a poplar tree in the place where Khoja Isḥaq Vali was staying, and some hawks had made their nest in it and were harassing the khan's pigeons. The khan was much aggrieved at this /17b/ but couldn't find any solution. He sent someone to His Grace to ask if he could direct his concentration to the capture of the hawks, so that his pigeons might be delivered from their grasp and the khan find peace of mind. His Grace was deep in meditation and lifted his head. "Does the khan think of me as his bird catcher?" he said. "Climb up and get those creatures," he snapped at Ḥafiẓ Niẓam. Ḥafiẓ Niẓam climbed up, caught them and came down, and gave them to the khan's man. The affair left a certain resentment in His Grace's mind, and he departed for the province of Ḥiṣar.[37] A few days later, the khan contracted an illness from which he eventually died.[38]

5. ISḤAQ VALI'S SOJOURN IN THE TARIM BASIN

Khoja Isḥaq Vali had evidently not received permission to instruct directly from Makhdum-i Aʿẓam but from His Holiness Mawlana Luṭfullah Chusti, who was a milk brother of Makhdum-i Aʿẓam. Permission had in fact been given from Mawlana Muḥammad Qażi to Mawlana Luṭfullah Chusti, but the spiritual transmission ran from Mawlana Muḥammad Qażi to Makhdum-i Aʿẓam, and Mawlana Luṭfullah respected this succession and pledged his allegiance to Makhdum-i Aʿẓam. After Makhdum-i Aʿẓam crossed into the eternal realm, the spiritual lineage then reverted to Mawlana Luṭfullah. Meanwhile, Khoja Isḥaq Vali had been studying in Bukhara. Upon receiving a sign from the Prophet, Mawlana Luṭfullah invited him from Bukhara, betrothed his daughter to him, and entrusted him with the spiritual lineage that had been left to him for safekeeping. He told his companions: /18a/ "Whatever you used to request from my master Makhdum-i Aʿẓam, you should now request from Khoja Isḥaq Vali." With this, he gave him a full dispensation.

Note that this account represents the view of the Isḥaqiyya. Devotees on the side of Khoja Ishan-i Kalan maintain that after Makhdum-i Aʿẓam the spiritual lineage ran via the most noble Khoja Muḥammad Islam (better known as Khoja Juybari), and from him it was transmitted to Khoja Muḥammad Amin, who is known as Ishan-i Kalan. They claim that from

Ishan-i Kalan onward, it will stay with them until Judgment Day. God only knows the truth![39]

Whatever the case, none of these descendants was entirely deprived of some share of this affiliation. Khoja Isḥaq Vali in particular had a perfect worldly pedigree, since he resembled the blessed visage of the Prophet. Because of this, Makhdum-i Aʿẓam used to say, "Every time that I see Muḥammad in my dreams, he appears in the guise of this child." Whenever he saw Khoja Isḥaq Vali, he would leap to his feet and bow before him. If one of his companions questioned this, he would explain his dreams and say with fondness that these bows toward his child were out of respect for the Prophet.

There is an anecdote from Abd al-Laṭif Sulṭan, one of the khans of Urgench, who was among the most pious men of his age and a leading deputy of Khoja Isḥaq Vali.[40] /18b/ He relates: "One day I was sitting reading a biography of the Prophet when an ecstasy overcame me and I lost consciousness. I saw the leader of the saints, Muḥammad, appear in front of me, and all around him lights were flashing and going in and out of his shirt. After a while, I came to and went to attend on His Grace. I saw him sitting there with the same appearance as the Prophet. Around him lights were flashing and entering his shirt and disappearing. I was astonished and perplexed. His Grace immediately raised his head. 'Sulṭan,' he said, 'why would you be surprised? We belong to the Prophet's bloodline. If on some occasions we resemble our forefather, what is there to marvel at?' I was immediately blown away by these manifest secrets, and I apologized."

There is also an account of how Khoja Isḥaq Vali graced Kashgar with his presence, at the invitation of Abd al-Karim Khan.[41] Abd al-Karim Khan went out and greeted him with deference and accommodated him in Kashgar. However, the bird of kingship had already flown from the khan, and because of this, the khan didn't appreciate His Grace's presence. He ignored him, and for forty days no meeting took place between them. Eventually the khan sent him a pony with an old saddle.[42] When His Grace saw this, his mood soured. "We came at his invitation," he complained, "and this is how he treats us? Obviously he intends to expel us from this region." Three days went by before the khan sent a letter stating that His Grace /19a/ should depart his domains. With all his companions and household, His Grace traveled throughout the Kirghiz and Kazakh lands. A number of miracles occurred there: with his prayers, the dead came back to life, the sick were restored to health, springs flowed in the deserts, and idols emitted the sound of the Divine Word—all manner of strange and wonderful things. He destroyed eighteen temples of idolatry, and 180,000 infidels entered the faith and obtained guidance from him.[43]

Eventually Abd al-Karim Khan sent someone to His Grace to ask forgiveness, and he made his way back to Kashgar. In fact, though, the khan's disrespect had not diminished, and because of that, His Grace didn't set aside his resentment either. One morning, Muḥammad Sulṭan came into His Grace's presence, exhibiting faith and loyalty. His Grace said, "My son, before long the kingship of this province will fall to you." Muḥammad Sulṭan arose with his devotion confirmed and requested a recitation of the opening verse of the Quran. "O Grace," he said, "my first offering to you will be my soul. On top of that, all of these provinces will be dedicated to you." The next morning, Abd al-Karim Khan left on campaign for Ganzhou with thirty thousand men.[44] After they had traveled for seven days, a whipping sandstorm and flashes of lightning arose one evening from the direction of Ganzhou. Abd al-Karim Khan heard the neighing of horses and suspected an ambush, so he abandoned his camp and fled, even though it was nothing more than a lightning storm. Prior to this, His Grace had said, "Abd al-Karim Khan is exerting himself in vain. The conquest of Ganzhou will be the work of Muḥammad Khan." Now His Grace immediately instructed Muḥammad Khan: "Go quickly, the victory is in your hands." Muḥammad Khan /19b/ went to the city of Bulghar with five hundred men, and captured and killed its khan while he was in his garden.[45] He took possession of that region, then came before His Grace and dedicated his conquests to him.

This incident only increased Abd al-Karim Khan's hostility, and any pretense of hospitality was done away with. One day while His Grace was engaged in training Muḥammad Khan, someone made mention of Abd al-Karim Khan. "Have faith in God Almighty," His Grace said, "that we may be freed from his tyranny." So saying, he bowed his head, and tears fell from his eyes. The companions also began weeping and crying and entered into meditation.

Mulla Sangin Khalifa describes what he experienced next:

"All of a sudden I lost consciousness, and I saw myself in a garden, the like of which does not exist in this mundane world. The Prophet was sitting on a platform by the side of a pond. His Grace was standing in front of him and telling him about Abd al-Karim Khan's impropriety. The Prophet looked up and saw a stork sitting on a poplar tree. 'Strike that stork,' the Prophet said, 'it's making too much noise.' His Grace hit its neck with a stick, and it fell from the tree to the ground.

" 'God is great!' I blurted out aloud."

" 'Praise be to God,' His Grace said, 'the Prophet has delivered us from Abd al-Karim Khan's wrongdoing.' Then he turned to me, 'Mulla Sangin, did you have a vision?' I was astonished and apologized. Three days later, news came that /20a/ Abd al-Karim Khan had died, and the kingship had passed to Muḥammad Khan."

Much have we experienced how in this temple of retribution,
Whoever fell out with drainers of the dregs fell down.[46]

He who wounds the heart of one of God's friends,
Without doubt has cut his own thread with his own hand.

In sum, Khoja Isḥaq Vali spent a total of twelve years in Aqsu, Kashgar, Yarkand, and Khotan. He led many people along the right road and promoted Muḥammad's Holy Law. He trained several of his followers to the level of perfection before eventually returning to Samarqand.

6. THE SONS AND GRANDSONS OF ISḤAQ VALI

Here it is fitting to tell a story involving Ushtur Khalifa, a companion and guide to the forlorn, whom His Grace had appointed in his own stead as deputy in Kashgar. After a period of time, Muḥammad Khan's dedication was starting to wane, and he declared that since his fathers and forefathers had always been faithful to Sulṭan Alp Ata, he would go and request assistance from him as well.[47] Setting out with a large procession, he went and slaughtered some horses, cows, and sheep, cooked up a huge stew, and was in the middle of reciting prayers. Ushtur Khalifa, who was a strong and determined man, set off boldly in pursuit of him. In the midst of that large gathering, he climbed atop Sulṭan Alp Ata's tomb and wrestled it with hands and feet. Everyone who saw this was astonished, the khan included. Right then a huge dragon suddenly appeared and attacked the deputy. Just as the deputy was brandishing his sword at the dragon, His Grace manifested and swung his own sword at the dragon's head, cleaving it in two. The khan, along with everyone else, witnessed this miracle with his own eyes and fell at His Grace's blessed feet, sobbing and full of apologies. /20b/ The khan dedicated all his property to him, along with the revenue of certain cities, and renewed his faith and devotion.[48]

Come now, heart, let's make straight for the beloved,
We'll renew our pledge and commitment.
Each soul needs but one beloved, what would I do with a second?
Let's sacrifice ourselves for the one we have chosen.

There is also a story concerning Abdullah Khan's brother Rustam Sulṭan, who came on campaign from Bukhara to Kashgar with an army fifty thousand strong.[49] Muḥammad Khan was then in Yarkand and oblivious to what was going on, but once His Grace had alerted him in a dream vision, the khan made his way to Kashgar and fortified the city. The opposing army came and laid siege to it, and Muḥammad Khan realized that before this force, his own army was like a drop of water in the face of an ocean. He had no choice but to beseech the court of He Who Lacks Nothing and cry out in supplication. All of a sudden, His Grace came into view, smiling and in good cheer. "There should be victory tomorrow, God willing," he said. "You must assuredly give battle, for the triumph will be yours." So saying, he vanished.

The next morning, Muḥammad Khan rode out with five hundred cavalry and routed the enemy. His Grace had warned him not to pursue them, however, for if he were to do so, then none of them would make it back alive.

In the end, Rustam Sulṭan made his way home and sent a donation of two hundred *tangga* of silver to His Grace in Samarqand. Then he went to see Abdullah Khan. "What was the reason this defeat befell you?" Abdullah Khan asked.

"By God," Rustam Sulṭan replied, "I swear that our entire army saw Khoja Isḥaq Vali, /21a/ dressed in white and riding a white horse, charge out of the citadel with a hundred thousand men wielding lances and other weapons. They came in pursuit of our army, but His Grace restrained them. Had they given chase, not a single one of us would've made it back alive."

Abdullah Khan felt bitter resentment toward His Grace, and he took this enmity with him to the grave. Muḥammad Khan, by contrast, dedicated more provinces to His Grace out of gratitude for this victory. This was the third time that Muḥammad Khan made offerings of these cities to His Grace.

This story is drawing out. I had best condense it, lest I lose sight of my original purpose. Eventually His Grace passed from the mortal realm to the eternal world and was buried in Isfiduk.[50] Isfiduk is separated from Dahbid by a canal: Isfaduk lies to its north, while to the south is Dahbid, the location of His Holiness Makhdum-i Aʿẓam's luminescent shrine. The reason they didn't bury Khoja Isḥaq Vali in Dahbid alongside his illustrious father was something Makhdum-i Aʿẓam once said: "According to the Prophet, anyone who is buried between himself and U̱sman will be admitted to Paradise, and this is why they buried U̱sman in the Baqiʿ Cemetery. Likewise, it's been revealed to me that anyone who is buried between me and my son Khoja Isḥaq Vali /21b/ will be admitted to Paradise." Because of this, he stipulated in his will that they should bury him in Isfiduk.

The reason they relocated his shrine to Bagh-i Buland was that when His Grace was seven years old, Makhdum-i Aʿẓam led all of his companions down to the Kuhak [Zarafshan] River, which was in a state of flood. Two of his deputies entered the water, but the current surged and they couldn't get across. They were left there helpless. Khoja Isḥaq Vali was seized by a divine inspiration, and he came and struck the river with a whip. The river split into two, and a dry pathway emerged in the middle, allowing them all to cross. Makhdum-i Aʿẓam quipped: "My child, you've taken liberties with this river in my presence. The river won't give up without eventually having its revenge." Thus it came to pass that one day the king of Samarqand was told that the river was encroaching on Khoja Isḥaq Vali's shrine, and he exhumed his body and reburied him in Bagh-i Buland.[51] Bagh-i Buland was the king's garden, and he assigned his entire property and gardens to the shrine as a pious endowment (*waqf*). To this day, it remains in the possession of His Grace's descendants.

Khoja Isḥaq Vali left behind two sons. One of them was a Simurgh of the mountain of unicity, a Homa of the sky of happiness, and a shining sun of the community and religion: Khoja Quṭb al-Din, whose offspring /22a/ now tend to the shrine in Bagh-i Buland.[52] The second was a blessed and unique escort on the Path of Guidance, Khoja Shadi (his original name was Khoja Yaḥya). In the land of Kashgar his grace-filled tomb is situated in the capital of Yarkand. Another son by the name of Khoja Shahbaz died in Aqsu when he was only seven years old. When it was decided to relocate Khoja Shahbaz's body to the Golden Shrine in Yarkand, the people of Aqsu requested that a tomb remain there for them, and he was interred there, where his imposing shrine still stands.[53]

When Khoja Isḥaq Vali was departing these cities, he appointed deputies to each of them: Ushtur Khalifa in Kashgar, Khoja Qasim Khalifa in Yangiḥiṣar,[54] and Yusuf Khalifa in Khotan. In Yarkand, the capital of Moghulistan, he assigned Khoja Shadi to his position before departing. For a time, Khoja Shadi led those who were lost in ignorance along the Path to Truth, and while occupying the seat of guidance he trained a number of people to perfection.

At that time, one of Ishan-i Kalan's sons, who was a mine of humility and meekness and a source of honesty and purity, Pole of the Chiefs (*nuqabā*) and Aid of the Nobles (*nujabā*),[55] Khoja Muḥammad Yusuf arrived in Kashgar. With him was his son, a wellspring of divine grace known as Khoja of the Horizons (Khoja Afaq), whose original name was Khoja Hidayatullah. ("Afaq" here refers to the entire world. They call him Khoja Afaq because from East to West he was renowned for his saintliness, and all the world's people /22b/ bound the belt of service to him.) The people of Kashgar honored them greatly. At that time, Abdullah Khan was ensconced in Yarkand, while his son Yolbars Khan was in Kashgar and Nur al-Din Sulṭan was in Aqsu.[56] Yolbars Khan was defiant and wavering in his loyalty toward Abdullah Khan, while to Khoja Muḥammad Yusuf, and particularly to His Grace Khoja Afaq, he was highly solicitous. One day the sultan saw from the portico of his palace that a party was approaching on foot, with one man riding a donkey. "Who are they?" he inquired. His companions informed him that this was Khoja Muḥammad Yusuf, and the sultan requested that they provide him with a thoroughbred horse and a gold saddle. Khoja Muḥammad Yusuf got off his donkey and mounted the horse, but then dismounted and got back on the donkey, allowing Khoja Afaq to ride the horse instead.

"Khoja Afaq, my son," he asked, "how do you imagine yourself?"

"I see myself like a world-conquering king," he said.

Thus it was that Khoja Afaq lived out his life in the fashion of a king. Even Khoja Shadi assigned his property and pious donations in Kashgar to Khoja Muḥammad Yusuf and Khoja Afaq. All the ranks of Kashgar's population, led by Yolbars Sulṭan, swore allegiance to them and became their devotees.

The grasping hand of fate then took hold of Khoja Shadi. He drank from the cup of EVERY SOUL SHALL TASTE DEATH [21:35] and resigned himself to destiny's command. There was such grief in Yarkand it felt like the dawn of Judgment Day. With Ismaʿil Khan at the fore, all the scholars, wisemen, amirs, and people of the kingdom held a mourning ceremony and buried him to cries of "O my heart! What grief!"[57] He left two Makhdumzadas behind. One of them /23a/ was Khoja Ubaydullah, who was the fruit of the tree of guidance and a sapling by the stream of happiness. The other was Khoja Abdullah, a king of the clime of sayyidhood and an emperor of the sultanate of honor. There were also some well-trained deputies who saw to the exoteric and esoteric training of these two infant Makhdumzadas. For his part, Ismaʿil Khan treated them both with respect and recognized the two Makhdumzadas in the position of their illustrious father, to whom the khan had previously pledged his devotion.

> O King, a request I have to ask from you:
> That how you treat the noble, you treat the lowly too.
> He may be small, but know that he is large in God's eyes,
> His eminence is from the prayers of the people.

Whether it was due to an invitation from the khan or for the purpose of reciting the opening of the Quran at the mourning ceremony, Khoja Muḥammad Yusuf had come from Kashgar to Yarkand. The khan and all the kingdom's people greeted him and treated him hospitably. Eventually it crossed the khan's mind that he too might pledge his devotion to Khoja Muḥammad Yusuf, and this became known among the people. The khan resolved to gather all the scholars and amirs the following morning and announce his decision.

That same day, Khoja Shadi's deputies came into the khan's presence carrying the two Makhdumzadas and humbly petitioned him, "O righteous king, we ask for justice! Is it in accordance with the Holy Law or royal justice that someone infringe on someone else's property and wealth?"

"What's going on?" asked the khan.

"Everyone, from the khan down, had sworn allegiance to our master," the deputies said. "Even though our master's body is no more, his spirit is still present. And besides, there are these two Makhdumzadas who, while still young, are mature in their deeds. There are also some deputies. We might be humble in appearance, /23b/ but we've received our license from a fully accomplished guide. Praise be to God, instead of leaving our master's seat empty and vacant, we are still promoting the Path of the Khojagan to some extent. Now we learn that tomorrow the khan apparently intends to swear allegiance to Khoja Muḥammad Yusuf. What could possibly be the reason for someone to shun their own master and adopt a different one? If it is firm proofs and miracle-working that you desire, then we must disappoint you, for our patrons are God, the Prophet, and our spiritual guide. If you insist on doing this, then please permit us to leave, we will take the Makhdumzadas and our master's remains and all depart."

The khan became angry and confused, unable to make a decision either way. "Deputies," he said after a while, "you should meditate on this tonight." Lowering his head, he went on, "Khoja Muḥammad Yusuf should also meditate on this. It might do some good. Let me give you my answer in the morning. Dervishes know best the business of dervishes; everyone is an expert in their own craft."

Every saint can see a saint,
And Ali can see Muṣṭafa.[58]

That evening the dervishes meditated so intensely that they cut themselves off from the lower realm and ascended close to God. They summoned up all their energy into spiritual fists and struck blows at one another. In particular, Ushtur Khalifa's son Abd al-Aziz Khalifa took on the appearance of a wild camel, with bloodshot eyes in a divine revelry, sometimes coming to consciousness and sometimes fainting again. It was he who inspired everyone else.

According to the narrator of this story, that night Ismaʿil Khan had a dream in which he saw a large white /24a/ camel enter the city from outside and approach the Golden Shrine. A small camel came out of the cemetery and started struggling with the larger one. Grappling and wrestling, the small camel eventually bested it. When the khan woke up, he sensed that circumstances had changed. That morning Khoja Muḥammad Yusuf departed for Kashgar without meeting the khan. He traveled a day's journey to a place called Topluq in the Yangiḥiṣar region. The following evening, as is intended by the saying DEATH IS A BRIDGE THAT CONNECTS FRIEND TO FRIEND, he crossed from this mortal world into the eternal realm.[59] TRULY WE ARE GOD'S, AND UNTO HIM WE RETURN [2:156].

Khoja Afaq came down from Kashgar to retrieve his blessed remains, and he buried them in the neighborhood of Yaghdu. Lamentations arose from the people of Kashgar, and their shouts and cries touched the heavens.

Within Yarkand, the Makhdumzadas and their deputies continued to make progress. The faith and loyalty of those who had sworn allegiance was strengthened, and those who had not yet pledged themselves did so. After some time, Ismaʿil Khan exiled Khoja Afaq from Kashgar and installed his son Babaq Sulṭan there.[60] These cities flourished to an extent that had not been seen in the reign of any khan prior to this, nor has been since. For twelve years, the common folk had no idea whether there were any soldiers in the land at all. Words like "cruelty" and "tyranny" were simply unheard of. The religious scholars and learned men made great accomplishments, and Muḥammad's Holy Law was dignified.

One day the khan observed from the top of the citadel that the scholars were coming toward the palace. He immediately leapt to his feet and performed a prayer of thanksgiving. "O God of the two worlds," he said in his entreaty, /24b/ "what honor you've brought to this shamefaced one, that these wise and learned men should approach my residence without any invitation. How can I ever fully express thanks for this grace? If I had a hundred thousand tongues, I still wouldn't be finished before Judgment Day." While he was occupied with giving praise and thanks, the scholars hesitated and became slightly anxious. Then the khan gave permission for them to enter. He expressed his apologies and made plain his gratitude, and the scholars were relieved.

Come, cupbearer, get the cup of pleasure circling around,
It is the season of joy and mirth, the age of the just king.

Khoja Ubaydullah died while he was still young.[61] The elder Makhdumzada, Khoja Abdullah, lived for some time and spent his days dispensing guidance from the position of spiritual preeminence and leading the people to truth. Yet he too died before he reached the age of forty. He left behind two Makhdumzadas. One of them was the bloom of sayyidhood Khoja Ay (Moon), whose actual name was Khoja Shuʿayb. The other was a chair of the assembly of virtue, a luminary among those who follow the Path, and a chief of the clan of sayyids, Khoja Kün (Sun), whose name was Khoja Danyal. For a while they lived in full honor, and the khan and everyone else recognized them as their Makhdumzadas and held them in the highest esteem.

7. THE EXILE AND RETURN OF KHOJA AFAQ

Let us now take up the story of Khoja Afaq, who had been expelled from Kashgar by Ismaʿil Khan.[62] He left Kashgar and traveled from city to city, making his way through Kashmir before arriving in a region called Ju, which is part of the kingdom of China.[63] /25a/ Among the Chinese infidels in these parts were some Brahman shaykhs who, instead of spiritual exercises and miracle-working, performed confidence tricks. Through slight of hand, they had established various sects among the infidels. There was a place of worship there, similar to a dervish lodge, where all the infidels had convened. They were engaging in all sorts of miracle-like subterfuges and had hung up their silk tassels on particles of light.[64] When Khoja Afaq entered, all of these tassels fell to the ground. The infidels were astonished and wondered who this man could be. Eventually they all went into meditation, and Khoja Afaq also ascended to the realm above. At some points, the infidels got the upper hand, and sometimes Khoja Afaq. In the end, they all sought refuge in their faith, but there was a mountain blocking their path, and from top to bottom they couldn't find a single gap in it. In a state of helplessness, the infidels gave up and asked, "Who are you? Where have you come from?"

His Grace said, "I am a scholar and a khoja of the Muslim tribe. In particular, the people of Kashgar and Yarkand are my disciples and devotees. Recently someone came and deprived me of these cities and drove me out. My request is that you instruct someone to restore this homeland to my hands."

"It would be very difficult for an army to go from here to there," the Brahman replied, and instead he wrote the following letter to the Qalmaqs:

> Boshogtu Khan,[65] this Khoja Afaq is a noble man and fully accomplished in his own religion. He is said to be the khoja of Kashgar and Yarkand, but a man named Ismaʿil Khan has usurped his ancestral lands and expelled him. You should go with an army /25b/ and take back his domains for him, for otherwise he will be unable to do so himself.

His Grace took this letter and conveyed it to the Qalmaq *törä*.[66] Out of deference, the *törä* acted on the instructions and personally led his army on a campaign against Kashgar. Rumors spread among the people of Kashgar that Khoja Afaq was on his way with an infidel by the name of Sengge.[67] Ismaʿil Khan's son Babaq Sulṭan went out with an army to confront them, but the Qalmaqs emerged victorious, and Babaq Sulṭan was stuck by an arrow and martyred. In the end, the people of Kashgar submitted. They organized affairs in Kashgar and then continued toward Yarkand. From Yarkand, Ismaʿil Khan came out before them with a great army and readied for battle, but as fate would have it, victory did not fall to the khan's side. The governor of Yarkand was hit by an arrow and martyred, and from this the khan clearly perceived that luck was not with him and that the opposing force would carry the day. If they fought on, he realized, it would cause the people great suffering. With this in mind, the khan went out to meet the enemy army with thirty retainers and left these final instructions for the city's inhabitants: "You should appoint the two Makhdumzadas to guide you in maintaining the city and insist that you will only open the gate on condition that they not interfere with religious affairs and that they appoint officials from among you. Otherwise do not open it." Once these conditions were accepted, they opened the gate. Khoja Afaq was installed on the throne, and in Kashgar they appointed his elder son Khoja Yaḥya, whom they used to call Khan Khoja. They took Ismaʿil Khan and all his followers back with them, and it was because of this that the Ili mountains became the place of residence of the khans.

When the Qalmaqs /26a/ were on their way back, Khoja Afaq consulted with the people of the kingdom and decided that these Qalmaqs shouldn't go home without some compensation for their service, so he gave them a donation of a thousand robes of honor and a thousand *tangga* of silver.[68] Subsequently, the number of people distorting the faith increased by the hour, and thus it came about that this innovative impost on the commoners is yet to be abolished, and may well not be until the end of time. Khoja Afaq became ensconced on the throne and dove into the ocean of gnosis. Yet his standing as a khoja did not sit well with worldly rule, and a consensus was reached to bring Ismaᶜil Khan's younger brother Muḥammad Emin Khan from Turfan and enthrone him. Muḥammad Emin Khan had a sister whose name was Khanim Padishah, who was betrothed to Khoja Afaq, and Muḥammad Emin Khan pledged his spiritual devotion to Khoja Afaq. Subsequently the khan campaigned into the Ili mountains and came back with many Qalmaq captives, including several *töräs* who fell into his hands. After some time, the Sufis became overbearing and headstrong, and all sorts of incidents started to occur. His Grace took no notice of all this, because he was intoxicated in meditation of God, but Muḥammad Emin Khan fled in fear for his life, and eventually one of his own retainers martyred him. TRULY WE ARE GOD'S, AND UNTO HIM WE RETURN [2:156].[69] Khoja Afaq consolidated his position on the throne once again.

8. THE MARTYRDOM OF KHOJA SHUᶜAYB

Here it seems appropriate to continue the story of the two eminent Makhdumzadas, Khoja Shuᶜayb and Khoja Danyal.[70] At the time when His Grace Khoja Afaq took up the throne of the sultanate, these two venerable Makhdumzadas saw that the behavior of the Sufis and ecstatics had gone awry and they were acting corruptly. They realized that time was precious, so they took some of their own following as companions, /26b/ bade farewell to the rest, and withdrew and took up residence in Kashmir. Sometime afterward, a couple of their deputies were on a pilgrimage to Yarkand's Golden Shrine one evening, when they ran into a mad Sufi who hauled them before Khoja Afaq with all sorts of abuse and mistreatment.

"Who are you?" His Grace inquired.

They replied, "We are men of the Makhdumzadas, the descendants of Khoja Isḥaq Vali."

His Grace rebuked and punished his Sufis and treated these deputies with great respect. "We belong to the same generation," he said. "Given that there was never such conflict and dispute among our forefathers, why should there be any enmity between us? Let's get rid of the skeptics who stand between us, and the dispute will subside."

> O Lord, keep the skeptics and ill-wishers at bay,
> So that we're delivered from the hostility of both.

His Grace then inquired, "Did these Makhdumzadas have any lands and canals as their endowments?"

The deputies replied, "The khan made offerings to them of the village of Fayżabad in Kashgar, Toqquzkent in Yarkand, Aq Saray in Khotan, and Aq Yar in Aqsu, and the income from these lands used to be expended on their Sufi lodge (*khānqāh*)."

"Then they should restore to you the proceeds from these lands according to the old precedent," His Grace ordered. "And if you have any companions, you should reunite with them and go about your business with full honor. You may even send someone to the Makhdumzadas so that they come too. Whatever we have by way of material or spiritual possessions, we will share with them." Owing to the great magnanimity he thus exhibited, the dependents of the deputies who had scattered to various parts /27a/ reassembled and took up their position at the Golden Shrine in Yarkand. They spent the revenue from these lands on their expenses, and they also sent gifts to the Makhdumzadas. For some time, they enjoyed considerable status, and no one did them any harm. On several occasions, the deputies sent letters to the Makhdumzadas, with this message:

> These are the circumstances your servants find themselves in: His Grace has shown us much favor, and he always says that the Makhdumzadas should come and share in the prosperity of this kingdom. It would be best if you were to honor us with your presence.

After letters like this had gone between them many times, the message eventually had an effect on the Makhdumzadas. Their interest in moving back was stirred, but with every step they took in that direction, they still couldn't entirely shake their feeling of unease. Finally, destiny brought them to Sanju, and from there they wrote this letter:

> O sunshine of the zenith of happiness, and moonlight of the night sky of honor! O unique page in the book of the world, Khoja Afaq! With your permission we have arrived in Sanju with Yarkand as our destination. In the first place, we belong to the same generation of our family, and thus share the obligations of kinship. Secondly, in Islam there is no principle of tricking or deceiving others. Our forefathers were long engaged in expounding the Holy Law. The people must have picked up this bad habit from someone else. Such people need to receive instruction both from you and from us. If you were to put our mind at ease by sending a note of safe passage bearing your seal, we will proceed in safety.

When this letter reached His Grace, he rejoiced, and in reply he wrote out a letter of safe passage and affixed his seal to it. It said:

> The Makhdumzadas must naturally be allowed to proceed. Anything that God Almighty bestows on us, /27b/ we shall share with them. We will not interfere with them in any way. Their affairs will be restored to the state they were in previously. Nay, they will be superior to that, for while the khans were no relatives of theirs, we have the obligations of kinship between us, and to disavow that connection would be a sin and an act of rebellion.

When this letter reached the Makhdumzadas, they felt reassured and set off for Yarkand. Yet their doubts were still not entirely dispelled. In the end, Khoja Shuʿayb said, "O brother Khoja Danyal, although we're approaching our destination of Yarkand, my unease hasn't diminished. Every time I take a step forward, it pulls me back one step. These kingdoms loom before my eyes like a river of blood and a storm of grief. Even though I can allow myself to go, I won't allow you to, lest our lineage come to an end. This is how my destiny seems to me." He assigned a few people to accompany his brother Khoja Danyal and sent him on his way. Khoja Shuᶜayb himself took a few companions and made it to the edge of the Tiznab River, where that evening four hundred deranged Sufis came out and martyred him.[71] TRULY WE ARE GOD'S, AND UNTO HIM WE RETURN [2:156]. They stuffed his dead body into a saddlebag and threw it into the river.

For a while, no one could reveal this corrupt deed to His Grace. Those who were his loyal disciples simply carried on with their prayers and worship and kept it to themselves. But there was one bold and noble-minded man among the associates of the Makhdumzadas, who one day dressed himself in black sackcloth and smeared black on his face, rendering himself an astonishing sight. /28a/ After His Grace had finished a recitation from the *Masnavi*, and before the prayers and exultations, he made his way into their midst and started performing a mystical dance (*samāᶜ*). Everyone was curious. "Who are you?" His Grace asked. "What is this state that has taken hold of you?"

How have you come to this condition, what has overcome you?
If not because of some weighty pain, then why this state of mind?

"I am one of the men of the Makhdumzadas," the man replied. "With your permission, and on your promise and oath, the Makhdumzadas made their way here, but when they reached the banks of the Tiznab, four hundred people went out and martyred them. When a pledge from you is worth nothing, then what do you expect us to do?"

When paganism arises from the Kaaba, what remains of Muslimdom?[72]

"O no!" His Grace cried out when he heard this grievous news, slapping his knees in rage. Angrily he said to the fanatics: "You murderous zealots, this will have consequences not just for you, but for me too. You've given me a bad name that will last until Judgment Day. This deed of yours won't go unpunished. Soon someone will come along and slaughter you like sheep as well." And thus it was that after Khoja Afaq's death, Aqbash Khan rounded up several thousand fanatics and slaughtered them in the watercourse of a mill, making the millstone run with their blood.[73]

The marketplace of revenge will always be bustling.

His Grace rode out with all the scholars and amirs to the bank of the Tiznab in mourning. They saw that the river had receded from the place where the Makhdumzada's body had been thrown, /28b/ and the saddlebag was lying in a dry patch. His Grace personally dismounted and retrieved the bag, tears streaming from his eyes the whole time. Sobbing and crying, they reverentially loaded his corpse onto a camel and carried it back to Yarkand. Everyone gathered to say prayers and bury him at the Golden Shrine.

9. KHOJA DANYAL SEEKS REFUGE IN TRANSOXIANA

We return now to the story of Khoja Danyal, who on his brother's advice had fled in fear of the fanatical Sufis. His route took him to Samarqand, and when he reached Dahbid, he fell before the tomb of Makhdum-i Aʿẓam, weeping like spring rain. "O spirit of my great forefather," he cried out, "what is this destitution and ruin that has befallen me, wandering from door to door, unable to find a place of refuge? That I should lose my brother and our family endure such bloodshed and hardship! What wrong have I ever done to be reduced to this condition? Forgive me my sins!" Appealing again and again until his face was soiled, he eventually fell asleep. A vision came to him of spirits, including those of Makhdum-i Aʿẓam and Khoja Isḥaq Vali, and they said to him, "Khoja Danyal, raise your head, do not grieve. Be patient and act according the hadith, PATIENCE IS THE KEY TO HAPPINESS. As Ali has said:

> WHEN SOME /29a/ MISFORTUNE AFFLICTS YOU,
> REFLECT ON THE SURA "DID WE NOT EXPAND,"[74]
> AND THAT EACH HARDSHIP COMES BETWEEN TWO INSTANCES OF EASE.
> WHEN YOU THINK UPON THIS, YOU'LL FIND JOY.

For every difficulty you face, that is to say, there will be two joyful events. Son, in a short while the position of khoja and the throne of those kingdoms will pass to you and your offspring." With this they vanished. Khoja Danyal woke up greatly relieved by these consoling words. He went to Bagh-i Buland and paid his respects to the luminescent shrine of his great-grandfather, Khoja Isḥaq Vali, and resided there for a while.[75] Afterward he went to Khujand and became a local headman (*kadẖudā*).

The Venerable Khoja Yaʿqub, who was a key to the treasure trove of divine gnosis, chief among the truth-seekers, and a worthy heir to the prophets and the apostles, was born in Khujand. From conception until his birth, and from that time until he grew to maturity, he manifested many miracles. Space would not allow me to describe them in detail, and the patience of my readers would be tested, so I have decided to omit them.

The reason they called Khoja Yaʿqub "Khoja Jahan" is that he received his training from the spirit of the chief of the Khojagan and lord of the world, Abd al-Khaliq Ghijduvani. He himself was known as Khoja Jahan, and therefore Khoja Yaʿqub came to be known in the same way. Some also say that when Khoja Danyal took his son to Balkh, there was a prominent holy man in that city who was known for performing miracles. They paid him a visit, and this saint looked upon Khoja Yaʿqub with his insightful gaze. "My impression of this son of yours is that he will be a champion," he discerned. /29b/ "He will combine esoteric with exoteric knowledge, and will be without equal in wisdom and learning. In composing poetry, he will have no peer in his age, and he will be admired around the world for his words and deeds. You should name him Khoja Jahan." It may have been for this reason, then, that he was given this name. He would often frequent the shrine of Shaykh Musliḥ al-Din Khujandi to request assistance, and he received many blessings and insights from this shaykh. As he alludes to in his poetry, if he ever had any difficulties in his studies, this shaykh would resolve them for him:

> *I too derive some of my ability from the dust of Khujand.*[76]

On occasion, he would host gatherings with men of science and learning in Samarqand, Bukhara, and Balkh, and he would show them the utmost respect. In the words of Akhund Mulla Mashhuri:

> One might say that Adam descended to earth from Paradise,
> When Mashhur set out from the city of Balkh for Yarkand.[77]

10. THE FALL OF KHOJA AFAQ

Let us turn again to the story of Khoja Afaq. Seated on the throne of the Yarkand sultanate, he was dispensing kingly rulings to those seeking justice in accordance with the shariʿa of Muḥammad. At other times, he would occupy the shaykh's chair and instruct his disciples in the ethics of the Path and hold meditation (*ẕikr*) circles. Sometimes he would conduct recitations from the *Maṡnavi* and explain the truths of gnosis, exhibit love for the beloved, and become drunk on God. His assemblies of one or two thousand companions would turn themselves upside down in blind intoxication.

> Cupbearer, pass the festive chalice from lip to lip today,
> You won't find such a spiritual king in an age like ours.
> A single glance from this monarch's eye was enough for both worlds,
> For he was an emperor of guidance (*hidāyat*) in the position of Mavlavi.
> /30a/ Like the sultan of gnosis, Mawlana Rumi,
> He tailored the garb of the *Maṡnavi* to his own lofty stature.

Khoja Afaq had two sons by Khanim Padishah: Khoja Ḥasan and Khoja Mahdi.[78] In particular, His Holiness Khoja Ḥasan was a pole in the heavens of miracle-working and center of the circle of guidance, a bloom in the rose bed of happiness, and a fresh sapling of the tree of sainthood. For Khoja Afaq, this son's existence was a blessing and a point of pride. He would constantly say, "On that day that I took these kingdoms with the support of the Qalmaq army and occupied the throne of the sultanate, in my embarrassment and shame I felt I would never be able to raise my head before God and the Apostle. Glory to God that with the existence of this child, I have made recompense for my dishonor, and my black face has whitened."[79]

Sometime after this, Khoja Afaq departed the mortal world for the realm of eternity. TRULY WE ARE GOD'S, AND UNTO HIM WE RETURN [2:156].[80] They brought His Grace's body and buried him in Kashgar in the neighborhood of Yaghdu, and with all the mourning it seemed like a new Judgment Day was dawning. Khanim Padishah set herself up in Yarkand with her sons, while Khoja Yaḥya took control of Kashgar. A few days later, Khanim Padishah came to pay her respects at the shrine with the scholars and amirs of Yarkand, including the *aʿlam akhund*.[81] Khoja Yaḥya came out to meet them, following which they visited the shrine and paid their respects. Khoja Yaḥya spent the night in the city and in the morning went out to Ḥażrat Mazar to entertain Khanim Padishah.[82] /30b/ At one point, the *aʿlam akhund* of Yarkand, Akhund Mirza Barat, took Khoja Yaḥya aside. "Khoja Yaḥya," he said by way of advice, "governing a kingdom is difficult, and with a woman like

Khanim Padishah it will be impossible. The threats we face are many: Kirghiz to this side, Qalmaqs to that, our enemies are all lying in wait. If you were to go to the capital Yarkand and assume the throne, and Khanim Padishah and the princes were to stay here in Kashgar praying at the shrine, then these enemies would be unable to find a foothold, and the kingdom might be secured."

In response to this proposal, Khoja Yaḥya asked, "Wouldn't people criticize me for contesting the capital with my mother just as soon as my father had died?"

The akhund spoke again, "Humility is of no use in affairs of state. With humility, the kingdom will come to ruin. And when rulership has slipped from your hands, regrets and misgivings will be of no use." While this was going on, Akhund Mulla Taqi caught wind of things and joined in the discussion. They came up with a plan of action and then went their separate ways, but Akhund Mulla Taqi's wife found out about their conspiracy and divulged it to Khanim Padishah. Khanim Padishah became suspicious and conceived a plot to assassinate Khoja Yaḥya. She stationed a few men with swords in hand, and when Khoja Yaḥya came the next morning, Khanim Padishah rebuked him bitterly: "Khoja Yaḥya, what's the meaning of having me lodge here at the shrine while you sleep in comfort inside the city? I'm not just a guest but your mother too. /31a/ Wouldn't it be good manners for you to stay a couple of days and spend a night with me here before I go back? Which of your fathers and forefathers were khans? It was *my* fathers and forefathers who were khans, while yours used to pray for them. It would be pointless for you to lay claim to the khanate, would it not?"

To this upbraiding, Khoja Yaḥya responded with disdain: "I'd remained in Kashgar thinking that it might be of assistance to you and His Grace. But if not, I'll happily withdraw somewhere else and pass my time praying." At this point, a shrewd man named Laṭif Bakavul realized that things were getting of hand, and he immediately gave a signal. Khoja Yaḥya got himself out of there in a hurry, and Khanim Padishah departed immediately for Yarkand. One night after she entered Yarkand, a few fanatics went and martyred Akhund Mirza Barat with an axe.

How strange people are, that because of a grudge,
They put an axe in the top of Mirza Barat's head.

Six months after His Grace Khoja Afaq's death, Khoja Yaḥya was martyred at Khanim Padishah's instigation. He left behind three sons, and two of these were also killed. One son, Khoja Aḥmad, was swifted away and kept in Tüshük Tagh.[83] The fanatics also killed Sayyid Beg,[84] who had been governor of Kashgar, and Khanim Padishah appointed Akhund Mulla Taqi as governor in his place. A few days after this, they brought forth Khoja Aḥmad and elevated him to the khanship, and Akhund Mulla Taqi escaped and made his way to Yarkand.

Meanwhile, as khan in Yarkand, Khanim Padishah installed her son Khoja Mahdi, whom they referred to as Padishah Khoja. During this period, a great deal of bloodshed occurred, /31b/ so much so that they gave Khanim Padishah the nickname Madame Executioner. One night, six months after the death of Khoja Yaḥya, the fanatics assassinated her too. She had gone to bed wearing chainmail and the blade couldn't penetrate it, so they lifted up the edge of her robe to stab her. "This is all Khoja Mahdi's doing!" she cried out before giving up the ghost.[85]

With the kingdom thus left vacant, Muḥammad Emin Khan's younger brother Aqbash Khan came and took control of these territories. In Yarkand, he slaughtered a thousand fanatics like sheep and ground grain in a mill driven by their blood. In Kashgar, he installed his son Sulṭan Aḥmad Khan and arranged for him to marry one of Khoja Yaḥya's daughters. At that time, Qalandar Beg's son Muḥammad Emin Beg was governor of Kashgar.[86] Aqbash Khan expelled the princes who remained in Yarkand to India and sent an invitation to Khoja Danyal:[87]

> Khoja Danyal! Previously our fathers and forefathers were devoted disciples of your fathers and forefathers and relied on the strength of their prayers to administer the kingdom. Now in our reign too, you should come to these parts and give guidance to those who are lost.

11. KHOJA DANYAL ESTABLISHES HIS RULE IN YARKAND

Accepting this letter's invitation, Khoja Danyal traveled with his household from the city of Khujand to Kashgar. With Arzu Muḥammad at their head, the Kirghiz came out to greet him and invited him into the city.[88] He didn't enter, though, nor did the people of Kashgar welcome him. They already had a khoja, they said, and didn't have any need for him. With apologies, the Kirghiz then escorted him to Yarkand. The entire population of Yarkand, with the governor at the fore, /32a/ greeted him, led him into the city with much ceremony, and confirmed him in the position of khoja. A few days after this, they decided that they needed a khan as well, believing it would be impossible to maintain the kingdom without one, and by consensus they invited Hashim Sulṭan from among the Kazakh khans.[89]

In Kashgar, meanwhile, Khoja Aḥmad was confirmed in his office. From among the Kirghiz, Arzu Muḥammad served as *qarakhan*,[90] with Qarazangi Beg and Jarub Beg as governor and deputy governor, respectively. The entire administration of the kingdom was in their hands.[91] Sometimes they raided the people of Yarkand, and sometimes they came like thieves in the night, taking captives and inflicting great suffering on the ordinary folk. One day it was determined that Qarazangi Beg would take five hundred heavy cavalry, and Jarub Beg five hundred well-armed soldiers, and ride out for Yarkand. They organized for one of them to stage a surprise incursion by the Golden Gate and seize and bind the Kazakh Hashim Sulṭan before falling back. The other would enter by the Khanqah Gate and capture governor Alim Shah Beg the Fat and deputy governor Shah Jaʿfar the Stubborn and bring these men out, along with Khoja Danyal.

By the time these two irreligious Kirghiz were nearing Yarkand, news had got around that an enemy army was on its way and was close to entering the city. Khoja Danyal, Alim Shah Beg, and Shah Jaʿfar Beg each took charge of securing one gate, assigned others to the rest, and stood in a state of heightened alarm. Hashim Sulṭan, by contrast, was still in his cap, nightgown, and sandals. Events caught him by surprise, but he immediately took a staff from the major domo and mounted a lame horse that was standing around with its saddle on. /32b/ Ordering the Kazakhs who were nearby to mount up, he rode out to confront the enemy.

The two sides came face to face before the city gate. The Kirghiz Jarub Beg brandished his lance and spurred his horse toward the sultan, and the sultan likewise drove his lame horse onward without hesitating. Jarub Beg was about to skewer the sultan with his lance when the sultan struck the lance with his staff and broke it in two. Then he wheeled around and hit Jarub Beg on the head with his staff. His skull split open, and he fell to the ground.

Ardor is what a man needs, not a blade at his waist,
Without that, a hen's feather is as much use as a sword.

In the same spirit, Makhdum-i Aʿẓam would often recite these lines in the Turki language:

If high-mindedness is an ally to a man,
Then in the end he will obtain his goal.

Hashim Sulṭan laid low a few more Kirghiz with his staff in the same fashion and ran them into the ground. The Kirghiz were dismayed and recoiled backward. Hearing word of Hashim Sulṭan's bravery, Alim Shah Beg and Shah Jaʿfar Beg mobilized the army, with Khoja Danyal at its head. They dressed the sultan in royal garb and readied the instruments of war. At that moment, news came that Qarazangi Beg had arrived before a gate with five hundred men. Immediately they hurried to confront him, and a great battle took place. When it finally became dark, cries of "mercy!" from the army of Kashgar filled the heavenly dome, and the army of Yarkand also set aside their vengeful blades.

My luck is upside down, my fortune is reversed,
/33a/ Mercy from this affliction, O shah and sultan, mercy!

The next morning, the Kirghiz sent an emissary to negotiate peace terms on the basis that they would no longer violate the frontiers of Yarkand nor do the people any harm. They requested that Jarub Mirza, who had fallen into enemy hands, be returned to them, and they promised to release three thousand Yarkandis whom they had captured. Khoja Danyal, Hashim Sulṭan, and everyone else agreed to this, but when they searched among the army, it was discovered that Jarub Mirza had not been taken prisoner. Then they looked among the dead bodies and saw that Jarub Mirza had died when struck by Hashim Sulṭan's staff. They brought him out and cleaned his wounds, bound him to a piece of wood, and dressed him. Then they sat him on a lame horse, secured his hands and feet, and set off leading the horse by the reins. Watching from the distance, the Kirghiz noticed that Jarub Mirza was unable to lift his head. They reasoned among themselves that since the mirza was such a bold and courageous man, he was obviously mortified at falling captive to the Sarts, and therefore he was approaching without raising his head.

From the one side, they delivered this enlivened corpse, and the Kirghiz for their part gave up the three thousand captives. By the time these captives had rejoined the army, the Kirghiz had discovered that the mirza was but a stiffened corpse, and they departed with shouts of grief and mourning. /33b/ From that point on, they never again dared to come against Yarkand. Khoja Danyal and Hashim Sulṭan struck up the *shadiyana* rhythm loudly, gave thanks for the victory, and directed their attention to festivities and worship of God.[92]

After some time, certain naysayers exhibited hostility to Khoja Danyal and Hashim Sulṭan and issued threats against them. The sultan was overcome by anxiety and withdrew with his retinue to the edge of the Kazakh lands. Khoja Danyal then spent a period of time occupying the Yarkand throne himself.

12. THE ISḤAQIYYA AND THE JUNGHARS

Let us now take up the story in Ili. While the Qalmaqs had been in a state of disunity, Muḥammad Emin Khan had plucked up his courage and, with Khoja Afaq's instigation and blessings, had led a raid and carried off thirty thousand Qalmaq captives. The Qalmaqs bore a long-standing grudge at this, and were anxious to take revenge. Once they had restored stability, they realized that the chaos and disarray among the Muslims presented them with an opportunity, and they descended on Yarkand in force. Khoja Danyal saw with foresight that he had no capacity to oppose the infidel army in battle. Helplessly, in accordance with the hadith, FLIGHT FROM THAT WHICH CANNOT BE OVERCOME IS AMONG THE CUSTOMS OF THE APOSTLES, he eschewed war and strife and went out to meet the infidels in submission. The infidels for their part restrained from tyranny and cruelty and accorded him respect, confirming him once again on the throne of Yarkand.

When the infidel army finished their business in Yarkand and made for Kashgar, /34a/ they took some soldiers from Yarkand and also persuaded Khoja Danyal to accompany them. The Kashgaris gave battle for a few days, but ultimately they too were unable to resist and reluctantly opened the gates and surrendered. Khoja Aḥmad fell into the hands of the infidels. At first they intended to kill him, but Khoja Danyal cautioned them: "If this Muslim land is necessary for you, beware not to kill their khojas, because they are descended from the Prophet of the Muslims. They won't allow you to kill him—even their wives and children would prefer to die in hand-to-hand combat with you." The infidels took this advice, and they refrained from executing him. After they had settled affairs in Kashgar to their liking, instead of giving Khoja Danyal leave to go to Yarkand, they took him back to Ili. They then sent someone to Yarkand to bring his family and retinue to Ili and settled them there in comfort, while they chose people that they preferred for the governorships of Yarkand and Kashgar. They shipped Khoja Aḥmad off like a prisoner and kept him under strict surveillance on the outskirts of Ili, but with God's blessing Khoja Danyal lived with dignity and honor in the land of the infidel.

A wise man will be revered and respected in every region,
Cursed is that place where an ignorant man is esteemed.

For seven years he resided there in this fashion.[93]

Dear reader, heed now some salutary signs, and observe the generous bounty of the Creator: /34b/ At that time when Muḥammad Emin Khan raided the Ili region and took thirty thousand infidels captive, he also carried off certain members of the *törä*'s family, most of whom became Muslims. He presented a beautiful daughter from the *törä*'s family to Khoja Danyal, and Khoja Danyal brought her into the fold of Islam and took her as his wife. A drop of spring rain settled in her womb, and indications emerged that a royal pearl, a priceless gem, was forming.

It was at this time that the Qalmaq army came on its campaign against Kashgar and Yarkand. They retrieved all those who had been taken prisoner, regardless of whether they were now Muslim or non-Muslim, and took them back to their own tribes. They assigned this girl to marry one of the *törä*'s Qalmaq chiefs, but whenever the groom came close to her and tried to consummate the marriage, he would have a seizure and be struck dumb and remove himself again. She thus remained pure until she was finished with her pregnancy. On the day that she gave birth, it was like the river of life emerging from the realm of darkness, or a world-illuminating sun rising at the crack of dawn. They witnessed a pure son come into being, who had the look of Yusuf of Canaan about him. They clothed him in fine brocades and set about bringing him up. Before long, his intellect matured. He obtained an education in the Qalmaq fashion, and the infidels would often praise the child's intelligence. Until he reached seven years of age, no one knew that /35a/ he was the son of a Muslim, and his mother had no way to divulge this secret. She was always pained by this, but she couldn't find a Muslim to reveal it to, since her tribe was several months journey from the *törä*'s camp and the Muslim settlements.

As luck would have it, one day the itinerary of one of the Muslim court merchants (*bāzargān*) brought him to this tribe.[94] As he made his tour, he eventually set foot in this woman's camp. When she suddenly realized that a Muslim had arrived among this tribe of infidels, she was overjoyed. This verse gives an appropriate description of her state of mind:

> Suddenly last night that sweet round face came to my forlorn heart,
> A ray of illumination shining from his bright cheeks.
> A visitor who was nowhere to be found has arrived at the house of my heart.
> Rejoice, O heart, for soul has come at last to your body!
> Be glad, O grieving soul, for eternal life has arrived!

Eventually she contrived a private meeting with the merchant, and she produced her son and revealed her secrets. She had the merchant write out a letter for her and pressed it into his hands. "Take this and deliver it to Khoja Danyal," she said, "and explain my circumstances to him. If you fail in this, you'll be responsible for the apostasy of one or two people, and you'll stand disgraced before the Prophet on Judgment Day."

This merchant delivered the letter to Khoja Danyal. As soon as he became aware of what it said, Khoja Danyal knew it to be true, and he was struck by a painful longing for his child. He immediately took the letter and went with the merchant to the *törä*'s palace and explained the situation. /35b/ The *törä* had the letter read out, and he listened to the merchant's testimony. He then appointed one of his own retainers, along with Khalifa Ubaydullah and Mulla Mashhuri (also known as Akhund Mulla Ibrahim) from Khoja Danyal's following, to head a group of people with these instructions: "If the situation is indeed as described, bring the child and entrust him to these Muslims. If those people don't acquiesce, bring the husband along with the wife and child. Otherwise, if this is a mistake, present these Muslims for punishment as liars."

Acting on this commission, the men came to the Qalmaq tribe and investigated the affair. The woman spoke openly, but her husband wouldn't divulge a thing, and they didn't show them the child at all. Instead, they pointed out the Muslims to the child from afar and said to him, "Look, the cannibals are coming; they're going to say that you're their child and take you away and eat you." They so terrified the boy that he couldn't even bring himself to look at the Muslims. The Qalmaqs also won over the Qalmaq official in the party, so that the Muslims couldn't raise any objections. They came up with a plan to say that this woman was falsely claiming this to be the child of Khoja Danyal because Khoja Danyal was a very handsome and charming young man, and she had been smitten when she set eyes on him.

> I don't know if he is a houri, an angel, or a pari,
> We've never seen such a beautiful youth among mortals.[95]

In the end, they made their way back to the *törä*'s palace without properly concluding the investigation. The Qalmaq husband was himself a member of the *törä*'s family, /36a/ and there was a strong bond between them. He fell sobbing and crying at the feet of Khung-Taiji[96] and pleaded with him: "O *törä*, king of the age! Have mercy on this long-standing servant of yours. If you try these White Turbans according to their Holy Law, they will inevitably produce evidence and remove this beloved son from me.[97] I don't have any son other than him, and I love him dearly. Without a doubt, I will burn up in longing for him."

Woe, a hundred thousand times woe, I am parted from the one I love,
I am separated from that tall one with rosy cheeks.
No one knows what kind of companion I have lost,
I am a distressed nightingale, and I have left the rose bed.

"How would it be," he continued, "if you were to take pity on this despondent slave of yours, adjudicate in my favor, and free me from this grief?"

Take pity on this body, which has been burnt by sighs of woe,
Otherwise, the flame of my grief will scorch the entire world.

Seeing no alternative, the Qalmaq judges (*jarghuchi*) conspired on a scheme to ensure that the boy would end up with the Qalmaqs. The *törä* decreed that next morning the Muslims should present themselves for an audience in their own dress and turbans, and the Qalmaqs likewise in their own garb. That morning a party of Muslims led by Temür Khan, Erke Khan, and Khoja Danyal drew up rows and seated themselves on one side, while the chiefs of the Qalmaqs sat opposite them.[98] They seated the Qalmaq plaintiff higher up and spoke words of warning to the child—for example, "These ones in white turbans are the people-eaters. Beware, a thousand times beware! Don't go near them or they'll catch you and eat you. Make sure you run and sit in your Qalmaq daddy's lap." /36b/ After rehearsing this, they brought him into the audience. On the Muslim side, hope was all but lost, but Khoja Danyal fixed his concentration on the court of the Lord and requested the aid of his illustrious forebears. He left the conscious realm and dived into a sea of divine witness. The *törä* asked this seven-year-old child: "Boy, is your father this Qalmaq? Or is it the khoja? Which one of them is your daddy? Go and sit in his lap." The child made straight for the Qalmaq—everyone could see which way he was going. But when he came close, he suddenly burst into tears, fell into Khoja Danyal's embrace, and fainted. Shouts and cries from people on both sides rose to the sky, and all at once they were carried away in involuntary wailing.

If this makes no impression on their hearts, then tell them,
How my flood of tears inundated the face of the earth.

Khung-Taiji wept a great deal himself, then spoke: "Khoja, justice has been done. It's evident that you were right. I will also grant you the position of khoja and the rule of these four cities. You may go and reside in your own city." With this, he gave him leave to depart. Freed from his detention at the hands of the infidels, Khoja Danyal offered thanks and praise to God. He left Khoja Jahan in the *törä*'s service and made his way to Yarkand with much pomp and ceremony. /37a/ Taking custody of his child, he dressed him in Islamic garb and held great festivities for his circumcision. On account of his handsome features, Khoja Danyal gave him the name Khoja Yusuf.[99]

Khoja Danyal occupied the throne of the Yarkand sultanate for a number of years, and his authority also extended throughout Kashgar, Aqsu, and Khotan. He guided the people and prevented them from going astray, and he ruled on their plaints without making any infringement on the noble shariʿa. He dedicated his life to worship and thanksgiving to God Almighty. Khoja Yusuf meanwhile busied himself with his studies, and in a short space of time he obtained an ample share of learning. During the time of Khoja Afaq, the Qalmaqs had levied a tax of one hundred thousand silver *tangga* on one hundred thousand people, and they continued to take this poll tax (*jizya*) of a hundred thousand *tangga* from Moghulistan.[100] Sometimes they would go to Ili for meetings with the Qalmaqs. This state of affairs persisted for seven years.[101]

Khung-Taiji had a daughter of marriageable age, and he decided to wed her to the son of the *törä* of the Torghut Qalmaqs. He invited Khoja Danyal and all the other amirs and officials from the Seven Cities (Yettishahr) to the marriage ceremony. They had no choice but to comply, so they made the journey to Ili. The infidel Khung-Taiji requested supplies for the wedding from the Muslims, and they offered him all that they had, but still the infidel was not satisfied. He was greedy for cloth from India, fine pearls, and expensive gemstones such as diamonds and emeralds, /37b/ and the Muslims didn't have anything that was appropriate. Eventually they were given an ultimatum: "If you don't provide the necessary items by tomorrow, I will slaughter Khoja Danyal along with the rest of you."

O Muslims, what state of affairs is this, that the world,
Would upturn a hundred Muslims before a single non-Muslim?

Desperate for some remedy for these terrifying threats from the infidel, the amirs and officials of the kingdom all threw themselves at Khoja Danyal's feet. "Khoja," they said, "you must find some way to avert this calamity! Your forefathers used to deal with difficulties like this. You should also be able to find some solution! If not, we are at a loss, for this infidel intends to kill all of us."

Khoja Danyal lowered his head, then raised it again after a while. "Muslims," he said, "this evening let us all as one beseech the court of the Merciful and the spirits of the Khojagan. It may be that they will deliver us from this trial."

That night, the Muslims assembled in a certain location. With heart and soul, they appealed to the court of the Lord and fell about crying and wailing. It was midnight when Khoja Danyal raised his hands in supplication, and the Muslims all held their hands open and said AMEN. It was not until the break of dawn, when they said GOD IS MOST GREAT, that they stopped praying, and Khoja Danyal pronounced these hopeful tidings: "O Muslims, it may be that God has delivered us from the hands of the infidel. Stand firm in the hope that our entreaties have been heard." /38a/ After some time, a shout rang out that Khung-Taiji (A CURSE BE UPON HIM!) had died, and in his place Galdan-Tseren had become *törä*. Upon hearing this news, the Muslims all went to the palace of the infidels and found out what had happened: Khung-Taiji's wife had poisoned her husband with the intention of making her own son the *törä*. Galdan-Tseren had been born to a different wife, and she intended to kill him too, but one of his brothers brought word to him. Galdan-Tseren had then mobilized his officers and told them what was going on, and with their support he had killed his stepmother and younger brothers, seized the throne, and become *törä*.[102] God put some of His grace in the heart of this infidel, and he decreed that the Muslims could return to their various places of origin and carry on according to the old precedents. He said to Khoja Danyal, "Khoja, you may return home too. I will entrust you with the position of khoja and king in these four cities. You should act even more loyally and steadfastly than you did during my father's reign." So saying, he gave permission for everyone to leave. Khoja Danyal led them back to their homeland, and they gave thanks to God and performed praise and worship.

A period of time went by in this fashion. They spent the income they received from the lands and canals that the khans had donated to Khoja Isḥaq Vali, but owing to the weakness of Islam and the strength of the infidels, they were obliged to deliver the Qalmaqs the tax revenue (*baj u kharāj*) that these kingdoms generated.[103] /38b/ In the end, in accordance with the rule that EVERY SOUL SHALL TASTE DEATH [21:35], Khoja Danyal sipped the cup of death from the wine-server of time and resigned himself to his fate. By way of testament and thanksgiving, he said, "I have entrusted all my children, infants and adults, as well as my wives, to the mercy of the Lord and the spirits of my forefathers." He was particularly mindful of Khoja Jahan. "My dear son," he said to him, "I have consigned you above all to the care of my estimable forefathers. Don't be remiss in training these young children. Show no laxity in serving Almighty God, as far as you are able, and do not neglect the precepts of the noble shariʿa. Be resolute in your studies and your actions. The Prophet left us knowledge and deeds as his legacy, not dirhams and dinars. I could see no alternative but to obediently submit to these infidels, and I was not in a position to wield the blade of Islam. I have no choice now but to make this final journey with this wish unfulfilled. You, though, should bring this desire of mine to fulfillment. Perhaps God will display His grace and mercy and grant you a precious opportunity, a moment of disturbance and disruption among these mortal enemies. Then you should swing the sword of Islam at the infidels without restraint, make recompense for my black face of shame, and take revenge for the Muslims. In that way you'll uphold the honor of sayyidhood /39a/ and feel no shame before God and the Prophet on Judgment Day." With this, he ended his testament and gave up his spirit to the Lord. TRULY WE ARE GOD'S, AND UNTO HIM WE RETURN [2:156].[104]

For a time, it seemed as if Judgment Day was dawning. Shouts and cries filled the revolving dome of heaven, and the sun was hidden behind a dark curtain. Khoja Danyal's loyal devotees fainted as if they were candles being snuffed out. The people of the city and the population of all the kingdoms gathered to mourn him, and they buried him with full honor in the Golden Shrine.

Khoja Danyal was survived by five sons and a number of daughters. Among his sons, the first was Khoja Jahan, the second was Khoja Ayyub, the third was Khoja Yusuf, the fourth was Khoja Khamush (whose original name was Khoja Niẓam al-Din), and the fifth was Khoja Ubaydullah. Khoja Jahan exhibited great kindness toward these children and took responsibility both for their worldly education and their esoteric training. For their part, these sons recognized Khoja Jahan in the place of their illustrious father and did not stray in their obedience to him. Khoja Jahan was confirmed on the throne of the Yarkand sultanate, while Khoja Yusuf took the throne in Kashgar, Khoja Niẓam al-Din in Aqsu, and Khoja Ubaydullah in Khotan. These holy men all adjudicated the petitions of their subjects in accordance with the shariʿa and promoted the Islamic faith.

Khoja Jahan in particular held frequent gatherings throughout his life with the religious scholars and pious men of culture. With his soothing words, /39b/ he would enliven the souls of those present who were afflicted by grief and grant them rich favors. Sometimes he would hold audiences with the amirs and pillars of state, and displaying the regalia of rule, he would exercise justice and judge the petitions of the people according to the Holy Law. On other occasions, he would hold readings from works of biography and history and listen to the stories of the great prophets and beloved saints, the authoritative imams, and bygone kings. He would remember them with benedictions and dedicate prayers and recitations from the Quran to their triumphant spirits. Sometimes he would bring in volumes of ghazals and ma̲snavis, and explicate their truths and induce states of ecstasy, so that the people in the assembly would spin on their heads like moths and offer up their very selfhood to him as tribute. Other times, he would take hold of a thread of verse and improvise odes that were fiery enough to spark a bonfire of hearts, and heart-wrenching rhymes that could set souls in motion. In response to the intricate ghazals of his predecessors, he would compose salutary replies in five- and six-line stanzas. Sometimes he would occupy the position of the king of poetry and adjudicate among the works of the poets and versifiers of the age. To the authors of those he preferred he would show kingly favor, clothing them in royal robes and honoring them with a seat by his side. Each week, on Tuesdays and Wednesdays, he would inspect the madrasas /40a/ and visit the classroom of the most learned Akhund Khoja Isḥaq, who was known by his nickname of Khoja Akhund. Whichever of his quick-witted pupils excelled in rhetoric and debate, he would praise them and admit them to pride of place at his gatherings, lavishing them with generosity. At the same time, he would reprimand any dim intellects or blind know-nothings with his advice, and inspire them with looks of admonition. He would serve up all sorts of foods and delicacies to satisfy his companions. At other times he would converse with dervishes and disciples and instruct them on how to navigate the Path.

Thus all manner of people, great and small, made entreaties for this generous monarch and gave thanks for his happy reign. "God only knows," they would say, "whether there has ever been such a time as this in the past, or ever again will be in the future?" Some likened it to the reign of Sulṭan Ḥusayn Mirza, but others argued that while this age did indeed resemble that one, there were differences between the two sultans.[105] Sulṭan Ḥusayn was the son of a mirza, they explained, and in certain of his qualities and achievements he was not the caliber of this king, who in his lineage descended from the Lord of the two worlds, His Holiness Muḥammad. There is a hadith /40b/ attributed to the Prophet that says HONOR MY POSTERITY: THE PIOUS ONES FOR THE SAKE OF GOD, AND THE WAYWARD ONES FOR MY SAKE. This noble hadith is highly applicable in the case of these heirs of his.

13. A DISCOURSE ON GENEALOGICAL AND SPIRITUAL LINEAGES

Lineages come in two forms: the worldly lineage and the spiritual lineage. Someone's worldly lineage refers to a genealogy in the form of X *ibn* Y—the lineage that comes into being because so-and-so is the son of so-and-so. The spiritual lineage is the pedigree that is formed by the transmission of the sciences and practices of the Prophet. There are three categories to this kind of lineage. The first category is the manifest lineage, which is created through exoteric learning and public actions and does not contain any element of esoteric knowledge. Those in this category are known as "manifest scholars." Those in the second category have a portion of esoteric knowledge but do not possess any exoteric knowledge, or knowledge of technicalities and precepts; they demonstrate insight and miracle-working because of their inner purity. These are called the "Shaykhs of the Turks" (*mashāyikh-i Turk*).[106]

My idol, who went to no school and could not write a line,
With a glance became the preceptor of a hundred professors.[107]

The third category combines the exoteric sciences and the esoteric sciences, without in any way abandoning the precepts of the shariʿa, a commitment to pious deeds, and adherence to tradition. Externally, those in this category constantly observe the Holy Law, while their inner being exhibits the qualities of the Path and Truth. They are known as the "firmly grounded scholars" (*ulamāʾ-i rāsiḫīn*). God said: AND NONE KNOW ITS INTERPRETATION SAVE GOD AND THOSE FIRMLY ROOTED IN KNOWLEDGE [3:7], which means "No one knows the interpretation of the allegorical verses apart from God himself /41a/ and the firmly grounded scholars."[108] The hadith that THE SCHOLARS OF THE COMMUNITY ARE THE HEIRS OF THE PROPHETS is fitting in respect to this category. They have inherited from the prophets not wealth but knowledge and deeds.

The branches of learning associated with the Prophet are of two types. The first is the knowledge that is linked to prophecy, called the science of the shariʿa. The second is the knowledge that is tied up with sainthood, called the science of the state of being (*ḥāl*), or esoteric science. These fortunate individuals have a share of both these types of learning; otherwise it would be inappropriate to describe them as heirs of the Prophet, since an heir is one who obtains a share of the entire property of the deceased in accordance with their rights. If someone comes into possession of some, but not all, of his father's property—for example, if he has a rightful claim to inherit his gold but cannot lay claim to his silver—then it would inappropriate to describe that person as his son.

In Khoja Jahan these two lineages combined, and he was extremely well versed in both the exoteric sciences and esoteric sciences.

Should you ask his scholarly pedigree, he is the second Naqshband,
And if you ask his bloodline, he is of the family of Muḥammad.

Similarly, it has been said that if the spiritual lineage transmitted through these scholars and sayyids descended from Ali were suddenly to be lifted from this group, then there would no individual or living thing who could play the same role. Therefore, they are the deputies of the Prophet, such that the stability of Islam and the grounding of the Path and Truth, indeed the very ordering of the world, are dependent on them. The hadith that THE SCHOLARS OF MY COMMUNITY ARE LIKE THE PROPHETS OF THE BANI ISRAʾIL /41b/ is about them. So too is THE SHAYKH IN HIS TRIBE IS LIKE THE PROPHET IN HIS COMMUNITY.

The succession of Khoja Jahan's worldly lineage is as follows: he is Khoja Yaʿqub Khoja Jahan, son of Khoja Danyal, son of Khoja Abdullah, son of Khoja Shadi, son of Khoja Isḥaq, son of Makhdum-i Aʿẓam Aḥmad Khojagi, son of Sayyid Jalal al-Din, son of Sayyid Burhan al-Din, son of Sayyid Khoja, son of Sayyid Burhan al-Din Qilich, son of Sayyid Kamal al-Din, son of Sayyid Jalal al-Din, son of Shah Ḥasan, son of Shah Ḥusayn, son of Sayyid Muḥammad, son of Sayyid Aḥmad, son of Ubaydullah, son of Abdullah Afżal, son of Abdullah Iʿraj, son of Sayyid Ṭalib, son of Imam Ali Riża, son of Imam Musa Kaẓim, son of Imam Jaʿfar Ṣadiq, son of Imam Muḥammad Baqir, son of Imam Zayn al-Abidin, son of Imam Ḥusayn, son of Ali and Faṭima al-Zahra, who was the daughter of His Holiness Muḥammad.

The explanation of his spiritual lineage is as follows:

As is indicated by the verse AND WE SEND DOWN OF THE QURAN THAT WHICH IS A CURE AND A MERCY FOR THE BELIEVERS [17:82], the Quran is the word of the True Beloved and is a healing and mercy for all believers and Muslims. It settled first in the blessed heart of Muḥammad, and there was nothing left behind in the divine realm apart from what was forthcoming in the Quran. As God said: NOR ANYTHING MOIST OR DRY BUT THAT IT IS IN A CLEAR BOOK [6:59]. The practice of the divine was such that the blessing and mercy of the Lord's court could not reach anyone other than through the agency of someone who had attained perfection. Thus, that perfect individual was Muḥammad. There was nothing left behind in the unseen realm /42a/ that did not manifest within His Holiness.

All that God from the Court of the Exalted Power
Poured into the noble breast of His Chosen One.[109]

Following this, His Holiness became the conduit for this supreme grace to others. There is a hadith that THE QURAN HAS AN EXTERIOR AND AN INTERIOR, AND THE INTERIOR HAS SEVEN INTERIORS. Superficially, the Quran consists of the mundane sciences of the shariʿa, which he consigned to the breasts of the exoteric scholars, while the interior of the Quran is made up of the essence and truth of the shariʿa, and he bestowed this on the luminous souls of the esoteric scholars of the Path, the friends of God.

I selected out the kernel of the Quran,
And threw the skin before the unworthy.

Know and be aware, sincere student, that His Grace assigned the exterior and interior of the Quran, which is a cure and a mercy for the believers, to eighteen people from among his family and companions who had the aptitude for its meaning. Among these eighteen people, the most virtuous and talented was Abu Bakr Ṣiddiq. Because of his complete dedication to His Grace, the fire of love burned his liver, and every time he let out a sigh the smell of roasting flesh would fill an entire city neighborhood.

Every mournful sigh that arises from his breast
Is smoke which carries the scent of roast liver.[110]

On account of his ability and capacity, His Grace poured the sweet juice of meaning into the pure breast of Abu Bakr Ṣiddiq, his intimate companion in the cave, his true pupil and faithful friend.

He poured all this into the breast /42b/ *of Ṣiddiq,*
So that truth flowed from him as long as he lived.[111]

Abu Bakr then discharged this curative elixir of insight into the breast of the noble and steadfast Salman Fars, in recognition of his talent. From Salman Fars it flowed to that light of the garden of faith and beloved of the truth-seekers, Qasim b. Muḥammad b. Abu Bakr Ṣiddiq. He then transmitted this healing potion into the luminescent breast of the bygone khoja and enemy of the impious, Imam Jaʿfar Ṣadiq. The respected imam entrusted this enlightening concoction to the renowned sage and revered teacher, the

Sulṭan of the Gnostics Bayazid Bistami. Sulṭan Bayazid then caused this river of truth to flow into the breast of Shaykh Abu l-Ḥasan Kharaqani. Shaykh Abu l-Ḥasan in turn directed this limitless ocean of love into the breast of Shaykh Abu l-Qasim Gurgani, and from him it went to Shaykh Sarmadi Khoja Ali Farmadi, and then into the breast of the master of Hamadan, the authoritative theologian Shaykh Abu Yusuf Hamadani. From him it lodged in the breast of the lordly pole and khoja of the world, Khoja Abd al-Khaliq Ghijduvani. The noble Khiżr adopted him as his son and attended to his spiritual training, so while his guiding instructor was Shaykh Abu Yusuf, the focus of his devotion was Khiżr himself.[112]

Khoja Abd al-Khaliq Ghijduvani is referred to as the "head of the circle," and he left behind four of his contemporaries as deputies. First was Khoja Aḥmad Ṣiddiq, then Khoja Arif Rivgari, Khoja Avliya-yi Kalan, and Khoja Aḥmad Yasavi. Khoja Aḥmad was first to occupy the position of shaykh, while the other two [*sic*] were in his service. Afterward, they inherited the position. Khoja Arif issued a diploma to Khoja Maḥmud Faghnavi, /43a/ and Khoja Maḥmud switched from practicing silent remembrance (*ẕikr*) to vocal remembrance and went about his work.[113]

The scholars of Bukhara asked Khoja Maḥmud, "What is the purpose of performing the vocal remembrance?"

Khoja Maḥmud said, "My intention is that those who are sleeping should awake, that the negligent take heed, and that those who are lost find the path. It is consistent with true repentance and is the foundation of all happiness."

Mawlana Ḥafiẓ al-Din said, "His intention is correct, so it is permitted for him."

From Khoja Maḥmud this meaning came to Khoja Ali Ramitani, and he directed it toward the most accomplished guide of the era, Khoja Muḥammad Baba Sammasi. After him it made its appearance in Amir Sayyid Kulal, who was preeminent among those who have attained perfection and states of being. From him these true secrets shone forth in the pride of the shariʿa and adornment of the Path, Khoja Baha al-Din Naqshband.[114] The Great Khoja's capacity was wide and strong, and he was not satisfied with this quantity alone. God in His utmost grace appointed the spirit of Khoja Abd al-Khaliq Ghijduvani to assist him. In the same way that God had manifested grace from His court within the Prophet, He did so again for the final time in the soul of the Great Khoja in Bukhara. As Mawlana Abd al-Raḥman Jami has said:

The coin that was struck in Yathrib and Batha,
Was minted for the final time in Bukhara.
None profited from that coin's inscription,
/43b/ *Other than the pure heart of Shah Naqshband.*[115]

In the *Nafaḥat al-Uns*, the Great Khoja [Baha al-Din Naqshband] is reported to have said:

Each night I would pay a visit to the shrines of Bukhara, such that I would be lost to myself. In a dream I saw the wall of a mosque was rent on the side facing the direction of Mecca (the *qibla*), and a large throne was visible. On that throne a blessed being was seated, with a yellow curtain drawn before him. All around the throne there was a crowd. It became evident that these were the friends of God from the past. "Who are they?" I wondered.

At that point one of the group came forward and said, "That great one is Khoja Abd al-Khaliq Ghijduvani, and these are his deputies." He indicated each one of them by name: Khoja Aḥmad Ṣiddiq, Khoja Arif Rivgari, Khoja Avliya-yi Kalan, Khoja Maḥmud Anjir Faghnavi, and Khoja Ali Ramitani. When he came to Khoja Muḥammad Baba Sammasi, he said, "You've seen this one while he was alive. He gave you a cap and was your shaykh. Do you recognize him?"

I said, "I do."

After this the gathering told me, "Take heed, the Lord of the World Khoja Abd al-Khaliq Ghijduvani will say a few words, and in traversing God's Path you have no choice but to comply with them." I was eager to meet the khoja, so they raised the curtain from between us. /44a/ I greeted him, and he returned my greetings and cast his transformative gaze on me. He then said a few things having to do with the beginning and middle stages of the Path. One of these was that at all times one must be steadfast in conforming to the shariʿa, act in accordance with the tradition and divine ordinances, and abstain from taking license and indulging in innovation, until such time as the tradition and ordinances are well established.[116]

The Great Khoja gave up the practice of vocal *ẕikr* and withdrew from discoursing with Sayyid Amir Kulal. The amir took this as a reproach, but on the instructions of Khoja Abd al-Khaliq Ghijduvani, the Great Khoja didn't pay any mind to the fact that Sayyid Kulal was put out. The dispute between them reached the point that Sayyid Amir Kulal prohibited his companions from associating with Khoja Baha al-Din, saying that Khoja Baha al-Din was a magician and belonged to an evil sect. Among his disciples, he took an oath from one named Shaykh Amir Ḥusayn that he would never sit in Baha al-Din's company. This Amir Ḥusayn used to sell boots, and it so happened that one day Khoja Baha al-Din turned up at his shop, intending to buy a pair. The instant that Amir Ḥusayn set eyes on him, he ran into the shop and slammed the door shut.

"Come out here and do business with me!" the Great Khoja said.

"My master Sayyid Amir Kulal made me swear that I wouldn't sit with you," Shaykh Amir Ḥusayn replied.

/44b/ "Simple enough," Khoja Baha al-Din said, "come outside and do business with me standing up!"

Amir Ḥusayn took out some boots, and started to transact with him while standing up. They bargained over the price, and in the end the Great Khoja struck a deal and made his purchase. "You engage in such trickery and deception just to sell a pair of boots," he said, "what will become of you in the end?" With this, he continued on his way.

Shaykh Amir Ḥusayn was completely dumbstruck, and he abandoned his shop and set off after the Great Khoja. He stumbled in like a madman while the Great Khoja was sitting with his companions Khoja Yusuf and Khoja Muḥammad Parsa. The khoja gave him a bemused look. "Come, Amir Ḥusayn," he said. "I have obtained a ruling (*fatwá*) for you from the imams and mujtahids." The substance of the ruling is as follows:

> The shaykhs have said: If someone traveling on the path of eternity, having sworn allegiance to one master should swear allegiance to another without rejecting the first, is it in accordance with the Holy Law and the Path? They have determined: It is permitted and allowable, because all the people of God are bound by the same rule, they share a common outlook, and their goal is the same.
>
> *There is only one Kaaba—even if there are a hundred roads to it.*
>
> Contention is nothing but the habit of a dervish. It is like seeing double, being cross-eyed, and indulging one's animal nature. If for some reason this individual rejects his first master, then his dedication to the second

master is also invalid. The rejection of one is the rejection of all, and the acceptance of one is the acceptance of all. The shaykhs have recorded this question concerning the Path /45a/ in their books, although GOD KNOWS BEST.[117]

Subsequently this infinite river of Truth flowed from Khoja Baha al-Din Naqshband into the blessed heart of Mawlana Yaᶜqub Charkhi, and from him the curative sea of mercy crested in the heart of the initiate of the secrets, Khoja Ubaydullah Aḥrar.

One who knows the freedom of renunciation,
Is Khoja Ubaydullah Aḥrar.
Ubaydullah's glorious destitution
Served its turn at emperorship of the world.[118]

Khoja Aḥrar's blessed heart was extremely capacious and receptive and was not satisfied with this amount. He received assistance from the spirits of the Great Khoja and Shaykh Abu Bakr Qaffal Shashi, and from many other friends of God, so that the divine secrets emptied out entirely in his heart.[119] From Khoja Aḥrar this noble lineage came to adorn Muḥammad Mawlana Qażi, and from him this door of divine grace was flung open to the heart of the chief of Arabia and Persia and the best of the community, Makhdum-i Aᶜẓam Khojagi. From Makhdum-i Aᶜẓam this sea of divine grace divided into two streams. One of them flowed as a deposit into the confines of Muḥammad Islam Khoja Juybari's heart. From him it was entrusted for safekeeping to Ishan-i Kalan Khoja Muḥammad Amin. Following this, it stirred in his beloved brother Khoja Baha al-Din and was then entrusted to his child Khoja Hashim Dahbidi. /45b/ Following this, it manifested in his brother Khoja Muḥammad Yusuf, and from him it emerged in his honorable son Khoja Afaq.

I don't know where this lineage raised its head.

As for the other stream, it flowed from Makhdum-i Aᶜẓam as a deposit for safekeeping to Mawlana Luṭfullah Chusti. From him this lineage stirred in Khoja Isḥaq Vali. After him it manifested in his son Khoja Shadi, and then it came to light in his son Khoja Abdullah. Following this, it expressed itself in his bright-minded son Khoja Danyal, and from him it came to adorn his accomplished son, that imbiber of divine union, Khoja Jahan Khoja Yaʿqub.

The pen has reached this point and snapped its nib.

WERE I TO ADVANCE FROM HERE THE DISTANCE OF A FINGERTIP,
I WOULD BURN UP.[120]

The introduction is finished, the pen is satisfied with it.[121]

It then became evident that Khoja Jahan was the pole of the age, a true saint, and was engulfed in a sea of witness. Although in public he surrounded himself with a veil of sultanhood and presented himself in the guise of a religious scholar and poet, such that someone who was ignorant would not know or recognize who he was, nevertheless men of insight and those aware of the truth could tell that the bird of his soul was surveying the plain of Paradise and nesting on a branch of the Lote Tree, and that the divine grace and mercy of the Lord had established its court in the inner chambers of his heart.

The late Akhund Shah Abd al-Qadir, who was the leading scholar and chief mufti of Yarkand, is said to have related the following:

There was one holy /46a/ night, which had a hint of the Night of Power or the Night of Desires about it.[122] Midway through the evening, I had refreshed my ablutions, performed the thanksgiving prayer, and recited an entreaty for forgiveness, but had not yet fallen asleep. In that state, I lost consciousness. In a dream, I saw a huge, tall building, whose dome rose higher than the celestial vault of the sky and whose ceiling, columns, and walls my gaze could barely take in. From the building's dome, rays of light were streaming out with such intensity that the sun and moon which light up the world were but novices by comparison. With a hundred humble entreaties, I was eventually admitted to the building. I went in and observed from a niche that on top of a royal dais a throne of gold had been erected, decorated with rubies, diamonds, and various jewels, the like of which was unimaginable to any mortal. Seated on this throne was a blessed figure for whom the sun, or indeed a hundred thousand suns, would be no more valuable than a speck of fragrant dust from his sandals. In front of him were seated two noble princes, one of whom was dressed in green, the other in red. Around this great throne had been set up four half-thrones, on which four luminescent men were sitting. Surrounding them was a great crowd seated row upon row, in numbers beyond reckoning.

Gazing at this sight, I was lost to myself. After a while, I came to my senses and asked someone who this was on the throne and /46b/ who these other people were. He told me, "That one on the large throne is the lord of the two worlds, Muḥammad, and those on the half-thrones are his four great companions—the rightly guided caliphs. The rest of the assembly are his companions and the saints of the community. From that time until now, they have met to appoint someone to the position of pole whenever the incumbent pole leaves the world."

Right then, two people led in Khoja Jahan Khoja Yaʿqub. He kissed the ground respectfully and introduced himself with a bow.

His Holiness returned the greeting. "Come forward, my son," he said. He kissed Khoja Jahan's brow and said, "My son, your capacity for the trappings of polehood is superior to that of anyone else; you are best suited to this lofty position." So saying, he dressed him in the pole's robe, and the entire assembly applauded him. Then he instructed them to give his old robe to Khoja Jahan's servant.

I immediately ran forward, and they gave me his clothes, which I put on. Khoja Jahan pleaded, "O Prophet of God, this is an extremely high position, and this humble servant of yours is so wretched and lacking in ability. This puts me in an awkward position. What should I do?"

Muḥammad said, "Son, this is a gift from God, and to whomever He gives it, right there and then his ability will rise to the necessary level.

Receptivity is not a necessary condition for His bounty.
Nay, His bounty is the necessary condition for receptivity.[123]

Don't worry, God and the spirits of the saints of the community will be your patrons. The task will get easier, God willing."

At that point, I came to myself. I saw that I was seated facing the *qibla* reciting my entreaty for forgiveness, /47a/ but my nose was filled with a perfumed scent. I immediately set off for the palace, intending to announce this joyous news. But here was an astonishing sight: the usual custom was to lock all the gates and take the keys inside, but this evening I simply opened the nine gates and walked in. The chains were all lying undone; not a single one of them was locked. I don't know whether it was because of some miracle that the locked gates had opened or it was simply by chance that they had left them unlocked that evening. In any case, I arrived in front of the library and Khoja Jahan's private quarters. I saw that a candle was burning, but the door wasn't open. Out of humility I hesitated for a moment, so as not to enter without permission, when all of a sudden a voice came from within the room: "Come in, Akhund." At this summons, I entered. He had just finished a thanksgiving prayer and was in the midst of his supplications when he called out to me. I bowed and congratulated him.

The khoja and pole of the age said, "Akhund, why the delay with these congratulations? You should have said this in that assembly you witnessed."

I was dumbstruck. "Forgive me, king of the world," I said.

The khoja took pity on me. "Akhund, explain the dream that you had," he said.

"My apologies," I replied, "but *Where there is clarity / what need is there for explanation?*"[124]

"Indeed," said the khoja, "but just so that you find some peace of mind." So I explained my dream, but I didn't mention that I had been given his old robe, not wanting to seem greedy.

The khoja said, "Akhund, /47b/ why didn't you mention the clothes that were given to you?"

"I'm sorry," I stammered. "On your blessed shoulders you had an embroidered and studded cloak. You took it off and discarded it to me. I bowed and put it on."

I had faith before this, but I did have my doubts. With this, my belief increased a hundredfold. With repentance and humility, I pledged my devotion, and my heart lit up like a torch.

"This is a secret," the khoja said, "it must be kept hidden. Be careful not to divulge it to anyone."

> [*Letting out the secret from behind the veil is not expedient.*]
> *If it were, in the licentious gathering no rumor would be left unspread.*[125]

I didn't reveal this secret to anyone as long as the khoja lived, but now that he's hidden to the world, I've decided to tell the story.

Every time Akhund Shah Abd al-Qadir related this story, he would weep and cry. Certain charismatic spiritual guides came to Yarkand, and the akhund gave his peers, apprentices, and his sons leave to pledge their devotion to them, but he himself departed the world maintaining his old loyalty.[126]

According to Abdullah ibn Masʿud (MAY GOD BE PLEASED WITH HIM!), the Prophet of God said, "Verily God /48a/ has three hundred chosen servants whose hearts are the same as the heart of Adam. He has forty servants whose hearts are the same as the heart of Moses, seven servants whose hearts are the same as the heart of Ibrahim, five servants whose hearts are the same as the heart of Gabriel, three whose heart is the same as Michael's, and one whose heart is the same as Israfil's."

When this lone individual leaves the world, then they select someone from the three and appoint him in his place. When someone from among these three dies, they choose someone from the five, and so on in this fashion. They call the three hundred the Good (*akhyār*), and they call the forty the Substitutes (*abdāl*). They call the seven the Pious (*abrār*), and the affairs of the seven climes are entrusted to them. They call the five the Pillars (*awtād*), they call the three the Chiefs (*nuqabā*), and they call the one the Pole (*quṭb*) or the Aid (*ghaws̱*). They all know one another, and in everything they do they require each other's permission.[127] They are always present in the world, and every binding and loosing, every appointment and dismissal, and every promotion and demotion among the people of the world is due to them, for they have been entrusted with spiritual rule. Each appointment and each dismissal, indeed every affair, is first instantiated by them in a spiritual sense before it will come to pass in the external world. Every day they all follow the pole in performing the dawn prayer at the Kaaba. They report to the pole on the day's events and handle the world's affairs with the pole's permission.[128]

There are also the *maktūm* saints—i.e. those who are hidden—/48b/ numbering four thousand. These do not know one another, or even know themselves, for they are unaware of their own state of being. These are the saints of the world, as the Prophet is said to have said of them: BY THEM SUSTENANCE IS PROVIDED, RAIN FALLS, AND INCIDENT IS KEPT FROM THE FACE OF THE EARTH. This is all thanks to their blessed existence; were it not for presence of this prestigious group, then the world and its inhabitants would succumb instantly. WERE IT NOT FOR THE RIGHTEOUS, THE SINNERS WOULD BE DESTROYED.

The world is maintained by the existence of the elect,
And stays in place thanks to their grace.
Were it not for their presence on the face of the earth,
Then this mortal world would be as SCATTERED DUST [25:23].

One of the elders of the Path has said, "I once witnessed a gathering of pure spirits in the hidden realm and offered them my greetings. They greeted me in response. I asked them, 'What sort of lineage do you have?' They said, 'We are Sufis, and there are seven gradations among us: The students, disciples, wayfarers, journeymen, fliers, and attainers, and the seventh rank is that of the pole, of which there is only one.' "

There are two kinds of pole. One is the Guiding Pole (*quṭb-i irshād*), whose heart is the same as that of Muḥammad, and who is referred to as the "everyday pole." The other is the Substitute Pole (*quṭb-i abdāl*), whose heart is the same as that of the Holy Israfil. They call him the "fixed pole," or the "reclusive pole." The everyday poles have wives and families, they own property, and they have friends and enemies. They are the deputies of the saints in summoning people to God. /49a/ People don't know who they are; only those whom God has guided will know them. On this there is a hadith from the Prophet: MY SAINTS ARE BENEATH MY DOMES; NO ONE KNOWS

THEM OTHER THAN ME. That is to say, "My saints and my friends are behind a curtain; no one recognizes them apart from me," although one can know them with God's approval.

Every saint can see a saint,
And Ali can see Muṣṭafa.

It has been said that the reclusive saints are in the position of attendant (*khādim*), while the everyday saints are in the position of adviser (*vazīr*). Outwardly they are among the people, while inwardly they are with God. If one of the reclusive saints commits a sin, then the everyday pole requests forgiveness for them, and pronounces their forgiveness. They serve as proof and example of spiritual guidance for the wayward pupils. Certain saints received a revelation that God said, "If I gave this world and the next to a single person, I would expect nothing in return. I would only expect something from someone to whom I introduced My friends." And some of the greats have said, "Just as there are two poles in the heavens, the north pole and the south pole, so too there are two poles on earth—the substitute pole and the guiding pole." The reclusive saints have always been present, and were so before the era of the Prophet. At the time of his emergence, the substitute pole was Uways Qarani's uncle Iṣam Qarani, who was a manifestation of the Merciful, and for that reason His Holiness said, VERILY I FIND THE SCENT OF THE MERCIFUL COMING FROM THE DIRECTION OF YEMEN. The substitutes have complete liberty in eating and drinking, making ablutions, taking medicine, performing prayers, and carrying out the tradition of Muḥammad. They do not dwell for long in any one place, /49b/ and only take up residence somewhere if they become sick. The poles are fixed in their locations, and they are long-lived. Khoja Khiżr and Khoja Ilyas converse with the pole; in most respects, they show him honor and emulate him in performing prayers.

Certain identifying signs were explained to the pole of the poles, and aid to God's friends, Khoja Baha al-Din Naqshband, and he listed these signs in these couplets:

There are three signs of sainthood: The first of these
Is that when you gaze upon his face you will be drawn to him.

Second is that in gatherings when he discourses on meaning,
He deprives everyone of their seflhood once again.
Third is that a saint is truly the most distinguished in the world,
So that no evil deed will come from any of his limbs.[129]

That is to say, there are three signs of sainthood. The first is that when you look at them intensely, your heart will inevitably be drawn to them, and you will immediately recognize them as a friend. The second is that in any gathering when they talk about spirituality, they send everyone into a trance with their words, so that people's hearts lose all interest in the world. The third is that a saint is distinguished among the people of the world, and no low deed can come from any of their limbs. Their entire being and all their words and deeds are in harmony with Muḥammad's Holy Law.

Several other signs and indications of sayyidhood have also been established. Imam Ṭaḥawi is better known as the nephew imam, because he was the son of Imam Shafiᶜi's sister. This notwithstanding, he embraced the Hanafi school of Imam-i Aᶜẓam, who was a light of the community and a paragon of the shariᶜa. His reason for doing so was that Imam Shafiᶜi's sister /50a/ died during childbirth, while the child was still in her womb and showing signs of life. According to the school of Imam-i Aᶜẓam, it is permitted to cut open the stomach of a woman who has died for the sake of the child. Even if it harms the corpse, the survival of one is the greater good. "A live cat is worth more than a hundred dead lions," as the saying goes. They therefore had recourse to the authority of Imam-i Aᶜẓam, cut open her corpse on its left-hand side, and took the child out. They raised the child, and he became a scholar of religion, adopting the name Imam Ṭaḥawi.[130]

At that time, Imam Shafiᶜi's was the dominant school, and it was particularly widely disseminated among Imam Ṭaḥawi's family. Yet Imam Ṭaḥawi gave up the Shafiᶜi school, and chose instead the school of Imam-i Aᶜẓam. "I'm disgusted with a school that would cause the death of someone like me," he said. He popularized the Hanafi school and became its leading representative. Every hadith that he accepted should be accepted, and may serve as a guide to action, while any hadith that he rejected cannot. Within the Hanafi school, his words have the status of authoritative proof.

In his book entitled *Ṭaḥawi*, Imam Ṭaḥawi relates the following anecdote:[131]

Abu l-Fażl Bukhari once said, "I asked the pride of the nations, the upstanding Imam [Hanafi], 'Is it possible to know the descendants of the Prophet from their features? How should one adjudicate someone's claim to sayyid descent?' "

The imam said in reply, "There are several distinguishing signs of a descendant of the Prophet. The first is that they have a mild disposition and never look askance at anyone. The second is that they keep quiet about people's failings. The third /51a/ is that they control their temper. The fourth is that they forgive people their sins and don't seek revenge. The fifth is that they refrain from fornication or sodomy and don't keep young lovers for evil deeds. It is just as the Prophet has said: HE SHALL NOT SODOMIZE OR BE SODOMIZED; i.e., 'My offspring won't be a catamite, and won't do evil things with catamites.' Confirmation of the first sign is found in the verse AND TRULY THOU ART OF AN EXALTED CHARACTER [68:4], which means 'Verily, O Muḥammad, you have a perfectly pleasant disposition.' Therefore, anyone who has a bad temper, by the consensus of all the authorities, their connection to the Prophet is invalid. Likewise, in the case of someone who publicizes the flaws of others, there is consensus that his connection is invalid. If someone loses their temper and flies into a rage, in their case too, the view is that their connection is in error. And someone who commits fornication or sodomy, by consensus their connection is also false. Telling lies, spreading gossip, or slandering others is not the conduct of the offspring of the Prophet, and anyone who displays these bad habits, their genealogy too must be faulty."

The holy imam also said, "Understanding this question is essential for Muḥammad's community, for during the end times many people will claim they belong to the line of the Prophet and will let their locks hang down like a sayyid and an Alawi. Whenever they exhibit the aforementioned marks and signs, /51b/ they should be believed and accorded respect as descendants of the Prophet, but if these signs are not present, then they should not be believed, and it is not necessary to honor them. It is similar to the well-known situation of people suspecting everyone of being Khiżr. This issue will come up a lot in the end times, but since people are now unaware of it, they distort their faith and exaggerate their deference to these people beyond all limits."

In the book entitled *Muḥiṭ*, the following is related:

There are many indications of sayyidhood. Among these are that a sayyid will never be given to illicit or deviant acts and will not distort the affairs of the shariʿa, because an inclination toward illicit acts or distortions of the Holy Law has been prohibited, and anyone who exhibits a tendency toward either of these is not among the sayyids—i.e., their claim to sayyidhood is invalid. Likewise, having an inclination to that which is deviant is a form of corruption, and corruption is evil. They too are not among the descendants of the Prophet, as is established by the hadith: THE SON IS HIS FATHER'S SECRET, and therefore gives an indication of his interior state. If the father's inner being is pious, then the child will be pious, but if the father's interior is corrupt, then the child will be corrupt and wicked. Given that without doubt the Prophet's interior was of the utmost righteousness and capability, then for any offspring whose inner state does not match that of the Prophet, their claim to the lineage is questionable and in doubt.

If someone claims to be a sayyid among the people,
/52a/ *You needn't believe them even if they look like a saint.*[132]

In a similar vein, Mir Sayyid Sharif Jurjani[133] has said:

If someone has no hint of the Prophet about them,
Then the only fruit their tree will produce is infamy.

14. THE VIRTUES AND QUALITIES OF KHOJA JAHAN "ARSHI"

This discourse is going on for too long; I must continue toward my goal. Suffice it to say that all the signs and indications described here, whether of sainthood or sayyidhood, were verified down to the last detail in Khoja Jahan and his family. Outwardly and inwardly, there was not the slightest doubt as to their identity as sayyids. With them the hadith THE SON IS HIS FATHER'S SECRET found complete confirmation.

Akhund Mir Abid al-Din, who was an eloquent nightingale in the grove of words and chair of the assembly of insight, once told the following story:

During my studies at the Royal (*Khānlïq*) Madrasa in Kashgar, when I took it upon myself to practice spiritual exercises and gain knowledge, I would occasionally seek insights from Arabic books, and sometimes I would try to compose verse in Persian or Turki. Throughout this whole time, I was hearing stories about Khoja Jahan, who was the foundation of our peace and security, and I was seized with a constant desire to serve him. In the end, a pilgrimage to the Two Holy Shrines helped bring this about. Having decided to make this journey, I had gone as far as Yarkand. There was no question of its being possible to kiss the threshold of his majesty's court and have an audience with him. /52b/ Yet as soon as he caught wind, he said that the companion and pupil from Kashgar should come and see him. I went to his presence and humbly kissed the ground before him. It was an honor well above my station.

Then he started questioning me. "What have you brought me by way of gift?"

"Forgive me, king of the world," I said. "How could an ant possibly bring a gift into the presence of Sulayman?"

"Did the ant not present the leg of a locust," the khoja replied, "as was appropriate to the occasion?" I was struck dumb and lowered my head in shame. I didn't realize that I was expected to bring a couple of ghazals of poetry.

The learned men and poets of the age were all gathered there, and these lines from Khoja Kamal Khujandi[134] came up:

> *Scholarship and piety are nothing but pretense, meaning is something else,*
> *A man of meaning is one thing, the field of meaning is something else.*[135]

Khoja Jahan said, "Scholars, give me an interpretation of this couplet." They all analyzed it to mean that "scholarship and piety, devotion and abstinence, etc., all of this is meaningless pretense, and true meaning is something different. A man of meaning is different from the field of meaning." But the khoja wasn't convinced by this reading. Indeed he objected, saying, "if a man of meaning is on the field of meaning, then he should be brave, otherwise he should not be on the field, so a man of meaning and a field of meaning are not different things." All the scholars fell silent. They fetched a few copies of Khoja Kamal's divan and saw that this was indeed the intended meaning.

On the morning of the following day, it was announced that everyone should present themselves again. A group went, and he ordered a huge dish of pilaf to be prepared and dedicated it to the spirit of Khoja Kamal. They read the same verse:

> /53a/ *Scholarship and piety are nothing but pretense, meaning is something else,*
> *A man of meaning is one thing, the field of meaning is something else.*

Everyone said, WE CONCUR and WE AFFIRM THIS. In the interpretation too, no emendation was necessary, and the meter was not questioned. To summarize the meaning, it is that wherever pious learning is devoid of meaning, then it is mere hypocrisy and pretension, and wherever pure meaning is found, then hypocrisy and pretension have no place. Thus it became evident to all that these lines had been distorted in transmission, and Khoja Kamal's noble spirit had come and instructed them as to the original phrasing.

The conversation in this gathering ranged across various subjects, until eventually the khoja posed this question: "What is the reason for the opposition and discord that is plaguing the scholars of this age? Have things always been this way, or is there something about the times?"

Akhund Haji Abdullah, who was an authoritative scholar and an expert in both law and ethics, replied: "Permit me, O king of the world. The times have indeed changed, and the portents of Judgment Day are becoming more frequent by the day. Their level of theology has declined, and their faith in Islam has weakened, and because of this they gossip and connive against one another and cause strife and dispute. Our predecessors were not like this."

So saying, he launched into the following story:

"During the reign of Abdullah Khan, there were two exemplary scholars living in Yarkand, Akhund Zihni and Akhund Yaʾsi by name.[136] Each of them had incomparable religious learning and wisdom, and between the two of them there had never been the slightest offense or enmity, or the least complaint. The khan would constantly give thanks to God that in his age and his domains there were such noble individuals. /53b/ One day, the khan took these two men out for a hunting trip, so as to test them. As they rode, the khan came up alongside Akhund Zihni and asked, 'Why is it that the horse you ride is so playful and well-paced, while Akhund Ya'si's horse is heavy-footed, lame, and timid? Did you each impart your own personality to your horses, or what?'

"Akhund Zihni humbly replied, 'Forgive me, king of the world, the reason for this is that Akhund Ya'si is such a blessed individual. God's gaze is constantly brightening his soul, and with his inner purity he brings the tyranny and heresy of the world into the light of Guidance. All who fall within his purview are endowed with comfort in this life and the next, and anyone who is rejected by him will carry the collar of misery and misfortune in both worlds. Because of this, the horse he is riding treads with great deference and trepidation, since if he were to suddenly take a rude or arrogant step, then this rebuke might fall on him. The horse prides himself that it is a sufficient honor in both worlds to have such a blessed individual sit on its back. But the horse that I am riding is offended to have someone so clumsy and unfortunate as myself on his back. If the sins of this ignorant and wayward man were to pass to him, he thinks, would he then be destined for the same ignominious end? This is why he's bucking and pulling at the reins.'

"The khan listened to his reply. 'I see,' he said.

"After a while, the khan rode up to Akhund Ya'si and asked him the same question. In reply, the akhund said, 'Akhund Zihni /54a/ is such an eminent scholar, he is a repository of divine grace and mercy and a deputy of the Prophet. He implements the precepts of the shariʿa among the people, enjoining what is good and forbidding what is illicit. He is divine in his qualities and appearance and exemplifies the hadith QUALIFY YOURSELVES WITH THE QUALITIES OF GOD! The wealth of this world, or indeed a hundred thousand worlds, wouldn't be enough to corrupt his sharp mind. His horse is thinking that with such a great man on his back, how could he simply tread the ground, and not soar up into the heavens like the Buraq and pace across the sky?[137] Thus in his pride he is prancing and rearing up in the field. But the horse I am riding is weighed down with shame and asking why he must carry this devilish and insignificant man with sins as onerous as a mountain on his back? Better he had not been born than encounter such misfortune! It's because of this humiliation that he's being lazy and awkward.'

"Having heard such succinct replies and witnessed such humility, the khan commended the akhunds for their piety and virtue. In good cheer, he granted both of them robes of honor and thoroughbreds with golden saddles and performed a special prayer of thanksgiving."

When Akhund Haji Abdullah finished relating this anecdote, Khoja Jahan similarly presented him with a robe of honor and praised him.

/54b/ Akhund Mulla Mir Abid al-Din also relates:

When I had composed a couple of ghazals, I brought them into his presence. He quite enjoyed them, and he offered me storage space and study quarters in a madrasa that he had constructed. Yet my thought of making the pilgrimage to the Two Shrines still hadn't gone away; in fact, it was continuing to grow in strength. I was in a very awkward situation, because he had shown me a lot of honor. Every week, on Mondays and Wednesdays, he would come to the madrasa and put on a large feast for the students and listen to some lessons before leaving. Among the students, he paid particular attention to me, and while he was checking our lessons, he would single me out for distinction. In the end, I had to present to him my letter of leave for the hajj. A frown crossed his face, and he bowed his head in meditation. After a while, he raised his head again and said, "My friend, I searched for you among the hajj caravans and the pilgrims, but I couldn't find you. It seems it won't be your lot to make the pilgrimage." I left crestfallen, and my heart could not reconcile itself to this disappointment.

Khoja Jahan had a beloved son by the name of Khoja Ṣiddiq, who rivaled the sun in beauty and intellect. His fine personality gave an indication of the nature of Muḥammad, and his insight was such that Plato and Aristotle would have proudly served as his lowliest apprentices. He had a sound and straightforward mind, and if someone encountered a phrase as impenetrable as a steel ball, /55a/ he would cleave it in two with the spade of his quick wit. In liberality and goodness, Ḥatim and Barmas were his two deputies, and in justice Nushirvan and Baḥram were his trainees. Whenever a difficult word came up, people would say "this is Ṣiddiq's specialty," and he would turn his eyes to the ceiling and immediately grapple with it. At that time he was studying the *Aqa'id*[138] and was only eighteen years of age, but in terms of inquiry and analysis his education was already complete, and he had an endowment higher than that of a madrasa graduate (*ṭālib al-ʿilm*). His appreciation for poetry was such that by the time the rest of his classmates had memorized a verse, he would have interpreted its meaning and be able to discourse on it. On each occasion when he was composing poetry, he would extemporize a couple of ghazals and write them down. All his peers would congratulate him on his acuity and intellect. "If he were to perfect this skill," they surmised, "his works would surpass those of Naṣir Ali, Shawkat, Bedil, or Bekhud.[139] Set against his divans, those of others would be erased and annulled." In those days, the food, clothing, and all the expenses of the students were borne by him.

Akhund Mulla Mir Abid al-Din continues:

I presented my request for permission to make the hajj to Khoja Ṣiddiq. Through certain intermediaries, I received his permission, and after readying my supplies for the journey, I set off. But when I had traveled a few days, it became evident that heavy snowfall in the mountains had blocked the roads. All the caravans were turning back, and I had no choice but to turn around too. Overwhelmed with shame and embarrassment, /55b/ I retraced my steps. Khoja Jahan composed this ghazal and had someone deliver it to me:

Those with authority profit from a calm mind,
But when will the taste of dignified men ever please the restless?
Traveling in the homeland offers such surprises,[140]
For monarchs it is all the same as the dust of their street.
The lads are drunk and jovial, each day is a festival for them,
Those keeping the fast know nothing but revelry.
From all the drinking I fainted in the lane of the wine worshippers,
How would I know myself from quaffing such sweet draughts?
In tranquility you won't find the patience you seek, Arshi,
Don't pin vain hopes on those who lack restraint.[141]

When I heard this ghazal, I burst into tears and expressed deep regret. In the end, I came before him in humility. "Did you come up with an appropriate reply to my ghazal?" he asked. "Forgive me, Holiness," I submitted, "Khoja Naṣir Ali seems to have said it best:

One can't confine those who are restless to the prison of the homeland,
The shroud is a wild ride across the desert for those on this terrifying journey."[142]

With this exchange, the gathering came to an end.

Every time the akhund told this story, he would express remorse that in his ghazal he had hinted at his own sainthood and perfection. "We wasted our youth in ignorance," he would sigh with regret.

The story goes that Khoja Jahan once became so heartbroken and forlorn that for several days he refused to grant an audience to anyone. No one knew what the reason was: neither his kin, nor his dependents, nor anyone else could find a way to see him. Eventually, he instructed his family and following /56a/ to assemble. When they had all presented themselves, Khoja Jahan began to shed tears before them like spring rain. Everyone was surprised and perplexed at this scene, but no one had the audacity to ask why he was crying. After a while, he himself explained in his own precious words:

"O kinsmen, know that a group will arise from the east, and with battle and strife they will seize the throne and subdue these cities. At that time an unlucky star will position itself above us, and victory will fall to that side. There will be much bloodshed, and in the midst of this they will capture us all, separating father from son and mother from daughter. Some of us they will slaughter like sheep, others they will shoot. Some of us they will burn, others they will strangle with rope, and others they will martyr by stoning. Whether kinsman or disciple, none of us will survive. So come, children, let us hold our own mourning ceremony and weep at our own predicament, for in those circumstances there will be no one left to mourn for us, and no one to cry at our condition."

O heart, prepare for the calamities coming to your soul,
So many hardships, such violent trials are on their way.
No one will weep at your condition nor mourn for you,
Hold your own mourning and cry, for dragons are on their way.

"Thus, we will carry on the tradition of my illustrious forebears, His Holiness Imam Ḥasan and Imam Ḥusayn. Indeed, what is coming to us in this desert of misfortune will be a hundred times worse than the suffering they endured on the Karbala plain. The land and sky will cry for us, the angels of heaven and earth will mourn, /56b/ and Judgment Day will be renewed on our account. Such trials and tribulations will beset our friends and relatives too, and they will find no refuge. Just like the verse THAT DAY WHEN A MAN WILL FLEE FROM HIS BROTHER, AND HIS MOTHER AND HIS FATHER, AND HIS SPOUSE AND HIS CHILDREN [80:34–36], brother will flee from brother, father from son, and mother from daughter. The nooks and crannies of the mountains will become their home, and they will only find rest in remote deserts and secluded islands. Famine and plague will despoil these lands, such that men will vie to eat human flesh. Without anyone left to bury them, skeletons will pave the streets in place of cobblestones. Corpses will pile up in every lane, and from their foul stench vapors and miasmas will infect people's minds and drive them to delirium. Then before long, by God's command, a huge army will come forth from the east and throw this first party into disarray and take revenge for us. Those people will have a hundred thousand regrets for what they have done to us, and will apologize and seek forgiveness. Fleeing from mountain to mountain and from plain to plain, in a worse condition than that which they inflicted on us, they too will attain the rank of martyrdom."

Much have we experienced how in this temple of retribution,
Whoever fell out with drainers of the dregs fell down.

After this, Khoja Jahan took a page from his book of poetry and gave it to Khoja Ṣiddiq. "Read this, dear son," he said. "The rest of what I have to say is expressed there." Khoja Ṣiddiq opened the page and saw that the he had reworked the foregoing into a heartrending *mus̱amman* of nine stanzas. Khoja Ṣiddiq lost all strength, /57a/ and in a tearful state he recited the *mus̱amman*. As his kinsmen and disciples listened to its description of the approaching events, they cried like the clouds of early spring, and the scene was one of profound mourning. Clasping one another, sobbing and sighing, they repeated the words THE AUTHORITY BELONGS TO GOD.

This is the *mus̲amman* of Arshi, pole of the poles:

The tyrannical wheel has done its final deed, O heart,
It has cut my breast to pieces and left a scar, O heart.
It would be better to give up on life, O heart,
Such grief it has inflicted on me, O heart,
So many calamities descend on me, O heart.
But what use is it to sigh and moan, O heart?
Where can I find someone to share my suffering, O heart?
If I tell a fraction of it, I'll be in tears, O heart.

Sighs and cries among the afflicted are my lot,
Among the birds, the mournful nightingale is my destiny.
It's not an illness, no doctor knows the diagnosis.
My rivals cheer and rub their hands in glee,
And I realize this is my approaching fate.
As I grieve, friends prepare to rebuke me,
In this hardship I am bewildered and alone,
Give up selfhood, and become self-aware, O heart.

I was on good terms with men of science and learning,
Parting from them in the blink of an eye, my confusion grows,
They'll miss me now, with a hundred regrets,
Voicing either their longing, or their pain at parting,
When they hear of my frailty and destitution in exile.
Being apart is no simple hardship, but extreme adversity,
I lack the strength to stand in this world.
Where will you find a keeper of secrets, O heart?

Eventually one day our souls will fall into death's trap,
Rendering us infirm and helpless, it will brook no cure,
/57b/ It will leave us no chance to voice our plaint,
Our predestined fate will not admit any change.
Our faith will stay above our heads as a parasol,
And our spilt blood will turn the face of the earth tulip red.

All our companions and friends will grieve for us,
While vampires drink our blood, O heart!

This treacherous sphere will break its promises in the end,
Wherever it finds an upright man, it inflicts its cruelty,
If it sees men of learning, it swings its violent sword,
And rains down a million arrows of trials and calamities.
Not to speak this grief burns the soul, but to speak it burns the tongue,
If you try to keep it secret, it will burn the heart.
But why grieve even if it kills me a hundred times? I cannot come back to life.
Such trials you have afflicted me with, O heart.

From the east some friends will follow on our trail,
Vagabonds, humiliated in exile, will come looking for us.
Those who've bound tight the bond of fidelity to us,
Having fought years of conflict with the merciless ones,
Like Rustam they'll assail the bloodthirsty,
The ones who won't rest until they spill our blood.
Together they'll drive the vampires from their city,
In the blink of an eye there'll be no trace of them left, O heart.

For some months you'll be distressed and afflicted by sorrow,
Trampled by anguish and pained by mourning,
For some time you'll accompany the cold wind of grief,
Leaving behind this city of Yarkand.
But on Judgment Day you might finally find honor,
Admitted to His court and to His private chambers,
That day when you're ennobled, you'll appreciate the nobility of poverty,
Don't lose hope in God: remain supplicant, O heart.

Though you be wretched and mistreated in this ephemeral world,
Though they injure your soul and wound your heart,
Gladden your heart this instant, stop doing it harm,

/58a/ That monarch Muḥammad took pride in privation above all else,
And anyone of sober mind preferred solitude.
The one who holds the veil hid His treasure behind the curtain of poverty,
Fortune will favor those whom the stars choose to aid,
Have patience, O heart, and you'll be recompensed the same amount.

What does it mean to cry and make noise for the people of love?
Don't drag things out like a madman in describing your pain.
Instead of expressing these bloody tears and fiery sighs,
Take up residence in the hut of penury and resignation.
What use is there in sending up such smoke from a burning heart?
What's all this thrashing around on the plain of grief like a whirlwind?
It would be better for you to stay hidden from humanity,
O heart, you've exposed Arshi's pain for the last time.

After he finished reciting this poem, a cacophony of sobbing and weeping broke out among the gathering, and cries of "Woe!" enveloped the turquoise dome of the heavens. Eventually the commotion subsided, and they recited from the Quran and said prayers in praise of God. By way of advice to the assembled crowd, Khoja Jahan read them the following deed of reassurance (*tasillī-nāma*):

"O kinsmen, my purpose here is simply to apprise you of the fact that the rank of martyr is the highest and most lofty, and is a gift from God that He grants to whomever He wishes. Although martyrs generally sit below the saints, in some respects they rank higher than them, because there are certain qualities that have been substantiated in the case of the martyrs /58b/ and not of the saints. For example, GOD SAID: AND SAY NOT OF THOSE WHO ARE SLAIN IN THE WAY OF GOD, 'THEY ARE DEAD.' NAY, THEY ARE ALIVE, BUT YOU ARE UNAWARE [2:154]. That is, 'O people, don't say that someone who was killed in God's path is dead, for those people are alive in the company of God, though you cannot perceive them.' And likewise, Ḥasan of Basra has related: THE MARTYRS ARE ALIVE IN GOD'S EYES, AND IF YOU REQUEST SUSTENANCE FOR THEIR SOULS, THEY WILL BE ENLIVENED AND ENTERTAINED, JUST AS IF YOU REQUEST HELLFIRE FOR THE SOULS OF PHARAOH'S PEOPLE OR INFIDELS, THEN THEY WILL EXPERIENCE PAIN AND SUFFERING. It is also said that the souls of the martyrs manifest in the form of green birds. They nest on a branch of the Tuba Tree and partake of the bounties of Paradise and can fly off anywhere they like. And the Prophet has said: THE SAINTS WILL INTERCEDE FIRST ON JUDGMENT DAY, THEN THE APOSTLES, AND THEN THE RELIGIOUS SCHOLARS AND MARTYRS. And he has also said: WHEN A MISCARRIED FETUS STANDS AT THE GATES OF HEAVEN, IT WILL BE TOLD TO ENTER, AND IT WILL SAY, 'NOT UNTIL MY PARENTS ENTER WITH ME.' The purpose of all this is that martyrs are without doubt pure, and have the ability to intercede for someone else. /59a/ Each drop of their blood is recompense for all sorts of sins. There are many verses from the Quran and sayings of the hadith about them; it would take too long to explain them all. Let this be sufficient."

After Khoja Jahan had explained the status of martyrs, he spoke to comfort them:

"My children, stay resolute and firm. Death is the inheritance of every son of Adam, and it is not amenable to any ruse or tricks. GOD SAID: TRULY, THE DEATH FROM WHICH YOU FLEE WILL SURELY MEET YOU [62:8]. That is to say, in whichever direction you flee, it will confront you. By the command of EVERY SOUL SHALL TASTE DEATH [21:35], no one has ever found any alternative to quaffing the draught of death."

The world is a chalice, heaven its cupbearer, and death is the wine,
The people are those who quaff its draughts.
There is no deliverance for anyone,
From this chalice, this cupbearer, and this wine.[143]

"If it is our turn one day, then it will be someone else's the next. There is a hadith attributed to the Prophet that says, THIS WORLD IS A PRISON FOR BELIEVERS AND A PARADISE FOR INFIDELS. Indeed, this world has failed to keep faith even with the descendants of the Prophet. Had it done so, then it would've stood by those grandchildren of the lord of the two creations[144] and prince of both worlds, Imam Ḥasan and Imam Ḥusayn. But the pain and suffering that befell them was more than anyone else has ever experienced. People who had been in the presence of the apostle and guide Muḥammad sided with Yazid, and with their full knowledge and in plain sight they slaughtered Imam Ḥusayn on the plain of Karbala. If this is what the world has in store for the cherished offspring of the lord of two worlds, /59b/ then what is to become of the rest of us? Anyone who keeps this event in mind shouldn't be aggrieved by the trials of this deceptive and treacherous world. Divine fate won't ever be modified by substitutions and exertions, and nothing occurs that is not preordained. THE PAGES HAVE BEEN FOLDED UP, AND THE PENS HAVE RUN DRY. That is to say, the page of destiny has already been written out and folded away, and the pen has run out of ink."

You can't unpick the knot of fate with a fingernail,
Prepare instead for the nails of strategy to fall out.[145]

Will divine fate be made any different by human intervention?
Will a carving on stone be worn away by the rain?

"Although it would have been better to keep these secrets hidden, I've revealed them to you on account of my agitated state. But you should not divulge this to any outsiders, lest our enemies be strengthened."

With this, he finished his speech. Some intelligent individuals wrote a chronogram to record the date of this gathering, and it is said to have occurred in either the seventh or eighth year.[146]

15. ON KHOJA KHAMUSH

A description of Khoja Yusuf and a recounting of the stories associated with him would take a long time. God willing, this will be provided in more detail below, but here some mention should be made of His Holiness Khoja Khamush. He was an orthodox and pious man, naturally inclined to worship. He would fast during the day and hold vigils through the night, and both inwardly and outwardly he manifested not the slightest contradiction of the Holy Law. He held firm to the commands of the noble shariʿa, stuck to the thoroughfare of tradition and conformity, and chose the path of piety, refraining from indulging in *fatwas*. He spent his days reciting the Quran, or otherwise reading books. His original name was Khoja Niẓam al-Din, /60a/ but the holy Mawlana Niẓam al-Din Khamush was in his presence, and on this account they gave him the nickname Khamush. Khoja Khamush received a lot of training and assistance from Mawlana Niẓam al-Din and often made entreaties to him. His Grace Mawlana Niẓam al-Din was an extremely strong-willed man, as is described in following anecdote from Khoja Ubaydullah Aḥrar, which occurs in the *Nafaḥat al-Uns* and the *Rashahat Ayn al-Ḥayat:*[147]

[According to Mawlana Niẓam al-Din]: "The chief jurisprudent (*shaykh al-Islām*) of Samarqand was once a man by the name of Khoja Iṣam al-Din, who was my loyal devotee. When he became ill and death was at hand, his children and dependents greatly importuned me, so I tended to him at his bedside. I accessed the Preserved Tablet[148] and saw that his life had come to an end, with no possibility of reviving him. Nevertheless, I plucked up my courage and made own life guarantor for his corpse, and my spirit filled his body. Life returned to the jurisprudent, and he survived for twelve more years."

Some skeptics accused Mawlana Niẓam al-Din's sons of summoning spirits and disrespecting the jinn, and of having love affairs with the wives of certain members of the nobility. At that time, the governor of Samarqand was Mirza Ulugh Beg. When the issue came to his attention, he became angry and was determined to punish the Mawlana's sons, /60b/ but the Mawlana's sons had by this time caught wind of the calumnies and managed to get away. The Mawlana himself was wracked with anxiety. People encouraged Iṣam al-Din to intervene in the case so that the Mawlana would be shielded from it, but out of timidity he kept to himself and made no effort at all. Mawlana Niẓam al-Din says that he was indignant at this, and he withdrew his life-sustaining guarantee. The jurisprudent, who was seated among a group of disciples, immediately collapsed, and all that was left of him was a pile of dry bones. Everyone present at that gathering was astonished. Samarqand was filled with a hue and cry, and criticism was directed at Mawlana Niẓam al-Din. Mirza Ulugh Beg was furious. They stripped the Mawlana of his turban, sat him on the back of a horse, and brought him to the Mirza's palace. The Mawlana was seated there with his head bowed in meditation when the Mirza passed before him, and he didn't get up and pay his respects. The Mirza flew into a rage and hurled abuse at the Mawlana.

"I only have one thing to say in reply," the Mawlana said. "I am a Muslim. Should you believe me, well and good. Otherwise, do to me what you will." The Mirza was moved by these words, and he rose from his seat and freed the Mawlana. Khoja Aḥrar says that Mirza Ulugh Beg was deeply disturbed by this quarrel. Before long, Mirza Abd al-Laṭif came with an army on a raid and put Mirza Ulugh Beg to death.

/61a/ Khoja Aḥrar also says that His Holiness Mawlana Niẓam al-Din had great inner strength. If someone mentioned in the Mawlana's presence that so-and-so was a skeptic or had been behaving badly, then his countenance would change immediately, and he would draw a line on the wall or the ground with a piece of wood, and right away that person, wherever they happened to be, would fall down and die.

There is a story, for example, that one of the Mawlana's disciples started complaining to the Mawlana about a certain student who was always spreading rude gossip about the Mawlana. The Mawlana's mood altered. As it happened, right then the student in question appeared in the distance and walked past without showing any deference. The Mawlana was infuriated, and with a small stick he drew a picture of a tomb on the wall. That wretched cynic dropped dead immediately. The Mawlana withdrew, and people went and saw that the student had already consigned his deposit to the hands of the Holy Azrael.

In any case, Mawlana Niẓam al-Din has countless miracles and stories of willpower to his name, but it would be best to cut short my account.

> Come, Ṣadiq, gather up your words toward the original goal.
> All this talk is dragging the story out, you'll never reach the end.

Khoja Khamush likewise had immense strength of will, and anyone who tried to upset him in some way would be unlikely to get away unscathed. He took up residence in the city of Aqsu, and he handled the petitions of the common people in accordance with the Holy Law and promoted the noble shariʿa. The just and righteous Mirza Hadi Beg had a sister /61b/ called Ulugh Aylam, who was particularly virtuous and pure. Khoja Khamush took her as his wife, and she spent her life in his service.

Some time after this, Khoja Khamush made his way from Aqsu to Ili, where Khoja Yusuf was. After a while he was struck by an illness, which increased in intensity until it became clear that it was terminal. They brought Khoja Yusuf to his bedside, and Khoja Khamush delivered his last testament to him: "My kinsman, now is the time for my blessed journey, and I must ready my provisions for the road. But for this trip I need good deeds and meritorious actions, and I don't have any. There is a hadith attributed to the Prophet: WHEN SOMEONE DIES, THEIR DEEDS ARE TERMINATED, APART FROM THREE: A CONTINUING CHARITY, KNOWLEDGE FROM WHICH PEOPLE PROFIT, AND A PIOUS SON WHO WILL OFFER BLESSINGS. That is to say, 'Whenever someone dies, then all of their actions will come to an end, apart from three kinds. The first is an ongoing charitable endowment, such as a pond, a mosque, a madrasa, or a bridge. The second is knowledge from which the people derive benefit and learn from, and which will last until Judgment Day. The third is an upstanding son, who will say benedictions for his father and mother.' Sadly, I am departing without any of these. Whatever I have left in my possession, you should spend it in God's name on the poor, and then take the rest and build a madrasa in Yarkand. I am consigning Khoja Jahan, you, and of the rest of my kinsmen to God Almighty and our illustrious ancestors; I hope you will be satisfied with me. Please convey to Khoja Jahan /62a/ that I was honored by his patronage, and that he has more claims against me than hairs on my body, but now I have been unable to redeem any of my debts to him. I can only hope he will forgive me." So saying, he ended his testament and gave up his spirit to the Lord. TRULY WE ARE GOD'S, AND UNTO HIM WE RETURN [2:156].

Laments and cries of mourning filled the surrounds of Ili. There were various groups of Muslims there, including the entire clan of khans and the descendants of Khoja Afaq, led by His Holiness Khoja Mu'min.[149] These different parties of Muslims collaborated to shroud Khoja Khamush's body and prepare it for burial, and then assembled to pray for him, with Temür Khan serving as imam. Some thousand people from the common folk of Ili, along with the khans, khojas, and begs of the Seven Cities, contributed to a collection of alms. The neediest received two hundred *shang* of raw cloth, and everyone became rich on the abundance of charity.[150] They readied his blessed body and the burial casket and loaded them onto a camel to transport to Aqsu. Among the sons of Khoja Yusuf, an eminent sayyid by the name of Khoja Abdullah took the reins of the camel and led it down to Aqsu. The entire population of that city came out to greet them. They received his body with great respect and buried it temporarily in the shrine of Khoja Isḥaq Vali's son, His Holiness Khoja Shahbaz. /62b/ Sometime later, they took his blessed bones from Aqsu and transferred them to Yarkand for burial in the Golden Shrine. Khoja Jahan carried out Khoja Khamush's last will and testament and constructed the White Madrasa (*Aq Madrasa*). He provided generous pious endowments for it and apportioned the merit of this deed to Khoja Khamush.

16. ON KHOJA UBAYDULLAH

Khoja Ubaydullah, who was this saint's younger brother, was a particularly bold and daring young man, and had no equal in humility and piety. He married a sister of Erke Khan, and this princess bore him four sons, whose names were Khoja Shams al-Din, Khoja Yaḥya, Khoja Aḥmad, and Khoja Abid. To give a full account of the qualities of each of these sons would be excessive, but some mention of them will be forthcoming below, God willing.

For his residence, Khoja Ubaydullah had been assigned to Khotan, but before going there he deputized for his brother Khoja Khamush on the seat of guidance in the city of Aqsu, where he heard the plaints of the people in accordance with the shariʿa and implemented its precepts. As fate would have it, while he was doing so, he sipped the syrup of death, as is required by the Quranic verse WHEN THEIR TERM COMES, THEY SHALL NOT DELAY IT BY A SINGLE HOUR, NOR SHALL THEY ADVANCE IT [7:34].[151]

> The Creator put an intricate talisman around the fortress of death,
> And anyone who entered, /63a/ not a trace of them was found.[152]

They transported his blessed body and buried it in the Golden Shrine. In certain circles, it was rumored that the reason for his death was that the faithless and ill-willed Abd al-Wahhab, the leader of the skeptics, had surreptitiously poisoned him.[153] However, the holy family didn't give this suspicion much credence. "If this speculation is correct," they said, "then on the Day of Judgment, when the first and last have assembled, both of his two faces will be black with shame before our illustrious forefather, and he can account for himself there. Otherwise, if it is not true, we have no wish to bear responsibility for his death." Thus they kept silent and didn't pay this talk any heed.

In place of their father, Khoja Shams al-Din and his younger brother Khoja Yaḥya took up residence in Khotan, and they lived there handling public affairs in accordance with the shariʿa.[154]

17. KHOJA YUSUF'S ESCAPE FROM ILI

Let us now take up the story of Khoja Yusuf. He was a wise and articulate man, cultivated, orthodox, and pious. He was knowledgeable, versed in the ways of the world, free with his advice, and peerless in intellect. He was the foundation of peace and stability, and a worthy heir to the just kings. He served as an irrefutable example and evidence for the skeptical enemies and those given to innovation and deviation in their faith. Unique in his rectitude and discernment, he was without peer in handling the kingdom's affairs. Victory was his slave, and triumph was his retainer. The justice of Nushirvan and Baḥram merely mimicked his own, and the liberality and kindness of Ḥatim and Barmas were but a foretaste of his. /63b/ Every time that he encountered a foe, such was his good fortune that defeat would already be engraved on the enemy's brow with the pen of predestination. Every cynic who had the gall to speak against him was inevitably laid low beneath a hail of misfortune, and every traitor who conceived a plot against him was simply hacking at his own sapling with the axe of exertion. Every strategy that he devised came to fruition through divine intervention, yet some ignorant fools couldn't appreciate this and believed that he was changing fate by his own interventions. In truth this was not the case: his interventions were in accordance with fate, and things eventuated for that reason.

It is well when some device accords with fate,
But woe to any plan that contradicts it.

By night and by day, he was occupied with remembrance of God and recitation of the Quran, seeing to the needs of the common people, and eradicating the innovations and corruptions that his rivals had introduced. His constant orientation and credo were to bring peace to the kingdom, promote the work of the scholars and wise men, nurture the shariʿa, and support Islam. All the people of the kingdom, great and small, were satisfied with and supportive of him. In his managing of the kingdom, it was as if the kings of old were but his chief apprentices. The prosperity and happiness of this holy family, as well as their achievements, all depended on his existence, such that as long as he was on the throne of the sultanate, they were all held in high esteem, and no harm could come to them from any of the hostile conspirators. It was as if he was the patron of the entire saintly family: he would shield them from all their worries and anxieties /64a/ and would intercept their enemies and take care of them. Some adversaries would spend years preparing a devious trap, but this holy man would learn of it in advance with the light of insight, so that years of effort would go to waste, and as required by the saying HE WHO DIGS A PIT WILL INEVITABLY FALL INTO IT HIMSELF, they would fall victim to their own plot.

Many corrupt and irreligious men had been trying to introduce strange innovations among the Muslims, and increase the poll tax that the infidels levied on the Muslims, so as to curry favor with the Qalmaq *töräs* and their *jarghuchis*. Because of this, Khoja Yusuf spent most of his time in Ili teaching these good-for-nothing heretics a lesson and, to the extent possible, trying to preserve the Muslims from the tyranny of the infidels and distortions of their faith. A second reason for his coming and going from Ili was to observe the state of the infidels and seek an advantageous time, thinking that God Almighty might one day provide a window of opportunity when discord would strike these infidels from within. At such a time he intended to brandish the sword of Islam without any hesitation, rid the Muslims of this unjust oppression, liberate those various groups of Muslims who were captive in Ili—including the khans, the khojas, and everyone else—and declare Islamic rule openly. He always cultivated this desire for holy war in his heart, but the times did not allow for it, since the Muslims were lacking in strength to confront the infidels, and certain faithless individuals were loyal to the infidels /64b/ and harming to the people of Islam. Besides this, the infidels were strong and numerous. Even traveling at express speed for six months, it wasn't possible to cross their territory from one side to the other, and within these boundaries it was brim full of infidels. No one could imagine how they might resist them, or even get close to them.

O Lord, throw the infidels into disarray, and unite the tribe of Islam,
For the infidels have done much injustice to the people of the faith.

Khoja Yusuf had four sons, each one of whom was a prince of the realm of sayyidhood, a tall sapling in the garden of nobility, a conquering sultan of felicitous conjunction, and a Nushirvan on the throne of justice.

One was as bold as Rustam,
Unique among mankind in bravery.
Kindness and generosity was his motto,
And justice for the people his concern.

One was unrivaled in excellence,
With Aristotle and Plato his advisers.
Such a sharp and perceptive mind,
He was a wit among the quick-witted.

One was pole of the faith and religion,
What a noble and honorable man!
With Faridun's grace and Jamshid's temper,
He was replete with all the virtues.

One was a mine of humility and meekness,
Such a charming and courteous pupil.
So pure in appearance and disposition,
His countenance was a shining sun.

A full account of these four princes would take too long, particularly of the eldest prince, Khoja Abdullah. He had such courage and grasp of military affairs that if Rustam and Sam had been alive during his lifetime, they would without doubt have bound the belt of submission, /65a/ hung the deed of capitulation around their necks, and become his most humble retainers. He had such physical strength that if any kind of strapping foe ever had designs on him, they would be reduced to a quivering wreck. His second son was Khoja Muʾmin, who was an extremely pious religious scholar, who befriended the learned and sought out the wise men, and was of pleasing nature and mind. His third son was Khoja Quṭb al-Din, who was charming and handsome, with fragrant locks, cheeks like Jupiter, and a flowery face. His curly hair was a belt on which he hung hearts, and the ball of his eye was a blood-shedding killer. His ruby red lips with a half-smile were like a pistachio nut or a fresh bouquet, and his shining white teeth were like drops of dew on a flower bed, or whole pearls. His countenance made the sunshine jealous, and his glowing face was the envy of the moonlight. His fourth son was Khoja Burhan al-Din. Because he had such love for this young son, who was given to displays of coquetry, they called him Erke Khoja.

Khoja Yusuf installed some of these princes in positions of authority, and he had some of them accompany him to Ili, where they would probe the state of affairs among the infidels. They envisaged that there would come a time when they could draw the sword of Islam against the infidels once and for all, and the different tribes of Muslims would be freed from captivity; that they would carry on the tradition of *ghazat* and thereby obtain the status of holy warrior and enjoy honors in this world and the next.

On the final occasion when Yusuf /65b/ went to Ili, he saw that it was in a state of disarray owing to the discord among the infidel *töräs*, and he realized that the opportunity he had eagerly anticipated for years had arrived. It was a precious chance, and he knew that he needed to realize his ambition and advance toward this great accomplishment, but he didn't permit himself to reveal these thoughts to anyone and didn't take anyone into his confidence.

The governor of Kashgar at this time was the wise and resourceful Khosh Kifäk Beg.[155] He was extremely discerning and farsighted, a good source of advice, and unrivaled in his liberality and kindness. Yet his timidity could get the better of him. Because of this, Khoja Yusuf advised the Qalmaqs to send Khosh Kifäk Beg back to Kashgar, arguing that the Kirghiz were lying in wait in the surrounds, and they might do some damage to the city while it was vacant. With this, they sent Khosh Kifäk Beg back to Kashgar, instructing him to go and see to the city's walls and fortifications, construct lookout posts around it, and prepare the armory and ready it for battle, so that the Kirghiz would be unable to intervene.

Khosh Kifäk Beg arrived in Kashgar and carried out the tasks assigned to him. He repaired the city's fortifications and kept guard. The entire population wondered what the purpose of all this activity could possibly be, since for the time being there was no sign of the enemy army. Even Khosh Kifäk Beg himself couldn't see the point of it.

/66a/ Meanwhile, Khoja Yusuf secretly sent a letter to the Qipchaq Kirghiz in the surrounds of Ili, with the following message:

> Brave men of the Qipchaq! In days of old, your fathers and grandfathers had command of the army of Islam and wielded the sword of Islam boldly. They never submitted to the infidels. Indeed, they were faithful and loyal to our predecessors. The best form of worship is holy war: it is for this that brave men were brought into being. Should they die in infidel hands, they become martyrs, which is the highest rank of all, and if they kill, then they are holy warriors, and the status of holy warrior is a pride and honor for champions in both worlds. Should any wealth come to hand in the course of looting, then it is more licit than mother's milk or the sweat from one's own brow. Is it not a shame for true men to live out their long and honorable lives in grudging subordination to these wretched and impure infidels? I have hope in God that as my life is coming to an end, I may now whiten my black face, and swing the sword of Islam against the infidels without dissembling, and make recompense for my years of subservience. If divine grace aids you, then come at a certain date and time and lend support to the cause of Islam.

The leader of these Kirghiz was a man by the name of Umar Mirza.[156] He wholeheartedly endorsed the message, and wrote out a pledge of allegiance and gave it to the man who had delivered the letter. When the messenger returned with it, Khoja Yusuf was overjoyed and found renewed strength. /66b/ Yet there was no way for him to return to Kashgar without obtaining leave or offering an excuse. The infidels would not let him go without some pretext to gain their permission. Pondering this, he gave a letter to one of his personal servants and instructed him surreptitiously to go and spend a few days on his pasturage, then come back in a hurry announcing that he had come from Kashgar, and present this letter. In accordance with this command, in a few days' time, this servant came rushing in with the letter. Khoja Yusuf took him and the letter and went to see the *törä*. The infidel asked what was going on, and Khoja Yusuf read the letter to him. This is what it said:

> From Khoja Muʾmin, Khosh Kifäk Beg and all the Kashgar begs, our petition to the *törä* is as follows: The Kirghiz in this vicinity have united and

> made a compact that at such-and-such a date and time they will storm Kashgar from all four sides, loot it and take its people prisoner, and reduce it to dust. Now is the time for you to assist us; we must ward off this threat before it descends on us. Once it eventuates, regret will be of no use. If you have any use at all for this land and territory, then you must spare no effort to aid us, so that the Kirghiz cannot find a way in. Otherwise, Kashgar is lost.

When the Qalmaqs heard this news, they were at their wits' end. They deliberated among themselves and decided that it would be best to send an army, /67a/ but they saw no way to do so, since there was such discord within their own territory. In their helplessness, they determined that Khoja Yusuf should go and take care of the situation.

The infidel *törä* summoned Khoja Yusuf and addressed him: "Khoja Yusuf, you are a wise and resourceful man. You are privy to all our affairs—we have no secrets that you are not aware of. There is such endless chaos in our homeland right now, there is no likelihood of organizing a military campaign. Instead, you should take this affair to hand. If you go back to Kashgar and stand up to the Kirghiz with your own tribe of Muslims, it may be that simply with you there the Kirghiz will hesitate and be repulsed."

In his heart, Khoja Yusuf gave thanks to God Almighty and silently repeated to himself "praise be to God!" In a conciliatory tone he said, "O *törä*, have patience, don't be so disconsolate. There is no need for me to go. Instead, if my child Khoja Abdullah were to go, the situation might be resolved. If that proves insufficient, then let me go."

His advice was accepted, and with this decision, they equipped Khoja Abdullah with provisions. Khoja Yusuf told him discretely, "My child, my intention in this is that if I were to go back myself, these infidels would insist on keeping you here by their side, and it would be difficult for you to leave. Now you should go first and send a succession of people back with letters reporting that the Kirghiz are pressing fiercely, that they are on the verge of laying waste to the territory, and that panic has set in among the Muslims. Say that no one has the courage to stand up to them, and the land is so disturbed that with some small excuse they might reject the *törä*'s authority and submit to the Kirghiz. Say that you've been unable to resolve the situation /67b/ and settle the discord. God willing, in this way I will be given an opportunity to go to Kashgar myself. I have great hope in the Judge of Necessities that I will be delivered from the foul gaze of these infidels and liberated from submission to them, that I will promulgate the faith and raise the standard of Islam above the Muslims, put into effect Muḥammad's shariʿa, and call down a rain of refuge on the heads of the people." With these final instructions, he gave Khoja Abdullah leave to go, and they bade each other farewell.

Khoja Abdullah hurried on his way to Aqsu, where the people came out to greet him. He stopped in Aqsu for a few days and recruited some thousand soldiers from the surrounding towns. He picked out four hundred poor-quality and overweight horses from Khoja Khamush's herds and set out for Kashgar. The entire population of Kashgar came out to welcome him, and he ensconced himself on the throne of the sultanate in full honor. He then dispatched a series of letters to his associate, *aʿlam akhund* Haji Abdullah, along the lines that he had been instructed. No one else was privy to this correspondence. When his letters arrived in Ili, the infidels were struck by anxiety; they requested that Khoja Yusuf quickly take himself to Kashgar and resolve the issue, and they gave him permission to depart.

Khoja Yusuf went to his quarters in high spirits and gave thanks and praise to God. /68a/ When he had readied his supplies and tents for the journey, he loaded them onto huge camels, and with his entire retinue mounted on swift horses, he got himself out of there as quickly as a cold wind. In great haste, he had gone as far as one stage beyond the Muzart Pass when he ran into the governor of Ush, Khojasi Beg.[157] Khojasi Beg was an extremely wily and corrupt individual, but he also had a degree of sagacity about him. At this first encounter, he spoke humbly: "Congratulations, my king, on opening Islam."[158]

"The congratulations should be for the Almighty Lord," Khoja Yusuf said to himself, but didn't voice his opinion. They exchanged a few pleasantries, and Khoja Yusuf told him that Ili was presently in turmoil, that it was not an appropriate time to go, and that it would be better for him to turn around. But this schemer did not agree, and said he that would pay a visit anyway. He said goodbye and went on his way. With his discerning eye, Khoja Yusuf could tell that this heretic was on his way to the infidels to stir up trouble, and he sped onward to Aqsu, leaving his caravan train behind him. He spent one day in Aqsu, then set out for Kashgar. On the fourth night out from

Aqsu, he alighted in Kashgar. He had sent someone ahead from Fayżabad to tell the people of Kashgar to come out and greet him, but also to tell his son Khoja Abdullah not to leave the throne unoccupied. When this messenger brought the news, all the people were astonished and set off in a welcoming party. Khosh Kifäk Beg, the governor of Kashgar, hastened out to Daulat Bagh.[159] Some didn't go that far, but some went even farther. Khoja Abdullah exited by the side gate and met him on the field in front of the palace pavilion. To great fanfare, Khoja Yusuf entered the city and took up his place on the sultanic throne.

18. KHOJASI BEG SOUNDS THE ALARM

Let us now follow the story of the conniving Khojasi Beg. /68b/ On the day that he saw Khoja Yusuf on the Ili road, he could confidently ascertain from his bearing that he had ended his subordination to the infidels and that he was about to draw the sword of enmity against them. Khojasi quickly made his way to the palace of the infidels, where the *törä* was an infidel by the name of Dabachi.[160] "O *törä*," he complained to him, "it was wrong of you to send Khoja Yusuf back, there was no call to let him go. Before long he will break faith with you and draw his sword against us. On the day he crossed the Muzart Pass, he became your enemy. With such disorder in your domains now, it would be much better to have a man of good counsel like him by your side. What a pity! Still, there is no use in regret. With luck, if someone were to quickly go now, they might be able to catch up to him and bring him back. Otherwise you'll have to abandon hope of holding onto Kashgar and Yarkand."

Certain intelligent infidels had also opposed the idea of sending Khoja Yusuf away and had given the *törä* cause to regret his decision. With Khojasi's intriguing, the chagrin among the infidels only intensified. The *törä* assigned three hundred men to a particularly brave and quick-witted infidel and sent him off with instructions to chase down Khoja Yusuf and turn him around. If he would not come voluntarily, then they were to detain him and bring him back by force.

This infidel set off swiftly in pursuit, but he couldn't catch up, because it was God Almighty who had released Khoja Yusuf from his imprisonment among the unbelievers. When these infidels reached a station called Masjid, which is close to Fayżabad, Khoja Yusuf had already made it past Kimä.[161] /69a/ The infidels had no choice but to turn back disappointed. They went to Aqsu, where they conspired with the skeptic Abd al-Wahhab to send someone with this message: "Khoja Yusuf, the *törä* is summoning you. Amursana is apparently on his way with a large army. Before he arrives, you must make your way to Ili, for now is the time to offer assistance and help. If support is forthcoming, the *törä* will never forget it, and he will always uphold your authority. But if you fail to cooperate, then you should expect grief and ready the instruments of war."

This man arrived in Kashgar and explained the message to Khoja Yusuf. In reply, Khoja Yusuf explained that he could not set out because of a pain in his leg joints, but promised that he would go once his condition had improved. He dismissed the messenger, who returned to Aqsu. The infidel emissary's plot with Abd al-Wahhab thus came to nothing, and he made his way back to Ili in disappointment.

Khoja Yusuf gave praise and thanks to God and exerted himself in implementing the noble shariʿa. He administered the petitions of the common people in accordance with the Holy Law, held council with the religious scholars, and the whole time was fixated on the victory of Islam. He readied the armory and mobilized blacksmiths, fletchers, and bowyers to prepare the weapons of war. He reinforced the gates, particularly the palace gates, and was always at work on military installations. He was as vigilant as if it were the day of battle. Some irreligious men who witnessed this situation were shocked /69b/ and disturbed, while some pious men saw it and took inspiration, asking when that day would come when they would at last be able to swing the sword of Islam against the infidels without inhibition. Some days went by in this fashion.[162]

19. THE DEATH OF KHUDAYAR AND THE AFFAIR OF THE QALMAQ EMISSARY

Here it is appropriate to describe the events surrounding Deputy Governor Khudayar. He was a particularly ignorant man, weak in his faith, and sympathetic toward the infidels. Observing the activity of Khoja Yusuf, he was deeply perturbed, for he was not at all comfortable with the idea of the triumph of Islam and was thus always hoping that the infidels would subdue these cities once again and their rule be instituted as before. This was because he had obtained his rank by introducing illicit innovations among the Muslims in service to the Qalmaq infidels. While in Ili, he had boasted a great deal about the fact that he exercised authority over Khoja Yusuf and the rest of the saintly family, and never for a moment did he abandon the enmity toward them that was in his heart. Although he conducted himself appropriately in public, he was corrupt on the inside.

There was also a bald man by the name of Abd al-Sattar, a native of Artush, who was extremely deceptive and treacherous. He was always the cause of dissension and strife, and was constantly sowing disunity among the Muslims. At the instigation of the incorrigible skeptic Abd al-Wahhab, this Abd al-Sattar made his sinister way to Artush so as to stir up trouble. He had his own fortified compound there, and he set himself up inside. If anyone got wind of this and went to see him, he would detain them without letting them out. Eventually he /70a/ imprisoned a large crowd. The governor of Artush, a man called Niyaz Beg, hunkered down inside the city in fear.

Abd al-Sattar then dressed someone up in Qalmaq fashion, with silk tassels, belt pouches (*qafturğa*), and ringlets made of women's hair, and secretly got a letter out to Khudayar Beg. When Khudayar Beg was apprised of the letter's contents, he quietly summoned a few begs from among his close confidants and shared it with them. They saw that it bore the seals of Abd al-Wahhab and Khojasi Beg. It read as follows:

> To Khudayar Beg and the begs of Kashgar: our message is that a huge army from the Emperor of China is said to be on its way to the Ili region. There is great unrest inside Ili at present, and the Qalmaqs will not be able to resist them. However things turn out, you should find some way to capture Khoja Yusuf and kill him. If we are to remain under the Qalmaqs, this will be considered a service, and if we are to fall under the Emperor of China, it will likewise be a service. You should cleanse the territory of their presence and govern it as you see fit.

The begs, however, did not approve this plan of action—indeed, they opposed it. Counseling delay, they said, "Khoja Yusuf is such a canny man, it simply won't be possible to lure him into this trap. If he somehow finds out, we'll all be doomed, and we'll die for an unworthy cause."

Suddenly a thought occurred to them: "If we reveal this letter to our khoja, he will have no suspicions toward us and will show us even greater honor." They resolved to do just this, and went their separate ways. Yet death's grasp had already seized hold of the scheming Khudayar, and the sword of fate /70b/ had blinded him and drawn the curtain of God's rage across his view. Satan began to lure him astray, and he could think of nothing else than the destruction of Khoja Yusuf.

There was a man by the name of Shah Beg, from the district of Artush, who descended on his mother's side from a line of sayyids and whose father's side went back to a family of begs. He held a private meeting with his younger brother Mubarak Shah, to which they invited Khudayar. "Until we kill Khoja Yusuf," Khudayar told them, "our affairs will not progress. Tomorrow, on Friday, Khoja Yusuf will come to the communal prayers. Let's set a few snipers at the archway of the Friday Mosque. They should shoot him either as he's dismounting and entering the mosque or inside the mosque during the service. Shah Beg and I will stand by with five or six hundred well-armed men, and Abd al-Sattar should prepare five or six hundred men from Artush and take up a position outside the city gate. When the sound of gunfire rings out, we'll rush to the palace from one side while Abd al-Sattar Beg charges at it from the other. On Friday everyone will be busy either at the market or in the mosque, and they will be caught unawares. Once we've seized control of the palace, the city will be in our hands. Khosh Kifäk is a simple-minded outsider; he'll take fright and withdraw. If we raid the houses of those people with ties to the palace, we'll become wealthy. All power will be in our hands, and we can do with it as we please. Those who cause us trouble we'll either kill or put in prison, and the infidels will support us too." (At that time the custom was to garrison each city with fifteen Qalmaqs, whom they termed the *qarakhan*.) They wrote this conspiracy out in a letter, fixed their seals to it, /71a/ and gave it to Mubarak Shah Beg. "You should assist Abd al-Sattar Khoja," Khudayar said to him, "while Shah Beg will stay with me. Get away to Artush inconspicuously, and make sure to be ready at the appointed time." With this, they bade each other farewell.

Mubarak Shah Beg went away and consulted with Shah Beg. "Khudayar Beg's promise is to make me governor of Aqsu," he said. "But instead of becoming governor by disgracing myself in both worlds through such treachery, it would be better to give this letter to my khoja. He can just as well make me governor of Artush. If this plan failed to come off, we'd be finished." He left by the River Gate and took a few steps, then slowly made a fake and slipped into the palace by a side door. This Mubarak Shah Beg was married to a daughter of Akhund Mulla Taqi, whose name was Halima Banu. For this reason, Khoja Abd al-Majid, who was Mulla Taqi's son, was also privy to the goings-on. The three of them, including Shah Beg, had to make a choice. It was the time of the evening prayer when they arrived before the Golden Palace, and they appealed to the attendants for leave to enter. Someone went in and requested permission for them, and it was granted. Khoja Abd al-Majid went in and carefully explained what was going on. After a while, the two others also entered and gave their account of the situation, and they revealed the letter. Khoja Yusuf understood that things were exactly as they said. "God willing," he said, "God in His grace will render them captive to us, and not us to them."

What am I thinking, and what is heaven thinking?
My thoughts are raw, but heaven's are cooked.

Khoja Yusuf gave an order to his attendants that they should hide Mubarak Shah, and they immediately concealed him inside the palace. /71b/ He permitted the rest to leave and then instructed one attendant to summon his son Khoja Abdullah, and also to rouse Khoja Mu'min and Darvish Bakavul and the rest of the palace staff, since none of these people were present. Khoja Abdullah was lying fast asleep, with the door to his courtyard shut fast. He had such a quick temper, no one had the nerve to open the gate and wake him up. Khoja Yusuf became angry, and he told a brave attendant to quickly go and rouse him. This man went and banged on the gate of the courtyard and woke him up. Khoja Abdullah still lingered while getting dressed, for such was his nature that he wasn't afraid of anyone and never got anxious or hurried.

Eventually Khoja Abdullah presented himself with a bow. Khoja Yusuf was in a state of rage. "This beauty sleep of yours will cost me my existence!"

he let forth. "Don't imagine that you'll always have this abundance of sleep. Let's see if you last forty days on this throne once I'm gone!" (He said this at a time of day when prayers were particularly efficacious, and thus it came to pass that when Khoja Yusuf died, it was one day before his forty-day commemoration when Khoja Abdullah gave up the throne of Kashgar and fled with his family to Yarkand.)

Khoja Yusuf uttered these angry words and, without explaining the situation, dispatched people to retrieve Khoja Muʾmin and Darvish Bakavul, wherever they were. These two had gone out hunting with a few others and had made camp in Qaraqir.[163] By nightfall, someone caught up with them and brought them back. Khoja Yusuf sent for the entire palace community, one by one, /72a/ but only revealed the conspiracy to Khoja Abdullah, Khoja Muʾmin, and Darvish Bakavul—nobody else found out about it.

That night no one got any rest. Everyone associated with the palace strengthened the guard, and the next morning they tightened it even more. The begs who were coming for an audience, as well as the city folk, all saw this and were surprised. They wondered what was going on but couldn't work it out. For his part, Khudayar Beg could tell from this flurry of activity among the palace staff that they had definitely found him out. He fortified his own courtyard and readied his relatives and retinue with supplies. That day he didn't go to the palace, nor did Khoja Yusuf go out for the Friday worship, sending Khoja Abdullah and Khoja Muʾmin instead. The day went by in this fashion.

The following morning, Khoja Yusuf remained worried that unless he captured and imprisoned Khudayar, the world would not be at peace and might well come to ruin. There were in attendance at the palace a few brave men from the Qipchaq Kirghiz who belonged to the family of Khoja Yusuf's wife Bayan Aghacha. He identified ten of these men, and from these he chose three who were to his liking, and from these he put one in charge with these instructions: "When I say for the second time, 'Boy, add some tobacco,' come and bind Khudayar immediately, and lock him up in the prison." Having given these instructions, he hid them in a room off a dark corridor in the Golden Palace.

Yet Khudayar didn't come this day either. While the audience was in session, a couple of people went out to summon him, but he still wouldn't come. His relative Abd al-Raḥim was told: "Go and fetch him; /72b/ we need his advice here. What possibly reason is there for him not to present himself? Whatever the case, please bring him."

Abd al-Raḥim left to try to persuade him. Khudayar Beg had had a terrifying dream the night before, and his sister was also strongly discouraging him from going. Nevertheless, the hand of fate had seized hold of him. He plucked up his courage and spoke a few anxious words: "How could they dare touch a hair on my body? Am I some animal that they might trap me? Well, it won't be so easy to capture this beast!"

Mouthing these empty words in pride and defiance, Khudayar mounted and headed toward the palace. As he came through the palace gate, he saw that everyone was standing to attention with great ceremony. He regretted his decision to come, but it was of no use; he had no choice but to go in and join the audience. There he saw Khoja Yusuf seated on the throne of the sultanate in great majesty, with signs of wrath evident on his face, and he started to panic.

Soon enough, Khoja Yusuf upbraided him: "Khudayar, what breach of faith did we ever show you, that you should display such treachery and hostility toward us? Did you not already commit various sins against us in the past? Yet we forgave you those wrongdoings and responded by honoring you and contributing to your prosperity. In the end your cup was full to the brim, yet whatever good fortune came to you, you saw it as the product of your own strength or of your Qalmaqs, instead of something that we did for the sake of God. You've had many opportunities, now it is our turn."

/73a/ *The time of Majnún has passed and it is our turn—*
The turn of everyone is five days.[164]

With this he said, "Boy, add some tobacco." The Kirghiz were standing on guard and presented themselves immediately, among them a brave man by the name of Tuqal. Khudayar was sitting down with his hands folded. Tuqal grabbed both of Khudayar's arms with one hand, and with his other hand he simply lifted him up and took him to his shoulders, as if he were picking up an apple from the ground. Khudayar started to cry out, until he descended down the stairs and disappeared from sight.

All the attendants in Khoja Yusuf's presence drew their swords. Shouting and commotion broke out, and no one could control themselves. The begs who were sitting there were all struck with fear for their own lives, and none dared to obstruct this deed or ask what was behind it. A trembling took hold of all who were present, with Khosh Kifäk Beg particularly disturbed. His face took on the orange hue of amber, or of saffron, and streaks of yellow like Kashmiri gold could also be seen. When Khoja Yusuf saw what a state those seated before him were in, he started to console and comfort them. "Do not be afraid, O begs," he said. "My enemy was but one man, and he has received his punishment. There's no cause for anyone else to worry, you will be safe. Khudayar's family will also be safe. This has nothing to do with them."

When he finished speaking, Khoja Yusuf glanced at Abd al-Majid as if to ask, "How have you dealt with Khudayar?"

Either Abd al-Majid /73b/ failed to grasp what he was getting at, or he was part of Khudayar Beg's conspiracy and didn't want the secret to be divulged, or else he was simply hostile to Khudayar. In any case, he went and told the Kirghiz that their khoja was asking, "Why are they keeping Khudayar? They should execute him without any delay or hesitation!" Right there and then, the Kirghiz sliced his stomach open and tore him to pieces.

When Khoja Yusuf queried what they had done with Khudayar, the attendants explained the situation. Khoja Yusuf furrowed his brow but said, "Well, what's done is done. Inform the begs that we have killed Khudayar. Have the heralds announce to the kingdom that our enemy was a single man and the affair is now dealt with. Everyone else should feel secure and have no anxiety. Khudayar's sons should likewise not be worried or afraid. We will take care of them and treat them honorably. The enemy was their father; the rest are free from sin. If they do not feel at ease, open the gate for them and let them leave. No one should harm them at all. Let them do as they please."

This was conveyed to the begs, and the begs had the town criers carry the news from street to street. Khudayar's sons did not feel safe at all, so they fled the city. They traveled via Upper Artush to the vicinity of Lower Artush, where they met with the treacherous Abd al-Sattar. When Abd al-Sattar heard what had transpired, he too lost all strength and decided to take flight.

On the same day, Khoja Yusuf decreed to the kingdom that the army should prepare itself, and he mobilized a thousand men. Among the Barlas mirzas, there was a wise and ingenious man by the name of Mirza Danyal /74a/ (the father of the current deputy governor of Kashgar, Mirza Ḥaydar). He was appointed commander in chief of the army and sent off to Artush against Abd al-Sattar. Khoja Yusuf dispatched him with these instructions: "Let no one die in battle, and do not not harass him either. If he decides to leave, let him go. He'll eventually be caught; there's no need to take great pains."

Mirza Danyal left with this army and encircled Abd al-Sattar's courtyard several ranks deep. They stood there patiently while Abd al-Sattar fired off a few shots. In the end, he took his chances and escaped in the middle of the night, and the army didn't pursue him. The soldiers became rich with the spoils and then withdrew.

The schemers and conspirators took themselves via Kalta Yaylaq and Kelpin to Aqsu.[165] In Aqsu, they explained events to the skeptic Abd al-Wahhab and held council. Abd al-Wahhab wrote a letter to the Qalmaq *törä* which said:

> O *törä*, Khoja Yusuf and his family, and the entire population of Kashgar, Yarkand, and Khotan have turned against you and committed violence against your people. A man named Khudayar Beg devoted his entire life to your service and became deputy governor of Kashgar by your decree. If they have killed a man of his standing, what is to become of the rest of us? We always told you that these khojas would prove unfaithful to you and would not miss the slightest chance to strike at you, that they would definitely rebel when opportunity presented itself, but you did not believe us. Now this has come to pass. /74b/ It would be best for you to send an army and capture them. Otherwise, this kingdom is lost.

Abd al-Sattar and the sons of Khudayar took this petition and went to Ili, where they fell at the feet of the Qalmaq *törä*, crying and wailing. "O *törä*," they pleaded, "our forefathers served your forefathers for years on end and dedicated their entire lives to your service. For your sake they increased the *baj* and *kharaj* on the Muslims, and by your decree they became the deputy governors of Kashgar. Khoja Yusuf has now killed our father on your account, accusing him of being loyal to the Qalmaqs and communicating with them. We escaped before he could kill us and made it here with great difficulty. We are requesting vengeance for our father. You must provide us with an army, and we will go and take our revenge."

So saying, they presented the letter from Abd al-Wahhab. Having acquainted themselves with its contents, the Qalmaqs knew with certainty that Khoja Yusuf had broken with them. They were deeply remorseful about sending him back from Ili, but it was too late. It was felt that the best course of action would be for an army to go, but some wise councilors advised: "Now is not the time for a military campaign, since Amursana has gone to the emperor of China and there are rumors that he is advancing with a large army. It would be better at this point for some brave and eminent individual to go as an emissary. If they treat him as in the past, well and good. Otherwise, when the emissary returns, then the army should go /75a/ and teach them a lesson."

There had been some Qipchaq Kirghiz in the Ili district who were tending their flocks as subjects of the infidels. When Khoja Yusuf departed from Ili, he had written them a letter, calling on them to give aid to Islam. They had weighed the situation and taken the opportunity to remove themselves via Kucha to Khotan. The Qalmaqs were particularly aggrieved at this, so they decided to send an emissary on the pretext of retrieving them. A further consideration was that they had become accustomed to levying the *baj* and *kharaj* from these Muslim cities and spending it themselves. Some time had gone by without receiving any tribute or gifts from these cities, and their unsatisfied addiction was giving them a headache. Circumstances did not allow for them to send an army, for the *törä*s were disunited at this time and there was no stability to the kingdom such that they would be reliably faithful to each other. Each month, if one of them took up the throne, someone would come from somewhere else staking a claim to the position of *törä*. In the end, the wise and insightful infidels, along with certain faithless would-be Muslims, came to the decision to send an intrepid individual with three hundred brave cavalry, fully armed and equipped, in the form of an embassy, and that letters bearing their seals should be delivered to the governor of Kashgar Khosh Kifäk Beg, the governor of Khotan Ghazi Beg, and deputy governor Niyaz Beg, stating the following:

> You should provide support to our emissary, seize Khoja Yusuf and Khoja Jahan along with their family and retinue, and deliver them to Ili. Should you show any negligence in this affair, you will face the consequences.

They issued letters to this effect, and they assigned three hundred /75b/ champion infidels all clad in iron to the command of a renowned infidel with the title of *medechi*, and sent them off.[166] These infidels quickly made their way via Aqsu and Ush toward Kashgar, and from these cities certain people of little faith joined the infidels as companions.

News reached Kashgar that an emissary from the Qalmaqs was on his way. As soon as he heard this, Khoja Yusuf surmised that he could not have come without some objective in mind. Thinking that something must be afoot, he sent out Darvish Bakavul with five men to greet the emissary. When he gave him leave to go, he told him discreetly: "Observe how he carries himself: has he come with benign intentions, or for some sinister purpose? It should be evident from his deportment. Whatever turns out to be the case, write and keep me informed."

Darvish Bakavul was an intelligent man. His greeting party went out two stages, and he could see that the emissary was behaving seditiously, so he immediately whipped off a letter describing the situation. Khoja Yusuf quietly made an entreaty to God Almighty and requested aid from the spirits of the great saints, while in public he strapped on a bow and readied the arsenal. He mobilized the people attached to the palace and drilled five hundred brave soldiers. As the emissary approached, the locals came out to meet him, and he eventually entered the city. At the gate he saw a party of armed men standing guard, and he quivered in fright, but he could only continue into the palace. There he saw rank upon rank of men, all fully armed and clad in iron, standing on either side with a path running between them, as vigilant as if it were the day of battle. As the infidels entered the palace and took in this scene, they were completely at a loss. They gave up hope of ever coming out alive and regretted the decision to come. /76a/ Still, they had no choice but to proceed to the celestial audience chamber. There were nine gateways, and at each one a couple of infidels were detained and filtered out, so that only five or six eventually entered. Khoja Yusuf inquired as to the health of the *törä* and the situation in Ili. They explained things fully and freely, and Khoja Yusuf received them in a very relaxed fashion. The infidels were struck by divine awe and withdrew with the utmost humility. Khoja Yusuf said praise and thanks to God and issued a command to his servants: "Although they are infidels, they are nevertheless our guests. As the Prophetic hadith says, HONOR THE GUEST, EVEN IF HE BE AN

INFIDEL. Give them a place to retire and accommodate them in the emissary's quarters, and see to their needs and those of their mounts."

They put them up in a courtyard for envoys close to the River Gate, which is now the residence of the infidel by the name of Wanya.[167] The infidels invited Khosh Kifäk Beg and showed him the *törä*'s letter. "Since I am a Muslim, I fear God," Khosh Kifäk Beg told them. "If it were not determined by God to be my fate, then no *törä*, not even a hundred thousand *töräs*, would be able to touch a hair on my head. If not by divine will, then even a hundred thousand *töräs* united as one wouldn't be able to change my fortune in the slightest. These men belong to the bloodline of His Holiness Muḥammad, the lord of the two worlds. My ancestors have long eaten salt from their table, as have I.[168] I will never show ingratitude for this, nor will I earn myself a bad name in this world and the next by selling out the religion for worldly riches. Whatever happens, I will treat it as God's will."

To this rebuke /76b/ he added a warning. "Khoja Yusuf is an extremely clever man; he won't fall for this trick. Don't waste your time on such fruitless endeavors; you'll be the ones to suffer for it in the end."

Nevertheless, Muḥarram Beg, who was governor of Beshkerem, and Niyaz Beg, governor of Fayżabad, came secretly before the infidel envoy with a group of begs. "Whatever is to become of us," they declared, "we will not defy the authority of the *törä*.[169] We have attained our status thanks to the *törä*'s generosity. We have no need for this khoja. The khojas have ruined this land and its kingdoms. The prosperity of our homeland depends on you. On the day that we separate from you, we will be trampled beneath the feet of the Kirghiz. What we need to do is to find some ruse to capture Khoja Yusuf. Once we've seized him, then it will be straightforward to capture Khoja Jahan in Yarkand. He is a simpleton, but Khoja Yusuf is like a canny bird who will be extremely hard to lure into a trap. Our advice is that it won't be possible to take him in his own palace; you'll be repulsed. But if you were to invite him to this courtyard, he would be obliged to come. You should conceal a few brave men in the underground storehouse, some with guns, some with bows and arrows, and some with swords and knives. Then, when Khoja Yusuf enters and sits down alone, they should kill him with whatever comes to hand. If we don't capture and do away with him immediately, the world will come to ruin. Once we've killed him, we should display his body to the people /77a/ so that his friends and enemies will have no doubts, and they will feel compelled to come and pledge allegiance. With that out of the way, we'll take control of Yarkand in a single day."

Thus they outlined their plot, and the infidels took their advice and cheerfully set about preparing to host the guest. When word of this reached Khoja Yusuf, he made an appeal to God, and held up his hands in supplication to the great spirits. "O immortal and eternal One! This black-faced sinner was unable able to carry out your commands as he should have. I've frittered away my life in trivial pursuits and spent the time for submission and worship in vain. I've been firm in my submission to the infidels and wavering on the path of Islam. But you are kind and merciful! If the sea of your forgiveness were but to come into motion, a single drop of it would do away with the mountain of sins built up by a hundred thousand sinners like me. Look not at this sinful one's refractoriness and rebellion, O Lord. For the sake of your friend Muḥammad, make me staunch among these fierce enemies and infidels, and make the existence of this humble slave a vehicle for the victory of Islam. Do not allow the honor of the shariʿa to be besmirched!"

With much crying and wailing, he eventually fell asleep. In his dream, he saw a luminescent man approach him saying, "Son, why are you so disturbed? Victory will be on the side of Islam, don't be so downcast! The enemies will be overcome and laid low. Tomorrow morning, don't hesitate to go and make the visit, just as the enemies desire. Fear not, keep your head high." Khoja Yusuf immediately woke up, and while there was no sign of anyone, /77b/ the interior of the room was filled with the scent of perfume. In gratitude for this auspicious vision, he repeated his ablutions and performed a prayer of thanksgiving.

The next morning, the infidel emissary invited Khoja Yusuf to pay him a visit. Accompanied by two or three hundred armed guards, Khoja Yusuf entered the embassy's quarters, and in the eyes of the infidels each of these Muslims seemed like more than one man. "For sure they have come to arrest us," they concluded with dread. "This is the day of our destruction! Muḥarram and Niyaz must have been conspiring against us." Finding no opportunity to hatch any plan, they were overwhelmed by their nerves and struck dumb, their bodies trembling. Because of all this, they outdid themselves in service and hospitality before seeing their guest off. Khoja Yusuf gave thanks and praise to God and returned to the palace with a magnificent parade. The infidel emissary couldn't quell his anxiety. Indeed, it increased to the point where he lost the nerve to stay in Kashgar and he had no choice but to seek permission from Khoja Yusuf to leave. Khoja Yusuf approved his request and let him go, and this infidel set off for Yarkand with his evil designs. By a different road, Khoja Yusuf dispatched one of his close confidants with a letter for Khoja Jahan:

> The infidel emissary who is now approaching has come with thoroughly treacherous intentions. In Kashgar he tried to spring his trap of guile and trickery, but God Almighty in His grace /78a/ kept us sinners from falling into it. Disappointed at this, he is now making his way to Yarkand for the same subversive ends. Be vigilant and on guard! Be sure not to allow yourself any negligence toward this affair. Take all necessary precautions. As long as this infidel is within Yarkand, even if that fraud Ghazi Beg invites you a thousand times, you should not go to his house, and you should not endorse anything that he says. To be safe from the enemy's plots, you should mobilize the entire palace staff, prepare the arsenal, and post a guard outside the palace day and night. You must be especially wary of enemies in the guise of friends.
>
> When friendly eyes cast a hostile glance, it is hard on the heart,
> Enemies never gave you their sympathy and they won't take it away.[170]
>
> Much hurt has been done by enemies in the guise of friends,
> So be more cautious of friends than of enemies.

He also sent the following letter to Khoja Yaḥya and Khoja Ṣiddiq:

> O brothers, be attentive and aware! Don't become complacent at our good fortune or be satisfied with honor and luxury in this transient world. To whom has it ever been faithful, that it would keep faith with us? Don't imagine yourselves immune from the turbulence of the times. The world is full of trials.
>
> *Don't recline in security, even on a lofty mountain,*
> *There are a hundred leopards in hiding, and a hundred dragons at its peak.*

Don't be inattentive to the plans of our enemies, for even though they might be humiliated, they will rouse themselves again. As insignificant as they are, they will be on the lookout. Once they have enticed you into their lair, it will be no use expressing regret. One has to confront threats before they manifest themselves; nothing can be done in their wake. My message is that strong enemies are laying an ambush, and you must be on guard against them. His Grace Khoja Jahan is a simple dervish, and his heart is entirely free of guile. Because of this, he has occasionally mistaken the sweet tongues of our enemies /78b/ for the truth, and he puts everything down to trust in God (*tavakkul*). To be sure, trust in God is appropriate, but it needs to be in its place. God Almighty has ordained a cause for every event, such that it will occur through that cause. What is required of His servant is to put that cause into effect, and to trust in the cause that has been created. It is not fitting to neglect this cause in the name of putting one's trust in God. It is just as our Mawlana has said in his noble *Ma<u>s</u>navi*:

The Prophet said with a loud voice, "While trusting in God bind the knee of thy camel."[171]

Beware! A thousand times beware! Don't be inattentive toward Ghazi Beg's treachery. If the venerable khoja shows confidence in him, you must forestall him and not allow him to set foot outside the palace. Stay on guard at all times: keeping hold of a kingdom is no easy task. Many kings and princes have come and gone, who out of simplemindedness and ignorance failed to recognize the true state of their kingdom, or were oblivious to conspiracies, and thereby fell into a trap and lost their throne.

When these letters of advice arrived, Khoja Jahan and the rest of the princes took all necessary precautions and remained on guard, strengthening the defenses of the palace. When the emissary infidels entered Yarkand, they met Khoja Jahan inside the palace. Here too they were apprehensive when they saw that it was even more fortified than the palace in Kashgar. It occurred to them that one khoja was even more wily than the next, for they were completely prepared and seemed to have entirely broken with them.

Instead of expressing this, though, they said a few perverse words by way of greetings from their *törä*, and with great deference they invited him to Ili, expressing the *törä*'s fervent desire /79a/ for a reunion with his friend. For his part, Khoja Jahan gave a warm response but said that the decision whether to go to Ili would have to depend on God's will, and he directed the infidels to the emissary's lodgings. They resided there for a few days.

Khoja Jahan then spoke with Ghazi Beg, outlining what he saw as the best course of action: "For years now, we've spent our lives serving these wretched infidels and have held firmer to their commands than we have to those of God Almighty. Now our lives are coming to an end, and we don't have a single good deed to sustain us on the journey to the next world. What a disgrace for us to come before the Lord in this shameful condition! There is a hadith attributed to the Prophet, that HE WHO DIES WITHOUT KNOWING THE IMAM OF HIS AGE DIES IN IGNORANCE; that is to say, "If someone dies and still has not recognized that age's king of Islam, then that man has died an impure and ignorant death." Praise be to God that the Lord created us within the Islamic faith and endowed us with intelligence and consciousness. It is incumbent on us to distinguish good from evil and advance toward the good. The Prophet also has this hadith, that HE WHO ESTABLISHES A TRADITION IN ISLAM WILL ENJOY ITS MERIT AND THE MERIT OF THOSE WHO ACT IN ACCORDANCE WITH IT UNTIL JUDGMENT DAY, BUT FOR ONE WHO SETS A BAD PRECEDENT IN ISLAM, THE SIN OF IT AND OF THOSE WHO ACT ACCORDING TO IT WILL BE UPON HIM UNTIL JUDGMENT DAY. /79b/ Because of this, the best form of worship is to accomplish good works, and there is no deed that can compare with holy war. All those who have come before us have shown the way in this. They did not shy away from holy war in the slightest. There is also the noble verse of the Quran, AND IF THERE BE ONE THOUSAND, THEY SHALL OVERCOME TWO THOUSAND [8:66]; which is to say, if there are a thousand on the side of the Muslims, then they will be victorious over two thousand infidels. According to this verse, it is inappropriate for a Muslim to flee from two infidels, for he himself counts as one, and his faith counts as one. When the infidels are three, however, then it is incumbent on the Muslim to flee, and failure to do so would be considered stubborn. God willing, as long as there is no sign of discord among these Muslims of the Seven Cities, we will be able to resist the infidels. Indeed, at present there is instability in the territories of the Qalmaq infidels, and they have succumbed to disunity among themselves. They won't dare to bring an army against us. In Islam, it won't do to submit to unbelievers out of one's own free will. So come, my beg, let us turn against these accursed infidels. Let us raise the flag of Islam above our heads and wield the sword without hesitation."

So saying, he enjoined Ghazi to support the victory of Islam. Yet the Lord Almighty in His divine decrees had destined this man for misfortune and disgrace, and these words made no impression on him. Ghazi gave no hint of this, however, and pretended to be in complete accord, suggesting only that they postpone any action for a few days, until the disunity among the infidels manifested itself. Khoja Jahan accepted this advice and decided to wait.

/80a/ A few days went by, until eventually the infidel emissary presented the letter with the *törä*'s seal to Ghazi Beg and Deputy Governor Niyaz Beg. They embraced it enthusiastically and set about devising a conspiracy. In the end, they decided that it simply wouldn't be possible to capture Khoja Jahan in the palace, because there were seven hundred armed and equipped men keeping watch. But if the emissary pretended to be sick at his residence and they invited the khoja to pay him a visit, then he would have no choice but to come and check on his illness, and the Qalmaqs would be ready for him. Only by this ruse would they be able to capture him—they could see no other way. Agreeing to this plan, the infidel emissary went to Ghazi Beg's house and made noises pretending to be sick. Secretly they issued a command to the Qalmaqs who had previously been stationed as *qarakhan*, as well as to the Qalmaq merchants, to inform them of what was going on, and all the infidels took up arms in readiness.

Ghazi then went and personally invited Khoja Jahan to visit. "With respect, my king, would you come to my humble abode today and hold audience there? The infidel emissary has been struck by a grievous illness; its symptoms seem to indicate his imminent death. He is distressed, saying that there is a decree from the *törä* that he needs to deliver, and he would like to show you his seal, but he is dying. Moreover, by a certain reckoning today is New Year's Day (Noruz), and I have laid in supplies for the celebrations. How would it be if you spent the day there today?"

He invited him with all sorts of blandishments, and His Grace promised to go. Yet as soon as Ghazi had left, all the princes and the palace noteworthies discouraged him from doing so. /80b/ "With respect, my king," they said as one, "we have had long experience of this sly Ghazi's treachery. His entire modus operandi consists of deception, he is not to be trusted. The emissary's behavior has equally been suspicious, he seems in no mood to contain his aggression. Khoja Yusuf sent several letters from Kashgar on this very point. If now you were to go and the enemy made some sudden move, how would we reply to him?" They made endless objections to stop him from going.

Meanwhile, for the purposes of the deception, Ghazi had the infidel emissary drink a few cups of pomegranate juice, then laid him down on a rug and pillow. Khoja Jahan had an elderly and naive servant by the name of Muḥammad Abdullah Bakavul, who was the most long-standing member of his staff. Ghazi called him in and showed him the infidel emissary. He saw that he was moaning and coughing up blood and couldn't lie still on his bed. He looked to be in a very poor state. The infidel importuned him: "Please get the khoja to come and see me, I have something to say to him. This is a severe illness, there's no chance of recovery. Go quickly, he must come soon if we are to meet."

After they went outside, Ghazi emphasized, "You've seen what state this infidel is in, this is an emergency. The khoja should come quickly and listen to whatever he has to say, then I'll be at peace. I'm worried about my reputation too."

This Muḥammad Abdullah Bakavul was such a guileless man, he fell for this trick /81a/ and ran off to see Khoja Jahan. Facing the objections of all those warning him against going, the khoja responded by first immersing himself in the sea of divine truth and then spoke: "God willing, my hope is that in this day and age they will be unable to harm a hair on my head, but instead through the vehicle of their fraud and trickery, God will bestow on us some degree of enlightenment, which will bring us honor in this world and the next. In the Holy Book it says BUT IT MAY BE THAT YOU HATE A THING THOUGH IT BE GOOD FOR YOU [2:216]. That is to say, there are many things that you may hope to ward off, but which in truth are a blessing for you. Likewise there are many things that you may view as beneficial, and expect some good to come from, but which are in fact injurious to you. You may feel melancholy for a few days. There may be grief and heartache. Yet the Most Merciful Lord will assuage this grief and recompense you richly, just as Ali (MAY GOD ENNOBLE HIS VISAGE!) has said:

> WHEN SOME MISFORTUNE AFFLICTS YOU,
> REFLECT ON THE SURA "DID WE NOT EXPAND,"
> AND THAT EACH HARDSHIP COMES BETWEEN TWO INSTANCES OF EASE.
> WHEN YOU THINK UPON THIS, YOU'LL FIND JOY.

And likewise a poet has said:

> *The beauty of a deed is hidden by the enmity of those who perform it,*
> *It was the wheel of fortune that threw Joseph into the pit.*

"What is intended by this is that someone may bring an enemy down out of spite but the subtle import of that deed be lost on them. It is just like when the Holy Joseph's brothers threw him into the pit out of enmity, not realizing that through the experience of that pit he would go on to become the king of Egypt, /81b/ and that they would be obliged to present themselves before him."

Tears welled up in Khoja Jahan's eyes and fell like raindrops, and he continued strewing his gems of insight: "O family, you must realize that our fate is not in their hands. Before long, God Almighty will provide us with an opportunity to rebel against these infidels and whiten our black face, to take the sword of Islam in hand and wield it without restraint, and to renew the Islamic faith. Following that, a party will emerge from the east, who will bring these cities into their possession with little effort. At that time, the victory will belong to those people, and defeat will fall to us. Even if Rustam and Sam were to enter the battle on our side and display their skills, they would fall before children riding wooden ponies. And if Maḥmud's elephant were to take the field for us, it would succumb to the sting of gnats.[172] Our fate will be in their hands, and the elimination of our line will also be in their hands. They will have neither mercy nor compassion, for in their eyes bloodshed is a point of pride and the highest calling." With this, he recited a stanza from the eight-line poem that he had composed earlier.

Eventually one day our souls will fall into death's trap,
Rendering us infirm and helpless, it will brook no cure.
It will leave us no chance to voice our plaint,
Our predestined fate will not admit any change.
Our faith will stay above our heads as a parasol,
And our spilt blood will turn the face of the earth tulip red.
/82a/ All our companions and friends will grieve for us,
While vampires drink our blood, O heart!

One of Khoja Jahan's daughters had a son whom they used to call Qiran Khoja, although his original name was Khoja Ḥasan.[173] He was no more than six or seven years old, but every day he would manifest all kinds of miracles. Sometimes he would distinguish the shoes of those destined for heaven from the shoes of those destined for hell, and sometimes he would divulge hidden secrets while playing among the children. Khoja Jahan trained this child himself and took him as his adopted son. He was extremely clever. When he was displaying his various miracles, Khoja Jahan would feed him food from the bazaar, such was the extent of his frugality.[174]

This child was sitting in front of Khoja Jahan. He took him aside and kissed his forehead. "I wish this misfortune would afflict us alone and pass with our downfall," he said, "and that it wouldn't extend to innocents like you. For you have yet to taste any of the pleasures of this treacherous world or experience any of its comforts. But there won't be salvation for anyone from this great cataclysm. Neither I, nor you, nor anyone else will escape the grasp of this calamity: it will ravage the entirety of this clime. There will be neither friend nor enemy left here to collect our blood price or take revenge for us—neither kinsman nor foreigner, neither tyrant nor killer. All will face doom."

The impact of these words on his family members left them bereft of all patience and self-possession; it was as if Judgment Day had erupted inside the hall. All at once, cries of mourning arose, /82b/ and the sound of "Woe is us! What misfortune!" filled the heavens. Some were unconscious and lost to themselves, while others were agitated. Some were having paroxysms like half-slaughtered birds, and some were as fitful as if they were in the ecstasy of a mystical dance (*samāʿ*).

Muḥammad Abdullah Bakavul entered and explained the emissary infidel's symptoms and delivered the message that Ghazi had entrusted him with. Nobody was happy to hear this: it was as if he had poured boiling water into a cooking pot. Shihab al-Din Bakavul shot him a hostile glare, thinking to himself, "One day I'll get you back for this incompetence." This resentment lingered with him.

Yet Khoja Jahan did not yield to the assembly's remonstrations. He told them all to remain watchful and finished saying his piece. Then he took Khoja Yaḥya as his companion, assigned a large number of his servants to patrol the palace, and rode off with only a handful of people. Reciting the verse AND WHOSOEVER REVERENCES GOD, [HE WILL APPOINT EASE FOR HIS AFFAIR] [65:4], he made his way to Ghazi's house of disrepute. Ghazi greeted him with even more humility than in the past and led him inside, where he saw the infidel lying in bed. The conspiracy was obvious from his posture and bearing, and all the more so in the case of Ghazi, but Khoja Jahan did not let on and instead put his trust in God. After a while, a round of tea was brought in, and some infidels entered and invoked the *törä*'s decree to seize both Khoja Jahan and Khoja Yaḥya. They disarmed them and took them into the guest room, where they detained them. Then they fortified the outer gate and tied up all the servants who had accompanied them. Their intention was to prevent anyone sending word to the palace, so that they could go and take them by surprise /83a/ and capture the rest of the family too.

Khoja Ṣiddiq had led a group up onto the palace wall to watch what was going on. Ghazi's gate was clearly visible, and they saw a commotion break out and the gate slam shut. They knew for sure that he had sprung some trap and matters were getting out of hand. They, in turn, strengthened the palace gate and stood with their weapons at the ready. Right at that moment, some two or three hundred infidels and Muslims came running toward the palace, but they saw that the gate was shut firm. Those who led the charge were shot at from above and had no choice but to fall back. Taking advantage of this opportunity, thirty-five intrepid souls led by Khoja Ṣiddiq and Shihab al-Din Bakavul broke through the side wall of the palace and got themselves outside the city, withdrawing toward Khotan. They sent a servant by the name of Muḥammadi Mir Akhur to Kashgar to report to Khoja Yusuf.

My informant tells me that some five or six hundred men, including both infidels and Muslims, set off to catch Khoja Ṣiddiq and bring him back. They caught up with him on the banks of the Zarafshan River. Everyone raised their eyes to the heavens and cried out in supplication:

O God, I love you, that is all,
For there is no one like you.
O God, take hold of my hand in this trial,
O God, come to my rescue at this time![175]

Their entreaties were accepted at the Lord's court, and they all took courage and turned around. As they did, one infidel rode toward them hurling abuse. Expressing his intention for holy war, Shihab al-Din Bakavul nimbly took aim at his mouth with an arrow and let fly. /83b/ Before the infidel could get his head out of the way, it struck him in the mouth and protruded a yard's length from his neck, as if he were chewing on the arrow. The infidel was thrown backward off his horse, and his wretched soul took up residence in the seventh circle of Hell. On seeing this, everyone on the other side was awestruck and intimidated, and they turned in flight.

Khoja Ṣiddiq and his brave companions gave thanks and praise to God and continued on their way to Khotan. When they came close, they ran into one of Ghazi's staff who had also come to Khotan. They seized him and sent him off on a horse with this warning: "Go and make sure to tell that idiot Ghazi that he is not to harm our king or touch a single hair on his body. Otherwise we swear to God that we will round up all of Ghazi's kin in Khotan, take them out to the Yarkand Gate, slaughter them like sheep, and make a mill run with their blood. We will not leave a single inch of brick in the Yarkand city wall standing. If we don't massacre them all, my name is not Khoja Ṣiddiq."

When Khoja Ṣiddiq neared the city of Khotan, the whole population of the kingdom came out to greet him. He made a grand entrance to the city, then met with Khoja Shams al-Din and explained the situation to him. At that time, one of Ghazi's sons was governor of Khotan. They seized him and tied him up, and they also detained another of his sons and some of his relatives. Khotan was also full of Qipchaq Kirghiz who had come from Ili, led by a man named Umar Mirza. These they instructed to go and ransack the houses of Ghazi's sons, and then a command was issued for an army to assemble made up of all the Kirghiz as well as the men of Khotan. The army mobilized in a single day, /84a/ and Khoja Ṣiddiq set out for Yarkand with a force of six or seven thousand. They tied the hands and feet of all of Ghazi's retinue, including his sons, and entrusted them to the Kirghiz, setting up an old tent for them in the evenings. The Kirghiz carried them along with all sorts of abuse and mistreatment.

20. GHAZI BEG HAS SECOND THOUGHTS

Let us now turn to a story about Muḥammadi Mir Akhur. On that day, which was a Thursday, he was joined on the road by a member of Khoja Jahan's bodyguard (*ushaq*) named Yusuf.[176] The two of them traveled by night, and at midmorning on Friday they entered Kashgar by the side gate. They met with Khoja Yusuf and explained the situation to him. Khoja Yusuf struck his knees angrily, his passion was fired, and every hair on his body stood up straight. He instructed Khalifa Ṣabir to keep these two men hidden, so that the enemy not find out about them, and with his own retinue he went out to Qaraqir and set up camp. The elite of Kashgar came out and held a council. There was a rumor that a group of Kirghiz was approaching from Ili who might possibly find some way to harm his subjects, and since Yarkand was not entirely safe either, Khoja Yusuf gave a command for the army to assemble. He felt it was best that they carry themselves correctly and not give any indication of disunity.

In a couple of days, a large force was mobilized. Two days after this, they brought out Muḥammadi Mir Akhur along with Yusuf and entrusted them with a letter, which read:

> Ghazi, you bumpkin, you seem to have forgotten the way you used to behave. If you're simply ignorant, come to your senses. If you're asleep, wake up. If you touch a single hair on my brother's head, /84b/ I swear by the Prophet that if I fail to hunt down seventy generations of your family and slaughter them like sheep before the Qabaq Atqu Gate till the mills run with their blood, and if I don't take Yarkand's population captive and smash its city walls to smithereens, then my name is not Khoja Yusuf.

He didn't hold back with his threats; then he pressed the letter into their hands. "Deliver this to Ghazi," he said, "and don't hesitate to say a hundred times more than this. He shouldn't dare to even look at you with his treacherous eyes." These two men took the letter and set out for Yarkand. There were patrols on the road in one or two places, but they didn't dare waylay them.

When they arrived before the city gate, it was shut fast. "Open the gate," they shouted, "we bring a letter. Khoja Yusuf himself is on his way behind us with an army beyond all measure. Quickly, open the gate!" They raised such a cry that no one could sit idly by. The people of Yarkand were particularly upset at this state of affairs, and since they couldn't find an excuse not to, they simply threw open the gate without asking anyone's permission. The two men came into the city and entered Ghazi's residence without hesitating. They saw the infidel emissary sitting there, along with all the Qalmaqs and a group of begs. They handed the letter to Ghazi, who took it respectfully and read it, trembling with fear as he did. The Qalmaqs asked him about it, and these two men let fly with reproaches in the Qalmaq tongue, telling them that Khoja Yusuf had ridden out with an army ten thousand strong, and that he had also sent men to the nearby Kirghiz, who were rallying from all directions. /85a/ Neither the Qalmaqs nor any of the inhabitants of Yarkand had any strength left. Prior to this, the threatening message that Khoja Ṣiddiq had sent via Ghazi's servant on the road to Khotan had already arrived. In the face of these combined threats, they were at their wits' end, and they treated Muḥammadi Mir Akhur and Yusuf with the utmost deference. Following this, a letter from Khosh Kifäk Beg also arrived, in which he escalated the threats:

> Ghazi Beg, with your corruption the whole of Yarkand, along with seventy generations of your family, will come to ruin. For a couple of days of worldly renown, you've turned your face against Islam and aided the infidel and committed such injustices against the sons of the Prophet! Imagine how difficult your case will be before God and the Prophet in the next world. From the time of the wars of Yusuf Qadir Khan and the imams until now, we Khotanese have yet to shed our bad reputation, and now thanks to a couple of frauds and tricksters like you, the whole of our people will be disgraced.[177] With these disreputable actions of yours, the people of Khotan won't be rid of their bad name until Judgment Day. I'm

> fed up with being a fellow countryman of yours. Indeed, I'm sick of such a country. A world of shame has overcome me, as if I myself had committed this awful deed. To make up for this, you should immediately install Khoja Jahan on the throne and beg forgiveness for your sins. Otherwise this entire cataclysm will be on your shoulders.

Ghazi listened to these words and was plunged into misgiving and regret. When the staff of the palace heard about these letters, /85b/ they were emboldened and found the fortitude to strengthen the palace's defenses and carry themselves more confidently. As a trick, Ghazi dressed his own men up as Qalmaqs and led them into the room where Khoja Jahan was sitting and had them abuse him. Ghazi himself then pretended to intervene and turn them away, saying, "I am devoted to the khojas, better you harm me before doing any harm to them!" Ghazi spent his time engaging in contrivances such as this.

In the meantime, people brought word from Khotan that Khoja Ṣiddiq had seized all of Ghazi Beg's kin and household and was on his way with a large army of several thousand Kirghiz and Khotanese, and that he intended to slaughter those he had captured before the gate of Yarkand. When Ghazi heard these menacing words, he fainted. He had accommodated all the Qalmaqs in a park inside the city, and he decided to end his dealings with these infidels. That night he smuggled two swords in to Khoja Jahan and told him that if the infidels requested to execute him, he would not allow it, and that if they broke in, he should stand by the door and kill anyone who enters.

Ghazi called in not only his friends and acquaintances but also the elders of Yarkand, explained the situation to them, and asked for their advice. "These regions, and Yarkand province in particular, were the abode of Khoja Isḥaq Vali," they all told him. "This country will only flourish with the blessings and well-wishing of his descendants. /86a/ What will now eventuate from the stain of this treachery that you've carried out? What calamities will befall these lands? Khoja Jahan is a man of saintly qualities, and entirely meek and mild. To make recompense, you should trust in his mercy, swear an oath on the Quran, and ask for forgiveness. It may be that he will absolve you, that you will be reconfirmed in office, and that no injury will come to your fortune and wealth." Ghazi found this advice very much to his liking, and he sprang into action.

21. KHOJA YUSUF PROCLAIMS THE AGE OF ISLAM

Regarding Khoja Yusuf, I am told that on that day he sent off his threatening letter to Yarkand, he also dispatched Khoja Abdullah with five hundred men to Barchuq. The excuse was to intercept the Kirghiz of the Sariq Qalpaq who were coming from Ili, but the real purpose was that if suddenly the infidels were to take Khoja Jahan off to Ili, he could set an ambush and rescue him. While in Ili, Khoja Yusuf had made a pact with the Kirghiz who were on their way, and for that reason he had no anxiety toward them, and indeed he was anticipating their imminent arrival. Secretly he had been sending people to tell them to hurry up and the Kirghiz were rushing down, although the people were unaware of these secrets and were worried.

The Kirghiz came quickly /86b/ into Khoja Yusuf's service, and troops from around the kingdom were also assembling. To everyone's surprise, the Kirghiz assumed all the responsibilities of his staff and made them redundant. That day Khoja Yusuf summoned the scholars and amirs and the elite and commoners of the kingdom and admonished them: "Leaders of Kashgar, know that God created man so that they worship Him: I DID NOT CREATE JINN AND MANKIND, SAVE TO WORSHIP ME [51:56]. For how long will we remain in submission to the infidels and waste our lives serving them? When our lives come to an end, how will we confront the court of God Almighty? How will we reply to His questions in such a state of disgrace? Regret and misgivings will be of no use there; we need to take action in advance. It is God who created man: is it not a shame if we spend our lives following the command of His foul infidel enemies, instead of adhering to His command? He instituted holy war as a requirement for His servants. Glory be to God, at this time the Muslims now have the strength to stand up to the infidels, because they have been thrown into turmoil, and two groups of Kirghiz have rebelled and joined us. The first of these groups has now settled in Khotan, and the second /87a/ in Kashgar. Previously we had no choice but to submit, and therefore we remained loyal until this time. But now the right thing to do is to turn from these infidels. We should boldly loft the banner of Islam and draw the sword of victory against them, whiten our black face, renew our observance of the religion and Holy Law, and determine to enter the afterlife without shame. For countless years this desire for holy war never left my heart. I always wished that if only we could free ourselves from submission to these infidels, we would install Temür Khan on the throne of the sultanate and hand the affairs of state to him. We would withdraw and spend our lives in devotion, according to the old customs and precepts of our forebears, and make recompense for our years of service to the infidels. Glory be to God, it looks as if such a time has arrived, and I have hope now that my goal may be achieved. I need your opinions on this immediately. If you endorse this objective, come, let us renew our oaths and make a special pledge of allegiance."

As he delivered this fiery speech, the cries and shouts of the crowd rose up like a towering tornado and filled the dome of the heavens. All at once, everyone started weeping like the April rain. When they had eventually composed themselves, they replied: /87b/ "We have but one soul, but even if we had a hundred thousand, we would sacrifice them all for Islam, as an offering for its victory. If we die, we'll have no remorse, for we can hope that in the next life we'll be resurrected among the martyrs and holy warriors." Everyone eagerly swore allegiance and renewed their oaths and said congratulations. The eloquent and articulate *aʿlam akhund* Mulla Maḥmud recited the opening chapter of the Quran for their victory.

At that time, three hundred Qalmaqs of the Sharas tribe had come to trade and had set up camp in a field on the side of Sögät Mountain.[178] There were also some Qalmaqs inside the city.[179] Khoja Yusuf dispatched the army of Islam with this command: "Invite the infidels to embrace Islam. If they accept, well and good. Otherwise, you may kill them. This will be their punishment." He also sent someone into the city to have the town criers go from street to street proclaiming: "Now is the age of Islam! The age of Islam!" The kettle drums and the flutes struck up a happy tune, and the hearts of the enemies fell to pieces. Wherever two people met, they would first praise Islam before shaking hands. That day, whether freeman or slave, man or woman, all were so joyful they could hardly contain themselves, as if all their ambitions in this life and the next had been realized.

When the army of Islam reached their camp, the infidels realized what was going on and put up resistance. The Muslims, who were waiting for an excuse to harm them, attacked immediately, and within an hour they had massacred them. A few got away in the direction of Upper Artush, and it was decided not to pursue them. Inside the city, the Qalmaqs who were garrisoning the *qarakhan* guard post went unmolested. /88a/ These infidels had always been eager to bring advantage to the Muslims, and when the infidel emissary arrived, they had given Khoja Yusuf some hint as to his treachery and corruption. Because of this, he sent these infidels back to their own region safe and sound, telling them to report on what they had seen.

Everyone's hearts were set at ease. Even the Kirghiz, who had been anxious that Khoja Yusuf might trick them and deliver them to the Qalmaqs, became satisfied with affairs and directed their energies to the campaign against Yarkand.

22. KHOJA JAHAN PROCLAIMS ISLAM IN YARKAND

Those who have transmitted this story say that Ghazi was utterly aghast at the treachery he had committed. Terrified at the imminent threats from both directions, he couldn't come up with any alternative but to take the Quran into his hands and enter Khoja Jahan's quarters. Falling at his feet, he begged for mercy on the Holy Book and asked forgiveness for his sins. Out of respect for the Divine Word, Khoja Jahan forgave him his wrongdoing.

"O king of the world," Ghazi pleaded with him, "toward you my heart is at ease. But I fear the princes may try to hurt me in some way."

Khoja Jahan gave him his promise. "You have put the holy Word of God between us. I will not allow anyone to harm you. Any injury done to you will be the same as if done to me."

Ghazi cried, clutched the Quran to his breast, and swore a series of oaths. "May the Quran be my witness," he said, /88b/ "that I will spend the rest of my life serving your majesty, being friend to your friend, and enemy to your enemy. In public and in private, in word, deed, and conviction, I will commit no treachery. And if at any time if I fail to keep faith with this pledge, may the Word of God strike me down in punishment, and may my face turn black in this life and the next."

Khoja Jahan also took the Quran into his hands and made a vow. "I too will not break faith with you. May this noble Word of God be witness to my oath."

That day they erected a tall throne in Khoja Jahan's audience room and invited him to come and take up the seat of the sultanate. The scholars, amirs, and all ranks of Yarkand's population came and swore allegiance to him. Such was the excitement of that day, it was as if Judgment Day was dawning. Everyone who came and celebrated Islam and swore an oath burst out crying. No one was exempt from the exuberance, and their happiness gave way to tears of joy. Even the earth and sky were sobbing with delight, as were the mountains and oceans. The town criers were told to proclaim from street to street: "Now is the age of Islam, the age of Khoja Jahan!" Frenetic drummers made such merriment, it seemed as if the birds in the sky and the fish in the sea were coming to the boil. The scholars explained Quranic verses and hadiths to do with the victory of Islam, and the poets recited celebratory odes. Each group celebrated in its own way and made merry. /89a/ All the amirs requested that a command be given in relation to the infidel emissary and the Qalmaqs he led, so that they could execute them, but Khoja Jahan said: "It is impermissible to kill infidels in any situation other than battle. Instead, leave the infidels to themselves and expel them from the city, then let the army then give chase. If they convert, they will be safe. Otherwise, those who die in the fighting will die, and those who get away will get away. This is what the shariʿa requires. Furthermore, my dear son is in Ili among the infidels. If we persecute these infidels to any greater degree than this, it will not be good for him."

The amirs thus gave horses to each of the infidels and expelled them from the gate, while the army pursued them. Those that died in skirmishes along the way died, while the rest got away. On their way back to Ili, they joined up with a group of five hundred Qalmaqs who were coming to reinforce the infidel emissary, oblivious to what was going on. When the Muslims were done with this engagement with the infidels, they carried Khoja Jahan with all formalities to the palace and seated him on the throne of the sultanate. That day was New Year's Day (Noruz), and it seemed as if three New Year's Days had all come at once: the New Year of the victory of Islam, the New Year for the first day of the year, and the New Year of Khoja Jahan's release from imprisonment.[180]

When these affairs had been dealt with, Ghazi Beg said, "Apparently Khoja Yusuf has inaugurated Islam in Kashgar, and news has arrived that he intends to lead an army against Yarkand. If the princes saw fit, they might go and congratulate him on the opening of Islam and forestall his campaign. Khoja Ṣiddiq, meanwhile, has gone to Khotan. Word is that upon arriving there, he took my family captive and is now raising an army of

Kirghiz under Umar Mirza. /89b/ Could there please be a decree to one of the palace chiefs for them to go and transmit the good news, demobilize the army, restore my family to their place, and bring Khoja Ṣiddiq back?" Khoja Jahan approved of these proposals. He sent his son-in-law Khoja Umar off to Kashgar and dispatched Muḥammad Abdullah Bakavul to Khotan with a letter bearing his seal.

Khoja Umar made his way to Kashgar just as Khoja Yusuf was drilling his troops in Qaraqir with the intention of marching on Yarkand. When Khoja Umar arrived bringing the good news and his congratulations for Islam, Khoja Yusuf led all the amirs and religious scholars of Kashgar in applauding Khoja Umar on the opening of Islam in Yarkand. Everyone who heard these happy tidings said words of praise. Khoja Yusuf repeated his ablutions and performed a special prayer to express his thanks to God. He hosted Khoja Umar as his guest for a few days of festivities before sending him on his way again.

23. THE KHOTANESE ARMY ARRIVES IN YARKAND

We turn now to the story of Muḥammad Abdullah Bakavul. While making for Khotan at full speed, he ran into Khoja Ṣiddiq, who was coming along the road leading the Khotanese army. Muḥammad Abdullah Bakavul explained to him what was going on in Yarkand and reported the good news, showing him the letter instructing him not to harm Ghazi's family. But Khoja Ṣiddiq took no notice of what he was saying and did not credit the letter. Instead he began to abuse him, accusing him of conspiring with Ghazi and stringing Khoja Jahan along. /90a/ "You've even gone so far as to fabricate a letter to free Ghazi's family and relieve his worries! What more trouble will you cause us? What else do you have in mind?" Shihab al-Din Bakavul in particular was bitter that this man had persuaded Khoja Jahan to go with him to Ghazi's house. He would've liked to have punished him, but Khoja Ṣiddiq didn't permit any violence, for it was impolite to harm his illustrious father's retainer. He satisfied himself by issuing a command to give him a lame horse and have him straggle along behind the army unaccompanied. Picking his way along the road in great discomfort, Muḥammad Abdullah Bakavul regretted immensely that he had ever come.

A couple of days went by, and the eloquent and brave *aʿlam* of Yarkand, Akhund Mulla Umar Baqi, was also sent out. He too met with Khoja Ṣiddiq, explained events and delivered the good tidings, and showed him a letter regarding Ghazi's family.[181] But even the akhund's words and letter did not allay these people's suspicions. "Ghazi is a thoroughly deceptive individual," they said. "If he made some request to the akhund, he may have felt obliged to take him at his word and come. This seal is meaningless, since Khoja Jahan is imprisoned in enemy hands. They're hoping to defeat us through trickery or lure us into the city by deception." As a result, they didn't believe what the akhund was saying either and remained unconvinced.

In the end, they arrived before Yarkand in this state of uncertainty. All the elite of the city came out to greet them, but even then /90b/ they still weren't reassured. Finally, Umar Mirza sent some of his own courtiers into the city. When they came back reporting that they had seen Khoja Jahan ensconced on the throne of the sultanate, they were at last convinced and entered the city. The leaders of the Khotanese army, with Khoja Shams al-Din and Khoja Ṣiddiq at the fore, along with the Kirghiz led by Umar Mirza, fell at Khoja Jahan's feet and praised him for reviving Islam. The cries and wailing went beyond all limits. Khoja Jahan exhibited great kindness toward them and gifted them royal robes. Khoja Ṣiddiq had composed a *qaṣida* for the occasion, with praise for God and the Prophet, and mention of his Four Companions, and he took it out and presented it. When Khoja Jahan read it, he was delighted, and he kissed Khoja Ṣiddiq's brow and offered a benediction for him. Happily, this *qaṣida* will be included in this book, so that it survives for posterity:

The ocean of your qualities is without limit or measure,
In what is beyond there is nothing with such permanence as you.
Are you of space, or are you of time?
From ignorance, your pure essence is obscure to us.
Prophet of God, the universe was created for you,
O happy one! Proof of this is the verse IF NOT FOR YOU.[182]
When the Almighty reflected on your visage,
The verses of THE NIGHT and THE DAY[183] were revealed.
O THOU ENWRAPPED! [73:1] was a summons to your pure being,

And He also made you A MERCY UNTO THE WORLDS [21:107]
Tomorrow, /91a/ O interceder, when you sit on the throne of mediation,
Don't make a disgrace of this wayward servant.
Abu Bakr was the first to confirm the path of the faith,
And he alone was the Companion of the Cave during the exile.
Umar was one of a kind in the sphere of justice,
Without him Muḥammad's Holy Law would not have been divulged.
What need is there to describe this law, for there is the Lord of Two Lights (U̱sman),
A spring of humility and generosity, a mine of integrity and modesty.
How well His Grace Muḥammad spoke of the Lion King:
THERE IS NO MAN LIKE ALI, AND NO SWORD LIKE ZULFIQAR.
King Ḥasan drank poison and became a martyr,
The good-for-nothing Yazid was the cause of this martyrdom.
And King Ḥusayn became the martyr of Karbala,
How this family suffered among the schismatics!
But such pain would not have come to these two princes,
If the Lord did not thereby impart great insights.
One is that tomorrow he will intercede for the nations,
And one is that a martyr will achieve fame in this world.
He knows the unseen, AND GOD KNOWS BEST ITS LESSONS,
What would a deviant like me know of wisdom?
Without suffering and hardship there can be no happiness and joy,
The Creator made grief and pleasure as twins.
O Arshi! King and Emperor! Had you not been in pain,
Then the Islamic faith would not have come to fruition.
By your grace, hearts chilled with grief rejoiced again,
The flowers sprang up, as if spring had come in autumn.
Futuḥi! Stay vigilant, while giving thanks for your condition,
For a few days this friend and this land have been salve for your eyes.[184]

Khoja Jahan then addressed him. "My dear child, you're explaining the causes and lessons behind the poisoning of our great forefather Imam Ḥasan and the slaughter of Imam Ḥusayn on the field of Karbala. /91b/ But were you to see clearly the incidents and misfortunes about to befall you, I can't imagine what expressions you'd use to describe them. Who will interpret their meaning?" As he said this, tears welled up in his eyes like a cascade of pearls. Everyone present at the gathering fell silent, as if a voice from heaven sounded in their hearts crying out, THE COMMAND BELONGS TO GOD! After some time, Khoja Jahan delivered some comforting words to set them at ease, and to inspire them he recited a heartwarming verse from the divan of the insightful Amir Alisher, better known by his penname of Navaʾi.

Khoja Jahan organized festivities for the military officers who had come from Khotan and distributed favors and royal robes. A few days later, he put Khoja Shams al-Din in charge of the Khotanese army and gave them permission to leave. He appointed Umar Mirza his plenipotentiary vizier and accorded him high status, making him responsible for the entire province of Yarkand. He handled all of the kingdom's affairs by judging according to the shariʿa and providing justice to the common people. He offered thanks and praise to the court of the Lord and was always busy holding gatherings with the religious scholars and in worshipping God.

24. KHOJA YUSUF CALLS FOR SUPPORT

We return now to the moving story of Khoja Yusuf. When his distress regarding the immediate events involving his brother Khoja Jahan was relieved, he sent letters and envoys to the Kirghiz in the surrounds, encouraging them to support the army of Islam. /92a/ He sent Darvish Bakavul to Andijan with a letter containing the following message:

> Governors of Andijan province and leaders of the Kirghiz! Be it known that the cities of this land of Moghulistan submitted to the accursed and oppressive infidels for countless years, and the tyranny of these infidels toward the Muslims exceeded all bounds. Praise be to God, with divine support and assistance, and with His limitless grace on our side, we have made Islam triumphant. Turning against the infidels, we have struck a decisive blow. Should fortune favor us, our hope from the Lord Almighty is that we will launch a campaign against the infidel's own territory in

> Ili and take many years' worth of revenge for the Muslims. If you feel the same ardor, then lend your support to Islam.

He also wrote the following letter to Qubad Mirza, leader of the Qushchi tribe (*uruğ*) of Kirghiz, who on account of his extreme bravery was known as Bahadur Bi:[185]

> Qubad Mirza, your family have long been devotees and disciples of our forefathers. In particular, your father Ghalcha Bi served as commander in chief for that light of the assembly of guidance and shining star in the constellation of manliness, our great kinsman Khoja Ḥasan, and on several occasions he assailed these wretched infidels with the sword of holy war and annihilated them.[186] It is for holy war that brave men were fashioned. Should you concur, then venture forth with your tribe and obtain the honor of *ghazat* for this life and the next. Take your place among the ranks of the *ghazis* /92b/ in support of Islam. There is no limit to the merit that is accrued in holy war.

There was also a large group of disciples and followers of Khoja Ḥasan, the illustrious sayyid by Ali's line, who were led by Akhund Mulla Majid and Akhund Mulla Noruz.[187] He wrote a letter to them, to this effect:

> Companions of our eminent kinsman! For many years now you have been wandering in exile and banishment from door to door and town to town. You have been reduced to this situation because of the tyranny and injustice of the infidels. Praise be to God, we have struck these infidels a mighty blow and liberated this territory from submission to them. We have cleansed it of their evil presence, and with the sword of Islam in hand, we are now advancing against them. We are of one body and soul with your master and spiritual guide; there is no distance between us. We are drops from the same river, and crumbs from the same piece of bread. You must come and lend support to Islam and assume your rightful lands and status.

He sent Darvish Bakavul off on the road to Andijan with these letters in hand.

25. KHOJA YUSUF'S CONDITION DECLINES

Here it is appropriate to tell a story involving Khoja Yusuf's pious wife, who was known as Jamila Aghacha. She was particularly beautiful and eloquent, with hair like the hyacinth and an ambergris scent. She was tall with a slim waist, and had the eyes of a doe. If I were to do full justice to her description, /93a/ words would fail me. She was Khoja Yusuf's companion while he was in Ili, and on the final occasion when he came down from Ili, she escorted him as far as Aqsu. Khoja Yusuf then hurried on to Kashgar while she remained in Aqsu, and no opportunity arose for him to send a party out to retrieve her. The eternal skeptic Abd al-Wahhab took advantage of this and came after her. For several days, her house was besieged as they fended them off. Eventually, one evening the deputy governor and treasurer of Aqsu, a man named Mirza Qasim Beg, who was among the devotees of the holy family, got Her Ladyship safely away toward Kashgar by the Ush road.[188] God Almighty rendered the army of Abd al-Wahhab oblivious to this, and they arrived in Kashgar with much pomp and ceremony. The people of the city came out to meet them and brought them into the palace. Khoja Yusuf praised them for their bravery and daring, and to celebrate he held a party for several days and honored the visiting begs with gifts of kingly robes. Khoja Yusuf let the festivities drag on to an extent that Khoja Ṣiddiq has described in one of his five-line poems:

> Futuḥi, prepare the festivities! Come, fire-worshipper, /93b/ ready the wine!
> Don't put me to shame, whether my gaze is straight or cockeyed,
> Bring me the celestial goblet, be it night or day,
> Singer, strike up a tune, give us a melodious song,
> For every drop the pourer spills you'll get nine, for life's comfort has arrived.

Sometime after this, symptoms of swelling were noticed on Khoja Yusuf's body, which gave an indication that he was afflicted with dropsy. They immediately turned to treating it, and the doctors and physicians considered possible remedies. Yet, with his insight, Khoja Yusuf knew that his condition would not improve. He made almsgiving his priority, and inviting all the religious scholars, he gave them generous donations and requested a recitation of the Quran for the sake of the Prophet, the Khojagan, and His Noble Grace (*ḥażrat-i ʿālīshaʾn*).[189] After they had finished reciting, he asked the scholars for their attention, and in heartrending words he informed them that his life was coming to an end. The scholars all prayed and requested he be returned to health. To comfort him, they expounded verses from the Quran and the hadith, then retired in tears.

Each day the swelling in Khoja Yusuf's blessed body increased till it came close to his chest, and there was no sign of recovery. In his anxiety Khoja Yusuf said, "It would be better if I took myself to the grave of my forefathers. When the event occurs, it will be extremely difficult to move a body in this fierce summer heat." He instructed his retainers /94a/ to announce to the kingdom that they should assemble and hold a great feast, enough for the whole population to eat its fill.

They prepared a lavish feast with all sorts of gifts for the scholars and amirs, as well as for the common folk. When everyone had finished eating, Khoja Yusuf addressed the crowd: "O companions, today is the day for us to part and say our farewells. For years we have sat together in communion, and I have enjoyed the rights of eating and speaking with you. For a long time, I have heard your petitions and exercised authority over you. What I ask now is that if any of you have taken offense on my account, or been visited by any injustice, whether deliberate or otherwise, then in the name of God you forgive me and give me your approval. This is my allotted destiny. My heart has grown cold to the comforts and trivial desires of the mortal world and has set its sights on the next life. I must transport this body to our ancestral grave myself and resign myself to fate. Look upon my children as you do me. I consign them, and you, to God, the Prophet, and my forefathers for safekeeping. Goodbye, and farewell."

When he finished speaking, a cry arose from this crowd and filled the space from the palace pavilion to the emerald dome of the sky. Amid such a cacophony, no one was able to maintain their composure. After some time, everyone stood up and humbly entreated: "O king of the world! May the Lord grant health /94b/ to your blessed body! We are all your most humble servants. Your rights to us are more numerous than hairs on our body. It is we who should be requesting approval from you: your satisfaction with us is a bounty in both worlds!"

With much weeping, they dispersed to their homes, while Khoja Yusuf bade farewell to his kinsmen. He appointed Khoja Abdullah and Khoja Muʾmin as his deputies and assigned them to stay in Kashgar, while nominating his two sons Khoja Quṭb al-Din and Khoja Burhan al-Din (the one they called Erke Khoja) as his traveling companions. He determined which among his retinue would stay or go, readied provisions for his journey, and then decided to set out. The entire population of the country trailed behind him to send him off. He dismissed some of them at one location, some at the next. Then he kissed Khoja Abdullah and Khoja Muʾmin with tears in his eyes. "My treasured children," he said, "I entrust you to the care of God, the Prophet, and my forefathers. We have a reunion on Judgment Day to look forward to. What trials and tribulations await you! What hardships you're destined for, what grief and suffering you'll face! You remain here in the midst of murderous adversaries. Should you mourn for me, or at the calamities that will come to you? What kind of exile and destitution awaits you? Which bloodthirsty enemies will you fall captive to? /95a/ This is the start of your own mourning. You should weep for yourselves."

Sighs as my companion, tears for a friend, and heartbreak as my confidant,
O cheerful one, such is the way our parting must be.

This is but the start of love, don't mope and cry so much,
For this flood of dishonor will drown the whole world.[190]

On days of parting, O eyes, shed tears of blood,
Do you know from whom you are separating?[191]

With a final "Farewell, be safe in God's hands," Khoja Yusuf dismissed his children and set out for Yarkand by the Yopurgha road. It was the height of summer, and the heat gave an indication of the hardships of Hell—it was almost as fiery as the plain of Judgment Day. His illness was extremely critical, and his pulse was thinner than a thread. The physicians were anxious, and unable to move forward or go back, they stalled helplessly on the road.[192]

> It is difficult to reach the destination,
> For my eyes are blind, the night is dark, my horse is lame, and the road muddy.[193]

The next morning Khoja Yusuf called his assistants and asked them what the reason for the delay was, ordering them to get a move on. The doctors inspected his pulse, and there were small signs of improvement. They were surprised, but Khoja Yusuf said, "God Almighty has granted me this health. My hope is that instead of being left here in discomfort, I will undertake my final journey after pressing my face to the dust of my ancestors' graves, and with the honor of meeting my elder brother the king." With this, they continued on their way.

People hurried out from Yarkand /95b/ to welcome him, and eventually when he came close to the city, the princes too came out to meet him. They intended to carry Khoja Yusuf into the city on a palanquin, but he did not allow it. Dressed in royal regalia, with his belt tied tight, he rode into the city mounted on a swift steed. Everyone praised him for his courage and stamina.

Khoja Yusuf met Khoja Jahan in the yard of the palace, and they embraced with much weeping. Everyone else was kept out while he greeted his family and kin and reclined on the throne of honor in the great hall. Then the scholars and amirs and the rest of the population came in and recited the opening of the Quran in his honor. For most of the time he was there, Khoja Jahan sat by his bedside and tended to his illness. The princes also attended to him, as did the princesses. They had a sister whose name was Ulugh Azizim, who was especially beautiful and charming. She had qualities of Maryam and A'isha, and was a scholar and poet of great eloquence and intelligence. Her locks had yet to curl and had a musky camphor color. She was still chaste, no foreign dust had settled on her pure skirts, /96a/ no one had picked anything from her flower bed, and the crook of her curly locks had yet to trap any prey. Nonetheless she already had complete mastery of poetry, and oftentimes Khoja Ṣiddiq would study composition from her. Khoja Yusuf also had two daughters, the first of whom was the envy of the sun, and the second made the moon jealous. On account of one of them, the fairies would be so humiliated as to seek refuge on Mount Qaf, while the other put the houris of Paradise to shame. The name of the first was Zuhra Begim, while the second was Zubayda Begim, though they used to call Zuhra Begim "Sariq Babaqim," and Zubayda Begim "Qarghabash Khoja." Khoja Yusuf had betrothed Zubayda Begim to Khoja Jahan's young son Muḥammad Khoja, and six months after this, Muḥammad Khoja had gone off to Ili.

These two maidens were waiting on Ulugh Azizim, and the three saintly women were always present in attendance on Khoja Yusuf. His illness did not improve, and indeed his soul grew estranged from the mortal world, and day by day his desire for the next life increased. On some occasions, the spirits of the ancients would come and summon him and tell him that they were waiting for him. Previously, when he had been sick in Kashgar, he had conversed with the spirits in the same way. Sometimes of an evening, he would ride out with only a single companion and conduct gatherings with all these spirits in the field that stands before the shrine of Ḥasan Fażlullah Khoja /96b/ and listen to their advice before returning.[194]

In this illness too, the spirits were coming before him to say, "Son, we are all waiting in anticipation of your arrival, please come and join us soon. God Almighty has a number of designs in store that cannot come to pass while you are still alive, for your existence is hindering them. The time for those events is approaching fast, you must make your way hither. Please come and take up the position that has been designated for you." Because of these premonitions, Khoja Yusuf's gaze was always fixed on the next life and was cut off from the people of the world. He didn't grant an audience to anyone, and for the next three months his life went by in this fashion.

26. THE RISE OF AMURSANA AND RELEASE OF THE WHITE MOUNTAIN KHOJAS

Let us now continue the saga from the Ili region, where at that time an infidel by the name of Dabachi was *törä* of the Qalmaqs. His kingdom was in complete disarray, and because of this an infidel called Amursana, who also had a claim to the position of *törä*, withdrew his support and instead made a bid for the position himself. He escaped to the land of China, which is a bonfire of infidelity, with one spark from its flame of nonbelief enough to cause the ruin of the world. He met there with the Chinese emperor and complained about Dabachi. Requesting an army from him, he promised in return that he would deliver the poll tax and levies from the Ili region. The infidels of China had long been at odds with the Qalmaqs, and each had been plotting against the other, but until now an opportunity had not arisen /97a/ for either side to gain the upper hand.

In the end, the emperor of China smiled on Amursana and gave him an army. Amursana led this Chinese force out from China and headed swiftly toward Ili. Within Ili itself, word spread that Amursana was bringing a massive Chinese army, and at this news, Dabachi trembled in fear. Because his kingdom was so disunited, there was no strength left to draw up the ranks of the army and resist the invasion. He had no choice but to flee into exile, and set off with three hundred of his own well-armed retainers. Amursana arrived with the Chinese army and found the throne of Ili vacant, so he assumed authority and pacified the kingdom.[195]

The infidel Dabachi, meanwhile, couldn't decide the best direction to go in. Ultimately divine fate drew him to the city of Ush. He sent in a go-between to find out whether the people there would give them passage: if they would provide refuge, then they would enter the city; otherwise they would continue on their way. At that time, the governor of Ush was the treacherous Khojasi Beg. He realized this was an excellent opportunity, and he blandished the go-between and sent him back with positive assurances. Meanwhile, he armed and drilled the townsfolk to such an extent that each one would've been a match for a roaring lion or a seven-headed dragon, and hid them while he rode out to greet Dabachi with five hundred men. He dressed up his plot in such a way that the truth took on a false appearance. The simpleminded infidel failed to discern the trap, and he entered the city. When the infidels were entirely inside the city, they slammed the gates shut. Some of them they took captive in their quarters, and some in the streets. They tied them up /97b/ and quickly dispatched Dabachi and the rest of the prisoners to Ili as a gift to the officers and chiefs of Amursana's Chinese army. They were delighted and sent Dabachi onward to the Chinese emperor.[196]

Having settled affairs in Ili to some degree, they set about devising a plan to bring Yarkand and Kashgar to submission. Various suggestions were put forward. Some said they should mount a military campaign, but some felt it would be difficult: there was chaos among the Qalmaqs, and the Chinese army was worn out by its long march. It would be exhausting to get them there, they felt, and if somehow they did, Khoja Yusuf was a very wily man, and the Muslims were at full strength. It would be difficult to achieve victory, and in fact there was a distinct possibility of defeat. It would be better to leave that region alone, they said, while these parts came into the emperor's possession. Yet on the advice of Abd al-Wahhab, Khojasi and a few of his ilk put forward a different view. "Yes," they said, "to take an army there would be hard, but there is an easier solution which is the best of all. There are two khojas in Ili from among the khojas of Kashgar, who remind us all of our spiritual guide. The entire population was dedicated to their father and grandfather, the people of Kashgar most of all. What is required is for one officer from the Chinese force and one from the Qalmaqs to be appointed as envoys with a bodyguard, and for one of the khojas to accompany them. It should be proclaimed that the whole of Ili and the Qalmaq lands have submitted to the emperor of China, and that he has appointed these khojas as khojas of these cities. If this word gets around, then the White Turbans will become subjects of the emperor easily and without a fight. Once the kingdom has been pacified, then the emperor and *töräs* can decide whether these khojas should stay in place or not."

/98a/ This advice was to everyone's liking, and they acted on it. Khoja Aḥmad, who was among the sons of Khoja Yaḥya b. Khoja Afaq, had two sons who had been held captive at the hands of the infidels. From the day they were born until now, they had never been free from imprisonment.[197] Abd al-Wahhab and Khojasi were their devotees, and their purpose was to set them free. In liberating them, God Almighty ordained a number of designs that were dependent on their freedom, and without which the kingdom could never come to rest. Thus, by divine decree, the infidels assigned one envoy each from the Chinese and Qalmaqs to their majesties and sent them down from Ili with much pageantry. In the company of the envoys, they reached Aqsu, where the entire population gave them an ostentatious reception and pledged allegiance to them. Passing on from there, they arrived in the city of Ush, where the people treated them with the utmost respect and offered the same pledge. They halted there for a few days while they debated whether or not to go on. No one could confidently advise continuing to Kashgar, since God only knew whether they would be safe in that city with

Khoja Yusuf there. The people of Kashgar, Yarkand, and Khotan had by now regrouped, and the Kirghiz in the vicinity had apparently risen up and proclaimed Islam. They felt that it was simply impossible to go there with these infidel envoys and such a small and disorganized body of troops. "Should they somehow /98b/ decide to mobilize an army against us," they said, "they will pulverize these cities and turn them into SCATTERED DUST [25:23]."

27. THE DEATH OF KHOJA YUSUF

Let us leave them in this quandary while we listen to a moving story from Yarkand. Khoja Yusuf's illness was showing no signs of recovery. In fact, he was progressively declining. The flames of revolt were flaring up on all sides, and various disturbing rumors were circulating. Some said that the region of Ili had rebelled and an army had come from the emperor of China and installed Amursana on the throne; that they had transported Dabachi to the Chinese capital and a Chinese army was on its way via Aqsu to subdue Kashgar and Yarkand; that it had already conquered Ush and was coming to take these cities. Others said that the Qalmaqs had stabilized the situation, led an army via Aqsu and taken Ush, and now had their sights set on Kashgar and Yarkand. These kinds of demoralizing rumors spread widely.

Men of good counsel met to offer advice to Khoja Jahan: "Refuge of the world," they submitted, "all sorts of disturbing reports are spreading throughout the kingdom. We need to take this threat in hand before it eventuates. It won't be any use to regret things afterward. Khoja Yusuf's illness is severe. If the army sent by those people arrives here, they will throw us into disarray, and certain enemies and irreligious ones will start making noises. It won't do to exhibit weakness in governing the kingdom; /99a/ the custom is to show oneself confident before the enemy. The appropriate thing would be for the army to assemble and march on Aqsu and Ush. If those Muslims side with us and confront the infidels, and the army of Islam emerges victorious, well and good. We'll drive the infidels back as far as Ili. Otherwise, if the infidel army triumphs, then we'll withdraw. Should they pursue us here, then we'll resist them at close quarters to the extent we can."

Khoja Jahan remained silent as they outlined this advice and didn't give any obvious reply. Three days went by in this fashion. Certain farsighted men became agitated and kept trying to persuade him, and they also stirred up the young princes. At the end of three days, Khoja Jahan finally relented: "If the army is to go, let it go."

Yet when Khoja Yusuf heard about the campaign, he was firmly opposed to it and would not give his approval at all. "That infidel army wouldn't dare take a step in this direction of its own accord," he said, "but if our army is somehow defeated, then they will inevitably pursue it. It would be as if we had gone to invite them and led them here ourselves. Our army is combined with the Kirghiz, an unfaithful people who don't deserve our trust. Furthermore, my disease is serious, with no likelihood of recovery. Now is not the time for campaigning, while our allies are dispirited and our enemies are rejoicing. Now is the time for patience and forbearance."

He counseled delay, and Khoja Jahan was convinced, /99b/ but the people didn't permit Khoja Yusuf to make the decision. Khoja Jahan was obliged to call up the army, and simply didn't tell Khoja Yusuf.

An army of inestimable size was mobilized, and endless troops of Kirghiz also rallied. Khoja Yaḥya ended up in charge of the campaign.[198] Kissing him on the forehead, Khoja Jahan gave him leave to march out: "I entrust you to God and to our great forefather." Khoja Yaḥya readied the baggage train and set off for his destination.

At this time, Khoja Yusuf's condition became extremely dire. He summoned all his kinsmen to ask them for their approval and to deliver his last words: "I have consigned you all to God Almighty. If you wish to please me, serve my brother the king as much as you can, and make him satisfied." With this, he instructed those present to renew their faith, and some of them started reciting the Sura Ya Sin.[199] When they finished their profession of faith (*īmān u islām*), he bore witness, then gave up his soul to the Lord. Shouts and cries, and the sound of TRULY WE ARE GOD'S, AND UNTO HIM WE RETURN [2:156], rose to the heavens, and sighs and laments filled the city of Yarkand. The entire population of the city turned out to mourn him. The princes each with their retinue, and the courtiers, amirs, scholars, and various ranks of people expressed sorrow and pain, and as they cried and wept, these anguished lines by Mir Alisher were on everyone's lips:

> It is the day of parting, O eyes, shed tears of blood,
> Do you know who it is you are separating from?[200]

On the day of the Prophet's death, Her Holiness the Lady Faṭima Zahra embraced his blessed grave, wiped her eyes on his pure tombstone, and spoke a heart-wrenching poem. Khoja Jahan led all the princes and princesses in reciting it too:

> SUCH MISFORTUNES HAVE BESET ME, THAT IF THEY
> WERE TO AFFLICT THE DAYS, THEY WOULD TURN INTO NIGHTS.

That is to say, "I've been struck with such grief and mourning, that if such grief befell the daytime, it would be unable to endure it and would inevitably turn into dark night."

> Woe is me; such scars have burnt my heart!
> Amid a hundred tragedies, what pain I feel,
> Shall I express my anxiety for my soul, or my grief in this mourning?
> Has anyone else experienced the injustice done to me?

Crying the whole time, Khoja Jahan readied the body for burial. When they had finished with the full ritual washing, they placed his blessed body in the holy bier. Khoja Jahan himself served as imam and led the entire population of Yarkand in performing the funerary rites before the Golden Shrine. He then gave the scholars the opportunity to conduct the rest of the ceremony. On this occasion there was such an almsgiving in Yarkand—no one knows whether there had ever been the like of it in the age of the khans, or since then. All the men of learning became rich, and the poor and indigent received what they needed.

Khoja Jahan then addressed the crowd in his sweet voice: "My people, you should know that this grief and mourning are not for my kinsman Khoja Yusuf alone, but for myself, and for all my relatives and children. A time is coming when no one will be left to mourn for us, and those struck by grief will lack the strength to express it."

> Everyone should mourn for themselves, for the day will come,
> When those struck by grief won't have a chance to grieve.

Those who heard these dispiriting words were immediately moved to anguished wailing. A single affliction multiplied a thousandfold. Shedding tears the entire time, they concluded the burial ceremony, said benedictions and praise and recited the Quran, and then went home. A number of scholars from Kashgar, led by the estimable Akhund Mulla Maḥmud, had come to tend to Khoja Yusuf's illness. The day after they arrived, the nightingale of his pure spirit broke free from the body's cage and took flight from the highest heaven to the realm of the angels. On the third day of mourning, they received permission to depart for Kashgar. They, along with the servants who had accompanied them, went back with a bounty of newly acquired wealth.

28. KHOJA YAḤYA ADVANCES TOWARD THE ENEMY

Here I must tell a stirring story about Khoja Yaḥya, commander in chief of the army. On the day he led out the army of Yarkand and Khotan, along with the whole force of Kirghiz led by Umar Bi and Möngke Bi, they made good progress and alighted at the edge of Yangiḥiṣar.[201] At that time, the governor of Yangiḥiṣar was Tarkhan Niyaz, son of Jan Baqi Beg. Tarkhan Niyaz was extremely loyal and close to the infidels, such that when the infidel *medechi* came on his embassy, he had spent an evening conversing with him while he was on his way from Kashgar to Yarkand and had given his word to help the infidels. Conscious of this promise, he was on the lookout for an opportunity to make good on it. Although Tarkhan Niyaz was timid, his eyes and ears were constantly directed toward the Qalmaqs, and when he caught sight of this army, his sedition only increased. When Khoja Yaḥya saw the treacherous way he was carrying himself, he became suspicious. He immediately took him into custody and had him bound, but the Kirghiz were so aggressive that they killed him in the course of handling him. Chagrined by this, Khoja Yaḥya pacified the situation in Yangiḥiṣar to a certain extent, then took his army and continued toward Kashgar. He instructed the army not to make for the city but instead to go via Artush in the direction of Ush.

29. KHOJA ABDULLAH'S CORONATION IN KASHGAR

We return now to the story in Yarkand. After Khoja Yusuf crossed into the eternal realm, Khoja Jahan thought it unwise for this army to have set forth. Yet Ghazi and the rest of the amirs, as well as the Kirghiz and all the princes, wouldn't allow the army to turn back. In the circumstances, they felt it was better to press on. If they could engage the enemy before they found out about the prevailing confusion, then the enemy would be dispirited and their bravery and daring diminished.

A little help is enough for someone readying for a fight,
A bit of flotsam and jetsam can be a lifeline on the battlefield.

/100a/ Khoja Jahan didn't challenge the unanimous view of his advisers and so resigned himself to the situation. He immediately drew up official announcements on the mourning and the succession and gave these to one of the princes, his son-in-law Ṣufi Khoja. "Go to Kashgar," he instructed him, "and announce this decree and hold a mourning ceremony. Then, on the following day, summon the people of the kingdom, read this appointment decree, and confirm my son Khoja Abdullah on the throne." With these instructions, he gave him leave to go.

Khoja Naṣrullah took charge of equipping the mission, and the two men quickly made their way to Kashgar.[202] They entered the city in the company of Khoja Yaḥya and alighted in the palace. The whole of the kingdom's elite had come out to greet them. There were also scholars from Yarkand inside the city, who trailed along behind the princes as they entered the palace. These scholars recited the Quran and said prayers of blessing and praise. People intuited from these Quran readings that there was news of a death, and they suddenly burst into tears. The sound of wailing enveloped the plain of heaven, and the cries of woe filled the surrounds. After some time, they composed themselves, and the letter of mourning was presented to Khoja Abdullah. Khoja Abdullah gestured for the letter-reader to read it aloud. This is what it said:

> In accordance with the command that EVERY SOUL SHALL TASTE DEATH [21:35], there is no son of man, or indeed anything that lives, which will avoid the circle of death. Which of the prophets and saints, which of the wise men has ever evaded this trap and slipped the grasp of fate's hand? /100b/ Which ignorant and stubborn man has ever been singled out for special privilege? King and pauper, infidel and believer are alike in this,

no one is free from the condition of mortality. The revolving sphere will present its goblet to everyone in turn: should it offer it to someone today, then tomorrow it will be someone else's turn.

> Should someone have the longevity of Noah,
> One day he will depart, unfulfilled and with a million regrets.

Khoja Abdullah my son! All authority belongs to God, and it is obligatory to submit to one's fate. There is no alternative to patience and forbearance. How could a slave dare raise his voice in objection to his master's deeds? No amount of crying, rending your collar, or scratching your face and tearing yourself into pieces will be of any use. Indeed, that will simply be a sign that you have not resigned yourself to submission. Remember, my child, A HINT IS ENOUGH FOR SOMEONE INTELLIGENT. What you need to do is provide counsel and reassurance to your younger brother Khoja Muʾmin and your mother Bayan, and all of our retainers and dependents. The situation is extremely grave, and the well-being of those who remain is the highest priority. My hope from God Almighty is that as long as there is breath in my body, I will show no negligence in supporting you.

Listening to this encouraging letter, everyone was heartened. They stopped crying and wailing, and the large crowd dispersed. In the morning of the following day, a summons was issued to the whole population of the kingdom, and everyone in Kashgar, noble and common, /101a/ thronged around. From within the crowd, Ṣufi Khoja took out the decree and delivered it to Khoja Abdullah. Kissing the ground in humility, the letter-reader received it from Khoja Abdullah and read it out in a loud voice. It went as follows:

IN THE NAME OF GOD THE MOST MERCIFUL AND MOST KIND

I AM PLACING A VICEREGENT UPON THE EARTH [2:30]

A multitude of praise and acclaim is due to the Almighty and Most Merciful, who with the beneficence and justice of His wise sultan and virtuous amir has kept the common people at peace and at ease in this mortal world and shielded them from the injustice exerted by the powerful on the powerless. Countless thanks are due to that plenipotentiary emperor, who deemed that anyone who submits to the king of Islam in this visible realm will assemble beneath that king's flag and march into Paradise in the next life, and that whoever fails to submit to that king of Islam and thereby disgraces themselves in this world, will be liable to endless suffering on Judgment Day. It is as the hadith of the Prophet says: HE WHO DIES WITHOUT KNOWING THE IMAM OF HIS AGE DIES IN IGNORANCE, which is to say, "If someone dies without recognizing the king of Islam in their age, then without doubt they have died in a state of ignorance."

And may a hundred thousand blessings be upon that lord of creation and pinnacle of existence, His Holiness Muḥammad (MAY GOD PRAY FOR HIM AND GRANT HIM PEACE!), who guided the people of both worlds /101b/ by pointing out the Straight Path and, through the commands of the noble shariʿa, provided laws and precepts to the chiefs of the kingdom and the just amirs, thereby giving order to the affairs of state (MAY GOD PRAY FOR HIM, AND HIS FAMILY, AND ALL HIS COMPANIONS!).

People of Kashgar! For years we spent our lives in subservience to the infidels. Praise be to God, for some time now we have hoisted the banner of Islam above our heads and renewed the institutions of the faith and the nation. God Almighty has entrusted to us the throne of rulership in this kingdom. My kinsman Khoja Yusuf carried out dutiful service and has now given up the deposit of his life to its custodian. He has deemed his beloved son Khoja Abdullah fit for the throne and given him the title "Padishah Khoja." All those who display obedience to Padishah Khoja will be honored in this life and the next and find salvation. Anyone who refrains from doing so should know that in this life they risk having their property confiscated and their family imprisoned or killed, and in the next they will be put to shame before God, the Prophet, and my forefathers, and sentenced to damnation.

Khoja Abdullah, you must handle the people's affairs with justice and adhere to the noble shariʿa. We had previously announced that you should serve as commander in chief of the army, but now your brother Khoja Muʾmin should take the army of Kashgar and advance on the enemy with Khoja Yaḥya.

/102a/ Complying with the instructions of this decree, the large crowd that had gathered sat His Holiness Khoja Abdullah on a Carmanian rug (*zilča-i Kirmanī*). On one side was Khoja Yaḥya, while opposite him was Khoja Naṣrullah. All the amirs, led by governor Khosh Kifäk Beg, took hold of a third side, and on the last was the *aʿlam akhund* Mulla Maḥmud and the rest of the scholars. In unison they lifted him up and seated him on the throne of the sultanate, and then went out into the vestibule and celebrated by feasting the crowd on a huge dish of pilaf they had prepared.

Now ensconced on the sultanic throne, Khoja Abdullah issued a command that the amirs should equip an army from among their own following and set forth. The amirs readied their supplies for the journey and rode out. With his brother's permission, Khoja Muʾmin also prepared for the trip and rendezvoused with Khoja Yaḥya in the district of Beshkerem. As they inspected the army, they realized that the baggage train was too large—it was as if they were packing up an entire city and relocating it. Every time they decamped, they would be on the move from dawn to dusk. The princes surmised that at such a sluggish pace, they wouldn't get to their destination in time, and certainly wouldn't be in any state to confront the enemy. They therefore instructed everyone to lighten their load, but as much as the soldiers seemed to be less encumbered, in actual fact they were not.

Traversing the stages, they eventually approached Ush via the Aqsay road. Since obtaining his freedom from the hands of the infidels, Khoja Burhan al-Din b. Khoja Aḥmad /102b/ had been enjoying his leisure and was completely oblivious to what was going on. It didn't occur to him that troops might suddenly arrive from Kashgar and Yarkand. He was in this state of ignorance when the dust cloud of an enormous army came into view, and from within the dust several banners became visible, each of which indicated the presence of a thousand men.

The hearts of the rivals fell to pieces from fear,
As the dust clouds rose from the sultan's army.
Cowards fainted as their souls fled their bodies,
And they deviated from their religion and faith.

30. THE BATTLE OF USH

Let us leave Khoja Burhan al-Din to assemble his troops and keep watch, while we continue the story of Khoja Muʾmin and Khoja Yaḥya. They led their army close to the city of Ush, deployed the advance guard, and halted. Upon consultation, they decided first to send an envoy, so that the enemy could give their response. If they submitted, well and good, but otherwise they would prepare for battle. To this end, they appointed an embassy consisting of Muḥarram Beg, governor of Beshkerem in the Kashgar oasis, and Tokhta Beg from Yarkand (who subsequently became treasurer of Kashgar), and along with them one of Umar Mirza's Kirghiz chiefs and one Kirghiz chief from Möngke's clan, each with their own bodyguards.[203] They wrote the following letter:

> Khojasi Beg![204] Endless ages have passed in which we have been loyal and subservient to the wretched infidels and bloodthirsty tyrants and have complied with their decrees and commands. Now, with the grace and mercy of God Almighty, we have established Islam, /103a/ turned our backs on the infidel, and drawn our sword against them. Our hope is that the Lord will bestow triumph and victory on us as Muslims. Our friendly advice is that you too should turn against the infidels and support Islam. These cities are the infidel's gateway to the cities of Kashgar and Yarkand. If you and the people of Ush were to aid us and pledge allegiance to Islam, then we will advance from here to Abd al-Wahhab in Aqsu. Should he too pledge his allegiance to Islam, then we will unite and keep this gateway shut tight. We will then send someone to probe the state of the infidels. If chaos still reigns among them, then we should take advantage of the opportunity and wage war against them. Should victory fall to us, we will annihilate them and summon them to the faith. If they convert, so be it, but otherwise we will take some of them captive and kill the rest. We will also free the sayyids and princes whom the infidels have long kept prisoner and return them to these parts. We will install the khans on the sultanic throne, and in accordance with tradition and precedent, our community of khojas will take up residence at the shrines of our forefathers

and engage in worship. Every governor should carry out his duties in the Islamic fashion.

It had always been our intention to repent from the despicable acts that we performed while serving the infidels in these years, to make recompense throughout the rest of our lives, and redeem our disgraced name by carrying out holy war. Khojasi Beg, you should unite with us in this pious deed /103b/ and make a pledge of allegiance to Islam. Tomorrow, on the Day of Judgment in the presence of the Lord Almighty, before our illustrious ancestor Muḥammad, you won't want to be left standing with a black face among the infidels. There is a hadith, ONE DIES ACCORDING TO THE WAY ONE LIVES, AND ONE WILL BE RESURRECTED ACCORDING TO THE WAY ONE DIES. This means "Howsoever a man lives his life, that is the way in which he will die, and howsoever a man dies, that is the way in which he will rise again on Judgment Day." There is also the hadith, ONE WILL BE RESURRECTED ACCORDING TO WHOM ONE ASSOCIATES WITH, which means "With whomever you associate in this world, you will come back to life with them in the next." To succumb eternally to the pain of Judgment Day for the sake of a few days of worldly luxury is not the action of a wise man. A wise man should instead choose the fortune of both worlds, and this is the fortune of Islam, not the bounty of the infidels, for that is empty and meaningless and only leads to destruction. If you now side with Islam, submit wholeheartedly and come out to welcome us, then we swear by the Lord that you will not be interfered with in any way. We will confirm you as governor of your region, appoint you commander in chief of the army in the Islamic style, and provide you with standard, drum, and horn. We will make you vizier of the entire kingdom and administer it on the basis of your advice and counsel. Our promise to your brother Abd al-Wahhab is the same. Otherwise, should you not side with Islam, then we have come against you with an innumerable army, made up of various divisions from Kashgar, Yarkand, Khotan, and Yangiḥiṣar, and several tribes of Kirghiz, including the Qipchaq, Toqquz Qipchaq, Sariq Qalpaq, Nayman, Chongbaghish, and Ottuz Oghul. Apart from this, Qubad Mirza, /104a/ better known as Bahadur Bi, is advancing behind us with thousands of men. With this inestimable force, we will reduce these cities to dust and imprison their inhabitants, for if despite their Islamic faith they oppose the Muslims and support the infidels, then according to the shariʿa it is permissible to attack them and either capture or kill them. Now is the time to ready the implements of war. We shall see whether the cupbearer of heaven hands the goblet of success to us, or to you.

O hard-hearted rival, ready the tools of battle,
You don't believe me; a hundred thousand warnings have no effect on you.
How long will it take for words to soften stony hearts?
Either divine fate will bring us triumph, or doom.

The appointed emissaries took this letter and set off, and delivered it immediately upon meeting Khojasi. Khojasi then led them to his own khoja, and they saw just what a palace of vice had been erected. Their army was intermingled with Qalmaqs and Chinese. Some of them had a Muslim appearance but an infidel manner, and their speech was completely infidelese. It was a strange gathering, without the slightest whiff of Islamic piety about it. They entered the court and observed that in the center, Khoja Burhan al-Din b. Khoja Aḥmad was sitting on the rug of honor. To his left and right were seated various tyrannical amirs, corrupt officers, and parties of merciless and vengeful killers, all ill-starred and wretched, without a trace of faith. /104b/ Treachery and enmity was obviously welling up from within them, and on their evil brows, storms of malice and envy were as visible as the sun.

From Kashgar this assembly included Shara Muḥammad Emin Beg,[205] his son Abd al-Raḥman Beg, Yusuf Beg, his brother Abd al-Sattar Beg, Musa Beg, and Khudayar Beg's son Muḥammad Emin Beg. From Yarkand there were the Qarghaliq governor Mirza Niyaz Beg, his son Mir Ivaż Beg, and Daulat Khoja. There were also the Aqsu governor Abd al-Wahhab Beg, his younger brother Umar Beg, and his sons Abd al-Sattar Beg and Abd al-Khaliq Beg, along with the begs of Aqsu, the governor of Ush Khojasi Beg, his son Muẓaffar Beg,[206] deputy governor Sart Beg, the governor of Kucha Allah Quli Beg, the governor of Sayram Muḥammad Yar Beg, and the Dolan governor Saʿadat Beg. From the begs of Ili there were Raḥman Quli Beg, Farman Quli Beg, Abd al-Raḥim Beg, Abdullah Beg the Kirghiz, and many other amirs.

From among the fanatical Sufis there were Mundi Ṣufi, Raḥmati Ṣufi,[207] Azhdar Niyaz Ṣufi, Nishtar Niyaz Ṣufi, and ignorant akhunds including Mulla Ivaż Akhund, Mulla Niyaz Akhund, Mulla Qutlugh Akhund, Saqal Akhund, Mulla Barat Akhund, Mir Noruz Khazinachi, Sariq Beg Yasavul, and Ilyas Mir Akhur. Besides these there was a large crowd of insignificant Sufis.[208]

Also present in that gathering was a man from the Qalmaqs by the name of Danjin Jaisang, who had previously served in Yarkand as *qarakhan*, and whom Khoja Jahan had expelled along with the emissary *medechi.* /105a/ That infidel had come bringing a thousand Qalmaq troops and a decree from Amursana. Finally, there was a Chinese man from the army of the emperor of China called Turumtai Hiya, who had come as ambassador with a party of subordinates.

The envoys entered this assembly, humbly kissed the ground, and presented the letter. It was received and read out, and when they were apprised of its message, they all resorted to mockery. "These Isḥaqiyya khojas of Yarkand have come here in vain," Khoja Burhan al-Din said. "They have no notion of their own capacities."

Don't step beyond your limit, this degree of perfection is enough,
For a wise man this is already a fortune without end.[209]

"Surely they can't be unaware that Amursana went to see the emperor of China and has brought back a Chinese army and assumed the throne as *törä* in Ili? And that Dabachi fled and came to Ush, but that they laid a trap for him and delivered him to the imperial army, who bound him in chains and transported him to the Chinese capital? Affairs in Ili have now stabilized. Across the six-month span of the Qalmaq territory, everything has been set straight. What's more, there are now several thousand Chinese troops in Ili, fully equipped and at the ready. Acting at the behest of the Chinese emperor, Amursana has given us the position of sultan and khoja in these cities, and he intends to expel the Isḥaqiyya khojas from their domain and remove them to Ili. The message to these khojas from the emperor of China and Amursana is that they must abandon Islamic rule, give up the sultanate of these cities, and come to Ili and beg forgiveness for their grievous sins from the *törä*, the amban, and the *jaisangs*. Should they fail to do so, we have with us Danjin Jaisang /105b/ with a thousand Qalmaq troops, and Turumtai Hiya with some Chinese. A force of ten thousand Qalmaqs is standing by at Aqsu.

With these men, we will go and deliver the emperor and Amursana's decrees, recruit more soldiers, and massacre the khojas down to the child in the mother's womb. Should I deviate in any way from these words, then I deserve the emperor's wrath." On this he swore an oath.

Listening to this threatening speech, the begs and Kirghiz who had come as envoys were at a loss. In essence, most of these envoys weren't particularly loyal, and there had in fact already been indications of their duplicity. They therefore declared their submission, transmitted the glad tidings of Khoja Yusuf's death, and pledged allegiance to Khoja Burhan al-Din. A few of them, including Muḥarram Beg, joined themselves to the Qalmaqs and didn't come back at all. Tokhta the Treasurer and some of the Kirghiz meanwhile rejoined Khoja Yaḥya and Khoja Muʾmin's army, each having promised to instigate a mutiny in their tribe and switch sides. The princes asked them what had transpired, and these charlatans greatly exaggerated the predicament they were in.

The princes plucked up their courage and spoke. "O people! In God's name we have proclaimed Islam, rebelled against the infidels, and struck them a blow. Should they rend us into a hundred pieces, we will never flinch from this vow /106a/ and will never give up. We have but one soul, but even if we had a hundred, we would sacrifice them before God and the Prophet for the sake of Islam. If our martyrdom is decreed to be at the hands of these men, we welcome it, for this is the tradition handed down to us by our illustrious forefather, His Holiness Imam Ḥusayn (MAY GOD BE PLEASED WITH HIM!). We will not tarnish the honor of the sayyid lineage. We will present ourselves on Judgment Day with our bloodied bodies in the ranks of the Karbala martyrs and request vengeance and restitution for our martyrdom from God and the Prophet. For a while, we have held the cup of pleasure and lived a life of leisure. If in riding the steed of fortune, we were ever negligent toward affairs of state, or if by giving free rein to wanton desire, our bodies became soiled by rebellion and sin, then we shall purify ourselves with cleansing martyrdom."

My soul is an offering, may God make martyrdom my lot,
It is a tradition I inherit from Ḥusayn of Karbala.
It will cleanse me of the dust of rebellion, why should I grieve?
Eventually one day death will ravage both body and soul.

"One shouldn't take any notice of threats such as these. To the contrary, wise men shouldn't even consider such nonsense intelligible speech. Khoja Burhan al-Din's words are entirely meaningless. It would've been much better if he had come to these parts of his own accord, without collaborating with the infidels. He is our kinsman, and we would've smiled on him and welcomed him with open arms. Whichever city's throne he chose, we would've confirmed him on it. We would've seen to his well-being and striven to deter his enemies as much as we could. /106b/ But instead he is coming to the land of Islam leading an army of infidels and threatening us with their decree. I've had enough of such relatives. We intend to abide by the command of the noble shariʿa, and won't allow ourselves to do anything that is impermissible and incorrect according to it. Let the revolving sphere of heaven hand the reins of desire either to them or to us. We had no prior knowledge that Khoja Burhan al-Din was coming this way. Indeed, our intention was that if everything went according to plan, we would liberate him from the infidels. We hadn't considered the possibility that he might show us such faithlessness. Nevertheless, one must submit to one's fate. Whatever is to become of us, it is destiny, and we will confront it squarely." With this, he bound the blade of enmity tight around his waist and strode out to face the enemy.

> I am resigned to fate, whatever it brings is my destiny,
> How much more must I endure at the hands of my callous beloved?
> I once hoped for fidelity from him, and more,
> But pain and hurt loom before me, and I give up.

The princes had a well-equipped army, with supplies and provisions for the battle and healthy mounts. They lacked for nothing. But their morale was flagging at the knowledge that Khoja Yusuf had died, that the Qalmaqs had reorganized themselves and dispatched an army, and also that the Chinese were assisting them by sending Burhan al-Din at the head of an invasion force. Thinking back to the earlier dominance of the Qalmaqs, which these cities had been unable to withstand, and the fact that a Chinese army that the Qalmaqs themselves could not resist /107a/ was now supporting them, they became uneasy. What could the outcome possibly be, they wondered, if they were bold enough to confront them? The men had had particular experience of the raids of the Kirghiz and Qalmaqs, and were completely enervated at the thought. Although they were eager for the spoils of war, they gave up any notion of taking booty from the Qalmaq army.

Khoja Burhan al-Din had given various promises to the men who had gone back and forth as envoys. "If at your instigation the troops from the opposing side, be they Kirghiz or others, join us and become our allies, we will write letters to the emperor and the *törä* and entrust the kingdom to them. From generation to generation, we will make them rich with recompense from the emperor and the *törä*. No one will have the slightest objection if they take as much as a horse's head of gold as booty. To any of the Kashgaris and Yarkandis who recognize us, along with the emperor and the *törä*, we will give a high official position with full honors and issue a diploma of *tarkhan* status with a red seal valid for seventy generations."[210] With commitments like these, he had sweet-talked the envoys and sent them off to the Kirghiz. When these corrupt envoys outlined these promises to the soldiers, some of those with weak faith were persuaded. In particular, the good-for-nothing Kirghiz switched sides with great enthusiasm.

Yet before these grim tidings had circulated throughout the army and the rot had set in, /107b/ they struck at the army of Burhan al-Din, and the casualties piled up. Several times they drove them against the gate of Ush. By that time, twenty-one Qalmaqs and locals had descended to Hell, never to be resurrected. More than this were wounded, as most of their horses were lame and their weapons of poor quality. They were on the verge of being routed, while only one man from the army of Islam had been martyred. Yet in this situation the Kirghiz tricksters advised the princes to retreat a little so that the Ush troops might advance: they would then surround the enemy and kill them to a man. It was so decided, and the army of Islam withdrew a distance. The Kirghiz took their chance, and in a feigned attack Möngke's tribe set out toward the Ush troops. They broke ranks and split off from all sides, joining up with the army of Ush. Khoja Yaḥya and Khoja Muʾmin saw that the army was ruined and that the opposing force was growing in strength and now moving to the offensive. The princes had no strength left to make a stand. With the enemy now outnumbering them, they took the necessary precautions. Acting according to the hadith, FLIGHT FROM THAT WHICH CANNOT BE OVERCOME IS AMONG THE CUSTOMS OF THE APOSTLES, they chose the path of flight and retreated.[211]

At this point, the zeal of the Ush soldiers multiplied a hundredfold, and they joined with the Kirghiz to give pursuit. They attacked so fiercely /108a/ that only a few people got away. Some had head wounds and others broken limbs; some were on lame mounts, while others were limping themselves; some were barefoot, and others were naked. Discarding their arms and provisions, they returned to Kashgar in a terrible state. Among the various tribes of Kirghiz that had been part of their army, some joined the Ush troops and came raiding from behind, while others accompanied the army in its flight, pillaging their way back to Kashgar.

May a million stones fall upon the Kirghiz,
Their lineage run dry and their homes burn down,
Don't make their acquaintance for they know no friendship,
Nor is there any faith in their compact.
They have no shame before God, nor before humanity,
Do not credit their faith in Islam,
Their act of submission is robbery, and banditry their skill,
Ingratitude is a virtue for their bankrupt sultan.
Their hospitality is an enemy; their kindness a killer,
Plundering one and striking at their guest,
O Ṣadiq, could people really behave like this?
Satan and the devils would be put to shame by these deeds.

Khoja Muʾmin and Khoja Yaḥya were mortified at the fact they had taken such a large army and been defeated by one so small, and had to abandon their weapons and baggage train during the retreat. Khoja Yaḥya took the soldiers of Kalta Yaylaq, Fayżabad, and Yarkand and made for Yarkand, while Khoja Muʾmin took the Kashgar troops /108b/ back to Kashgar. He sent someone in advance as a messenger, who arrived and explained the course of events to Khoja Abdullah, the one known as Khoja Padishah. He struck his knees in rage and beat out the *shadiyana* in shame. From the rhythm of the kettle drum, everyone in the kingdom deduced at once that the army had been defeated, because they had expected them to be gone for eighteen days, and this event was announced on the thirteenth.

That evening, Khoja Muʾmin entered by the side gate and met with Khoja Abdullah to explain the affair. Khoja Abdullah was greatly perturbed, but he tried to comfort Khoja Muʾmin. "For some time now, the star of good fortune has been favoring us," he said. "Now it seems that bad luck has replaced it. What can we do? Whatever fate brings us from above, we must prepare for it. Tricks will be of no use."

> Will divine fate be made any different by human intervention?
> Will a carving on stone be worn away by the rain?

Meanwhile, Khoja Yaḥya was making his way to Yarkand with the Yarkandi army. He likewise sent someone out in advance, who arrived and gave his report. "Such is our destiny, we are obliged to accept it," Khoja Jahan said, without evincing too much distress. "Whatever comes from God, there is no use trying to avoid it. We are his servants, and we will acquiesce to divine fate. There's no point remonstrating with it."

/109a/ These words put people's minds at ease, and certain men of initiative offered their advice. "Let's invite anyone who is left among the warriors of Möngke's tribe of Kirghiz, without telling them what has transpired. Let's say instead that those who went to Ush have done us a service, so we would like to entertain their family and friends as our guests and present them with robes of honor. When they come, we can seize them, and then send a raiding party out to their encampment and take everyone else prisoner."

Khoja Jahan consented to this, and they sent a messenger to the Kirghiz with this invitation. They succeeded in detaining four hundred cavalrymen inside the palace, and then sent troops to raid their camp. Some were captured, while others escaped. Most of these Kirghiz tribes withdrew to the mountains and started raiding the countryside around Yarkand, although Umar's people escaped in fright and did not join in the raiding.

In a state of embarrassment, Khoja Yaḥya came and met with Khoja Jahan. Khoja Jahan assuaged his feelings of guilt and gifted him a royal robe. Everyone was cursing the actions of the Kirghiz, but these ill-born Kirghiz were devious. By way of a ruse, they too wept and said, /109b/ "O king and refuge of the world! What a disgrace it is for men to shun the service of the Prophet's descendants and turn their face from Islam. They'll be repudiated in this life and the next, and a curse will be upon them for seventy generations. There were a few scoundrels among us who were orchestrating all this. We're disgusted with them, God is too, so let's give them their just deserts. We'll send someone in secret. If he's able to punish them for the sins for they have committed and strike a blow at them, well and good. Otherwise, we'll take their families captive and seize their property. In the end, they'll fall into our hands and we'll execute them. Then we'll go and get the people who escaped to the Yarkand mountains and have been raiding. We'll stand against the enemy and sacrifice ourselves for Islam." They made a hundred thousand promises and compacts and swore oaths on the Quran.

O lord is there any community,
As untrustworthy as these?
Though their eyes be full of tears and their tongue soft,
Their breast is stone and their heart is hard.

Khoja Jahan was a kindhearted and merciful man, and he was taken in by the words of these wretched men. Some tried to dissuade him, but the khoja could not imagine that Muslims would go back on their word, especially since they had taken an oath on the Quran. "Even if there are doubts about their Islam," he said, "there are no doubts as to mine. If they won't keep an oath sworn on the Quran, I certainly will." So saying, he gave back to these Kirghiz all their belongings and /110a/ mounts that the people of Yarkand had seized, and trusting in their loyalty, he sent them on their way. But just as soon as these deceptive infidels had left the city gate, they set about plundering and brigandage. They went off and joined the people in the mountains and came raiding the fields around Yarkand and taking prisoners. There was no way that the Muslims could stick their necks out in safety.

Khoja Jahan was deeply disturbed, and he cried out to the heavens. "O treasonous celestial sphere, what betrayal is this? How much more cruelty can I endure? How many more arrows of grief will you aim at me? Shall I tell you how I pine for my kinsman, whose forty-day mourning period is yet to pass? Or shall I tell you of the oppression of these evil Kirghiz?"

Heaven has inflicted injustice on this poor and hapless soul,
I have no strength to endure the calamities it has brought down.
Would that it had only caused grief for my single head,
But it has brought me enough pain for more than a hundred heads.

Mourning to this side, anxiety for my soul to that,
Heaven has rained down on me arrows of anguish.
All manner of misfortune has struck me alone.
O Ṣadiq, there was no limit to the trials that befell the king Arshi,
Heaven exceeded the injustice shown toward the Karbala martyr.

"If only in this hour of grief my kinsman Khoja Yusuf could be here," he continued. "He would find some solution to relieve my burden. /110b/ But it is clear now that our time has passed, and misfortune looms before us. Everything we intend to do produces the opposite result. Now the only option is trust in God. We are obliged to accept our fate." So saying, he put his faith in God.

When tyranny and injustice descend on me from heaven,
What can I do? There is no turning back now.
Now is not the time for action, the remedy is trust in God,
I won't tarry for a minute in this strife-ridden world.

31. KHOJA BURHAN AL-DIN ADVANCES ON KASHGAR

Let us now turn to a tale of woe from the city of Ush. On the day that Khoja Burhan al-Din defeated the army of Khoja Yaḥya and Khoja Mu'min at Ush, he was greatly enriched by booty and captives. He confiscated their weaponry, tents, camel trains, and provisions, and then reclined on the throne of honor. Witnessing this, his retinue and following ascribed it to a miracle, and their faith in him multiplied a hundredfold. Their greed was aroused, and they became drunk with desire for worldly possessions.

If fortune lends a hand, it can turn a dervish into a sultan,
Increasing his honor day by day.
If a lucky star shines on someone,
Though he be weak as an ant, it can make him Sulayman.
It can make him emperor, and fill his body with soul,
More than that: it can give his soul its beloved.

But should fortune frown on someone,
Though he be king of the world, it will bring him low.
Ṣadiq, shed your illusions in this throne of worldly fortune,
In an instant it will make a king a pauper, and a pauper a king.

A group of deviants led by Abd al-Wahhab Beg offered the following advice to Khoja Burhan al-Din: /111a/ "Now that we've defeated the army of Kashgar and Yarkand and achieved victory, the best thing to do would be to harass them from behind. If we can get those who switched sides and those still on the road to join us and advance on Kashgar, the Kirghiz will unite with us, and since most of the people of Kashgar are your disciples, they will also assist us. Kashgar will be ours without a fight. If we hold back at a time like this, they will overcome their confusion, regain composure, and mobilize against us. If we wait until then to act, they will show us no mercy and defeat us. The best option is for us to advance quickly. Should Kashgar fall, Yarkand will be easy."

Khoja Burhan al-Din and everyone else found this advice persuasive, and right away he issued a decree to load up the provisions and tents that had been captured from the Yarkand army and advance on Kashgar.

32. REINFORCEMENTS ARRIVE FROM ANDIJAN

Now for a story of strife from Kashgar. With their military defeat, Khoja Abdullah and Khoja Muʾmin were downcast spiritually too, and within the kingdom plots and conspiracies began to manifest themselves. At the rumor that Khoja Burhan al-Din was on his way, people from all directions went out to greet him. It was impossible to prevent them: for each one you might stop, ten more would get through. If you tried to prevent them from going discretely, they would simply leave publicly. It you openly prohibited them from going, then they would go in secret. There was simply no way to stop them.

Earlier, Khoja Yusuf had entrusted Darvish Bakavul with letters and sent him to Andijan to the companions of the Lord of the Felicitous Conjunction, Khoja Ḥasan, /111b/ who were led by Akhund Mulla Majid and Akhund Mulla Noruz, and also to Qubad Mirza. These men had accepted the invitation and come to Kashgar. When the akhunds entered the city and met with Khoja Abdullah, they expressed their condolences with a recitation of the Quran, and everyone wept. The mourning reached such a degree it was as if Judgment Day were dawning. After some time, Khoja Abdullah invited the akhunds to summon their own devotees and disciples and instructed them to keep watch on the city walls and in the streets. He sent some of his attendants off with gifts to welcome Qubad Mirza and assigned the rest of them to guard the fortifications and thoroughfares.

33. KASHGAR FALLS TO THE INVADERS

It is time to heed a story of the treacherous Abd al-Majid. Khoja Yusuf had patronized this man and treated him more intimately than his own son, such that all the palace servants were jealous of him. The *aʿlam akhund* Mulla Maḥmud had even told Khoja Yusuf in private, "My king, admitting Abd al-Majid to the palace and sponsoring him is akin to Ali patronizing Abd al-Raḥman b. Muljam in his own house, only to be betrayed by him.[212] There is not a whisper of fidelity in his essence. There is no way that he will not eventually commit some treachery, either toward you or toward the princes."

To this complaint /112a/ Khoja Yusuf replied, "I'm aware of this myself; the enemy is indeed crafty. But when his intention becomes known, we'll be able to repel any move."

Khoja Yusuf waited, therefore, and sure enough, in the hour of crisis Abd al-Majid exhibited his disloyalty. He advised all the amirs to rebel, and turned his back on the princes before anyone else did. He went out to greet Qubad Mirza but didn't allow any of the servants that Khoja Abdullah had sent to approach him. Qubad had come with the honorable intention to commit himself to service, but was led astray by Abd al-Majid's devilish whisperings.

> A devilish man is a hundred times worse than the devil himself,
> God called Satan "the furtive one" (*khannās*) because of his corruption.
> Everyone is wary of the devil's evil whisperings,
> But Satan worries about the whispers of a devilish man.

Abd al-Majid made all sorts of proposals to Qubad Mirza, and gradually wore down his resistance and deprived him of all initiative. Among the things he said was this: "O Mirza, *Become a friend to the conqueror, that thou mayst conquer: beware, do not become a friend to the vanquished, O misguided man!*[213] Khoja Yusuf has died, and his family and retinue have lost their leader. What's more, they took all of their weapons on a campaign against Ush, but were defeated and threw them away. The Kirghiz have all gone out to welcome Khoja Burhan al-Din.[214] You may have allied with these people, but they cannot rule the country. Instead of joining with them and becoming governor of Kashgar, it would be much better for you to reach an accommodation with Khoja Burhan al-Din. /112b/ When these princes abandon the city and leave, you can take the governorship without a struggle and confiscate the huge wealth that has long been accumulating at the palace and in the hands of Khosh Kifäk Beg and his associates. The booty will be all yours." Abd al-Majid outlined these various schemes, and as soon as he mentioned the word "booty," it was as if these low-minded Kirghiz simply melted. They discarded all their ambition and noble intentions and completely lost their free will.

Have there ever been any as ignoble as the Kirghiz down the ages?
Among the unfaithful, the wicked, the unreliable, and the treacherous?
Stingy and malicious, greedy and corrupt,
Among those without ardor, generosity, or modesty?
They're bloodthirsty tyrants, and for the sake of a dirham of booty,
They won't blink at murdering a hundred on the battlefield.

Abd al-Majid instructed these Kirghiz to give this account of themselves: "We are enemies to neither of these two khojas. Both of them are descendants of the Prophet and belong to the lineage of Makhdum-i Aʿẓam. We won't fire our arrows at either side, but will remain neutral." They gave this reply to Khoja Abdullah's servants and carried themselves like outsiders.

When Khoja Abdullah heard Qubad's disingenuous response, he was distraught, and he took counsel on the situation with his brothers. "O kinsmen," he said. "What are these troubles that are afflicting us? What misfortune has taken hold of us? We're not yet through the forty days of mourning for our father, and now these calamities occur. /113a/ Should I complain of my grief at losing him, or tell you my anxieties about our own destruction? My entire strength rested on this wretched Kirghiz Qubad, and he too has turned out to be worthless. If we're not going to confront these newcomers face to face, then I suppose we'll have to give up the city and leave. Should we decide to fight, we don't have the troops or morale to do so. The Kirghiz are entirely committed to their side, and many of the Kashgaris are their dedicated disciples too. There's a good chance that they'll come for us and deliver us up to them. Of course, if we flee without offering any resistance, we'll earn a bad reputation for ourselves and can expect to be criticized."

While they were contemplating their predicament, Khoja Burhan al-Din was making haste from Ush. He had come as far as the vicinity of Artush on the outskirts of Kashgar, where people came out to greet him. Khoja Abdullah hesitated whether to hold onto the throne, but felt he had to put up some show of bravery. Abd al-Majid sent a member of the palace staff in to him with this blunt message: "Khoja Abdullah should vacate the throne; its rightful occupant has arrived. It would be better he realize this for himself and give up. This is what the people of Kashgar want. Otherwise, things could get dangerous for him. For a wise man, a hint should be enough."

Khoja Abdullah was distressed at this impudence. Not long after that, Abd al-Majid himself went out to the field on the banks of the Tuman River and shouted at the portico of the palace at the top of his voice: /113b/ "Princes, what is the point of delaying?"

Khoja Abdullah was on the portico, and as soon as heard this, he picked up a bow and arrow and drew it a few times, before those who were present intervened to stop him. Abd al-Majid didn't calm down and kept charging around aggressively. Finding his composure, Khoja Abdullah yelled out: "O faithless, treacherous man. This treason that you commit toward us, you actually do to yourself. Remember: *wherever you eat the salt, don't break the salt jar*! We gave you salt, treated you well, and recommended you to our forefathers. Now for your own interests you claim that you'll dutifully serve those who are on their way. God willing, you'll come to a bad end, disgraced by the ingratitude you've shown us. You might regret it then, but it won't be any use. This ruination you're bringing down on us will be visited on you a hundredfold." And indeed, it came to pass that Abd al-Majid's property was confiscated, with some of his family and following taken captive and some executed.[215]

Khoja Abdullah thought to himself that there seemed no way either to hold his ground or to go out and stage a confrontation. In this helpless state, he consulted his mother and brothers, and they decided to evacuate. He also asked governor Khosh Kifäk /114a/ Beg for his opinion. "The truth is that there is no way to hold on here," he said. "It is time to go into exile. Don't imagine that there is any comfort and ease awaiting you, or that you will continue to rule as before. It is time to bid farewell and leave. And should you decide to leave, don't go to Yarkand, you won't survive there. Yarkand is itself in turmoil, and you won't be able to avoid it. If you were to fall into the hands of this group, they wouldn't hesitate to martyr you and bring your line to an end. The best thing would be to make for Andijan; we'll accompany you on the way. In that situation, the other side might feel more cautious and refrain from attacking Yarkand. There may yet be hope that in a while, by some means or other, we'll be able to retake these cities, or at least stave off the execution of those on our side who fall into their hands."

O king, now is the time of exile, of grief and separation,
Abandon your city and palace and set out for Syria and Iraq.
It is time to leave behind this unfaithful mundane world,
And give up this struggle of the celestial spheres.
How many luckless kings have occupied this sultanic throne?
Let it pass from you, let it come to someone else who desires it.
How long you have drunk the sweet wine of pleasure?
Now sip the poison of grief, don't put on airs!
With such an array of calamities and all sorts of incidents,
Wash your hands of your soul, it's time for goodbyes and farewells,
/114b/ Say, Ṣadiq, is there any hope of salvation at a time like this?
Facing the onslaught of the Chinese, Qalmaq, Kirghiz, and Kazakh.

Khoja Abdullah listened to Khosh Kifäk Beg's encouragement that he go to Andijan, then replied, "Governor, your advice is sound and reasonable, but it is not fitting to abandon my honorable uncle. If we leave in this way, he'll be unhappy with us. Winning the kingship of the entire world by displeasing him is impermissible for us, but dying with his approval will be an honor in both worlds."

> Hunting success, I chase the shadow of the bird of fortune,
> I thought it fell on my lane one day, but it was the shade of a wall.
> I seek carnal and spiritual desire from a mole on the lip,
> Deprived of that, my soul has only scars and tears of blood.

Delivering this reply, he bade farewell to Khosh Kifäk Beg. That night Khoja Abdullah assembled his own retainers and prepared his baggage train, then said goodbye to his confidants and initiates and left with his retinue by the side gate for Yarkand.

Since the death of Khoja Yusuf, forty people had been assigned to recite the Quran. Every night, ten of these forty would stay up all night reciting in a private room along a corridor in the Golden Palace. It was two days short of the forty when Khoja Abdullah chained the doors and left. Those reciting sat there unawares until dawn the following day, when they found the door shut tight. Bandits came /115a/ and prized the door open and entered. At the sight of this group of bloodthirsty cannibals wielding huge clubs, the akhunds were terrified. These men immediately entered and stole the rugs, Qurans, and bookstands, and the bewildered akhunds fled. They could see that the palace had been ransacked: the door to one room was broken down, another's was in splinters—it resembled an abandoned mosque in the desert. They got themselves out of there with great difficulty. Some of those akhunds are still alive, and to this day they say that they're yet to recover from the shock.

Meanwhile, those who were conscious of what was going on were helping themselves to people's property. For his part, Khosh Kifäk had decided to leave with his household and retinue and had exited the River Gate and gone to his courtyard on the banks of the Tuman River. Abd al-Majid informed the Kirghiz about this, who immediately cut them off and started attacking. They captured them with all their goods and belongings and imprisoned the unfortunate souls in a deep pit. Khosh Kifäk Beg, with his wife and some ten others, had been in the advance party and made it to safety. One of his sons, Aẓim Shah by name, hid in the depths of a cave. He concealed himself there for a few days, before he ran into a heartless servant who gave him up to Khoja Burhan al-Din. They held him for a couple of days before finally executing him.

Abd al-Majid, meanwhile, was alive to the situation. He sounded out the *shadiyana* drum while Khoja Abdullah was yet to leave the city, and all the townsfolk /115b/ knew there was a change in the world's affairs. Inside the city, such a commotion arose, with all ranks of the population stricken with anxiety (although some ignorant people were rejoicing). Early the next morning, Abd al-Majid stuck a peacock feather in his turban and came to the field in front of the palace. There he gathered the amirs and the scholars and boasted to them of his treachery. "Did you doubt that Abd al-Majid could get things done? Do you see now?"[216]

"You heretic," Akhund Mulla Maḥmud muttered to himself. "Do you have any idea what's coming to you? You should get moving before it arrives."

> Beware, you who do evil to others!
> Stop oppressing people, and you'll be free from worry.
> In the end, all who persecute face worse persecution,
> Choose virtue as your profession and be a prince among men!

The assembled scholars and amirs then went to meet Khoja Burhan al-Din. When they arrived and paid their respects, they could see there was something unusual about his side's deportment. Their speech was different, and their mannerisms were entirely different. They interacted among themselves differently, they looked different, and the relationship between shaykh and disciple was different. Their symbols of royal and religious authority were different, and their litanies and prayers were different. The way they greeted each other was different, as was the way they said goodbye. A meeting of sorts took place, and then they went back. The next day, Khoja Burhan al-Din began with a pilgrimage to the shrine of Ḥażrat Mazar, then entered the city of Kashgar in triumph and assumed the throne. The Qalmaq and Chinese envoys also came and took up residence. Inside Kashgar, a lot of violence and pillaging took place. /116a/ They accused many people of being Black Mountaineers and made threats against them, and some crazy Sufis and wild men who had been wandering in the wilderness gained prominent positions. The inhabitants of the kingdom couldn't voice their concerns about these people to Khoja Burhan al-Din, which demonstrated to them the value of the favor they had previously enjoyed. Some wise men came to regret their disloyalty.

> There are more incidents than the people had envisaged,
> There is more suffering than had been anticipated.

The eternal skeptic Abd al-Wahhab, Raḥman Quli, Abdullah the Kirghiz, along with the amirs of Kashgar and several mad Sufis and heretics put forward a proposal. "The army should continue on its way to Yarkand. Those khojas are quivering in panic. If we advance and deny them any rest, we will capture them easily. Otherwise, if quarter is given, they will find some way to cause trouble. They may even be able to harm us. The best thing would be to issue a decree for the army from Kashgar to assemble and march off." This advice appealed to Khoja Burhan al-Din, and he immediately ordered the army to rally and advance on Yarkand.

Qubad the Kirghiz had presented himself before Khoja Burhan al-Din and sworn to serve him loyally. In return, Khoja Burhan al-Din had promised to make him governor of Kashgar once Yarkand had been conquered. /116b/ He now appointed Qubad as commander in chief and instructed him to make for Yarkand. With Qubad leading them, the Kirghiz and the forces of Kashgar, Aqsu, and Ush, as well as some five or six hundred Qalmaqs and Chinese, all set off toward Yarkand.

34. THE BATTLE FOR YARKAND

Let us now continue the story from Yarkand. On the day when Khoja Abdullah and Khoja Muʾmin and their following entered Yarkand, Khoja Jahan gave up all thought of holding on and maintaining his throne. He instructed his entire family and retinue to relocate to a camp outside the city, and he went out with them and set himself up. From Yarkand he invited the scholars, amirs, and wise men, great and small, and put on a feast to in their honor. Then he rose to speak in farewell. "My people! Scholars, amirs, and subjects! Listen closely now. For ages I have enjoyed the right to eat and converse with you, and I have exercised rule over you. Whatever mistreatment you may have experienced as a result of my policies, whether in word or in deed, and whether deliberate or by accident, I ask you to forgive me. If you seek revenge, I will accept it, as will God. From the days of my forefathers until now, you have not shown the slightest hint of infidelity toward us. Even now, I hope your kingdoms will never lose their stability and prosperity until the end of time. May God grant you this good fortune. /117a/ The reason I ask for your approval is that Khoja Burhan al-Din of the line of Khoja Afaq, at the behest of the Chinese emperor and with his emissary, has come and conquered as far as the outskirts of Kashgar. There is a possibility that he will advance on Yarkand. If he manages to come this way and a battle occurs between us, it will cause suffering to the Muslims on both sides. We could submit to him, but by God we remain within Islam, while they have joined with the infidel and turned their backs on the faith. It is not appropriate for us to submit to infidels. In any case, they would not trust us, and it would end in conflict. It would be better for us to leave on the hajj with our kin and retinue, should God grant us this. For some time now, I have cherished a desire to visit the Holy Shrines, but circumstances did not allow it. Now is a suitable time. In the past, when their forefathers were ruling these lands and our forefathers came to prominence, their forefathers ceded to them the throne of guidance. Now we too have spent a while ruling from the throne and have no unfulfilled ambitions left. It is their turn."

The time of Majnún has passed and it is our turn—
The turn of everyone is five days.

"Our only intention is that everyone attains their desire. It is obvious that heaven's favor and the star of fortune /117b/ are on their side, and ill fate is on ours. It now seems that our best option is to avoid causing harm to ourselves and anyone else, and step aside for them."

As he spoke these moving words, a hue and cry rose up from the crowd to the heavens and filled the camp. After a pause, the scholars led by *aʿlam akhund* Umar Baqi and the amirs led by Ghazi Beg remonstrated with him. "O king, and refuge of the religion!" they said. "Without you this mortal life is impossible for us. If you decide to leave, you should take the people of Yarkand with you. Let us accompany you! Otherwise we can in no way reconcile ourselves to your abandoning us and leaving. They will definitely not come here; they will be content to take Kashgar alone. Previously their forefathers were satisfied with Kashgar, and they therefore see Kashgar as their familial resting place. Yarkand is the land of your forefathers—that's why they chose to be buried here. Let them throw the infidels at us, we'll give them their just deserts. Let them even accompany the infidels, we don't care, we'll meet them in battle. If we die, we'll be martyrs, and if we kill them, we'll be holy warriors. We have but one soul, but even if we had a hundred, they may as well be sacrificed for Islam. Let us die wrestling and stabbing at them. We'll never take a backward step or acknowledge their authority. How can the Holy Law allow you to simply give up and leave to their fate people who exhibit such resolve? Apparently they're on their way with infidel envoys and a decree. /118a/ But even if there weren't a decree from the infidels and they came as pure Muslims, we are Muslims and our king is a Muslim, and the shariʿa commands that it's impermissible for Muslims to wage war on Muslims. According to the Holy Law, the sin is theirs, not ours. The merit of holy war is greater than the merit of the hajj." They made every effort to prevent him from going and renewed their commitments with oaths on the Quran.

Since they had put their case in terms of the shariʿa, Khoja Jahan could see no alternative but to stay there and resign himself to his fate. Submitting to whatever God had in store for him, he reentered the city.

I'll submit to what comes my way as my fate,
There is not the slightest thing in the world that is not predestined.
If it's my destiny to die in enemy hands,
Would it be right to flee from it and save myself?
It is not I alone, but my descendants too,
Who inherit the weighty legacy of the Karbala martyr.
Sometimes even earth and sky become foes,
Were I to cry out a hundred times, I wouldn't get any reply.
I'll part not just from my house, but my soul too it seems,
As a hundred calamities and a multitude of misfortunes confront me.
I am thirsty, and the cup of death is circling my way,
The cry from the people rings out: DRINK, O THIRSTY ONES!
Ṣadiq, such injustice has been done to your emperor Arshi,
Abandon the people of the world, associate with them no more.

Khoja Jahan chose forbearance, put his trust in God, and brought the people from the surrounds of Yarkand into the city. /118b/ He saw to the city's defenses, appointed sentries and guards, and kept watch. It was reported that a cloud of dust had arisen from the direction of Kashgar, and within it waves of soldiers were coming into view. Khoja Jahan entrusted the affairs of state and command of the military to the unfaithful traitor Ghazi Beg, making him commander in chief and governor plenipotentiary, and all of Yarkand's affairs devolved to him.

Meanwhile, people started complaining to Khoja Abdullah. "How can we allow such cowardice and timidity? To shrink in fright and run away at some distant rumor that the enemy has arrived somewhere? Doesn't honor require warriors to give battle once or twice, and only then to flee out of necessity if the enemy triumphs? Otherwise, we should continue to resist as much as we can." These complaints were particularly directed at the worthless Ghazi. Khoja Abdullah and Khoja Muʾmin could hardly raise their heads from this embarrassing censure and were left in a dispirited and troubled state.

Which pain shall I express, which of my troubles?
I ask, has anyone else ever experienced such hardship?
Shall I tell of my grief, the anxiety of loss,
/119a/ Or shall I narrate the disastrous ruin of my house?
Will I describe to you the enemies attacking me from all sides?
Intent on killing me—a perilous trial.
All trouble is coming my way, while my miserly rival has no worries,
Every second he inflicts a million punishing wounds.
O Ṣadiq, is there any suffering that has not afflicted the princes?
Neither their following nor fortune kept faith with them.

Disorderly groups of men from the Kashgar army were streaming toward Yarkand. Those who arrived were taken prisoner and detained inside Yarkand. This situation carried on for ten days, and the number of captives reached five or six hundred, until on the tenth day Khoja Burhan al-Din arrived with much fanfare. It was calculated that Khoja Abdullah had come to Yarkand ten days after Khoja Yaḥya returned from the battle at Ush. Then another ten days had gone by before the Kashgar army began to show its face in a disorderly state, and it was ten days after that that Khoja Burhan al-Din arrived. With the princes leading them, two or three thousand brave cavalrymen issued from Yarkand to confront him. Khoja Jahan gave them a stern warning: "Beware, a hundred times beware! Don't fire an arrow at the Kashgaris. They are Muslims, and we are Muslims, and shooting at Muslims is not permitted by the Holy Law. You should hold off until they make some noise. After that, you may fire with the sanction of the shariʿa. Otherwise, anyone who shoots without permission will face my displeasure in this life and the next." /119b/ Given these instructions, when they drew up their ranks, they didn't fire a shot or charge around on the battlefield. They were patient and kept silent.

Some from the other side, by contrast, were putting on a provocative display. Sounding a battle cry of "*qit! qit!*" they commenced their advance, and this noise of "*qit! qit!*" filled the entire battlefield.[217] Hearing this, several men ran back to the city with the good news, Ghazi Beg's son first of all. Khoja Jahan heard these happy tidings and gave thanks. "For some time now, I had been troubled by the thought," he said, "that since they are Muslims they might attack with the cry of 'Allah!' Should this side also attack with the cry of 'Allah! Allah!' and battle take place between them, then what would become of them, and of us? This is exactly what I was worried about, but glory be to God, this anxiety of mine has been assuaged, and I'm now free from worry. Don't hesitate to give battle; let loose your arrows with fortitude. If you die, you'll be a martyr, and if you kill someone, you'll be a holy warrior. Give battle invoking God, the Prophet, and Ḥusayn the martyr." With this, he gave them permission to enter the fray.

When this news reached the battlefield outside, the men took inspiration, and with cries of "O God! O Prophet! O Ḥusayn!" they commenced the attack. /120a/ Sometimes charging from the right wing to the left, and sometimes from the left wing to the right, they were swimming in a sea of soldiers, and the sound of "Allah! Allah!" put the fear of God into the army of Kashgar. They had no strength to stand up to them—particularly to the bravery of Khoja Abdullah, which will be described below.

There were certain courageous souls from among the princes, such as the nimble and quick-witted champion Khoja Inayat, an impassioned man of sayyid lineage who was eager for martyrdom. He was Khoja Jahan's relative by marriage by one remove, and although he was elderly in years, his zeal was that of a young man. "What a pity it is," he always used to sigh, "that my precious life has gone to waste. I have no good deeds to my account, and I've never been able to realize my lofty intentions. If only there was a holy war to end my life with, I would drench this white beard of mine in blood and sacrifice my soul for Islam." Such was always his desire, and therefore this battle enlivened his spirit, and his fervor increased a thousandfold. On the battlefield, he was like a forest lion, displaying his prowess sometimes with a spear, sometimes with a sharp sword, sometimes with bow and arrow, and sometimes with a fearsome battle-axe. Whichever weapon the situation lent itself to, he would put it to use. He drove the enemy back as if they were fleeing before a lightning storm, and he piled up the dead bodies.

/120b/ Whatever you do in this world, make a good name for yourself,
You'll see its reward in the next life, this one won't last forever.
Even if you have Noah's longevity and Solomon's wealth,
Death's messenger will come one day, and you will die.
With which of its inhabitants did this mundane world ever keep faith?
There is neither eternity nor stability to it.
Shake out your skirts and divorce the old woman of time,
The young shouldn't accommodate themselves to the old, have you no shame?
If you are wise, O brother, shed the burden of selfhood,
Ruin yourself before death brings you low.
Abandon your household and sacrifice your soul to the beloved,
Wage holy war, tomorrow you'll find the rank of martyrdom.
O Ṣadiq, what good deeds the kings did while passing through!
They struck the mouths of the infidels who invoked Lat and Manat.

Another of the brave princes was that roaring lion Khoja Yaḥya. He was Khoja Jahan's nephew, although the affairs of the kingdom had been entrusted to him as if he was his son, since he was without rival in wisdom and counsel. He rode bravely across field as if on Ali's mule, and was unique in his courage and high-mindedness. Witnessing his exploits on the day of battle, Rustam and Sam would have been struck dumb.

If Rustam and his offspring were there that day,
As much as they cried out on the battlefield, it wouldn't make a sound.
If Tahmuras and Tahamtan present themselves, they'd better flee,
On the same pass /121a/ my swift rider will kill them both.
If he rains arrows down on the field, he'll spill their blood,
If ten million people charge from all directions,
He'll prance among the ranks: Give up your soul, pious one,
He'll raise a ruckus: Tear up your cloak of virtue,
Who are you, O Ṣadiq? And who is this king you praise?
To praise the king is the pauper's obligation.

One of the renowned champions from among the amirs was the deputy governor of Aqsu, Mirza Murad, who was like a tiger in the grove of bravery, or a fire-breathing dragon in the vanguard of the warriors of the age. He had previously come down with Khoja Yusuf from the infidel stronghold of Ili to Kashgar with the intention to wage holy war and bring about the victory of Islam. Then he had been obliged to accompany Khoja Abdullah to Yarkand.

Come, cupbearer, pass the goblet around,
I'll drink till I'm drunk and say a few words.
The fireplace of battle is warming up,
Cowards are burning there like it or not.
/121b/ While the brave champions who fight like lions,
Have become fireproof like salamanders.
Though fire burned the corpse of Nimrod,
For Abraham it was like a bed of roses.
While the cowards tire of life,
The heroes are only just waking up.
Like the Mirza, who became a forest lion that day,
A servant of the people who whipped up a storm,
It was if the Mirza became Maḥmud's elephant,
Destroying the train of the enemy.
Frothing at the mouth like a drunken camel,
And trampling people beneath his feet.
Sometimes to the right, sometimes the left, sometimes straight ahead,
That admirable man displayed his skill.

Like a wolf herding a flock of sheep,
The people fled to make way on both sides.
Causing such a disturbance among the people,
Firing needles of pain at their hearts.
Setting the retinue of the enemy in disarray,
And parting souls from their bodies.
A full account would have no end,
It wouldn't fit on the page were he to be described.
Come Ṣadiq, move toward your conclusion,
Who told you to dwell on these words?
Time is precious, finish your speech,
Do you want to do this tomorrow? Wrap things up.
Stop talking, time is valuable,
Who knows if there'll be a chance in the morning?
You have a fine governor in the kingdom,
He's shown an incompetent like you much sympathy.
His mother is particularly kind,
Incredibly wise, and a perfect Muslim.
Loyal to the beloved kings,
And a devotee of the shaykhs and saints.
A patron of fine poetry,
And an aficionado of stories and tales.
The saga of the saints in particular
Meets with her favor.
If the chief of the province is a patron of letters,
What luck it is, a rare honor!
If you don't compose something at a time like this,
What will you say on Judgment Day, O wordsmith?
So take a step toward your goal,
And begin your poem once more.
One of the champions was Mirza Qasim,
Who was completely fearless and unflinching.
In his courage he was unique,
There was a hint of Rustam in his bravery.
Fixing his concentration on God,
With the words "O Ḥusayn!" in his mouth,

He threw himself at the enemy without hesitation,
Cutting, slicing, and shooting with abandon.
What joy it is for someone to find martyrdom,
And obtain honor in both worlds.
Another of the mirzas was Mirza Sherdagh,
/122a/ Who laid a multitude of scars on the lions' chests,[218]
He was peerless in his bravery,
Cutting the heads of the Chinese and Qalmaqs.
Proudly charging into the battlefield,
Human souls were burning like chaff on his blade.
Was there any fear at all in his heart?
Even if he stood alone, God was his companion.
Mirza Abd al-Wahhab was one more,
Blessed with amazing strength,
Reciting "Allah, Allah,
O Prophet, O Ḥusayn the Martyr!"
And also from the palace staff,
One of the brave and honorable champions,
A hero without equal,
The daring Shihab al-Din Bakavul.
Commander in chief of the swift riders,
Or indeed, a high-flying royal falcon.
Bravest among the braves,
Rustam was not his equal.
Leading the dexterous cavalrymen,
He was a roaring lion among the ranks.
His illustrious forefather was Ushtur Khalifa,
Who manifested astonishing miracles.[219]
Shihab was his likeness,
An intoxicated camel just like Ushtur.[220]
People mourned as he struck his blows,
Raising a hue and cry on the battlefield.
Striking this way and that, he laid them low,
Advancing forward, he piled up mountains of dead.
With "Allah" his determined battle cry,
He left the enemy dazed and confused.

Other courageous men from the palace
Had the same martial vigor.
But were I to recount them by name,
This poem would never end.
There were also some Kirghiz warriors,
Urus was one, and Tuqal, and Khojam Yar,
Famous and daring champions all,
My account gives but a hint of one in a thousand.

Some of these brave men finished parading on the battlefield, then killed some and wounded others, unseating men from their horses and taking them captive. They drove Khoja Burhan al-Din's army back a distance of one *farsang*, /122b/ then returned to the city in triumph, where Khoja Jahan said a benediction for them. All the city's residents were happy to see that the army outside was small, and they imagined that the next day they would rally the troops and go out and smash the Kashgaris to smithereens. But then, from the pavilion of the palace and the city walls, they saw something going on outside: group by group, tribe by tribe, unit by unit, the army of Kashgar was descending on the city and surrounding the walls on all four sides. Everyone inside the city fainted. None of the princes allowed themselves any rest as they saw to the defenses. That night they made multiple circuits of the city, staying vigilant in the hope that if the city did not fall that evening, then perhaps it would be possible to hold out.

O Lord, will there ever be such tension as on this night?
From dawn to dusk there will be anxiety and misgiving.

Khoja Jahan also composed this ghazal:

When I examine the shape of the marble, its state has altered,
I wonder if it is having different thoughts too?
Futuḥi! Take refuge in Arshi's perfection,
When I look at the shape of the age, its state has altered.

/123a/ They made it through this terrifying night in safety, but Khoja Burhan al-Din's army had rallied in numbers beyond estimation, coming from Ili, Aqsu, Kucha, Ush, Turfan, Kashgar, and Yangiḥiṣar, along with several groups of Kirghiz, including men led by Qubad from the Qushchi tribe, Ṣufi Mirza, Ḥakim Mirza, and Umar from the Qipchaq, as well as men from Möngke's tribe and the Chongbaghish.[221] For a whole day and night, affairs stood this way, and then the soldiers broke up in all directions. On either the third or fourth day—the story varies in the retelling—they beat the drums of war, and a huge army from the city of Yarkand was mobilized. They drew up their ranks facing the Kashgar army, and two seas of soldiers fell into lines opposite each other. At a few places on either side, they struck kettledrums and sounded horns, creating a huge cacophony.

They strung the soul's dulcimer among the ranks,
Signaling that the heroes were advancing into battle.
The passion of the noble warriors was aroused,
They strode onto the battlefield rending their chests.
Crying out and attacking with abandon,
Lion-like they wielded the blade bravely.
While the womanly warriors, weak, effeminate,
And lacking ardor, fled from corner to corner.
Steeds with spirit were stirred into action,
But the mules grew tired of charging around.
The impassioned warriors were something to see that day, Ṣadiq,
But lizards are better than fighters without passion.

These two seas of soldiers organized their lines such that they picked out the best fighters and stationed some on the right and some on the left, while some they appointed as the vanguard in the center. In front of them they placed the artillerymen and musketeers, and then anyone who was timid and cowardly they assigned to the rearguard. The princes themselves took up position beneath the war banners and the dragon-shaped standards.

Brave men from both sides strode onto the field between the two lines, /123b/ sometimes surveying the right wing, and sometimes the left, Sometimes when they steeled themselves they would spur their mounts directly at the center and show off their horsemanship. The two armies gradually mingled, and like the convergence of two seas, it became impossible to tell them apart from a distance. Grasping and stabbing at one another, attacking sometimes with spears, sometimes with swords, and sometimes with bows and arrows, the battlefield became a fiery oven sending sparks up toward the sky, and a rain of death began to fall.

From the army of Yarkand arose a cry of "O God! O Prophet of God! O Ḥusayn, O martyr!" The enemies began to tremble, and their hearts were pounding. From Burhan al-Din's army, by contrast, there was no sound apart from "*qit! qit!*" because most of the army were Kuhistani—that is, mountain men (*taghlïq*)—as well as Qalmaq and Kirghiz, who were oblivious to the faith of Islam and had no affinity with it. Specifically, there were certain officers among them who were entirely indifferent to the religion and its precepts, and to the ruin of the Islamic faith. These included the incorrigible skeptic Abd al-Wahhab, the ill-fated Raḥman Quli, the corrupt Abdullah the Kirghiz, the faithless Abd al-Karim,[222] the ever-doubting Abd al-Sattar, and /124a/ the unscrupulous U̱sman, as well as Mundi Ṣufi, Niyaz Ṣufi, Sariq Yasavul, and certain Kashgari amirs and others.

Come, cupbearer, pass the goblet a second time,
It's time for the dulcimer and kettle drum.
I have some complaints against the tricksters,
Against the evildoers, or should I say bloodsuckers.
There were some leaders in that army,
Who were ignorant not just of piety but of faith itself.
They had not a care for the ruin of the shariʿa,
Not one of them was seeking the Path.
Night and day their business was war,
Making enemies for the sake of it and taking revenge.
Exerting cruelty on the people of God,
While their conscience turns a blind eye.
So devoted they were to evil deeds,
Leading someone astray was perfection to them.
They gave bad advice to stir enmity,
And divert from the right course of action.
Sowing discord between kings,
They were quick to cast aspersions.
If the vizier is a roguish man like this,
When the king says to take someone's cap, they slit his throat.

But a wise vizier is a blessing to kings,
With him they'll find peace in this life and the next,
Their reputation for justice will last until Judgment Day
They'll find limitless recompense for it in days to come.
If a vizier is a bloodsucking tyrant,
And a traitor given to infidelity,
He'll earn his king a reputation for injustice,
And the kingdom will never be at rest.
The common folk will resent the king,
O people, his kingdom will be ruined!
So many monarchs have enjoyed good fortune
On account of a wise and virtuous vizier.
Sulayman obtained honor and glory
Because of the miracle-working Asif b. Barkhiya.
Alexander's fame spread thanks to Aristotle,
Conquering land and sea with his strategies.
Nushirvan became /124b/ known as the Just Sultan,
But Buzurjmihr the Wise was the cause.
And Sulṭan Ḥusayn received his good name
From Mir Alisher Navaʾi of Herat.
There is no need to describe viziers of ill counsel,
Or to depict examples of them.
They brought their kings a bad reputation,
And themselves became lost in obscurity.
O God, whoever is in charge of a province,
Grant him a wise and knowledgeable vizier.
So neither the kingdom nor its inhabitants come to ruin,
And so there be pious observance of the Holy Law.
Glory be to God that now is such a time,
With all of God's people safe and secure.
Call a halt now, Ṣadiq, to these words of yours,
Where are you wandering off to? Come to your senses.
The enemy is pressing from all sides, time is tight,
With friend facing foe, the battle is at the crucial point.
Some of the warriors from the group just described
Were as bold as warlike lions,

Like the offspring of Ahriman,
Or devils from Mount Qaf.
One was a black demon, the other an Ifrit,
Raising a battle cry with the words "*qit*! *qit*!"
Throwing the Muslims into disarray,
Martyring a thousand and wounding a thousand,
It was a great calamity for the Muslims.
They inflicted torture like the deceptive Dajjal,
Massacring the Muslims and piling up the corpses,
Erecting mound after mound of martyrs.
They had no pity or compassion,
Within them was only vengeance and enmity
O God, would that there never be such people,
In the deserts and seas, on the plains and in the mountains.
Never allow a Muslim to encounter them,
An infidel would be ashamed at what they have done.

The battle intensified, and on both sides a great deal of bloodshed occurred. The army of Yarkand were already gaining the advantage when they fired the two European guns, nine hands in length, that had been left behind by Khoja Yusuf, and that Khoja Abdullah had brought from Kashgar. Up to a distance of one *farsang*, these guns never missed. /125a/ Khoja Burhan al-Din had occupied a hill called Bay Döbä, and when they fired—although the story varies—the shot is said to have struck the horse of the standard-bearer (because he was far off), causing the standard in one of his hands to fall.[223] Whatever the case, they were panicked and drew back from the hill-top. On seeing this, the warriors of Yarkand took courage, and in a frenzied charge, they drove the soldiers remaining on the battlefield backward and harried them from behind. It looked as if Khoja Burhan al-Din's army was about to be completely routed. In this dire situation, Qubad the Kirghiz intervened with his own troops and checked the men of Yarkand, who had no choice but to turn their reins and call off the pursuit. Eventually the sun set in the west and the dark red vault of the sky donned its bloody robe, and in accordance with the verse TRULY WE HAVE ADORNED THE LOWEST HEAVEN WITH LAMPS [67:5], the torches and lanterns of the stars appeared in the closest sphere. When it became late, both streams of soldiers beat the drum of withdrawal and retired to their camps. The army of Yarkand, led by Khoja Abdullah and Khoja Yaḥya the Holy Warrior, made a triumphant entrance into the city, and Khoja Jahan said blessings and felicitations for them.

When the first advance guard of this Kashgar army had reached Yarkand, the populace had secretly made a collective petition to Khoja Jahan. "King of the world," they advised him, "we bring you this petition in secret /125b/ and urge you to approve it. Our message is that Khoja Burhan al-Din, with the aid of the Qalmaqs and the envoy of the Chinese emperor, has brought all the lands of Moghulistan apart from Yarkand into his domains. Although Yarkand province stands alone, nevertheless it is the capital of Moghulistan, and as long as no treachery or deception occurs from within, it can resist and overcome the forces of its remaining cities. Such treachery will only come about, or will only have an impact, from two people that we have suspicions toward: one of these is Governor Ghazi Beg, and the other is Deputy Governor Niyaz Beg. Ghazi Beg's situation is that although he has little love for those on the side of Khoja Burhan al-Din, he essentially lacks all notion of loyalty. He won't shy away from selling out the religion for material gain. He has shown signs of disloyalty in the past, and it's impossible to take him at his word. He has plentiful resources, a large retinue, and knows every trick in the book. If he hatches some plot to betray you, he will bring it to fruition. As for the duplicity of Niyaz Beg, he has long been dedicated to Khoja Burhan al-Din and his forefathers, and has regularly sent them offerings. When we went to Ush, some of his family members joined Bahadur Beg's sons in breaking from us and switching to the side of Khoja Burhan al-Din, and they have now arrived as part of his army. Niyaz Beg is always speaking ill of the princes, so there is the possibility of a plot from both inside and outside. He too has a large family and following, and ample resources. If he conspires against us, it will be effective. Once that occurs, regrets will be of no use: this must be dealt with in advance. /126a/ Our advice is to seize these two men and detain them somewhere, so that they play no role in affairs of state. If God grants us victory, then we can restore them to their positions and set matters in train again."

Khoja Jahan replied in his eloquent way: "My companions and well-wishers, I appreciate that you are saying this out of devotion to me, and to these kingdoms. But I have shown these two much favor and given them the finest salt. As they say, *Wherever you eat the salt, be sure not to break the salt jar!* On several occasions, Ghazi Beg has sworn on God's name not to commit any treachery and put his hand on the holy Quran. He may decide to keep his oath and not betray us. He is a Muslim, and it won't do to harm a Muslim simply on the basis of suspicions. Even if he doesn't respect the oath that he swore on the Quran, I certainly intend to. Should he fail to keep faith and choose to rebel, then I will leave him in the hands of God and His Prophet, and he'll receive his due punishment in this world and the next. As for Niyaz Beg, the rights of kinship still hold between us, so perhaps he too will refrain from any treachery (Khoja Jahan had married one of Niyaz Beg's daughters by the name of Aʾisha Beg, and she was now in his service). In case some treason is committed, then I will refer him too to God and the Prophet, and to my fathers and forefathers, and the patronage that I have given him. He will receive his punishment in this life and the next."

Wherever you eat the salt, poet, don't take a step away,
Such a quality is a sign of madness, his condition has come to a head.

You who nibbled the salt, beware not to show ingratitude,
In the end this salt won't let you go without punishment.

The assembly importuned him. "If you don't believe us, then at least /126b/ have these two set up their tents and court inside the palace, so they carry out the duties of governor and deputy right here for a day and night. The kingdom will be put at ease."

"Very well," Khoja Jahan said, "I will allow this." That same day, they organized accommodation for them, and the governor and deputy governor moved in.

35. KHOJA BURHAN AL-DIN CALLS ON KHOJA JAHAN TO SUBMIT

Let us leave them there a few days to cook up their conspiracies and plots, while we follow the saga from the side of Khoja Burhan al-Din. My sources inform me that the day after this bloody engagement, Khoja Burhan al-Din reclined on the throne in his luxurious tent and summoned the pillars of state. At his right hand was sitting Abd al-Wahhab the skeptic, his younger brother Umar Beg, and his sons Abd al-Sattar and Abd al-Khaliq, the governor of Kucha Khudaberdi, his younger brother Allah Quli, Muḥammad Yar, the governor of Sayram Ali Beg, the Dolan governor Saʿadat, Raḥman Quli, Farman Quli, Abd al-Raḥim Beg, and the Kirghiz Abdullah Beg. Seated to his left were Shara Muḥammad Emin, his son Abd al-Raḥman, Yusuf Beg, his younger brother Abd al-Sattar, Musa Beg, the governor of Beshkerem Muḥarram Beg, the governor of Fayżabad Mir Niyaz, Abd al-Raḥim Beg, and Khudayar's son Muḥammad Emin. In front of him was Danjin Jaisang and Turumtai Hiya, and from among the crazed Sufis there was Mundi Ṣufi, Raḥmati Ṣufi, Azhdar Niyaz, Nishtar Niyaz Ṣufi, Mulla Ivaż, Saqal Ṣufi, Mulla Barat, Mulla Qalam, Mir Noruz Khazinachi, Sariq Yasavul, Ilyas Mir Akhur, and likewise from the Kirghiz there was Bahadur Bi [i.e., Qubad Mirza] of the Qushchi, and Ṣufi Mirza, Ḥakim Mirza, and Umar Mirza from the Qipchaq, along with Möngke and the rest.

In this assembly he raised a question for debate: "With what sort of ploy can we take this city of Yarkand? /127a/ How can we reassure ourselves toward it? Even if we choose to fight, without that side deciding to, they won't come out and do battle with us. If we approach the walls and fortifications, they'll open fire and prevent us from advancing. If for some reason they come out and fight, they'll have the advantage against us. In that situation they might well defeat our troops and put them to flight. What's the solution to all this?"

All those present kissed the ground in humility. "The best way to deal with this would be for an emissary from our side to visit them," they replied. "He should take as his companions one or two of the Chinese emperor's envoys and some of Amursana's people and deliver a letter. These khojas of Yarkand have had experience of the dominion of the Qalmaqs and been on the receiving end of their attacks. They've heard enough about the countless numbers and determination of the Chinese. Maybe they'll be intimidated by the envoy's letter, and either come out to meet us in submission, or else abandon the city and escape."

The advice that they outlined proved agreeable to all. They immediately wrote up a threatening letter and appointed Mulla Baqi Sartarash as envoy, with four Qalmaqs, two Chinese, and a handful of locals to accompany him. Riding up to the city gates, they announced their embassy and received permission to enter. They then came before the palace of His Holiness Khoja

Jahan, and with the utmost disdain, /127b/ the courtiers forced them to kiss the ground at several entranceways before leading them into Khoja Jahan's presence. As soon as these good-for-nothings set eyes on Khoja Jahan's majesty, they were struck dumb. When they eventually came to their senses and looked around, they saw Khoja Jahan ensconced on a gleaming nine-level throne, like a torch in the assembly of eloquence, or a sun in the sky of justice. To his right hand were the patrons of the shariʿa, and guides to both the highborn and low—that is, the estimable scholars, including the *aʿlam* of Yarkand Akhund Umar Baqi, Akhund Haji Abdullah, Akhund Haji Ubaydullah, Akhund Shah Abd al-Qadir, Akhund Mulla Abd al-Qahir, and the rest. On his left-hand side, the illustrious amirs each sat in their place, including Governor of Yarkand Ghazi Beg, Deputy Governor Niyaz Beg, Shah Yaʿqub Beg, Sulṭan Beg, and other Yarkandi amirs. From the amirs of Aqsu there was the family's loyal devotee Mirza Murad Beg, his younger brother Mirza Shah Murad Beg, his son Mirza Zulfiqar Beg, Mirza Sherdagh Beg, Mirza Niyaz Beg, Mirza Qasim Beg, and Niyaz Beg. From Kashgar there was Ufal Niyaz Beg, and from the Yarkandis there were various sayyids, *mingbegi*s and *yüzbegi*s, *mirab*s and *parvanachi*s, and scholars and amirs, all seated in rows.[224]

In front of him on half-thrones were seated the princes, /128a/ each of them a fresh cyprus in the grove of sayyidhood, and a new bloom in the sultanate's rose bed: Khoja Yusuf's cherished sons Khoja Abdullah, Khoja Muʾmin, Khoja Quṭb al-Din, Khoja Burhan al-Din (the one known as Erke Khoja), Khoja Jahan's son Khoja Ṣiddiq Futuḥi, his adopted son Khoja Yaḥya, and his sons-in-law Khoja Umar and Ṣufi Khoja. Among the rest of the princes were Khoja Naṣrullah and Khoja Inayatullah. One row behind these princes were Ivaż Khalifa, Abd al-Raḥman Khalifa, Ṣaliḥ Khalifa, Muḥammad Abdullah Bakavul, Shihab al-Din Bakavul, Polad Quzi Khalifa, Mirza Abd al-Wahhab, Mirza Abd al-Manaf, Muḥammad Vali Dorgha, Hamdam Bakavul, Muḥammadi Mir Akhur, Mulla Muḥammad Kerek-yaragh, and Tiläk Bahadur. From Khoja Abdullah's retinue there were Ṣabir Kerek-yaragh, Darvish Bakavul, Khojash Khoja, Khojam Naẓar Dorgha, Urus Mirza, Tuqal Mirza, Tursun Qashqa, and Aqyol Bahadur. From Khotan there were Shah Żiya al-Din Khalifa, Khoja Laq Khalifa, Tokhta Khoja, and Aq Burut. These and more of their followers were present. Sometimes sitting down, other times standing up, they displayed their devotion while gazing expectantly into Khoja Jahan's eyes.

The disreputable envoys kissed the honorable threshold a few times, wiped its dust on their eyes, and presented their letter with great trepidation. /128b/ With a glance, Khoja Jahan gestured to his secretary, who immediately took the letter and began reading it aloud in his eloquent voice. This is what it said:

> Khoja Jahan and men of Yarkand! I hereby inform you that there is a decree for you from the emperor of China first of all, and secondly from Amursana, that for centuries now these lands have belonged to the Qalmaqs. Indeed, the Qalmaq *törä* dispatched you here on the promise that you would regularly submit to him the poll tax, the *kharaj*, and the *baj*. Why do you now turn your backs on them and launch such treacherous attacks, and even consider it legitimate to kill them? What shortsightedness and naivety it is to engage in such vain endeavors and indulge these empty fantasies, which will only lead to ruin. Perhaps you are ignorant and have not been informed of some significant recent events. Dabachi, whom you deceived, has been dismissed from the position of *törä* and sultan, and furthermore has been exiled to China in chains and fetters. By decree of the emperor of China, Amursana has taken up the throne of the sultanate, and a large Chinese army has occupied Ili. All throughout the Qalmaq domains, order has been restored and affairs have been set straight. All those territories that were previously subject to them have now become subject to the emperor of China, and the poll tax, *baj*, and *kharaj* are due to him. He has sent us with thousands of men to take control of these lands /129a/ and transmit his and the *törä*'s decrees. Those who comply have nothing to worry about. But if someone rejects them, then we are to visit death and destruction upon them to the extent that we can. Should our strength prove insufficient, then he has sworn on his own religion that he will lead an immense army with hordes of Chinese and Qalmaqs, massacre the region's inhabitants along with their livestock, and dig up their land and throw it into the rivers to completely annihilate it. It would be wise for you now to immediately cease resistance and lead the populace out. We will kowtow to the emperor and *törä* and ask mercy for you. Maybe they will forgive you, and grant each of you a city to rule. This much we owe you on account of our bonds of kinship. But should you not abide by this advice, your crimes will be

upon you. Our army is made up of men from several cities and several tribes of Kirghiz, Qalmaq, and Chinese, and behind us troops are continuing to arrive. In a short while we will breach the city, destroy its fortifications, and set fire to all the dwellings. We will carry you and your families to the banks of the Zarafshan River, slaughter you like sheep, and make a river of blood flow. We will burn the bodies and cast the ashes to the wind, so that it serve as a lesson for everyone from now until Judgment Day that none should draw their sword against their emperor and *törä*.

/129b/ Brother, stop speaking and heed some advice,
How long will you exert yourself in worthless deeds?
Whatever you do, don't abandon your faith in Islam,
There's a world called the "afterlife" which they say is a delight.
Don't make a misstep while seeking worldly pleasures,
One day this ball will fall into the pit of destruction.
Any deed you do today, whether good or bad,
Count ten as one, don't expect anything more.
Don't converse with ignoble men, for their evildoing
Will leave you reviled and filthy in both worlds.
Don't you know? A wise companion is more precious than one's soul,
From him you'll rise to the pinnacle of authority.
But few ill-disposed men led the king astray,
And a bad reputation hung around his neck.
The people of the world are devious and full of tricks,
Ṣadiq! Seek wisdom and insight and see the colors of the rainbow!

When they reached the end of this treasonous letter, Islam's righteous king Khoja Jahan issued an angry command that they rip it up and throw it into the fire. His stewards immediately tore the letter into pieces and cast it into the hearth.

Khoja Jahan then creased his brow in rage and addressed these good-for-nothing envoys: "Your khoja, your emperor, and your *törä* are all talking nonsense. They seem entirely devoid of reason. There's a well-known saying, that if you think yourself a hero, then imagine your opponent a roaring lion. A wise man is someone who considers the consequences of his deeds.

For many years we had no choice but to submit to these wretched infidels. /130a/ We squandered our lives to make a living in this mortal realm. What we've done here is in recompense for this misspent existence. We have no expectations left from this transient world. For some years we indulged our desires on the sultanic throne, and each one of them was fulfilled. Our intention by these actions is not to acquire material wealth, but instead to obtain the merit of holy war, the deed for which real men were created. Even if the merit of holy war isn't evident to you, it is to us, for we have read the Word of God and the hadith of the Prophet and learned that this is the highest form of worship. Holy war or martyrdom will be our legacy. Whichever is bestowed upon us, that will be our fate. But no one should imagine that we will submit once again to the infidels. God willing, as long as there is life in our soul, we will wrestle, fight, and die with the unbelievers. There is no possibility of us surrendering."

My passion and boldness are not the same as before,
My strong arms are not what they once were,
Don't doubt that the enemy will advance toward us,
Second by second my ardor is not the same as it was.

Having thus admonished the envoys, Khoja Jahan permitted them to leave. These contemptible men removed themselves from the city in a state of boundless fear and anxiety, and went and reported what had occurred to Khoja Burhan al-Din. /130b/ He and his army were struck with disappointment and misgivings, and the Kirghiz were demoralized.

36. KHOJA JAHAN REPLIES TO KHOJA BURHAN AL-DIN

Let us leave these people in their forlorn state, while we continue the story of Khoja Jahan. After the envoys were dismissed, he summoned the pillars of state once more, assembling the same group of people described above, and gave his view of the situation.[225] "My people! Scholars, amirs, and subjects! With the honorable intention to please God and promote the noble shariʿa of His Holiness Muḥammad (May God pray for him and grant him peace!), we rebelled against the infidels, raised high the banner of

Islam, and wielded the sword of holy war against those wretched souls. Yet certain events have come to pass that indicate that our endeavors are not succeeding. The first of these was when we decided to campaign against Ush; right then my kinsman Khoja Yusuf died. He was always the one to decide affairs with his wise counsel, and we lost him. Then, because the Kirghiz miscreants betrayed them, the army sent to Ush came back defeated. The enemy's forces became well equipped with our own weapons and supplies and grew in strength. Secondly, because of the scheming of a few traitors in Kashgar, our children Khoja Abdullah and Khoja Muʾmin panicked and gave up the city and fled in this direction. Kashgar slipped from our grasp, /131a/ and the enemy became even more numerous. Among the Kirghiz we had generously patronized Umar, Möngke, and Ṣufi Mirza, with all their tribesmen, and equipped them well, but those ingrates too have sided with the enemy. Likewise, I had commissioned Darvish Bakavul, an old servant of my kinsman Khoja Yusuf, to invite the Kirghiz Qubad and his tribe from Andijan. Qubad too has proved himself faithless and sided with the enemy, and now has become a source of insecurity for us. Matters have reached the point that the Chinese and Qalmaq armies, with forces from various cities and several tribes of Kirghiz, are closing in on Yarkand. The content of the letter brought by their envoys has been divulged, and you have heard it. It seems to us now the best course of action would be to set out on a pilgrimage to Mecca with our family and dependents. Should God permit us to do this, well and good. Otherwise, if either these people or someone else come for us, we will obtain the rank of martyrdom. Whatever is to become of us, we'll be with our families. Once we have evacuated, no harm should come to the kingdom. It's evident that the revolving heavens have fixed an unlucky sign above us, and the star of fortune is moving toward the opposing side. Even if Rustam or Sam were to enter the battlefield on our side, there'd still be no chance of victory. Now is the time to resign ourselves to fate and withdraw. Should our allotted destiny be to die at the hands of these people, there's no need to grieve, for martyrdom will our reward. And if not, we shall find freedom."

/131b/ O faithless heaven, how deviously you revolve,
Now my complaint is against you, you charlatan.
Wherever there's some ill-natured ignoramus, you satisfy his desire,

But you betray those who are noble-minded and wise.
For vengeful tyrants you bring forth the star of fortune,
You take their side and grant them victory and triumph.
But to someone brave and virtuous you're a threat,
Like a trickster, you damn them with an evil sign.
You spill the blood of kings and princes without hesitation,
What a pitiless vampire you are.
You're an enemy to anyone with the slightest wisdom,
But you're a companion to a perverse skeptic.
O Ṣadiq, if this is what distinguishes the work of heavens,
What hope can you have? Of course you'll end up ruined!

As Khoja Jahan concluded this moving speech announcing his decision to go on the hajj, shouts and cries from the assembled crowd filled the heavens, and everyone fell into a loud weeping. When they eventually composed themselves, they appealed as one: "O conquering king! Victory and triumph are your two constant companions. Your Holiness has no need for such dejection and despair! How could you remove yourself from this dangerous situation but cast us into the fire? However this fire burns us, it will burn you too. Indeed, it will touch you more than us. Disunity will do us no good. Let us expend all our determination and resolve on this affair as one body and soul and lay down our lives for each other. /132a/ Either we will trap the ball of desire, or the enemy will carry it off. Of every possible strategy, the best would be for us to send an envoy to the enemy, and a letter be written containing admonitions that will cause their livers to melt and their hearts to crumble. Have a few wise men and some guards take a letter to them and bring back their reply."

This advice satisfied Khoja Jahan, and he issued a decree for the secretary to compose a letter. The scribes immediately prepared a letter, and Ṣaliḥ Khalifa was appointed to the embassy with a few companions.

Equipping his party, Ṣaliḥ Khalifa set off toward Khoja Burhan al-Din's army. Word of his approach reached Khoja Burhan al-Din, and in his own fashion he too assembled a stately audience, made up of various groups of Kirghiz, Qalmaqs, Chinese, seditious amirs, tyrants in the guise of scholars, bloodthirsty Sufi madmen, and others from the nobility and common folk. Ṣaliḥ Khalifa carried out his duties as envoy and presented the letter with a bow. Khoja Burhan al-Din signaled to the letter-reader to take it, and he removed it from its nine layers of wrapping and commenced reading its eloquent message. It opened with words of praise for God and the Prophet, and then went on:

> By the grace and benevolence of the Lord Almighty (MAY HE BE PRAISED!) /132b/ we have found the wherewithal to end our subservience to the infidels, raise the banner of Islam, and strike a blow against unbelief through holy war. Our hope is that by this deed of ours we shall obtain limitless reward in the next life and find salvation from the fires of Hell. The command of the Creator, the decree of the Prophet and Lord of Both Worlds (MAY GOD PRAY FOR HIM AND GRANT HIM PEACE!), and the verdict of the noble shariʿa is this: if you belong to the community of Islam, then how can you collaborate with the infidel in attacking us, causing such trials and hardships, and exercising such tyranny and injustice on the Muslims? It is the Word of the Lord that THE BELIEVERS ARE BUT BROTHERS [49:10], which means that a believer is the brother of a fellow believer, and therefore any treachery between them is wrong. The enemy of a believer is the enemy of God, and the enemy of God is an infidel. If someone from among the believers shows enmity toward a fellow believer, then he is not a believer, but an infidel. If it is your goal to gain a kingdom, then aiding the infidel is unnecessary. You should attack from that side, and we from this. The two of us will remove the infidels from our midst, and then whichever kingdom you desire, you will be confirmed on its throne. If you were greedy and set your sights on the entire territory, then we would approve that too, for we have our hearts set on the two Holy Shrines. We will leave this land and set out on a pilgrimage to Mecca, for we have no desire left in this mortal world, and it is now your turn to rule. Our goal is simply this: to erase all trace of the infidels from this Muslim land, and to obtain the merit of holy war.
>
> Since ancient times, our forefathers never acquiesced to the rule of infidels. Indeed, if holy war is a duty on the entire community, then for us it is a particular obligation. We come from the line of sayyids. If you're confident of this genealogy, then you must adhere to the traditions of our illustrious forefather, the lord of Arabia and Persia, His Holiness Muḥammad (MAY GOD PRAY FOR HIM AND GRANT HIM PEACE!), and act

on the ruling of the shariʿa. That tradition is holy war: it is a fortune for this life and the next. For anyone who has an ounce of faith in Islam, this is the final word. /133a/ If someone has no faith or interest in Islam, and doesn't yield to the commands of the shariʿa, then it is permissible for us to kill them. Should we do so, we'll be holy warriors. Should we die, we'll be martyrs. According to the ruling of the shariʿa, such an individual is an infidel, and there is no distinction here. Although they may be Muslim in appearance, and profess their faith, say prayers and even fast during Ramadan, they are an infidel. They are equivalent to the Qalmaqs or the Chinese, for they have seen fit to shed the blood of believers unjustly in service to the infidels. According to the shariʿa we have committed no sin, we have only established Islamic rule. The learned Saʿd al-Din Taftazani in his *Commentary on Nasafi's Aqaʾid* has instructed us that ONE WHO KILLS A BELIEVER BECAUSE HE IS A BELIEVER CAN ONLY BE AN UNBELIEVER. That is to say, someone who kills a believer because of his status as a believer, i.e. who kills out of enmity toward the religion of Islam, is nothing but an infidel, for hostility to the Islamic faith is unbelief.[226] If a Muslim exhibits hostility toward a fellow Muslim without serving an infidel, and spills his blood, then he will be a grievous sinner, but he won't be an infidel. You, however, have come on the command of the infidels leading an infidel army, even though you have the strength to fight and resist them.

To be sure, when the infidels are strong and the Muslims weak, then in that situation there is no choice, there is compulsion. But you have done things that no Muslim worth the name should do and violated the bounds of Islam. These are not the acts of Muslims, but the wrongdoings of infidels. The situation resembles an incident in the past /133b/ involving that gemstone of goodness and jewel in the crown of sayyidhood, the Ṣaḥibqiran and Holy Warrior Khoja Ḥasan (GOD'S MERCY AND BLESSING BE UPON HIM!), from the time he laid siege to the city of Yarkand for the victory of Islam, and surrounded it with a huge army. Yarkand was then under the dominion of the Qalmaqs, and there were a few Qalmaqs stationed inside the city for its defense. At the sound of the army of Islam, they panicked and fled toward Ili. Once Khoja Ḥasan had captured the city, he requested a ruling from the religious scholars of the day: "Those amirs who shunned the army of Islam and joined with the army of the infidel, is it appropriate in the eyes of the shariʿa to confiscate their property?" At that time the eminent scholar and jurist Akhund Mulla Niyaz Kalan was the *aʿlam* of Yarkand, and the mufti was Akhund Mulla Kifäk. These scholars cited a hadith from the *Hidaya*, and came up with the following opinion (*fatwá*):[227]

THE PROPHET (PEACE BE UPON HIM!) SAID: ONE WHO INCREASES THE SIZE OF A GROUP BELONGS TO IT, which is to say "If someone increases the size of a group's army, then he belongs to that group." Therefore, someone who lends support to the infidels to strengthen their army and increase it therefore belongs to the army of the infidel, i.e. they are an infidel.

The judicial ruling was issued, and they affixed their seals to it. On the strength of this ruling, the houses of those renegade amirs were raided. Their property was tallied up /134a/ and confiscated for the public treasury and divided among the army of Islam. Now too, according to this precedent, it is legitimate for us to spill your blood and seize your property. As long as we live, we will never submit to you, we will die fighting to the last. Even now inside the city there are people ready to grapple with you. Each Muslim counts for two men: his faith is one man, and he himself is one. By this reckoning, our army is greater than yours. There is a popular saying among the people, that even if a city's walls are made from paper, the people inside are weaklings, and their weapons are as thin as needles, as long as that city is not compromised from within, then it will not be taken from outside. So we will defend the city for a while. We have on hand stores of food, firewood, and water to last us several years. When we so choose, we will come out of the city and give battle; otherwise, we'll remain here at leisure. Should you attack, we will attack too. If we mobilized for battle now, we would need less than one out of a hundred of us, but in these circumstances everyone would prepare for battle, for when the army of the infidels confronts the army of Islam, it is a holy war and becomes incumbent on all humanity. Every husband must present himself for battle without his wife's permission, and every slave without asking his master. From east to west, anyone who hears will acknowledge their obligation to support Islam. This is what the shariʿa requires. /134b/ In the event of a clash such as this, either you will obtain the desired outcome, or we will.

When they came to the end of this profound letter, everyone was tremulous with anxiety. Those who had some sense of Islamic faith were particularly distressed—their whole body was shaking. Yet Khoja Burhan al-Din raised his head and addressed the envoys. "Your khojas are lecturing us too much. These pompous and threatening words have nothing to do with military affairs. We've come here not of our own accord, but by the decree of the Chinese emperor and of Amursana. Your teachings won't persuade them, and since they won't have any impact on them, they're not acceptable to us either. You're talking in vain and striving in pointless endeavors. Our position is on firm foundations, for it rests on two huge mountains. May the emperor and Amursana be well, now only this city of Yarkand remains behind these walls. Even if there were a hundred thousand cities like this, we would capture them with their help. We won't be inconvenienced by a long wait. If it's not taken today, then it will be tomorrow. And if not tomorrow, then the day after that. Eventually it will fall into our hands. It's not going anywhere." With this he dismissed the envoy, and since the day was already late, he assigned him some accommodation for the night.

Everyone was struck by the force of the envoy's letter. /135a/ Accompanying Khoja Burhan al-Din's army was a mountain man and court merchant by the name of Quzghun, who was Ghazi Beg's father-in-law, and who was a particularly devious individual.[228] Amid the despondency, he offered this advice: "My son-in-law Ghazi Beg has a wise vizier by the name of Ghiyas̱ Khoja, who is the one who handles all of his affairs. Ghazi never acts contrary to his advice. This man has now come out accompanying the envoy. If I were to invite him to my tent this evening and persuade him to side with us and win over Ghazi Beg, with such a ruse the city will be compromised from the inside and we'll be able to take it. Otherwise it will be very hard to achieve our goal." The plot he outlined was attractive to Khoja Burhan al-Din, and he gratified this trickster and fraud with all sorts of promises.

This heretic immediately led Ghiyas̱ to his tent, and throughout the evening he inveigled him with extensive hospitality, and conveyed promises from his khoja: "If Ghazi Beg abandons his own khojas in favor of us, and by some means betrays the city and delivers it to us, we will give him the governorship of Yarkand and put him in charge of all the amirs. His authority will extend across all the cities, and none will be able to contradict his decrees. As long as the rule of the Qalmaq *töräs*, /135b/ the Chinese emperor, and our own rule lasts, he will enjoy this hereditary office for seventy generations. If you can persuade Ghazi Beg of this, we'll also give you high position and a diploma of *tarkhan* status with a red seal for your descendants. If Ghazi Beg doesn't agree to this, however, and somehow the city falls to us, then we'll hunt him and his line down for seventy generations and slaughter them like sheep."

He concluded his promises and threats, had a letter written to the same effect, and handed it over. Ghiyas himself swore an oath on the affair. He explained that, to his knowledge, Ghazi had occasionally expressed hope that if he were to betray the city and give it up, Khoja Burhan al-Din might grant him the governorship again. The good-for-nothing Quzghun took these evil tidings as good news, and Khoja Burhan al-Din and everyone else rejoiced. They made sure that Ṣaliḥ Khalifa didn't catch a whiff of these plots, and the next morning they gave him leave to return with Ghiyas̱ at his side.

The envoys returned to the city safe and sound and explained to Khoja Jahan what had transpired on their mission. They also described the reception that their letter had received. Khoja Jahan expressed his resignation. "Whatever is ordained by divine fate," he said, "on my word /136a/ I am ready for it. I'm well past the point of being frightened by threats from people like this."

37. DEPUTY GOVERNOR NIYAZ TRIES TO TUNNEL OUT OF YARKAND

Let us leave Ghiyas̱ to start sweet-talking Ghazi Beg and now take up a story involving Deputy Governor Niyaz. His cousins, the sons of Bahadur Beg, along with Kucha governor Allah Quli Beg, his younger brother Muḥammad Yar Beg, his brother-in-law Shara Muḥammad Emin Beg, and other members of his family had come with the army of Khoja Burhan al-Din. These soulless individuals were always slandering the saintly family. Either they fixed a letter to an arrow and shot it in to Niyaz Beg, or some messenger went between them. In any case, this note said:

> Niyaz Beg, you and your family have long been our loyal devotees. You should now betray the city and deliver it to us. We will make you the commander in chief and governor of Yarkand, and the entire kingdom

will be under your authority. The governorship will be your hereditary legacy to pass on.

They made various false promises such as this, and at a few points they swore on the veracity of their words. They also threatened that if he didn't go along with them, then once they'd captured the city, they would kill all of his children and eradicate his line from the face of the earth.

When he became aware of this message, Deputy Governor Niyaz set about plotting to betray the city. He took counsel with a few close confidants, and they settled on the following plan: One side of his garden abutted the city wall, /136b/ with a thoroughfare in between that circled the city. If they dug a hole in a shed in this garden, then measured out thirty arm's lengths, they could make an entrance in a small hut outside the city wall and set up a gate with two flaps at either end of the tunnel. They would dig a tunnel large enough for two mounted men; when they'd finished it, they would inform Khoja Burhan al-Din's army, and in a single night around a thousand men could enter the city in turns. Then they'd combine these men with their own and charge at the palace, taking it by surprise. They'd go up to the drumhouse and strike up the *shadiyana* rhythm, and send criers out along all the streets to announce: "It is the age of Amursana and the emperor of China! It is the age of Khoja Burhan al-Din!" Then they would quickly take control of the four city gates, so that people could enter from outside, but no one could get out. Not a single creature would escape; they'd all be captured. It would be easy to take the city without any casualties.

Having decided on this plan of action, they set to work on the tunnel and exerted themselves digging it night and day. They removed the dirt during the night and filled two ice rooms that they had. The garden was empty, because it was the height of summer and not the season to spend time outdoors. At the entrance to the tunnel, they installed a doorway with two flaps, which was open by night and shut during the day. They had extended the tunnel some seven or eight arm's lengths toward the city wall, when a pious man among Niyaz Beg's staff became aware of the conspiracy. God Almighty gave him guidance, /137a/ and he immediately went to inform Khoja Jahan and point out the location of the tunnel. Niyaz Beg was called to the palace at once, and by surreptitious means Khoja Jahan sent someone to find out whether there actually was such a tunnel. The men who went saw the tunnel with their own eyes and came back and confirmed that it was true. Khoja Jahan ordered them to seize Niyaz Beg and lock him up, and they immediately took him into custody. Yet Khoja Jahan did not infringe on his family members, nor did he abuse or harm Niyaz Beg excessively. "Although he did not abide by his obligation of kinship," he said, "I will observe mine." Taking into account his duties to his father-in-law, he did not injure him. But henceforth he didn't allow his wife A'isha Beg, who was Deputy Governor Niyaz's daughter, to enter the palace at all.

As long as you're here, don't do harm to anyone,
Don't injure or abuse any soul.
Any pain you cause will backfire on you a hundredfold tomorrow,
So don't persecute someone else for your own gain.
Don't be devious and show disloyalty,
And commit such a weighty sin in both worlds.
Whatever you do, don't torture a poor man's heart,
In truth he is a king, don't treat him with such contempt.
You who took enemies into your confidence,
Don't befriend strangers, they'll betray your secrets.
An honest man is one whose affairs are unknown,
Have faith in him with heart and soul, don't shun him.
Any suffering and strife will come from the devious heavens,
Know yourself, swallow your pain, and don't show it to the enemy.
/137b/ O Ṣadiq, ask help from the spirits of saints past,
And don't be haughty: count yourself among the dogs of their dogs!

38. THE INTRIGUES OF ASHUR QUZI

It is time now for a story of some perfidious apprentices of the treacherous heavens. There was a cowardly man by the name of Ashur Quzi, who was originally one of the court merchants of the Qalmaqs. Khoja Jahan had patronized him and appointed him governor of Tagh Boyi.[229] Later, when Islamic rule was established, Khoja Jahan made him the royal provisioner, with the whole of Yarkand's affairs, including the resources of the palace, entrusted to him. He was practically the vizier of the entire kingdom; nothing could get done without his approval.

One can only marvel at the extent of this man's ingratitude. There were a few men, led by Khoja Maʿṣum and Mulla Ṣiddiq, who were sympathetic to the Qalmaqs and had some connection to them. They had initially been seized and put in prison, and spent a few days tied up there. Then word came to Khoja Jahan that the ground of the prison had become moist, with water seeping in, and that many of the criminals were in distress. Khoja Jahan instructed them to remove the criminals from the prison and assign each of them to be detained in someone's house, so they brought them up and divided them among the people. Ashur Quzi volunteered to take care of Mulla Ṣiddiq and Khoja Maʿṣum, and led them to his home. /138a/ While staying in Ashur Quzi's house for a few days, these men persuaded him to switch sides. One of Ashur Quzi's relatives had a servant by the name of Bay Polad, and through him he got a letter out to Khoja Burhan al-Din, which read as follows:

> I have repudiated my khojas, and recognized the authority of the Chinese emperor, Amursana, and Khoja Burhan al-Din. At dawn on Wednesday, have two thousand men charge on horseback toward the Yarkand citadel. Fifty or sixty men from our side will open fire toward the city, and another fifty will break down the city wall with spades and hoes and prepare an opening. The two thousand men should enter the city by that pathway. Then we will organize someone to go to the drumhouse and immediately beat the drums to announce: "It is the age of Amursana, the emperor of China, and Burhan al-Din!" In this way it will be easy to take the city while people are still unawares. None of the khojas or their entourage will get away; they'll all be captured.

When Khoja Burhan al-Din's people heard this, they were delighted, and Ashur Quzi was promised the deputy governorship of Yarkand. Bay Polad reentered the city by night and explained what had transpired. On the following day, which was a Tuesday, Ashur Quzi sent out his own servants and some others who were affiliated with Khoja Burhan al-Din and faithful to him. Then he consulted with his wives and sons. He had a wise and pious son by the name of Sulṭan Khoja, who was among Khoja Jahan's close retainers. He remonstrated and would not endorse the plan. "O father," he said, "what treachery and treason is this? /138b/ We'll never live down the sin of this affair. It is a serious crime to spurn Islam, join with the infidels, and enable their raiding and pillaging. Can you really countenance the idea of betraying the offspring of the Prophet like this? For years we have enjoyed the limitless generosity of these khojas of ours. We've eaten their salt and have obtained high office and wealth thanks to their patronage. To ignore all this and engage in such unseemly pursuits, and thereby earn ourselves a terrible reputation—these are not the actions of a human being! It would be much better to die with integrity than to become king of the world with this collar of ignominy around our necks. In this world they'll curse our name until Judgment Day, and in the next we'll face the anguish of Hell for all eternity. I have had enough of deeds like this, which sell out the religion for worldly gain. So has God."

Yet as much as he tried to dissuade them, his father said, "My son, this affair is decided, the time to forestall it has passed. Bay Polad has gone and brought back a signed compact. Tomorrow, on Wednesday, we should rise at dawn and prepare for eventualities." He showed him the letter, but his son continued to object and would not accept it. His father became enraged and lunged at him with his sword drawn, but his son evaded him and escaped. He made it out to the main street as they chased after him shouting "grab him!"

Racing toward the palace, Sulṭan Khoja entered without announcing himself and explained the situation to Khoja Jahan. Yet Khoja Jahan did not credit what he was saying. "You've decided to tell lies," he said. /139a/ "You've had a falling out with your father, and because of that you're making these serious accusations against him. How could he ever do such things?"

Sulṭan Khoja said, "Apologies, O refuge of the world, but there is not the slightest error in what I am saying. A plot is afoot, and it must be prevented. Delay will be a cause for regret." He swore an oath on the truth of what he was saying, and added, "Summon Bay Polad, and investigate these matters by interrogating him. If there is any mistake in what I am saying, then I deserve to be severely punished."

As he pressed his case, Khoja Jahan eventually discerned that there was truth in what he was saying, that this was no error. He ordered them to immediately bring Bay Polad. They presented him with hands tied before the throne, and Khoja Jahan drew his sword and brandished it at him. "You ingrate," he threatened him, "is this what is going on? Tell me the truth!

Whether you tell us or not, we'll kill you all the same, but it's better to die an honest man."

Bay Polad gave in. "Everything that you've heard is true," he admitted and explained the affair from start to finish. Khoja Jahan was enraged and ordered Ashur Quzi to be brought in. The two princes Khoja Quṭb al-Din and Khoja Abid set off to arrest him without causing a scene. Ashur Quzi was anxious at the fact that his son had run off in a rage /139b/ and had been unable to sit still at home. He was coming this way on his horse, wondering whether his son had divulged his secrets to anyone, when he ran into these princes. To reassure him, they said, "Ashur Quzi, we were just on our way to pay you a visit and hold a party. Did you find out and try to escape?"

"My apologies," Ashur Quzi replied, "I left the house completely unawares. Please do come now."

The princes declined the invitation: "We're on our way home now, but why don't you come to the palace too? Let's let go for a little outing. We'll take care of any work that needs to be done, and then see you home." With this, they led him toward the palace.

Once they reached the chancellery, they announced that they were arresting him by royal decree. They stripped Ashur Quzi of his clothes and brought him into Khoja Jahan's presence looking like a criminal. At the height of his rage, Khoja Jahan scolded him: "You wretched ingrate, where's that letter from your Qalmaq and your khoja?" Ashur Quzi wouldn't relent, so they decided to bring him face to face with his son, but his son didn't agree to a meeting, and even expressed his own willingness to die. As they increased the pressure on him, Ashur Quzi eventually confessed and described a chest, which some attendants went and fetched. Inside it was an envelope containing letter bearing a seal, which they took out and read. It described this conspiracy. Khoja Jahan ordered them to remove Ashur Quzi and imprison him, /140a/ and the courtiers bound him tightly.

The following day, Khoja Jahan assembled the entire population, including the scholars and amirs and the rest of the people of Yarkand. They sat Ashur Quzi in the middle of the audience hall, dressed in a tattered old cloak down to his knees, with his neck and hands bound with rough rope. Khoja Jahan described Ashur Quzi's treachery to those present in the assembly and addressed him in a fury: "You base, ill-born man. Didn't I once buy you from some Qalmaq and set you free? Didn't I aid you at various times of strife and save you? Did I not raise you to high office and assign the whole of my kingdom's affairs to you? I even trusted you with my own business and that of my family. For our food and clothing, we depended on you. You attained this honorable status thanks to us, but now you see fit to bring about our deaths, and the deaths of all of these people in the kingdom! You yourself should decide the penalty for this."

This heretic lowered his head, "The punishment for someone who has done such a thing is death," he said with resignation.

Khoja Jahan then /140b/ turned to the religious scholars and asked them: "According to the shariʿa, what is the punishment for someone like this, who has turned his back on Islam and aided the infidels?"

The scholars delivered a unanimous verdict: "The punishment for such an apostate is death."

Following this, Khoja Jahan addressed his high officials and the amirs of the kingdom: "What do you say?"

They all kissed the threshold and submitted: "O king of world, we have had enough of such deceitful men. Even if he was our father or our relative, he would still be our mortal enemy. We ally ourselves with God, the Prophet, and the king of Islam, not with thieves and reprobates. He has resigned himself to death, and the scholars have delivered their ruling. Even if that wasn't the case, to uphold authority and to serve as a warning, we would not be satisfied if you didn't kill him. There should not be any delay in carrying out the execution. This kingdom of Yarkand is a large city. Even if one or two hundred such men like him died, it wouldn't cause any weakness. One cannot maintain a kingdom without a firm hand. This man has done this today, but tomorrow it will be someone else, and the kingdom won't find stability. The enemy is strong; we must be on guard."

They urged him to quickly carry out the execution, but Prince Khoja Abdullah /141a/ said, "If we're to kill him, let's hang him tomorrow in the Friday bazaar. Everyone will see it with their own eyes and take heed." Khoja Jahan thought this was a good idea and delayed the execution to the following day.

Once the gathering had dispersed, Prince Khoja Abdullah summoned Governor Ghazi Beg and said to him, "The death sentence is entirely appropriate for this Ashur Quzi, whether in terms of the shariʿa, or in terms of pragmatic considerations. There is one issue, though, one sense in which execution may not be appropriate, which is that if someone else commits such treachery, sons will not inform on their fathers, or fathers their sons, or brothers their brothers. They might reconcile themselves to anything else except their execution, so they may decide to keep it secret, since if they report them they'll be killed. If Sulṭan Khoja were to beg forgiveness for Ashur Quzi's mortal sin, then we could favor him and confiscate the wealth in his house for the army, so as to supply us for holy war."

This suggestion appealed to Khoja Jahan, and he issued a command to this effect. The next day, however, the people of the kingdom again came to urge the execution. Khoja Jahan said, "His son Sulṭan Khoja has requested forgiveness from me for his father's sin, and I am now asking it from you."

He tried to allay the clamor for his execution, but the amirs insisted: "In an affair such as this, the kingdom won't come to rest without killing a few people. People won't learn their lesson." In the face of much importuning, /141b/ Khoja Jahan had Bay Polad and Khoja Maʿṣum hanged, and the hearts of the people were put at ease.

Don't stir up strife, take care to keep yourself innocent,
Put trust in God and stay above the riffraff.
Stop trying all these strategies, don't waste your efforts,
Keep yourself humble in the eyes of the world.
Don't do anything that will cause pain,
Whatever you do now, brace for something ten times as bad.
Don't mingle with the people of the world, they have no faith,
They'll come for you, so find some remedy in advance!
Don't seek worldly luxury, there's no rest for you here,
Unroll your prayer mat in a tranquil corner.
Ṣadiq, virtue has no significance in this age,
Acquire abundant wealth, or else stay the son of an akhund.

39. KHOJA INAYAT FALLS ON THE BATTLEFIELD

Let us now return to the story of Khoja Burhan al-Din, who was deeply disturbed that neither Deputy Governor Niyaz's compact nor Ashur Quzi's had borne fruit. Each day his men would charge at the city but be driven back.

From the city of Yarkand, there were also a few brave champions who would come out each day and pile up the enemy dead, charging at them with a cry of "O Ḥusayn!" They were like warlike lions swinging their claws at wild beasts, or seven-headed dragons spewing fire from their mouth, causing mayhem as /142a/ everyone scrambled to save themselves. All were struck dumb in astonishment. In particular, there was a brave warrior mounted on a piebald horse who was the spitting image of the Lion of the Lord Ali: Khoja Inayat. He was unique in his boldness, a tiger who broke ranks and a wrestling Rustam. The entire army of Khoja Burhan al-Din was distraught at his presence. They would always complain, "Woe, a hundred times woe, at this piebald-riding warrior. He'll wipe out our entire army one by one. If we were delivered from this skillful man, either by capturing or killing him, then we'd conquer the city of Yarkand. But as long as he's around, none of us will get out of here alive."

The bravery of one man can make an army bold,
And give the drinking glass a red tinge.

A few days went by in this fashion. Yet the stars of ill fate in the treacherous heavenly sphere were all positioned above the saints, and as an evil harbinger of this misfortune, one devious heretic stealthily took aim and shot at Khoja Inayat with a large cannon. It struck the right side of his face and broke his skull. Despite this he managed get off a shot, which flew and penetrated that heretic's chest, and he fell to the ground. Khoja Inayat lost consciousness and the world became dark to him. In his senseless state, he let go of the reins, but his piebald horse carried its master toward the city and brought him to the gate. /142b/ They let him through and conveyed him to his home, and on the third day he passed into the eternal realm.

Khoja Jahan and all the princes came and performed prayers for him in a huge mourning ceremony with much almsgiving, and they buried him in the Golden Shrine. "This mourning is not for Khoja Inayat alone," Khoja Jahan said, "but for all of us. This is the final sign that our age has come to an end. There will soon come a time when there will be no alms to give, or anyone to mourn for us and bury us. We must now hold our mourning ceremony ourselves and perform almsgiving while we still have our health." So saying, he made the people of Yarkand rich and wealthy.

Khoja Burhan al-Din's forces were delighted to be rid of this man riding the piebald horse, and each day they attacked with more ferocity than before. Yet when the champions of Yarkand confronted them, they couldn't stand their ground and had no choice but to withdraw defeated, because a divine zeal still prevailed among the army of Islam that was simply impossible to resist. Each day they built siege platforms at the level of the city wall or higher and climbed atop and shot at people on the walls and inside the city. But the next morning the brave men of Yarkand would go out and set fire to them with gunpowder. The flames would rise as high as the sky and they would be reduced to ashes, /143a/ and the timber that had been accumulated with difficulty went to waste in a flash. They would capture some of the people assigned to the siege platforms, some would be burned to death, while those who were quick enough would get away. These events occurred most frequently at the Qabaq Atqu Gate, and therefore this gate was Khoja Abdullah's assigned battle station. Some time passed in this fashion; Khoja Burhan al-Din's troops became extremely agitated and impatient, and the Kirghiz were also losing hope. None of them had the strength left to take to the battlefield.

40. SUSPICION FALLS ON GHAZI ONCE AGAIN

With that side in such a demoralized state, let us continue the story of the scheming Ghazi Beg. In faithlessness and treachery, he was truly without peer, and on the day that Ghiyas̲ brought Khoja Burhan al-Din's letters and started to cajole him, his conspiratorial juices stirred. He hardened his heart against the princes and dedicated himself to the side of Khoja Burhan al-Din. His battle station was along a wall at one of the gates, and he had full control of it. He would send out agents either through the gate or across the wall, and sometimes agents would arrive from outside and make pledges on the Quran, promising him the governorship of Yarkand. Some time went by in this fashion, until word of these secret dealings made its way to the princes and the staff of the palace. One by one, they brought it to Khoja Jahan's attention, /143b/ and they all gave him the same advice: "This Ghazi is an extremely deceptive and devious man. We've had long experience of his treachery. There's a well-known hadith that EVERYTHING THAT OCCURS TWICE WILL OCCUR FOR A THIRD TIME. This trickster's plots have been so frequent that there can be no doubt that he will betray you. What is needed is to seize this ingrate and his son and bind them, so that everyone's anxieties can be put to rest. If we don't take care of him in advance, he won't hold back from conceiving some plot against us. In the end we'll regret it, not that it will do us any good."

"My sons," Khoja Jahan replied to this counsel, "you're talking about conflict and double-crossing, but I am more interested in faith and piety. You speak in terms of strategies, but I speak in terms of fate. You're still thinking of ingenuity and imagination, but I have come to a position of resignation and trust in God."

> A heart that holds onto all kinds of desires won't find rest,
> I only stilled my soul when I entered the path of resignation.[230]

"Ghazi and I have placed our hands on the Quran several times. He has sworn oaths vowing not to show disloyalty toward me, and I have ratified his oaths and sworn to show confidence in him. Even if he doesn't keep his oath, for my part I will. Remaining true to one's oath is a sign of faith in Islam. There is a hadith from the Prophet that says HE WHO BREAKS HIS VOW HAS NO FAITH. I have need of faith, even if Ghazi doesn't. /144a/ Brave men who fail to remain true to their oath will be excluded from the ranks of the honorable and will forfeit the right to be considered men at all."

> A man's standing in the world lies in his words,
> Someone who breaks their word will receive no recognition.[231]

"One must also take into account that there are events within events, and secret designs behind everything that occurs. A servant of God must take heed of divine fate; nothing will come of exertions and strategizing. The inner truth of this affair will become known soon enough; right now there is no need for excessive analysis." So saying, he rebuffed the princes.

41. THE MEN OF YARKAND MARCH FORTH

Let us now continue the story of the trickster Ghazi. Not a night went by that this heretic didn't send a secret agent out to Khoja Burhan al-Din and inform him of events and intelligence from inside the city. Sometimes from this direction and sometimes from that, furtive spies would carry information on where there was some gap in the walls, or on locations where a breach could be made from outside, or on any other issue on which they might conspire to benefit Khoja Burhan al-Din's army and bring defeat to the army of the princes.

Some days went by like this, but they couldn't do any damage and failed to compromise the city in any way. Khoja Burhan al-Din became distressed, and the Kirghiz even more so. He secretly dispatched someone to Ghazi to elicit some plan from him: "We've become very anxious; how long are we going to sit here for? If you could outline for us some kind of plan that we can act upon and capture the city, or else if you yourself could try something, we'll make sure you are recompensed for this service from the *törä* /144b/ and will put the Six Cities (Altishahr) under your control."

Ghazi sent the spy back, telling him that he would send his reply the following day, and set about thinking up a trap or some deception. He ran through various ploys in his head. In the end, he decided that he would mobilize the Yarkand army and lead them out, then flee in retreat, thereby handing the city of Yarkand to Khoja Burhan al-Din.

He fixed upon this course of action and then went into Khoja Jahan's presence. "O just king," he pleaded, "how long will we stay imprisoned inside the city in this way, confined in a weak and helpless state? Eventually the time will come when the Muslims inside the city will start to suffer. People's mounts will go lame, and some might get hungry and slaughter them. Most of the population will be weakened by hunger and thirst and lose their courage and bravery. In that situation, everyone's abilities will be impaired, but regretting the situation then will be no use. While we still can, it would be better for us to enroll everyone between the ages of twelve and seventy into the army and all attack at once, and with a single blow rout the army of Khoja Burhan al-Din. That way we can be delivered from them."

His advice /145a/ seemed sensible to Khoja Jahan and everyone else, so the command went out that the Muslims should prepare for battle with the infidel army. Heralds went from street to street and lane to lane announcing, "O people! O nation of Muḥammad! O Muslims! Ready yourselves for battle, for the army of the infidel is at hand and is pressing its advantage against us. To fight now has become an obligation on all. Husbands should present themselves on the field of battle without gaining permission from their wives, and slaves without asking their master. Should you die, you'll be an exulted martyr, and if you kill, you'll be a holy warrior. If you avoid this fight, you'll earn the name of apostate and heretic and be liable to the censure of the noble shariʿa. Prayers be upon Muḥammad!"

As the shouts of the heralds rang out, Khoja Jahan ordered that they beat the drums of war, and they struck up the celestial music of Alexander's kettledrum, Jamshid's horn, the dulcimer of Giyumars son of Adam, and Kaykhusraw's clarinet. The thunderous and awe-inspiring sound tore the hearts of the duplicitous enemies into a hundred pieces. The champions and brave men steeled themselves, readied their equipment, and sharpened their blades, while some cowards were contemplating escape and trying to think of somewhere to hide.

42. GHAZI BETRAYS THE FIELD

Let us leave each man to spend the evening awake in his own way, while we take up the story of the deceitful Ghazi. During the night, /145b/ he dispatched a messenger with a letter to Khoja Burhan al-Din. Khoja Burhan al-Din, surrounded by his pillars of state, took the letter from the messenger and read it. This is what it said:

> Your most humble servant Ghazi submits that for a long time now I have been unable to conceive of a plan to take the city, and the strategies that I devised failed to produce results. Now, should fortune favor the emperor, Amursana, and Khoja Burhan al-Din, I have come up with a scheme that may come to fruition. Tomorrow morning everyone from seven to seventy years of age have decided to go out and give battle. After we've engaged once or twice, I will fake a maneuver from the right to the left, and whichever direction I go in, you should attack toward that side. Then I will break ranks and flee backward. At that point you can decide how to go about the massacre. I will take care of the remaining tasks inside the city, and you will see what services I perform.

When Khoja Burhan al-Din heard this news, he rejoiced with his followers, and they prepared for battle. He sent the messenger back with an abundance of promises. Meanwhile, in the city that night, fathers were farewelling their sons, and brothers farewelling their brothers. Their previous enthusiasm was at a low ebb, because the unlucky star that divine decree had fixed above them had reached its zenith, and from its influence tremors were making their way into their hearts, and a quivering into their bodies.

/146a/ In this anxious state, they caught wafts of the dawn breeze, and it lifted their spirits a little. They armed and equipped themselves and marched out the city gates. By the time they had been defeated and were retreating, the army still hadn't finished exiting the gates. Some who were good with numbers estimated this army of Yarkand to be close to forty thousand. For his part, Khoja Burhan al-Din, as in the past, drew up his left and right flanks, the center, and the wings, like pieces on a chessboard. Among his forces were men from cities such as Kashgar, Yangiḥiṣar, Aqsu, Ush, Kucha, Sayram, Bay, Shahyar, and the Dolan. Alongside these there were Qalmaqs, Chinese, and mountain men, plus various tribes of Kirghiz, including the Qushchi led by Qubad, the Toqquz Qipchaq led by Ṣufi Mirza and Ḥakim Mirza, the Taz Qipchaq led by Umar Mirza, as well as Möngke with his tribe, and the Chongbaghish. Yet in the face of the army of Yarkand, the army just described was but a drop in the ocean or a speck of dust before the sun.

The two seas of soldiers drew up their ranks facing one another, as if on both sides two imposing mountains had arisen. Swift and skillful cavalrymen rode across the battlefield, sometimes breaking through the lines on the right, and sometimes on the left, and creating a tumult. Even though Ghazi tried to prevent them, they drove Khoja Burhan al-Din's army backward a distance of several *farsang*. It almost seemed as if they were about to turn Khoja Burhan al-Din's army /146b/ into a pile of corpses. If they had all attacked at once, they might've reduced them to SCATTERED DUST [25:23]. Khoja Burhan al-Din's troops had completely given up the fight and were in a desperate state. No one had the strength to take a step forward, and Qubad had withdrawn with his people and was looking on. But then Ghazi made a couple of feints to the center and the left, pretending to scold his troops, and in this situation a few of Khoja Burhan al-Din's troops made to attack in Ghazi's direction. Taking advantage of the opportunity, Ghazi used this excuse to furl his standards and quickly flee backward. The Kirghiz saw this and charged after them. The Muslims in the army of Yarkand were confused and had no choice but to retreat: it was as though an army had descended from heaven to press them. They struck at the Muslims and laid out the corpses like stones in a valley, with blood flowing like rivers as far as the Qabaq Atqu Gate. People couldn't fit through the gate, so they trampled each other underfoot, and some were hauled up over the wall with ropes.

Instead of going into battle, Khoja Abdullah had remained in the guard tower above the gate, organizing for reinforcements to be dispatched and supervising the defense of the city. He was enraged when he witnessed what was going on, but there was work to be done at the gate and he couldn't leave. /147a/ Eventually he dropped down by rope from the city wall, and he and his retainers Tuqal, Urus, Khojam Yar, and Ichmish made some sorties into the fray with their spears. In fright, this horde of people divided to make way for them, and after they had gone through, they reunited as a single body. If they went charging in one direction, then the attack would come from a different direction. The forty or fifty thousand people who were in retreat couldn't bear to look back; they simply couldn't believe what was going on. Eventually Khoja Abdullah had to get back to the wall again. Until nightfall the slaughter of the Muslims continued. Those who got inside the gate were safe, but the rest perished, and the gate was shut fast. Throughout the night until dawn, they executed those who were half dead, stripped the corpses naked, and put them into pairs.

> There is no one so despotic as this tribe in the world,
> No tyrant has ever exhibited such cruelty.

43. THE EXODUS FROM YARKAND

Let us leave Khoja Burhan al-Din's army as they happily go about their pillaging and turn to a tale from inside the city. When the treacherous Ghazi broke ranks and came fleeing in, he fortified himself in his courtyard. That evening he didn't go to the palace, nor did he go the next day, and by morning word had spread among the population that it was Ghazi Beg who had thrown the army into disarray and fled. Within the city, the scene was one of grief and mourning. /147b/ Someone was crying for their father, someone else for their elder brother. One was mourning their younger brother, and another their son. No one was untouched by the grief; everyone was crying and weeping. Khoja Jahan, the princes, and all those attached to the palace were debating what the solution now was. They had nowhere to go, but no strength to stay.

> I have neither the strength to go, nor the resilience to remain,
> Such is the condition you've reduced me to, O heart.

They couldn't come to any decision. Several people were sent out to summon Ghazi, but he wouldn't agree to come. The day passed in this way and turned to evening, and again Khoja Jahan sent out his close confidants to go and tell Ghazi to come. He said that he would, but in the end he didn't. His behavior was becoming increasingly seditious.

Khoja Jahan then had them summon the *aʿlam akhund* of Yarkand at that time, who was Akhund Umar Baqi. "Akhund," he instructed him, "please go and convince Governor Ghazi to come. What reason is there for him not to? We've sworn oaths not to betray one another and have made vows on the Quran. Let him come for once and tell us what the best course of action is: Would it be better for us to stay inside the city, or should we evacuate it and leave? And if we leave, which direction would be best? For years we have eaten and spoken in common. In such desperate times, it would not do for him to turn his back on us. If someone fails to show faith in us, we won't show faith in him either. A believer is a fellow believer's brother. Our friendship is PURE IN THE FACE OF GOD, what need is there for dissimulation?"

> /148a/ *The sign of a friend is a bet on the day of need,*
> *Request a loan from a friend to try him out.*[232]

> *A companion is one who holds onto a friend's hand*
> *In his state of distress and despondency.*[233]

> When friendly eyes cast a hostile glance, it is hard on the heart;
> Enemies never gave you their sympathy, and they won't take it away.

"Selling out the religion for the sake of this transient world is not the act of a wise man. I could go on, but I'll keep this brief: a hint should be enough for someone intelligent." He finished talking and dismissed the akhund.

The akhund came and offered his advice to Ghazi. The conversation ran in all directions, and in the end they decided that it would be best for Ghazi not to go and instead to say in reply that he was afraid of the princes, that all sorts of troubling rumors were circulating, and that he needed to compose himself for a few days before going.

Some time went by, and servants came several times to fetch the akhund, but they didn't allow them to enter, and instead started to abuse them. Ghazi's attendants had gathered, and those in the city who were of bad faith were also mingling around, so as to prevent any outsiders' approaching that neighborhood. They had mustered the musketeers on that side of the city walls and brought them into Ghazi's courtyard, and if they met someone associated with the palace, then they would carry themselves in a hostile fashion. Servants who went and witnessed this reported it to the palace, and some started to openly rebuke Ghazi before Khoja Jahan, /148b/ urging him to seize and detain him. Khoja Jahan said:

A heart that holds onto all kinds of desires won't find rest,
I only stilled my soul when I entered the path of resignation.

"The time for action has come and gone, my friends. Don't curse him. Whatever is divine fate, I am ready for it. I made an oath on the Quran not to break faith with Ghazi. If he chooses to subject me to such trials and treachery, then I refer him to the Quran, my oath, and my forefather. Let's see whether Ghazi can hold onto power here for a year or even six months. Whatever is coming to us, it will come his way to an even greater degree. This whirlpool of calamities won't simply drown us alone, and the dragon of misfortune won't just breathe its fire at us. There'll be neither friend nor enemy left remaining here; neither infidel, nor Muslim; neither master, nor disciple. This conflagration will engulf great and small alike."

A wrenching love has arrived, drop your deceit wise man,
It has come like a lion tearing earth and sky, flee you fox![234]

This is simply the start of love, don't cry so much,
For this whirlpool of disgrace will conquer the whole world.

Akhund Umar Baqi eventually returned with Ghazi's devious reply and transmitted some threatening words from that side. Khoja Jahan kept silent while the akhund spoke and then gave him leave to depart. Again that evening, the princes, /149a/ the nobility, and their following held a few meetings before heading out to their battle stations. All kinds of plans were discussed. Some said it was better to stay inside the city, while some, including Khoja Abdullah and Shihab al-Din Bakavul, said they should immediately go and lay siege to Ghazi's courtyard and capture him. Once they had Ghazi, they said, it wouldn't be surprising if the enemies simply lost hope and retreated in disarray. Even if they didn't withdraw, they'd at least be able to hold onto the city.

Yet Khoja Jahan didn't endorse this idea and said to them directly: "With a strong enemy outside, and with our army having suffered such a resounding defeat, it wouldn't be wise to provoke a disturbance inside the city."

In the end, they made up their minds to leave immediately and travel through the night. Crossing the desert and the river, they would make for a cave in a certain mountain that had only one entrance, but inside of which there was a huge pasture with enough fodder and water to survive for a few years without any difficulty. With a single man sitting by the entrance with a musket, an enemy force of a hundred thousand wouldn't be able to come close. They reckoned that by the time the enemies realized and came after them, they'd be able to reach the cave. They had no idea what fate had in store for them.

When the Decree comes, the physician is made foolish.[235]

Acting on this plan, they prepared to evacuate. Some people's entire family were aware of what was going on, /149b/ while there were others whose fathers were in the know but whose sons remained ignorant inside the city. Some were on horseback, others rode camels, and there were some who had no mount at all and had to walk, without any equipment or supplies for the journey. In this disheveled state, they exited via the Maskhara Gate and took off down the Qarghaliq road. For a while they kept to the highway, before heading into the wilderness, since the Kirghiz were lying in wait along the road. With great trepidation, they entered indescribably wild terrain: it was too dense for the sun to shine in, or for the ground, or indeed anything in any direction, to be seen. Such was the urgency of the situation that if a father fell down, his son had no chance to help him up, and if a son was dying, his father could not comfort him. Men had no way to be men, nor wives to be wives. Fathers were oblivious to the condition of their sons, and mothers to that of their daughters. The terrain was harsher than the plain of Judgment Day. Wherever you tried to move, you simply couldn't get through. The trees had roots here and branches there, all intertwined with one another. Their twisted limbs spread across an entire *farsang* in a knotted embrace and blocked the way. It was beyond human strength to crawl through, and if someone somehow managed to struggle past one, there would be another one in front of them, even more intimidating. /150a/ Some people suffered cuts to their bodies, and others had their clothes torn. Every tree was left waving pieces of clothing like flags.

Besides these trials, the Zarafshan River, which because of its swift current was known as the Fast-flowing (Tezab) River, confronted them at several points.[236] The river was even more of a challenge than the jungle, because it was full of ice. The ice in the middle had only recently begun to flow, and it was piled up on the banks up to around the height of a man—sometimes more, sometimes less. In the channel itself there were ice floes, some of them the size of a house. If someone's mount was struck, a strong horse could occasionally stand up to it, but others would tumble helplessly into the water, plunging their riders into the river. Sometimes they would jump from the ice into the water, and by the time they came out, their saddle strap would've broken and slipped from their backs. Once they had fallen into the water with their saddlecloth, then it wasn't possible to ride them anymore—you'd simply freeze. Along with all these hardships, the good-for-nothing Kirghiz were in hot pursuit and would not leave them in peace. If anyone fell behind or strayed off in some direction, they would swoop in and capture them, or simply kill them. If you made it out of the jungle, then you faced the trial of the river, and if you got past the river, then you faced the trial of the jungle again, but the worst torment of all was the wicked Kirghiz.

Bring me a glass of wine, cupbearer,
I'll say a few words about the cruelty of the universe.
I have some complaints to make about times past,

A story of what the saints went through.
Such calamities struck these princes,
All of them upstanding and highborn,
The woes of the world from start to finish,
Were brought down upon them one by one.
Has what befell them ever occurred to anyone else?
/150b/ Which infidels or Muslims experienced this?
Mortal enemies and men with evil hearts,
Black-tongued serpents and scorpions,
Prevailed against them,
All traitors and bloodsucking fanatics.
By nature they have no pity,
They live luxuriously off the blood of others.
A description of their evil would never end,
Whatever one says, it's enough, O people!
I'd be embarrassed to give an account of them,
It's obscene to relate something so obscene.
So I'll describe instead that Ṣaḥibqiran,[237]
Stories and depictions of him are more to my taste.
With those saintly families fleeing,
Seeking refuge from the enemy's horsemen,
They withdrew to a wasteland of nonexistence,
Abandoning their land and home with ill-fated steps.
Not just a wasteland but a jungle of calamity,
Not just a jungle but the claws of lions.
Thorny trees like needles,
Striking their limbs like sharp daggers.
Or the talons of tigers,
Slicing through as if they were arrows.
Or shall I make mention of the river,
I've much to say, but it would only give a hint.
Everything became topsy-turvy in this time,
Without differentiating good from bad,
Once a river drowned the men of Pharaoh
And let the tribe of Moses pass safely,
But now it drowns the tribe of Moses,

And lets the men of Pharaoh cross without harm.
Cut short your words, O Ṣadiq,
Whatever the outcome of this affair, it is predetermined.
You could complain at heaven for a hundred years,
And still not finish, there's no end to it!

44. GHAZI BEG SEIZES CONTROL OF YARKAND

While these princes and their families make their difficult way through the wilderness, let us follow the story of the ill-willed Ghazi Beg. On the night when the princes evacuated the city and withdrew, the treacherous Ghazi immediately told his own associates to go and drum up the *shadiyana* rhythm. All around the city, from street to street, the criers announced: "It is the age of the emperor of China, /151a/ Amursana, and Khoja Burhan al-Din!" Ghazi sent some of his own sons with lavish tribute gifts out to Khoja Burhan al-Din with this message:

> As well as bringing about the defeat of the khojas, I have rebelled inside the city with my own kinsmen. I have declared against the khojas and intimidated them into leaving. An army should quickly pursue them and give them their just deserts. This is not my responsibility; it is now up to you. If they manage to get away to somewhere defensible, it won't be in your interests. Indeed, if one of them remains alive anywhere, you won't be able to rest easy in these parts. It is up to you what to do.

When Khoja Burhan al-Din became aware of this message, in high spirits he summoned his retinue and explained what had occurred. He chose Möngke from among the Kirghiz, one *jaisang* from the Qalmaqs, along with the Yarkand governor (*sic*) Raḥman Quli, the Yangiḥiṣar governor Abdullah the Kirghiz, Sariq Yasavul, Mulla Yoldash, Abd al-Wahhab's son Abd al-Sattar, Bahadur Beg's son Shara Muḥammad Emin, Emin's son Abd al-Raḥman Zarqi, as well as their retinues, and other swift and merciless evildoers, and dispatched them with an army in pursuit: "Quickly go and block their path," he said, "and bring them back captive. On no account should you show them any kindness, you'll feel my wrath if you do." With these final instructions, he sent them on their way.

45. DEPUTY GOVERNOR NIYAZ IS FREED

Let these impure men set out, while we have a story /151b/ from inside the city, where Deputy Governor Niyaz was tied up inside the palace. As soon as the princes exited the palace gate, he freed himself from his restraints and took control of the palace's affairs. One of Khoja Jahan's wives, A'isha Beg, was his daughter. He took possession of her entire quarters and everything inside, while Ghazi took the rest, and the people of the city also enriched themselves.[238]

46. THE FLIGHT OF THE KHOJAS

We turn now to those foul individuals who had taken off in pursuit. With urgency and haste they picked up the trail, and by dawn they had caught up with the princes. The devotees of the holy family were freezing in the cold. Some had plunged into the water and come out. Some had children in their arms. Some people were walking with their families; others were leading them on horseback. They were in a state of utter disarray when the enemies came upon them from all sides. The party of the princes had originally consisted of around a thousand people, but some had fled and others had met with misfortune, and so only four or five hundred remained. Among these, none had the strength to withstand the enemies, apart from that roaring lion and hard-hitting Rustam, Khoja Abdullah. /152a/ With inspirational courage and a few brave souls as his companions, he would sometimes throw himself at the center, and sometimes to the right and left, or strike from behind. On whichever side the enemy pressed, he would boldly present himself.

Apart from these heroic individuals, everyone else was so anxious at their own plight that they couldn't even bring themselves to look at the enemy. One of Khoja Jahan's wives, whose name was Sharifa Aghacha, was with child, and it so happened she went into labor that night. Sharifa Aghacha was the kindliest of Khoja Jahan's wives. He spent all his private retreats with her, and all the servants had their needs met through her interventions. Khoja Jahan was so devoted to her that he would recite his poetry to her. It hadn't been possible to leave her behind, so they had brought her out with them, accompanied by a number of chaperones. It was quite a spectacle: a piercing cry and a sound of moaning that would melt a stone. My informants tell me that when the time came, the lady had no choice but to dismount and lie down to give birth. When she was in that condition, one of her own entourage came and stole her horse and left. The bloodthirsty enemies were closing in from behind, and in front of her the princes had no knowledge of what was going on. They had no capacity to retrieve her, /152b/ and no one had the wherewithal to heed to her cries. She was simply left there helpless and lost.

47. LAST STAND ON THE BANKS OF THE ZARAFSHAN

Let us continue the story of the princes. That imperious Rustam, that vision of the roaring Lion of God, Khoja Abdullah was still confronting this mass of staunch enemies. Wherever they attacked, he would exhibit his prowess; not one of his shots failed to lay low some notorious foe. This was how things stood until the time of the evening prayer, with people clashing from both sides. In those circumstances, the Zarafshan River again loomed before them. Enemies in front had already stolen a march and occupied the best positions along the river, with their muskets aimed and at the ready. The loyal devotees were unable to make use of the good terrain, so despite the difficulty, they threw themselves into the river. Just at that point, when those at the front were already in the water and those behind were still approaching it, the enemies lying in ambush redoubled their assault. Witnessing this, Adil Shah Darkhan's son Ismaʿil Beg, who was one of Khoja Jahan's close retainers, took a group of people and switched to the enemy side.[239] Seeing this, those on the Muslim side despaired, while the enemies gained strength and spurred their horses into the fray. Khoja Abdullah urged his horse on and took up a position in front of them, but the enemies continued to hurtle forward, oblivious to him. He let off one shot, but still they took no notice. /153a/ He took aim a second time, and this shot struck someone, the arrow flying through his cuirass and burying itself in the ground.[240]

Upon seeing this, the enemies were bewildered and took a step back. This wretched soul had been the commanding officer of the army, and no one had ever been able to best him in a test of strength. He had entered the melee hurling foul abuse at the princes, and had the blood of several Muslims on his hands. His armor consisted of two waistcoats, two thick tunics, chain-mail, and a steel cuirass. When the enemies saw the arrow go through this armor and lodge in the ground, they were struck dumb, and lost all strength. Khoja Abdullah swiftly rode in and seized the reins of that evil man's horse, and he retrieved his helmet from where he lay and tied it to his belt. He struck at him with his battle-axe, and the ring of the axe caught on his chainmail. The man was pulled along for a few paces, before the mail came loose and he fell back to the ground. The Muslims dragged his body to the river and threw him in. As it carried him away, a cry of despair arose from the enemies, and some of them ran to fish the sinner's body out of the water.

The Muslims were now divided into three groups: one party had made it across the river, one was still in the water, and one was left on this side. Khoja Abdullah was shouting: "If you're a man, stay on this side, don't flee! Put yourselves in the firing line! Whether you flee from these infidels or not, /153b/ they'll kill you. If you're taken alive, they'll kill you. There's no choice other than death. Instead of dying with indignity, it's better to die fighting back." But his calls to arms had no impact on anyone except a few of his retainers. Everyone was worried about themselves and had no thought for anyone else. If anyone escaped the enemy's grasp, they gave up on them, since they knew that once they were put to flight, the enemy would eventually round up everyone else. They were traveling with their whole families, and as fast as they moved, they were still slower than the pace of the enemy, who were riding well-fed mounts and traveling by the only good road. If they decided to all attack the enemy at once, then even if the enemies eventually triumphed, they might have struck them a few blows, but they had no strength to do this. Although Khoja Abdullah was a brave and mighty man, he was no match for a hundred men, let alone a thousand. Before he had dealt with one side, they would attack from a different flank and pile up the dead.

If the ants unite as one,
They'll tear the skin off a fierce lion.

Though a lion is superior in boldness and bravery,
Should fate decree it, even ants will lay him low.

Khoja Abdullah raised a great cry, but in the end, since no one was taking any notice, he threw himself into the river in disgust. When the enemies /154a/ saw this, they assailed the Muslims left on the riverbank, among them Khoja Yusuf's young son, whose name was Khoja Burhan al-Din but who was known as Erke Khoja. A foul infidel came and smote him so hard that his blade went right through him. The prince fell unconscious from his horse and obtained the rank of martyrdom. His blessed body was trampled beneath the feet of the enemies, but the bird of his soul alighted on the tree of Paradise. TRULY WE ARE GOD'S, AND UNTO HIM WE RETURN [2:156]. That infidel then turned back and hacked at his head with his moon-shaped battle-axe. A man named Mulla Yoldash was also killed by an arrow to the head. Watching this, the Muslims lost their nerve, and everyone threw themselves helplessly into the river.

Particular mention must be made of that young lion and champion of the battlefield, Khojam Naẓar Khoja, whose eyes went dark to this world when he saw his prince being martyred. He seemed drunk and unconscious like a rabid camel, with bloodshot eyes like a male lion separated from its mate, unable to tell black from white. He let off such a volley of spears and arrows, no one would believe me if I described it, for the enemies were so numerous, made up of Qalmaqs, Kirghiz, mountain men, and locals, each one of them a renowned warrior. In despair, Khojam Naẓar Khoja picked up Erke Khoja's blessed body /154b/ and carried it away on his horse. The enemies came after him in pursuit, and in the circumstances he estimated that he wouldn't make it across the river, for there was mud and ice to evade which was piled up to the height of a man. He thought it better to leave the body on dry land than in the river, even if in the hands of the enemy, so he laid it down and dove into the water. Khoja Abdullah was also in the river and caught sight of his brother's body. He took one brave glance at it and did not look at it again.

A large number of people had entered the river by the same path. When they were still in the calm section, the swell rose up from behind, surging until it carried the Muslims away. A great hue and cry went up as they were engulfed. The enemies on one bank seized some of the Muslims who were swept back from the other side. Many were martyred, but some made it safely to the opposite bank. Khojam Naẓar Khoja was floating downstream, with some enemies chasing him. One hefty foe struck at him from behind, but he was wearing two suits of chainmail and a thick tunic, and the spear didn't have any effect. He got his two feet into his stirrups and lifted himself up onto the saddle and went about twenty or thirty paces without falling off. People who were observing from both sides looked on with admiration. But just at that point, another strong enemy /155a/ came up and struck directly at his side, and he fell limpid from his horse into the river. He was swept downstream for forty or fifty paces. On both sides of the river, the tall ice was impenetrable, and besides his clothes he was wearing two coats of mail, a woolen tunic, and two jackets, which made it impossible to lift him out. Khoja Abdullah realized the situation and took his bow from its case and broke it. He took hold of one end and held the other end out to catch the prince and pull him in. He saw that all of his limbs were on the verge of freezing, so he immediately stripped off his clothes and dressed him in his own waistcoat.

48. THE PRINCES YIELD TO THE ENEMY

As for the other families, although the princes had all made it to the other side of the river, the Muslims saw that none of them had their parents with them, or their children. /155b/ Most noticeable was the fact that Erke Khoja was missing. They all cried out in mourning, enough to bring heaven and earth itself to tears, and cause rocks to melt. In the midst of all this, Khoja Abdullah cast an angry glare at the princes and nobles: "You fools, why are you moping and crying? Would you really weep this much at the death of a few children? What will you do when many more than this die? When you yourselves die, what will you do?"

> Mourn for yourself, for you will die a sinner,
> Why cry for a child who has died innocent?

"O people! Anyone among us who falls into the hands of these murderous enemies must wash their hands of life and not give a thought to surviving.

If you have any life left in you, stand firm and be brave! Don't be taken alive by this group, for whatever you do, they'll kill you. In particular, if you belong to the line of sayyids, stand up to the arrows of the enemy. Don't fall captive to these vampires, for they'll kill you without hesitation, and with abuse and ignominy. Don't forfeit your honor, and you'll die an easy death, without suffering torture and pain." As he stood there proclaiming this, the crying subsided a little. Yet each was still anxious at their own fate. In one direction there was fighting, in another there was crying and wailing, and elsewhere people were starting to negotiate.

By way of invitation to peace talks, a few deceptive tricksters from the enemy shouted out from across the river: "O Muslims, why expose yourselves to these hardships and cause such suffering? Why endure pain for no purpose and bring about your downfall? Come, turn back from the grave, and resign yourselves to fate. The khojas on both sides originate from the same source, there is no alienation between them. Affairs will be decided according to Khoja Jahan's wishes. If his desire is to visit the Holy Shrines, then we will prepare his baggage and see him off to India, and then welcome him back with respect. If he desires these territories, then let him choose either the throne of Yangiḥiṣar or Khotan and take up residence there. Talk the princes down from their rage and present this truce to them in an attractive light, so that they may accept it. If you don't believe us, we hereby swear on the Quran." The three commanders—Abdullah the Kirghiz, Raḥman Quli the Mountain Man, and Sariq Yasavul—each swore a solemn oath on the Quran.

Muḥammad Abdullah Bakavul, Sayid Khalifa, Shihab al-Din Bakavul, and Mirza Abd al-Wahhab /156a/ presented the question of peace negotiations to Khoja Jahan. All the princes and members of the holy family assembled, and since no one could see any alternative, they had to resign themselves to fate and accept. Only Khoja Abdullah's rage had yet to subside. "God," he said, "would you grant this most humble and recalcitrant slave one more arrow, that I may entrust my life to the Keeper of Souls, rather than die with ignominy in the hands of these bloodthirsty tyrants? This rain of arrows on the Muslims has freed them from the toils of life. Why shouldn't it do the same for me?" So saying, he discarded his helmet and fought on. A flying arrow struck him in the eye, but it did not bring him death.

Khoja Jahan said to him by way of advice: "My child, turn away from the grave and resign yourself to fate. This rank of martyrdom will be our legacy. Don't look at anyone else, look into my face."

"Grandfather," Khoja Abdullah replied, "give permission for a few of us to leave behind our kinsfolk and our encumbrances, maybe God Almighty will grant us a way out and we'll be delivered from these murderous enemies. If we make it to safety, they won't be able to harm you at all. But if all of us /156b/ fall captive to these people like this, they won't keep a single one of us alive, they'll massacre us all. One can't credit the oaths of these faithless and untrustworthy men. We need to take a lesson from the affair of Ghazi Beg. I say this not out of fear of death. Right now, death looks preferable to me than the throne and crown of the seven climes. I am proposing this for two reasons. The first is that the line of our forefathers and ancestors must not be wiped off the face of the earth. The second is that I cannot stand the thought of falling into the hands of these evildoers and dying with indignity. My sense of pride simply won't allow me to do that."

> If you cut me into a hundred pieces with vengeance's sword, so be it,
> But I will not submit to the abuse of my miserly rivals.

Yet Khoja Jahan spoke again, as if he was preaching: "Yes, my son, everything you say from start to finish is true and correct, but seeking some remedy against heavenly fate is not the way of wise men. You are talking about that fate which is pending, from which it is permissible to flee or seek some solution, but this fate is irresistible and fixed, and there is no response to it other than submission. Since divine destiny has been determined for us in this way, do we have any choice but to acquiesce? Martyrdom will be our legacy. Praise be to God that we have not tarnished our family name but have obtained our inheritance. At the end of our days, we have carried out the tradition of the Karbala Plain. /157a/ Listen closely, my children: this mortal world is meaningless, and good fortune in it will not last. But there is no end to the bounties of the next life. One of the requirements of faith is to make plans in advance for the world to come, and to hold firmly to those plans. This mundane realm is no place for believers. There is a hadith from the Prophet, which says THIS MORTAL WORLD IS A PRISON FOR THE BELIEVERS, AND A PARADISE FOR THE INFIDELS. He who endures the toils of this world for the sake of the comforts of the next will profit, but he who prefers the comforts of this world and indulges his rebellious desires, and thereby falls victim to the tortures of the afterlife, does himself harm. O child, despair not, since out of this misfortune we can hope to accrue all sorts of ranks and stations in the next life, the extent of which God only knows. In accordance with the verse EVERY SOUL SHALL TASTE DEATH [21:35], there is no man, nor any creature at all, who will not sup the sweet wine of death. If it is someone's turn on this occasion, then next time it will be someone else's. In this matter there is no question of precedence. There is no difference between going now or going in the future—everyone will die in the end. But a death such as this won't always come to hand. Though now it looks like a trial, its pleasure and delight will be obvious after we die. Confronting hardship is a comfort. As much pain and suffering as there will be in the hands of these enemies, its recompense /157b/ will be greater than that. Now is not the time for heroism and daring, it is the time for patience and forbearance."

Every issue has a time and every subtlety a place.[241]

"The more patience and forbearance you have, the higher the rank you obtain will be. God Almighty has promised in his own words that he will befriend those who have patience: AND GOD LOVES THE PATIENT [3:146]. Refrain now from fighting, and replace resistance with resignation. Whatever has been preordained for us, let us prepare for it."

By the time he finished his speech, the princes were all in tears. "O great father," they said, "we are resigned, and God is satisfied. Now whatever is our final destiny, we will bow our heads before it. However much pain and suffering awaits us, we will endure it. We will give ourselves up to the hands of these enemies, and whatever is to become of us, we yield to it. We recognize it as an act of God, not of one of his creations." With this they reconciled themselves to the situation and humbly entered into negotiations with the enemy. Yet as much as Khoja Abdullah was persuaded, his sense of honor and nobility were not.

Amid this confusion, the enemies crossed the river. Raḥman Quli the Mountain Man, Abdullah the Kirghiz, /158a/ Sariq Yasavul, and some other officers came before Khoja Jahan. They paid their respects, then launched into a treacherous speech, presenting the same platitudes as before.

Although Khoja Jahan was well aware of the duplicity of these scoundrels, he had no choice but to going along with them. "We have fallen captive to you," he said, "the choice is now up to you. Whatever you decide to do, we are prepared for it."

> A heart that holds onto all kinds of desires won't find rest,
> I only stilled my soul when I entered the path of resignation.

"You may not find what we're saying convincing," these tricksters said, "unless Khoja Yaḥya hears it directly from the mouth of Khoja Burhan al-Din. Why doesn't Khoja Yaḥya go as an envoy in this affair, receive his commands directly, and come back? No one else is appropriate for this task."

Khoja Jahan could find no response to this deceptive request, so he helplessly gave in to it. He called in Khoja Yaḥya, kissed him on the forehead, and gave him permission to leave. "Go! I have entrusted you to the Lord Almighty and to my illustrious forefather Muḥammad." Khoja Yaḥya embraced all the assembled princes and requested approval from them one by one, and with tears in his eyes he departed into the midst of these mortal enemies.

The day was late, and one can only imagine the plight of this holy family's devotees. No one had anyone else to rely on, each one cherished their own sweet soul. Most of the Muslims had been drenched in the river, their clothes were soaked and freezing, and since coming out they hadn't had a thing to eat. They were all anxious at their own condition. Some had lit large bonfires to dry their clothes; /158b/ others had slaughtered and roasted their horses and were eating them with their families.

Khoja Abdullah noticed that four people were missing from among the princes: two members of the holy family itself, and two from among their children and wives. It wasn't known whether they had been martyred or not. He spoke sternly to the enemy commander: "If you intend to massacre us, reunite us before you kill us. We can't abide seeing our family members captive in the hands of outsiders. We're your prisoners, the choice is yours, but you should put us out of our misery by killing us first. Whatever happens after that, so be it, but while I remain alive, I won't allow you to behave in this way. As long as we still draw breath, we'll face this in each other's arms. We won't consent to peace terms in these circumstances."

The leader of the oppressors immediately sent messengers with announcements around the tents, and it turned out that these people had fallen into the hands of the Kirghiz. They were brought back safely and entrusted to the princes.

The Muslims spent the night crying disconsolately, while the enemies passed it with revelry and merrymaking. The troops had ringed the surrounds so tightly that no creature, not even a worm or insect, could find a way through.

Under this watchful guard, it was after midnight when Khoja Abdullah came into the presence of Khoja Jahan, leading by the hand Khojam Naẓar Khoja, /159a/ Ṣabir Kerek-yaragh's son Tokhta Khoja, and Shihab al-Din Bakavul's son Mirza Ḥaydar Khan. "Father," he said, "we belong to the line of sayyids and khojas. As much as we requested leave from you, it was not granted. But how would it be if these three children of the household were permitted to go, so that even if our lineage is wiped out, the line of our long-standing companions and the deputies of our forefathers will not be, and they will remain to say prayers for us?"

Khoja Jahan consented to this request. He recited the opening of the Quran for them and gave them his blessing: "I have entrusted you to God Almighty and to my forefathers." Khojam Naẓar Khoja seated these two children on his horse, one in front and one behind, and they departed on a single horse. From the strength of the prayer, one can see the ingenuity of God Almighty: the bloodthirsty enemies had surrounded them several rows deep, so that sentry calls were always within earshot. Yet the Creator threw dust in the eyes of this treasonous group, so no one was aware of anything. These three continued on their way and got themselves to a Kirghiz encampment.

It was just like the story of old, when Muḥammad, chief of the saints, was going into exile from Mecca to Medina, and ranks of infidels were lying in wait all around him. A revelation came down: "Escape from the violence of these infidels, take Abu Bakr as companion and hide in such-and-such cave. /159b/ The infidels will be oblivious and unable to find you, then you can give them the slip and get away to Medina."

"Brother," His Grace said, "at the Lord's command, Gabriel has outlined his design." The Prophet took a handful of dirt, blew the opening verse of the Quran into it, and strew it in the direction of the infidels. He witnessed the power of God Almighty, such that all the infidels were struck dumb like corpses. With composure, the Prophet and Abu Bakr evaded the infidels and made their escape. On this occasion, a verse was revealed: AND THOU THREWEST NOT WHEN THOU THREWEST, BUT GOD THREW [8:17]; that is, "O Muḥammad, you did not throw this handful of dirt, for while it appeared as if you threw it, in truth it was God who threw it."[242]

49. A NIGHT IN CAPTIVITY

Let God Almighty keep these three sons of deputies safe in his protection, while we describe the situation among the princes. They spent the night in great hardship, and the next morning the enemy commanders came and said to them, "You must now move on from here to Yarkand to meet with Khoja Burhan al-Din. Whatever he commands, so it will be. Whichever city he bestows upon you, you will take up residence there."

They dressed up their deceptions in the form of guidance, but the princes with their insight knew they were simply concealing the abuse and mistreatment they had in store for them, the extent of which /160a/ God only knew. "You won't be needing your baggage and weapons anymore," they added. "Instead of carrying them with you, give them to us. We'll take care of them." With this ploy, their supplies were confiscated. Seeing no choice but to comply, the princes returned and prepared for the trip.

They were driven along the road until the time of midday prayers, when they were made to camp in a dry riverbed in a place called Aqtam.[243] All along the way, heralds were shouting out that those who aided the sinners were also sinners, and those who accompanied them were also sinners. Because of this, no one dared to even look at them, nor they at anyone else. When the princes alighted, they had neither food to eat nor fuel to light a fire. The hunger was bad enough, but it was compounded by cold and thirst. Worst of all, their souls were aflame at the cries of their young women. They sent someone to the enemy commander: "On what basis can you subject us to such mistreatment? Even by the customs of the infidels there is severe punishment for killing small children. It is simply not done." After many entreaties, they were brought a few wet branches of oleaster shrub, but as much as the companions tried to light them, they wouldn't catch fire. Even if they managed to get a flame going, there was no dry kindling to light the wet wood. They slaughtered a couple of horses /160b/ and tried to cook the meat, but it didn't work. In distress, they beseeched the court of the Lord and sat there enduring the cold, hunger, and thirst. In this way, they eventually made it through the night with great difficulty. The next morning, the commander came and began to rudely move the princes along. Along with confiscating anything that was in their possession, they took their healthy mounts and transported them on lame horses instead.

50. A FINAL LAMENT

Let us conclude with a story about Möngke's tribe of Kirghiz. These foul infidels came up from behind and raided so fiercely it was like the dawn of a new Judgment Day. As much as the enemy army tried to restrain them, they took no notice. "We were the ones who first caught these criminals," they said, "and incurred the trouble associated with that. Why should someone else get the booty and we go back disappointed and empty-handed? *I am a Quran reciter, but my brother reads.*[244] What would be the point in that?" Thus, they took no notice of anyone else and set about mutinous plundering. The Muslims had no strength to refuse them the items they demanded. They stripped them down, sometimes taking their hats, sometimes their clothes, and sometimes their shoes. They showed them no mercy and weren't worried in the slightest that they might freeze to death in the harsh cold. At times they ripped children from their mothers' breasts, and other times they simply speared them and abandoned them.

With these trials and humiliations, they were driven along the road until the hour of the midday prayer. They made camp in a newly constructed courtyard, with walls in some places /161a/ as high as a man, and in some places lower than that. Inside, a kind of cellar with corridors had been constructed, whose walls were even lower. Livestock had been kept here, leaving it entirely putrid and filthy. Each prince occupied one room with his retinue and tried to tidy the place before settling down. Their circumstances here were even more dire than before, with nothing to eat or drink, and nothing to light a fire with. They couldn't put up with the wails and cries of their women and children. It was enough to break hearts and melt rocks, but it didn't make the slightest impression on their enemies.

Quickly, cupbearer, bring me that glass,
On a subject like this it's better to be blind drunk.
I've reached my wits' end with all this talk,
Did the Qalmaqs ever do things like this?
A strange condition has beset me,
My tongue has lost the strength to speak.
Tears fall from my eyes one by one,
My heart and soul have melted, O hard-hearted one.
My pen has cried and rent its breast,
And moistened the face of the page.
When have such acts of cruelty ever occurred in the past?
Could an infidel exhibit tyranny such as this?
He brought about such vice and corruption,
And the world descended into conflagration.
These kings were descendants of the Prophet,
A crown of the human race.
They struck the infidel senseless without mercy,
Wielding the blade of Islam openly.
Promoting the command of the shariʿa,
They levied taxes and tribute from the tyrants.
Prayers, fasting, pilgrimage, and alms,
All acquired great popularity in their reign.
Scholars obtained respect at that time,
And honor was shown to men of poetry.
In justice Khoja Jahan was truly unique,
His equity put Nushirvan to shame.
Time's midwife has never delivered the like of his nobility,
In virtue, he was a sea of generosity.
/161b/ The people of the world grew rich on his account,
A slave named Stingy (*bakhīl*) became a Ḥatim.[245]
If I were to describe his qualities for a hundred years,
It wouldn't end—in short, he was a sage.
The purpose of these words is not to flatter,

There is no need to provide a description of the sun.
My point is that with kings such as these,
Those aware of the secrets of truth,
Is it permissible to inflict on them pain and cruelty?
To kill them in torturous ways?
Grown-ups, youths, and some still breastfeeding,
And countless women and girls,
Were among this group,
But in the onslaught of these vampires,
Neither infidel nor Muslim showed mercy,
Neither the good nor bad took pity.
But surely you err—were there even any Muslims?
How could Muslims display such cruelty?
What do you mean by distinguishing good from bad?
They were all the worst of the worst,
Pigs among violent pigs.
If there was a single humble Muslim there,
Would they ever commit such injustices?
But look, they claim to be Muslims,
Such were the astonishing topsy-turvy times.
They call this infidel band,
This group of non-Muslims, "Muslims."
What's more, they refer to their spiritual guide,
A representative of the Path and of Truth.
They receive his favor as if it's the eight paradises,
If he smiles on them, they consider it a joy.
Anyone who rejects him they treat like a denizen of Hell,
Truly those who have faith in him are evil.
GOD FORBID, has there ever been the likes of these?
There have never been such calamities as this.
Is this not treachery, a betrayal of the religion?
A scandal among the Muslims?
These actions are nothing short of heresy,
Abomination doesn't get worse than this, O people!
See what sort of justice these people profess,
From top to bottom is it nothing but enmity and impurity.

If someone regards these deeds as permissible,
Then you cannot call them a Muslim.
It is error, sin, and blasphemy without doubt,
Anyone who doubts this, their faith is in question.
When someone commits a sin in this world,
/162a/ In the past or at this time,
If someone hears about it and denounces it,
And is scandalized by actions like theirs,
They should call them a Muslim according to the Holy Law,
Their soul will partake of the pleasure of faith.
But if someone hears of this and does not decry it,
Or even once says "what good things they did!"
They have not an ounce of faith by the shariʿa,
They are non-Muslims among the Muslims.
But there are many in this time,
Vulgar, heretical, and vile troublemakers,
Who take lawbreaking as their friend,
And remain faithful to their sinful heroes.
"Whatever they did," they say, "it was well they did it,
They did it knowingly though they did a lot.
Such deeds are a tradition we inherit from them,
Though we commit heresy, it is from them."
O God, to this mass of people,
Deprived of the sea of guidance,
Give your blessing and make your aid their companion,
Direct them and give them an inkling of the Path.
They know not what they do, they have gone astray,
Illuminate the way for them, they are lost.
When will they realize the obscenity of all this?
Could they really adopt this as their creed?
Do they know the difference between God's people and heretics?
How could they credit innovation as tradition?
Unless this deed was done out of ignorance,
From the force of obstinacy and bestiality.
Bring them to the right road,
Accept my plea for forgiveness for them all.

Save them from disbelief and the sin of rebellion,
Show favor and absolve them.
Deliver them from their wayward condition,
Bring them from disorientation to guidance.
O Lord, approve this entreaty,
And provide everyone with their needs.
Bless this black-faced rebellious soul,
And give my tongue strength to speak.
I'll tell of the trials of the saints,
And of the mourning at their misfortune and suffering.
Their devotees and disciples will weep and wail,
And bring the world to commotion.
Tearing their collars and rending their breasts,
They'll pour dust on their heads in misery.
Remembering them with benedictions,
They'll make the spirits of these saints glad.
Cry, O friend, for it is a time of martyrdom,
/162b/ Take pity on them, whether you were there or not.
Whoever lets a tear fall from their eye.
Can hope to avoid the fires of Hell.
It was a harbinger of the end of time,
Like Karbala, but a hundred times more terrifying.
From the beginning of time until the end,
Nothing like this has occurred among mankind.
O God, from now until Judgment Day,
Lift this suffering from the heads of the people.
Ward off these tribulations for the sake of the saints,
Don't bring down this misfortune on anyone else.
Let this mourning end with them,
And the world's people be delivered from such trials.
Come, Ṣadiq, conclude this story of yours,
Take yourself off, and the rest of your words too.

ABBREVIATIONS

Ch.	Chinese
EI^2	P. J. Bearman, Th. Bianquis, C. E. Bosworth, E. van Donzel, W. P. Heinrichs, et al., eds., *Encyclopaedia of Islam*, 2nd ed. (Leiden, Netherlands: Brill, 1960–2005).
EI^3	Kate Fleet, Gudrun Krämer, Denis Matringe, John Nawas, and Everett Rowson, eds., *Encyclopaedia of Islam, THREE* (online edition).
IPN ANRT	Institut pismennogo naslediia, Akademiia nauk Respubliki Tajikistan
IVAN RUz	Institut vostokovedeniia, Akademiia nauk Respubliki Uzbekistan
IVR RAN	Institut vostochnykh rukopisei, Rossiisskaia akademiia nauk
Ma.	Manchu
Mo.	Mongolian
NMAT	Alisher Navoiy, *Mukammal asarlar to'plami*, 20 vols. (Tashkent, Uzbekistan: Fan, 1987–2003).
QXMD	Zhongguo diyi lishi dang'anguan and Zhongguo bianjiang shidi yanjiu zhongxin, eds., *Qingdai Xinjiang Manwen dang'an huibian* (Guilin, China: Guangxi shifan daxue chubanshe, 2012).
SVR	A. A. Semenov et al., eds., *Sobranie vostochnykh rukopisei Akademii nauk Uzbekskoi SSR* (Tashkent, Uzbekistan: Izdatel'stvo Akademii nauk UzSSR, 1952–1987).

TAHartmann Martin Hartmann, "Ein Heiligenstaat im Islam: Das Ende der Caghataiden und die Herrschaft der Choǧas in Kašgarien," *Der Islamische Orient: Berichte und Forschungen* 1, no. 6–10 (1905).

TAUyghur Muhämmäd Sadiq Qäshqäri, *Täzkirä'i Äzizan*, ed. Nijat Mukhlis and Shämsidin Ämät (Kashgar, China: Qäshqär Uyghur Näshriyati, 1988).

TKSawada Sawada Minoru, " 'Tazukira i hōjagān' Nihongo yakushi," *Toyama Daigaku Jinbun Gakubu kiyō* 61–69 (2014–18).

TKShaw Robert B. Shaw, "The History of the Khōjas of Eastern-Turkistān Summarised from the Tazkira-i-Khwājagān of Muḥammad Ṣādiq Kāshgharī," supplement to *The Journal of the Asiatic Society of Bengal* 66, part 1 (1897).

NOTES

INTRODUCTION

1. For the history of the Junghar-Qing conflict, see I. Ia. Zlatkin, *Istoriia Dzhungarskogo khanstva (1635–1758)* (Moscow: Nauka, 1964); Fred W. Bergholz, *The Partition of the Steppe: The Struggle of the Russians, Manchus, and the Zunghar Mongols for Empire in Central Asia, 1619–1758* (New York: Peter Lang, 1993); Peter C. Perdue, *China Marches West: The Qing Conquest of Central Eurasia* (Cambridge, MA: Belknap Press of Harvard University Press, 2005); Onuma Takahiro, *Shin to chūō Ajia sōgen: yūbokumin no sekai kara teikoku no henkyō e* (Tokyo: Tōkyō daigaku shuppankai, 2014).
2. For studies of Makhdum-i Aᶜẓam, see Vika Gardner, "Makhdūm-i Aᶜẓam, Aḥmad," in EI³; Victoria R. Gardner, "The Written Representations of a Central Asian Ṣūfī Shaykh: Aḥmad ibn Mawlānā Jalāl al-Dīn Khwājagī Kāsānī 'Makhdūm-i Aᶜẓam' (d. 1542)" (Ph.D. diss., University of Michigan, 2006).
3. On the Tarim Basin Makhdumzadas, see Joseph Fletcher, "The Naqshbandiyya in Northwest China, Edited by Jonathan N. Lipman," in Beatrice Forbes Manz, ed., *Studies on Chinese and Islamic Inner Asia* (Aldershot, UK: Variorum, 1995), 1–46; Alexandre Papas, *Soufisme et politique entre Chine, Tibet et Turkestan: Étude sur les Khwajas Naqshbandis du Turkestan oriental* (Paris: Librarie d'Amérique et d'Orient, Jean Maisonneuve successeur, 2005); Alexandre Papas, "Khojas of Kashgar," in *Oxford Research Encyclopedia of Asian History* (2017); Devin A. DeWeese, "Āfāq, Khwāja and the Āfāqiyya," in EI³.
4. Rian Thum discusses this genre of texts in *The Sacred Routes of Uyghur History* (Cambridge, MA: Harvard University Press, 2014).
5. See Florian Schwarz, *"Unser Weg schließt tausend Wege ein": Derwische und Gesellschaft im islamischen Mittelasien im 16. Jahrhundert* (Berlin: Klaus Schwarz Verlag, 2000); A. A. Khismatulin, "Khojagan," in *Islam na territorii byvshei Rossiiskoi imperii: Entsiklopedicheskii slovar'*, ed. S. M. Prozorov (Moscow: Vostochnaia literatura, 2006), 1:417–25.

6. See section 48. In the 1850s, Valikhanov found "a descendant of one of the shaykhs of Danyal Khoja" to be the leading representative of the Black Mountain faction in Kashgar. See Ch. Ch. Valikhanov, "O sostoianii Altyshara ili shesti vostochnykh gorodov Kitaiskoi provintsii Nan-Lu (Maloi Bukharii) v 1858–59 gg.," in *Sobranie sochinenii v piati tomakh* (Alma-Ata, Kazakhstan: Glavnaia redaktsiia kazakhskoi sovetskoi entsiklopedii, 1985), 3:180. Imam Ali Qunduzi's *Tavarikh-i Manẓuma* (IPN ANRT 204, fols. 327a–328a) also mentions two hereditary leaders of the Black Mountain community in the mid-nineteenth century.
7. We find the same formula, for example, in a local translation of Firdausi's classic *Shahnama* (IVR RUz 1953). This is the Khoja Khamush translation, dating to 1194/1780–81, of an unknown prose version of the *Shahnama*.
8. Gayretcan Osman, "Muhemmed Sadik Kaşgari Üzerindeki Araştırmalar," in Muhammet Kuzubaş, Salih Okumuş, and Nuh Doğan, eds., *T. C. Ordu Üniversitesi Uluslararası Klasik Türk Edebiyatı Sempozyumu* (Ordu, Turkey: Ordu Üniversitesi Yayınları, 2013), 287–92. An image of this *waqf* document can be found in Sugawara Jun, "Sōshutsu sareru 'Uiguru minzoku bunka': 'Uiguru koten bungaku' no hukkō to bobyō no 'hakken,' " *Ajia yūgaku* 1 (1999): 83.
9. Other studies by Uyghur scholars offer dates of 1725 and 1849 for Kashghari's birth and death, giving him an unlikely lifespan of more than a hundred and twenty years. See, for example, the introduction to the Uyghur-language edition of the *Taẕkira-i Azizan*: Muhämmäd Sadiq Qäshqäri, *Täzkirä'i Äzizan*, ed. Nijat Mukhlis and Shämsidin Ämät (Kashgar, China: Qäshqär Uyghur näshriyati, 1988), 1.
10. See TKSawada, 1:65.
11. Iusupbek Mukhlisov, *Uyghur klassik ädäbiyati qolyazmilirining katalogi* (Ürümchi, China: Shinjang yärlik muziyigha täyyarliq körüsh bashqarmisi, 1957), 42 (#62).
12. QXMD, 164:392–394.
13. See *Qing shilu* (Beijing: Zhonghua shuju, 1985–1987), 24:673 (QL50/9/27).
14. Jarring Prov. 439, fol. 7a.
15. IVR RAN C569, p. 8.
16. IVAN RUz 9470 (SVR 5, #3469).
17. On these two works, see Paolo Sartori, "Between Kazan and Kashghar: On the Vernacularization of Islamic Jurisprudence in Central Eurasia" (forthcoming). A brief description of the *Zubdat al-Masaʾil* is given in I. A. Saidakhmedov, M. Iu. Iunuskhodzhaeva, and G. Iu. Astanova, "Agiograficheskie sochineniia kak istochnik dlia izucheniia dukhovnoi i politicheskoi zhizni Vostochnogo Turkestana," in *Iz istorii Srednei Azii i Vostochnogo Turkestana XV–XIX vv*, ed. B. A. Akhmedov (Tashkent, Uzbekistan: Fan, 1987), 158–59. Kashghari's *Adab al-Ṣaliḥin* has since been reprinted in Uzbekistan: Muhmmad Sodiq Qoshghariy, *Yakhshi kishilar odobi (Odob-as-solihin)* (Tashkent, Uzbekistan: Yangi asr avlodi, 2002).
18. M. Qutluqov, *Muhammad Sodiq Koshghariy* (Tashkent, Uzbekistan: Özbekiston KP Markaziy komitetining birlashgan nashriyoti, 1968), 9.
19. Muḥammad Ṣadiq Kashghari, *Zubdat al-Masaʾil wa-l-Aqaʾid* (Istanbul: Shirket–i Iraniyye, 1309/1891–92); N. S. Lykoshin, "Kodeks prilichii na Vostoke (Adab-ul-salikhyn)," *Sbornik materialov po musul'manstvu* 2 (1900): 23–83.
20. Emine Gürsoy-Naskali, ed., *Ashābu 'l-Kähf, A Treatise in Eastern Turki*, Memoires de la Societe Finno-Ougrienne 192 (Helsinki: Suomalais-Ugrilainen Seura, 1985); Mukhlisov, *Uyghur klassik ädäbiyati*, 42 (#64); Muhämmäd Sadiq Qäshqäri, *Äshabul*

kähf täzkirisi (Ürümchi, China: Shinjang Uyghur Aptonom Rayon az sanliq millät qädimki äsärlär ishkhanisi, 1994). On this shrine, see Shinmen Yasushi, "The History of the Mausoleum Aṣḥāb al-Kahf in Turfan," *Memoirs of the Research Department of the Toyo Bunko* 61 (2003): 83–104.

21. IVR RAN C569, p. 8.
22. See L. V. Dmitrieva, ed., *Katalog tiurkskikh rukopisei Instituta vostokovedeniia Rossiiskoi akadamii nauk* (Moscow: Vostochnaia literatura, 2002), 336. Dmitrieva also lists Kashghari as the author of a translation of Muʿin al-Miskin Farahi's *Rawżat al-Waʿiẓin*, a fifteenth-century collection of hadith with accompanying commentary. This is to confuse him with Muḥammad Ṣiddiq Rushdi, also an important eighteenth-century translator. The incomplete Saint Petersburg manuscript described by Dmitrieva is the same work as IVAN RUz 8880, which has been catalogued under the title that occurs in its inside cover, *Qiṣṣat al-Sharifat al-Musawiyyat* (SVR 7, #5498).
23. Mulla Musa Sayrami, *Tarikhi Hämidi* (Beijing: Millätlär Näshriyati, 1986), 110.
24. Central Asian Documents, Houghton Library MS Turk 70.
25. Rähilä Dawut, *Uyghur mazarliri* (Ürümchi, China: Shinjang khälq näshriyati, 2001), 89–90.
26. Edmund Waite, "From Holy Man to Villain: Popular Historical Narratives About Apaq Khoja Amongst Uyghurs in Contemporary Xinjiang," *Inner Asia* 8, no. 1 (2006): 5–28; Thum, *Sacred Routes*.
27. Saguchi Tōru, "The Revival of the White Mountain Khwājas, 1760–1820 (from Sarimsāq to Jihāngīr)," *Acta Asiatica* 14 (1968): 7–20; Laura Newby, *The Empire and the Khanate: A Political History of Qing Relations with Khoqand c. 1700–1860* (Leiden, Netherlands: Brill, 2005).
28. On this dispute, see Wu Mu and Zhang Fengfeng, "Lun Qian-Jia nianjian Xibuchake Bulute," *Zhongguo bianjiang shidi yanjiu* 26, no. 3 (2016): 42–52.
29. For example, Henry G. Schwarz, "The Khwājas of Eastern Turkestan," *Central Asiatic Journal* 20, no. 4 (1976): 266–96.
30. Valikhanov, "O sostoianii Altyshara."
31. Henry Walter Bellew, "History of Kashgar," in *Report of a Mission to Yarkund in 1873*, ed. Sir D. T. Forsyth (Calcutta: Foreign Department Press, 1875), 1:106–213.
32. "Fall of the Mussulman Dominion in Kashgharia," *The Pioneer*, March 21, 1876, 3–4; March 22, 1876, 3–4.
33. Robert B. Shaw, "The History of the Khōjas of Eastern-Turkistān Summarised from the Tazkira-i-Khwājagān of Muḥammad Ṣādiq Kāshgharī," supplement to *The Journal of the Asiatic Society of Bengal* 66, part 1 (1897). The British Library shelf mark of Shaw's draft Chaghatay text is 14456.h.19.
34. Mu-han-mo-de Sa-di-ke Ka-shi-ga-li, "Hezhuo zhuan," *Minzushi yiwen ji* 8 (1980): 53–136; Ma Dazheng, ed., *Qingdai Chahetai wen wenxian yizhu* (Ürümchi, China: Xinjiang renmin chubanshe, 2013), 136–217.
35. Martin Hartmann, "Die osttürkischen Handschriften der Sammlung Hartmann," *Mittheilungen des Seminars für orientalische Sprachen, Berlin* 7, no. 2 (1904), 5 (#40), 13 (#122).
36. M. A. Salakhetdinova, "Sochinenie Mukhammed-Sadyka Kashgari 'Tazkira-i Khodzhagan' kak istochnik po istorii Kirgizov," *Izvestiia Akademii nauk KirgSSR* 1 (Istoriia) (1959): 93–125.

37. Qutluqov, *Muhammad Sodiq Koshghariy*; I. Saidullaev, "Istoriko-literaturnoe proizvedenie 'Tazkirai Khodzhagan' Mukhammeda Sadyka Kashgari," *Izvestiia Akademii nauk KazSSR* 1 (1979): 41–45.
38. Mukhammed-Sadyk Kashghari, *Tazkira-yi 'Azizan*, trans. A. Sh. Nurmanova (Almaty, Kazakhstan: Daik-Press, 2006). See also A. Sh. Nurmanova, "Mukhammed-Sadyq Qashghariding "Tazkira-yi 'Azizan" shygharmasy: derektanulyq zertteu," *Izvestiia NAN Respubliki Kazakhstan* 3 (2007): 8–14.
39. Sawada Minoru, "'Tazukira i hōjagān' Nihongo yakushi," *Toyama Daigaku Jinbun Gakubu kiyō* 61 (2014): 59–86; 62 (2015): 89–118; 63 (2015): 33–57; 64 (2016): 81–106; 65 (2016): 21–44; 66 (2017): 55–82; 67 (2017): 31–60; 68 (2018): 27–43; 69 (2018): 33–50.
40. Mu-han-mo-de Sa-di-ke Ka-shi-ga-li, "Hezhuo Zhuan," in *Zhongguo xibei wenxian congshu*, ed. Gansusheng guji wenxian zhengli bianyi zhongxin, erbian vol. 39 (Beijing: Xianzhuang shuju, 2006).
41. Note, for example, the recent publication of a facsimile of a manuscript of the short recension held in private hands: Coşkun Kumru, "Muhammet Sâdık Kaşgârî'nin Tezkire-i Hâcegân Adlı Eserinin Transkripsiyonu ve Değerlendirilmesi" (Yüksek Lisans Tezi, Pamukkale Üniversitesi, 2016).
42. For catalogue description, see Günay Kut, *Supplementary Catalogue of Turkish Manuscripts in the Bodleian Library* (Oxford: Oxford University Press, 2003), 87 (#126).
43. See Kut, *Supplementary Catalogue*, 88 (#128); A. M. Muginov, *Opisanie Uigurskikh rukopisei Instituta Narodov Azii* (Moscow: INA AN SSSR, 1962), 87 (#129); SVR 3, #2721.
44. Kut, *Supplementary Catalogue*, 87 (#127); Hartmann, "Die osttürkischen Handschriften," 5 (#40).
45. Seyyed Hossein Nasr, Caner K. Dagli, Maria Massi Dakake, and Joseph E. B. Lumbard, eds., *The Study Quran* (New York: HarperOne, 2015); Jalal al-Din Rumi, *The Mathnawí of Jalálu'ddín Rúmí*, trans. Reynold A. Nicholson (Leiden: Brill, 1925).

IN REMEMBRANCE OF THE SAINTS

1. This is a line attributed to Muḥammad's companion Abu Bakr, frequently cited by Ibn Arabi.
2. Ma. Osman; Ch. E-si-man 鄂斯瑞 (d. 1788). After the Qing conquest, U̱sman was briefly governor of Aqsu, then served alongside his father Hadi, who was governor of Yarkand. Because of Hadi's involvement in the Gao Pu corruption scandal, the Qianlong emperor decided to appoint his son to Kashgar and not to Yarkand.
3. Ma. Ūdui; Ch. E-dui 鄂對 (d. 1778). His official Qing biography identifies his father as Polat and his grandfather as Mirza Niʿmat. The family is said to have held the governorship of Kucha in the Junghar period, and prior to the Qing conquest, Hadi is described as deputy governor (*eshikagha*) of that oasis. Hadi and his son received the aristocratic title of *beise*, and in the nineteenth century his line was promoted to *junwang*. For his official Qing biography, see Gertraude Roth Li, *Manchu: A Textbook for Reading Documents* (Honolulu: University of Hawai'i Press, 2000), 327–35. On this dynasty of Kucha "wangs," which survived into the Republican period, see Mämtimin Ba'izi, "Kucha wanglirining näsäbnamisi," *Shinjang tarikh materiyalliri* 48 (2006): 85–105; Xu Fulu, *Xiyu wangshi: Xinjiang zuihou yige wanggong 200 nian de jiazu jiyi* (Beijing: Huawen chubanshe, 2006).

4. In the Islamic world, the nomadic Chaghatayid elite were known as Moghuls (i.e. Mongols), and Moghulistan originally referred to the steppe region north of the Tianshan (see C. E. Bosworth, "Mogholistān," EI[2], 7:218). In Kashghari's day the term Moghul was falling out of use, but Moghulistan had become a common designation for the Tarim Basin and its surrounds.
5. The Huma is a legendary bird often depicted as similar to a phoenix. It is said that anyone on whom its shadow falls is destined for kingship.
6. In *juan* 6 of Qi-shi-yi's *Xiyu wenjianlu* (Edo: Senshōbō, Kansei 13/1800–1), Raḥima (Ch. Re-yi-mu 熱依木) is accorded a prominent role in events surrounding the initial Qing capture of Kucha and the 1765 Ush (Uchturpan) rebellion.
7. Kashghari's discussion of Makhdum-i Aʿẓam here is translated from the third chapter of the *Jamiʿ al-Maqamat*, a Persian hagiography of Makhdum-i Aʿẓam written by the saint's grandson Abu l-Baqa and dating to 1026/1617–18. This section corresponds to fols. 31a–34a of IVAN RUz 72 (SVR 3, #2571). On this and other hagiographies of Makhdum-i Aʿẓam, see B. Babajanov, "Biographies of Makhdum-i A'zam al-Kasani al-Dahbidi, Shaykh of the Sixteenth-Century Naqshbandiya," *Manuscripta Orientalia* 5, no. 2 (1999): 3–8. At around the same time as Kashghari was writing, a certain Muḥammad Ṣiddiq Yarkandi translated many of these same passages for inclusion in his White Mountain hagiography, the *Majmuʿat al-Muḥaqqiqin*. See Jürgen Paul, ed., *Katalog sufischer Handschriften aus der Bibliothek des Instituts für Orientalistik der Akademie der Wissenschaften, Republik Usbekistan* (Stuttgart: Franz Weiner Verlag, 2002), #36. This entire section is omitted from Group B texts, which substitute a short discussion of Khoja Jahan's spiritual lineage and genealogy.
8. The *Haftyak*, literally "one-seventh," was a textbook consisting of selected verses from the Quran.
9. On Khoja Aḥrar, see Hamid Algar, "Aḥrār, Khʷādja ʿUbayd Allah," EI[2] Supplement, 50–52.
10. The Kendir Pass, now better known as the Kamchiq Pass, lies along the main route between Tashkent and the Ferghana Valley. (Note that most manuscripts write Kandūr, but the *Jamiʿ al-Maqamat* has Kandir.)
11. From the *Divan-i Arshi*, ghazal #45 (Khoja Jahan Ärshi, *Divani Ärshi* [Ürümchi, China: Shinjang khälq näshriyati, 1995], 47.)
12. Abu l-Baqa, *Jamiʿ al-Maqamat*, fols. 34b–35a.
13. Abd al-Khaliq Ghijduvani's resting place of Ghijduvan lies roughly fifty kilometers to the northeast of Bukhara.
14. Abu l-Baqa, *Jamiʿ al-Maqamat*, fols. 35b–36a.
15. On the Sufi notion of "states of being," see L. Gardet, "Ḥāl," EI[2] 3:83–85.
16. Abu l-Baqa, *Jamiʿ al-Maqamat*, fols. 37b–39a.
17. Aḥmad the Moghul, also known as Sulṭan Aḥmad Khan b. Yunus Khan (d. 1504), was a ruler of the eastern Chaghatayid domains in the late fifteenth century. According to works such as the *Baburnama* and the *Tarikh-i Rashidi*, he earned the epithet Alacha ("killer") for his bloody raids on his Qalmaq Mongol neighbors.
18. This is a slight adaptation of Quran 2:18, substituting *lā yaʿlimūna* ("they will not know") for *lā yarjiʿūna* ("they will not return").
19. Abu l-Baqa, *Jamiʿ al-Maqamat*, fols. 3a–6b.

20. A legendary enumeration of the Seven Sultans evidently varied according to local tradition. Steingass cites one version as (1) the Sulṭan of Khorasan, (2) Sulṭan Ibrahim Adham, (3) Sulṭan Bayazid Bistami, (4) Sulṭan Abu Saʿid Abu l-Khayr, (5) Sulṭan Maḥmud Ghazi, (6) Sulṭan Sanjar Mażi, and (7) Sulṭan Ismaʿil Samani. See Francis Joseph Steingass, *A Comprehensive Persian-English Dictionary* (London: Routledge & Kegan Paul, 1963), 1503. While Satuq Bughra Khan is not included here, he is mentioned in other Central Asian sources as one of the seven. See, for example, Scott C. Levi and Ron Sela, eds., *Islamic Central Asia: An Anthology of Historical Sources* (Bloomington: Indiana University Press, 2009), 276.
21. On the hagiographic tradition surrounding Musliḥ al-Din Khujandi (or Maslaḥat al-Din Khujandi), see Devin DeWeese, " 'Stuck in the Throat of Chingīz Khān': Envisioning the Mongol Conquests in Some Sufi Accounts from the Fourteenth to Seventeenth Centuries," in *History and Historiography of Post-Mongol Central Asia and the Middle East: Studies in Honor of John E. Woods*, ed. J. Pfeiffer and S. A. Quinn (Wiesbaden, Germany: Harrassowitz, 2006), 34–36.
22. On Sulṭan Sayyid Burhan al-Din, see Devin DeWeese, "Aḥmad Yasavī in the Work of Burhān al-Dīn Qïlïch: The Earliest Reference to a Famously Obscure Central Asian Sufi Saint," *Asiatische Studien / Études Asiatiques* 67, no. 3 (2013): 837–79.
23. This anecdote involving Babur is missing from Group C texts. There, section 3 opens with a lengthy list of epithets of praise for Makhdum-i Aʿẓam, noting that "sixty fully qualified deputies remained after him to continue explaining the Path."
24. The event described here is the battle of Panipat (1526). A version of this anecdote occurs in the *Jamiʿ al-Maqamat*, fols. 73a–75a, and also in Muḥammad Ṣadiq Hamadani's *Ṭabaqat-i Shahjahani*. For discussion, see Muzaffar Alam, "The Mughals, the Sufi Shaykhs and the Formation of the Akbari Dispensation," *Modern Asian Studies* 43, no. 1 (2009): 149–50.
25. These lines initiated an ongoing correspondence between the Mughal emperors and the family of Makhdum-i Aʿẓam. In 1615, his grandson Khoja Hashim Dahbidi cited them in a letter to Emperor Jahangir, and Jahangir improvised a matching verse in reply. See Jahangir, *The Jahangirnama: Memoirs of Jahangir, Emperor of India*, trans. Wheeler M. Thackston (New York: Oxford University Press, 1999), 182.
26. For the text of the *Risala-i Baburiyya*, see Victoria R. Gardner, "The Written Representations of a Central Asian Ṣūfī Shaykh: Aḥmad ibn Mawlānā Jalāl al-Dīn Khwājagī Kāsānī "Makhdūm-i Aʿẓam" (d. 1542)," Ph.D. diss., University of Michigan, 2006, 708–732.
27. Although four wives are mentioned here, only three of them are discussed.
28. The term *īshān* is the Persian third-person plural pronoun ("they") and is a respectful form of address for Sufi shaykhs and learned religious figures in Central Asia.
29. Satuq Bughra Khan was a tenth-century ruler of the Qarakhanid dynasty best known for the legend surrounding his conversion to Islam. For the earliest surviving version of this narrative, see Scott C. Levi and Ron Sela, eds., *Islamic Central Asia: An Anthology of Historical Sources* (Bloomington: Indiana University Press, 2009), 73–76. On legends surrounding him and his shrine in Artush, see Fernand Grenard, "La légende de Satok Boghra Khan et l'histoire," *Journal Asiatique* ser. 9,

vol. 15 (1900): 5–79; Hamada Masami, "Le Mausolée et le culte de Satuq Bughrâ Khân," *Journal of the History of Sufism* 3 (2001): 62–87. On the Qarakhanids, see C. E. Bosworth, "Ilek-Khāns or Ḳarakhanids," EI², 3:1113–17.

30. In his account of Isḥaq Vali, Kashghari relies mainly on the Samarqandi author Muḥammad Ivaż's *Żiya᾽ al-Qulub*, a work completed in 1012/1603–1604. References here are to Houghton Library, MS Persian 95, where this section is found on fols 4b–5b. For a study which situates Isḥaq Vali's activities in the Bukharan khanate and its surrounds in the context of Uzbek dynastic politics, see Thomas Welsford, *Four Types of Loyalty in Early Modern Central Asia: The Tūqāy-Tīmūrid Takeover of Greater Ma wara al-nahr, 1598–1605* (Leiden: Brill, 2013).
31. A similar anecdote occurs in Kafshin Khoja's *Iqd al-Guhar* (Bodleian Library MS Ind. Inst. Pers. 117), fols. 26b–27a.
32. Muḥammad Ivaż, *Żiya᾽ al-Qulub* (Houghton Library, Manuscript Persian 95), fols. 5b–6b. Kashghari attributes this final anecdote (involving the gift horse) to Muḥammad Qasim, but in the *Żiya᾽ al-Qulub* it is clearly a continuation of Akhund Mulla Saʿid's narration.
33. This narration (*naql*) is slightly abbreviated from the *Żiya᾽ al-Qulub* (fols. 8b–12b).
34. Balkh is an ancient city in the north of Afghanistan. The Greek designation for this region, Bactria, derives from an earlier version of the same toponym. Now mostly in ruins, Balkh has been eclipsed by neighboring Mazar-i Sharif.
35. On Chusti, see B. Babajanov, "Mawlānā Lutfullāh Chūstī—An Outline of His Hagiography and Political Activity," *Zeitschrift der Deutschen Morgenländischen Gesellschaft* 149 (1999): 245–70.
36. On Mawlana Khurd Tashkandi (d. 975/1567), see Hamid Algar, "From Kashgar to Eyüp: The Lineages and Legacy of Sheik Abdullah Nidāī," in *Naqshbandis in Western and Central Asia: Change and Continuity*, ed. Elizabeth Özdalga (Richmond, UK: Curzon Press, 1999), 5–6. A biographical notice can be found in Shaykh Zinda Ali's *Ṣamarat al-Masha᾽ikh*, IV RUz 2619 (SVR 3, #2669), fols. 396a–399a.
37. The town of Ḥiṣar lies a short distance to the west of Tajikistan's capital Dushanbe. At this time, it was under the rule of a minor Uzbek dynast by the name of Temür Sulṭan.
38. The death of Pir Muḥammad Khan of Balkh is dated to 974/1566–67. See Thomas Welsford, "Rethinking the Ḥamzahids of Ḥiṣār," *Asiatische Studien* 65, no. 3 (2011): 814.
39. Group C texts state that Isḥaq Vali received his license directly from Makhdum-i Aʿẓam and omit this paragraph outlining the viewpoint of Ishan-i Kalan's partisans.
40. Muḥammad Ivaż, *Żiya᾽ al-Qulub*, fols. 19a–19b.
41. Abd al-Karim Khan reigned from 967/1559–60 to 1000/1591–92 (following O. F. Akimushkin, "Khronologiia pravitelei vostochnoi chasti Chagataiskogo ulusa [liniia Tugluk-Timur-khana]," in *Vostochnyi Turkestan i Sredniaia Aziia: Istoriia, kul'tura, sviazy*, ed. B. A. Litvinskii [Moscow: Nauka, 1984], 156–64, 224–25). The other significant hagiographic work on Isḥaq Vali, Shah Muḥammad ibn Ḥisam al-Din Payravi's *Jalis-i Mushtaqin*, says that it was Abd al-Karim Khan's brother Ṣufi Sulṭan (Ibrahim Sulṭan) in Kashgar who first invited the saint to the Tarim Basin (IV RAN A232, fol. 38b). Isḥaq Vali's arrival in the Tarim Basin can be tentatively assigned

to the late 1580s. According to the hagiography of Khoja Khavand Maḥmud, Isḥaq Vali was in Balkh in 994/1585–86, and a second meeting between the two men occurred in 1006/1597–98. This would allow for a twelve-year sojourn spanning the death of Abd al-Karim Khan (as described below). See D. Damrel, "Forgotten Grace: Khwâja Khâwand Maḥmûd Naqshbandî in Central Asia and Mughal India" (Ph.D. diss., Duke University, 1991), 61.

42. All manuscripts I have examined have *ṭūṭī aṭ* ("parrot horse"), a corruption of the *Żiyaʾ al-Qulub*'s original *tātū*. My translation restores the Persian original.
43. On Isḥaq Vali's exploits among the Kirghiz as portrayed in the *Żiyaʾ al-Qulub*, see J. Fletcher, "Confrontations Between Muslim Missionaries and Nomad Unbelievers in the Late Sixteenth Century: Notes on Four Passages from the 'Ḍiyāʾ al-qulūb'," in *Tractata Altaica*, ed. W. Heissig (Wiesbaden: Harrasowitz, 1976), 167–74. A variety of sources give Isḥaq Vali primary credit for the conversion of the Kirghiz to Islam, e.g. Nadr Muḥammad Khojam's *Kashshaf al-ʿArifin*, IV RUz 11420 (SVR 10, #6963), fols. 16b–18a.
44. The Prefecture of Ganzhou (Ganzhoufu 甘州府) lies at the western end of the Gansu corridor (now Zhangye 張掖).
45. The reference here to Bulghar is difficult to interpret. Usually referring to the Volga region, there is no toponym by this name in the vicinity of the Tarim Basin. It does not occur in other accounts of Muḥammad Khan's campaigns.
46. Ḥafiẓ, *The Collected Lyrics of Háfiz of Shiráz*, trans. Peter Avery (Cambridge: Archetype, 2007), 105; Rashid Ayvażi, ed., *Divan-i Ḥafiẓ: Bar Asas-i Hasht Nuskha-i Kamil-i Kuhan* (Tehran: Nashr-i Ṣadduq, 1376/1997), 1:144.
47. On this local saint of Turfan, see Ho-Dong Kim, "The Cult of Saints in Eastern Turkistan—The Case of Alp Ata in Turfan," in *Proceedings of the Thirty-Fifth Permanent International Altaistic Conference* (Taipei: Center for Chinese Studies Materials, 1993), 199–226.
48. Group B texts offers a different account here and show direct borrowing from the *Anis al-Ṭalibin* of Maḥmud Churas (Bodleian Library MS Ind. Inst. Pers. 45, fol. 91b). This text says that Isḥaq Vali offered up the life of his son Shahbaz Khoja to ward off the attacks of Alp Ata (cf. TKSawada 1:78–79).
49. This is Abdullah Khan b. Iskandar of the Shaybanid Dynasty, who ruled in Bukhara from 1557 until his death in 1598. Oleg Akimushkin dates this campaign against Kashgar and Yarkand to 1594–95. See O. F. Akimushkin, "Kashgarskii pokhod uzbekov pri Abdallakh-khane," in *Iranskaia filologiia. Kratkoe izlozhenie dokladov nauchnoi konferentsii, posviashchennoi 60-letiiu professora A. N. Boldyreva* (Moscow: Izdatel'stvo Akademii nauk USSR, 1969), 5–9.
50. Iṣḥaq Vali died in 1008/1598–99.
51. The Bagh-i Buland was a Timurid-era garden to the north of Samarqand. See Lisa Golombek, "The Gardens of Timur: New Perspectives," *Muqarnas* 12 (1995): 137–47. For a brief description of Isḥaq Vali's tomb, see "Mazar khodzha Iskhaka Vali bin Makhdum-i-Azama," *Spravochnaia kniga Samarkandskoi oblasti* 6 (1898): 197.
52. A family tree of this branch of the family is given in Komilkhon Kattaev, *Makhdumi A'zam va Dahbed* (Samarqand: Sug'diyon, 1994), 43.
53. The Golden (Altunluq) Shrine was the royal grave complex in Yarkand, located close to the Chaghatayid palace and the city's main mosque.

54. An independent Sufi community developed around Khoja Qasim on the outskirts of Yangiḥiṣar, as described in his hagiography, the *Nataʾij al-Arifin*. On this text, see Alexandre Papas, "Un manuscrit inconnu à propos des soufis de Kashgarie conservé à la Bibliothèque Nationale Firdawsi (Tadjikistan)," *Studia Iranica* 35, no. 1 (2006): 97–108.
55. These terms refer to the hierarchy of saints in Sufi thought, which is introduced in section 13 below.
56. The Chaghatayid Abdullah Khan reigned for approximately thirty years, from 1048/1638–39 to 1078/1668.
57. Kashghari's narrative has now moved into the reign ofIsmaʿil Khan, brother of Abdullah Khan, who established himself in the oasis of Aqsu with support from the Oirat Mongols and patronized Isḥaq Vali's grandson Khoja Muḥammad Abdullah (Shah Maḥmud Churas, *Khronika. Kriticheskii tekst, perevod, kommentarii, issledovanie i ukazateli O. F. Akimushkin* [Moscow: Nauka, 1976], 91). Ismaʿil seized the Yarkand throne from Abdullah Khan's son Yolbars in 1670.
58. A line from the *Valadnama*, by Rumi's son Sulṭan Valad (Tehran: Muʾassasa-i Nashr-i Huma, 1376/1997–98), 90.
59. Group B adds the location of the khan's death as Topluq in the Yangiḥiṣar oasis (TKSawada 1:85).
60. Khoja Afaq's presence in western China is attested from as early as 1671, meaning that his expulsion must have occurred soon after Ismaʿil Khan's accession to the throne. See Joseph Trippner, "Islamische Gruppen und Gräberkult in Nordwest-China," *Die Welt des Islams, New Series* 7, no. 1 (1961): 148.
61. According to the *Tazkira-i Abd al-Mannan* (IV RAN A231, fol. 14b), Khoja Ubaydullah died nine months after the passing of Abd al-Karim Khan, hence in 1592.
62. This section varies considerably across the three groups of texts. For analysis, see Minoru Sawada, "Three Groups of *Tadhkira-i Khwājagān*: Viewed from the Chapter on Khwāja Āfāq," in James A. Millward, Shinmen Yasushi, and Sugawara Jun, eds., *Studies on Xinjiang Historical Sources in Seventeenth–Twentieth Centuries* (Tokyo: Toyō Bunko, 2010), 9–30.
63. *Jū* here is believed to refer to Lhasa, reflecting Mo. *J̌uu* "Tibet, Lhasa," which derives from Tibetan *jo-bo* "elder brother, lord," the name of Tibet's most sacred statue of the Buddha, which is housed in the Jokhang temple in of Lhasa (cf. Ma. *Joo*; Oirat *Zü*).
64. The word here is Chaghatay *jalā*, from Mo. *J̌alağa* "tassel, crest, thick silk thread" (Ferdinand Lessing, ed., *Mongolian-English Dictionary* [Bloomington, IN: Mongolia Society, 1980], 1028).
65. This refers to the Choros aristocrat Galdan Boshogtu (b. 1644, r. 1678–1697), on whom see Arthur W. Hummel, *Eminent Chinese of the Ch'ing Period (1644–1912)* (Washington, DC: U.S. Government Printing Office, 1943–44), 1:265–268; Christopher Atwood, *Encyclopedia of Mongolia and the Mongol Empire* (New York: Facts on File, 2004), 193–94.
66. Deriving from the Old Turkic *törü*, the original meaning of *törä* is "rule, political authority." In Oirat Mongolian, it retained this sense, but for the Muslims of the Tarim Basin, it became the title by which they referred to the Junghar sovereign. The title was subsequently taken up by elite Muslim families in the khanate of Kokand.

67. This seems to refer to Baatar Khung-Taiji's son Sengge (r. 1653–70), but as others have noted, any such reference would be anachronistic as Sengge died in 1670. According to Maḥmud Churas, Sengge had played kingmaker on an earlier occasion in Yarkand, when he briefly installed a son of Yolbars Khan on the throne around 1668 (Churas, *Khronika*, 94–95). It may be that the two episodes became conflated in local memory. Galdan's encroachment on the Tarim Basin commenced in the late 1670s, and in 1679 the Qing court learnt that he had taken control of Hami and Turfan. Scholars disagree on the precise date of the expedition that resulted in the installation of Khoja Afaq in Yarkand, but 1682 seems the best fit for the available data.
68. Group B texts describe this impost as four thousand per month, while Group C gives the total as one hundred thousand *tangga*. See Sawada, "Three Groups of *Tadhkira-i khwājagān*."
69. Muḥammad Emin Khan was killed some time around 1104/1692–93. Sources such as the *Tarikh-i Kashghar* identify his chief protagonist at this time as Khoja Yaḥya in Kashgar (O. F. Akimushkin, ed., *Tārīkh-i Kāshġar: anonimnaia tiurkskaia khronika vladitelei Vostochnogo Turkestana po konets XVII veka* [Saint Petersburg: Peterburgskoe vostokovedenie, 2001], fol. 102a), whose support probably included Kirghiz. Muḥammad Yusuf Munshi states that in 1102/1690–91 Muḥammad Emin Khan sent a request to Subḥan Quli Khan in Bukhara for support against the Kirghiz who were overwhelming his kingdom. See Muḥammad Yusuf Munshi, *Tazkira-i Muqimkhani* (Tehran: Miraṣ-i Maktub, 2001), 247.
70. Here and in the following section, Group C has a considerably abbreviated and much more partisan narrative. It tells that the Makhdumzada (i.e., Khoja Muḥammad Abdullah) died in Kashmir. Khoja Afaq invited his sons Shuʿayb and Danyal to return to Kashgar, but they declined, instead taking their father's body to Dahbid for burial. Khoja Shuʿayb then took up Khoja Afaq's invitation but was killed as soon as he reached Sanju. The narrative is much more hostile to Khoja Afaq, who is depicted as always intent on killing these rival khojas. For doing so, he "soon went to fuel the fires of hell." See TAHartmann, 216.
71. The Tiznab River (some manuscripts have Tezab, or "fast-flowing"), one of the main waterways of the Yarkand oasis, runs parallel to the Yarkand (Zarafshan) River to the east of the city.
72. Dihkhuda's dictionary identifies this as an Indian aphorism. Ali Akbar Dihkhuda, *Lughatnama* (Tehran: Muʾassasa-i Lughatnama-i Dihkhuda, 1377/1998), 12:18402.
73. This image of slaughtering enemies and making a mill run with their blood occurs at various points throughout Kashghari's narrative and is a trope of Islamic historiography.
74. The opening words of Sura 94 of the Quran: "Did We not expand for thee thy breast, and lift from thee thy burden that weighed heavily upon thy back?"
75. Sources on Khoja Danyal's activities during his sojourn in Transoxiana are scarce, but one text produced within his circle of associates, Muḥammad Yusuf b. Muhtashim Yarkandi's *Majmaʿ al-Asrar* (written 1107/1695–96), tells us that along with his inherited spiritual lineage, Khoja Danyal also affiliated himself to one Khoja Shams al-Din. Shams al-Din was a grandson of Khoja Hashim Dahbidi (d. 1636) and therefore theoretically a member of the "rival" Makhdumzada

lineage descending from Khoja Muḥammad Amin (the same line as Khoja Afaq). See IVAN RUz 5468 (SVR 11, #7525), fol. 108a.

76. All manuscripts I have examined read *ḫāk-i Ḫujand*, but the only accessible manuscript of the Persian section of the *Divan-i Arshi* reads *ḫāl-i Ḫujand* ("Khujand's mole"), a more conventional trope for the allure that a saint exerts on his devotee. IPN ANRT 2277, fol. 21b.
77. These lines are not found in Mashhuri's published divan, Ibrahim Mäshhuri, *Divani Mäshhuri* (Kashgar, China: Qäshqär Uyghur näshriyati, 1985).
78. Group C omits mention of Khoja Mahdi (TAHartmann, 217).
79. Group B excludes all mention of Ḥasan and gives the impression that Khoja Afaq was taking pride in his son Mahdi. These texts erroneously describe Ḥasan as Mahdi's son (TKSawada, 2:99, 103).
80. Khoja Afaq died in 1694.
81. The *aʿlam akhund*, or simply *aʿlam*, was the leading jurisprudent of a city or region.
82. Ḥażrat Mazar is the Yaghdu shrine now known as the shrine of Afaq Khoja (among Uyghurs) or the tomb of the Fragrant Concubine (among Chinese).
83. Tüshük Tagh ("mountain with a hole") is the geographic feature also known as Shipton's Arch. See Eric Shipton, *Mountains of Tartary: Mountaineering and Exploration in Northern and Central Asia in the 1950s* (London: Hodder & Stoughton, 1950), 88–101. According to Qing sources, in the eighteenth century, the natural archway was associated with the Prophet Luqman and was a site of annual religious rituals. See Jianping Wang, "Islam in Uighur Society as Recorded by Chinese Gazetteers in the Late Qing Dynasty," in *Central Asia on Display: Proceedings of the VII Conference of the European Society for Central Asian Studies*, ed. Gabriele Rasuly-Paleczek and Julia Katschnig (Münster, Germany: Lit, 2004), 318.
84. On the assassination of governor Sayyid Beg, see Mir Khal al-Din Katib Yarkandi, *Hidayatnama* (IVR RAN C560), fols. 194b–196a. Group B texts say that "Qalandar Beg's son Muḥammad Emin Beg" was governor of Kashgar, while Shah Ṣaʿid (*sic*) Beg was governor of Yarkand, and that both were killed (TKSawada, 2:102).
85. Group B does not implicate Khoja Mahdi in the murder of Khanim Padishah.
86. According to the *Tarikh-i Kashghar*, Qalandar Beg was installed as deputy governor of Yarkand during the period of Khoja Afaq's tenure in Yarkand. Group B adds that Jarub Beg (from the Kirghiz) was deputy governor.
87. The princes referred to here must include Khoja Afaq's surviving son, Khoja Ḥasan, but probably also members of Khoja Afaq's wider family. It is known that the family of Khoja Afaq's brother Karamatullah, for example, spent time in exile in India during this period.
88. Group B adds Qarazangi Beg and Jarub Beg. The *Tarikh-i Kashghar* (fol. 103a) refers to Arzu Muḥammad as the *atalïq* (tutor) of Sulṭan Aḥmad.
89. Aqbash Khan was killed in 1107/1695–96.
90. A Mongolian term meaning "guard post," not to be confused with the Qarakhanid dynasty. The *qarakhan* was the small Junghar garrison and, by extension, the officer in charge of it. According to a memorial from 1765, the *qarakhan* (Ma. *harahan*; Ch. Ha-la-han 哈喇罕) was responsible for maintaining population records and collecting tribute from the Tarim Basin (QXMD, 76:74–82). The period of Kirghiz dominance described here commenced around 1700. In 1701, a letter reached the Qing

court from Hami, stating that "in spring of last year all the Burut (i.e., Kirghiz) joined Arzu Muḥammad in an attack on Kashgar from Andijan. Khan Khoja's son Khoja Aḥmad colluded with the Burut and let them into the city, and the Burut killed those in Kashgar who were sympathetic to Tsewang Rabtan." Zhongguo diyi lishi dang'anguan and Nei Menggu daxue Mengguxue xueyuan, eds., *Dayičing gürün-ü dotuγadu yamun-u Mongγol bičig-ün ger-ün dangse* (Hohhot, China: Nei Menggu renmin chubanshe, 2005), 16:340–41.

91. On the activities of these Kirghiz, see M. A. Salakhetdinova, "Soobshcheniia o kirgizakh v 'Khidaiat-name' Mir Khal' ad-Dina," *Izvestiia Akademiia nauk Kirgizskoi SSR.* Seriia obshchestvennykh nauk 3, no. 2 (1961): 133–40.
92. The *shadiyana* refers to festive music; versions of it have today been incorporated into the Uyghur classical repertoire. Judging from its use here, the *shadiyana* did not exclusively announce good tidings but might also indicate the arrival of important news and the coming and going of the city's ruler.
93. It is difficult to establish a chronology of these events, but if we calculate backward from information that Kashghari provides in the following sections, Khoja Danyal's exile to Ili may have occurred around 1713.
94. The word used here, *bāzargān*, carries a more specific meaning than its standard dictionary definition of "merchant." Under the Junghars, the Bazargan were a select group of official merchants who carried out trade on behalf of the Junghar aristocrats. Within the Junghar social system, they may be thought of as akin to an estate group.
95. NMAT, 5:62.
96. *Khung-Taiji* is a Mongolian title deriving from the Chinese *huangtaizi* 皇太子, "crown prince." Among the Junghar Mongols, the use of this title indicated the Junghar ruler's nominally subordinate status to the khan of the Khoshud. The *khung-taiji* referred to here is Tsewang Rabtan (1643–1727), who was given the title *Erdeni Joriqtu Khung-Taiji* by the Dalai Lama in 1694. On Tsewang Rabtan, see Hummel, *Eminent Chinese of the Ch'ing Period (1644–1912)*, 2:757–59. On titulature among the Junghars, see Junko Miyawaki, "Did a Dzungar Khanate Really Exist?," *Journal of the Anglo-Mongolian Society* 10, no. 1 (1987): 1–5.
97. White Turbans here mimics the Mongolian terminology for the Muslims, the "white hats" (Mo. *čaġan malaġaitan*).
98. Erke Khan was the son of Abd al-Rashid Khan II, who had briefly reigned alongside Khoja Afaq in Yarkand before being deposed, and Temür was Erke's son. This lineage, one of the few branches of the Chaghatayid royal family that can be traced into the eighteenth century, resided in Junghar captivity in the Ili region. A report from the 1750s describes Temür Khan as living in Kuitun 奎屯 on the northern flank of the Tianshan (QXMD, 9:401–5). After the Qing conquest, the family was relocated to Beijing.
99. In the Islamic tradition, Yusuf of Canaan represents the ideal of masculine beauty.
100. A Qing report on the tax system in the Tarim Basin from 1759 says that Yarkand paid one hundred thousand *tangga* to the Junghars annually, while Kashgar provided sixty-seven thousand *tangga* as well as quantities of grain, cotton, and saffron. For discussion, see Wang Dongping, *Ming Qing Xiyushi yu Huizushi lungao* (Beijing: Shangwu yinshuguan, 2014), 3–20.

101. Judging from the following anecdote, which describes the death of Tsewang Rabtan in 1727, the return of Khoja Danyal and his sons to the Tarim Basin took place around 1720.
102. The basic account here, that Tsewang Rabtan's death coincided with the arrival of emissaries from the Volga for matchmaking negotiations, is confirmed by other sources. Tsewang Rabtan had already married one of his daughters to a son of the Kalmyk Ayuki Khan (d. 1724) and was in the process of arranging more such royal weddings. The Kalmyk wife of Tsewang Rabtan's referred to here was Seterjab, and the son she supposedly hoped to install on the throne was Luuzang-Shonu, who became a thorn in the side of Galdan-Tseren in the following years. On these events, see I. Ia. Zlatkin, *Istoriia Dzhungarskogo khanstva (1635–1758)* (Moscow: Nauka, 1964).
103. The *bāj* was a customs duty levied on caravans, while the *kharāj* was the land tax.
104. According to a chronogram by Khoja Danyal's son Khoja Yaʿqub (Jahan), Danyal's death occurred in 1142/1729–30. *Divan-i Arshi*, MS Supplement Turc 969, fol. 73a.
105. This refers to the Timurid Ḥusayn Bayqara (r. 1470–1506), whose rule in Herat was regarded as something of a golden age in Islamic history.
106. On the *mashāyikh-i Turk*, see Devin DeWeese, "The Masha'ikh-i Turk and the Khojagan: Rethinking the Links Between the Yasavi and Naqshbandi Sufi Traditions," *Journal of Islamic Studies* 7, no. 2 (1996): 173–88.
107. Ḥafiẓ, *The Collected* Lyrics, 219; *Divan-i Ḥafiẓ*, 1:214.
108. On the significance of this verse in the Sufi tradition, see Toby Mayer, "Traditions of Esoteric and Sapiential Quranic Commentary," in *The Study Quran*, ed. Seyyed Hossein Nasr, Caner K. Dagli, Maria Massi Dakake, and Joseph E. B. Lumbard (New York: HarperOne, 2015), 1662–65.
109. Farid al-Din Aṭṭar, *The Speech of the Birds: Manṭiqu'ṭ-Ṭair*, trans. Peter Avery (Cambridge: Islamic Texts Society, 1998), 39.
110. Ṣaʾib-i Tabrizi, *Divan-i Ṣaʾib Tabrizi*, ed. Muḥammad Qahraman (Tehran: Shirkat-i Intisharat-i Ilmi va Farhangi, 1985–1991), 2:1061.
111. Aṭṭar, *The Speech of the Birds*, 39.
112. Khiżr ("the green man") is a figure who often turns up in legends and hagiographies at opportune moments to perform good deeds. See A. J. Wensinck, "al-K͟h aḍir (al-K͟h iḍr)," in EI², 4:902–5.
113. On the Sufi practice of remembrance, see L. Gardet, "Dhikr," EI², 2:223–27.
114. See H. Algar, "Naḳshband, Khʷādja Bahāʾ al-Dīn," EI², 7:933–34.
115. Abd al-Raḥman ibn Aḥmad Jami, *Maṣnavi-i Haft Avrang* (Tehran: Miraṣ-i Maktub, 1997–99), 1:484.
116. Abd al-Raḥman ibn Aḥmad Jami, *Nafaḥat al-Uns min Ḥażarat al-Quds* (1336/1957), 385.
117. For discussion of this ruling, see Jürgen Paul, *Doctrine and Organization: The Khwājagān/Naqshbandīya in the First Generation after Bahā'uddīn* (Berlin: Das Arabische Buch, 1998), 57.
118. Jami, *Maṣnavi-i Haft Avrang*, 1:486.
119. Abu Bakr Qaffal al-Shashi (291/904–365/976) was a prominent Shafiʿi jurisprudent from Tashkent (Shash).
120. This is a line from Abu l-Ḥasan Bakri's prose account of the Prophet Muḥammad's nighttime ascension to heaven (the *miʿraj*). See Frederick S. Colby, *Narrating*

Muḥammad's Night Journey: Tracing the Development of the Ibn ʿAbbās Ascension Discourse (Albany: State University of New York Press, 2008), 221.

121. This intrusion into the text may indicate that this section was originally part of a separate work.

122. The Night of Power (*laylat al-qadr*) occurs toward the end of the Islamic month of Ramadan, which is when Muḥammad's ascension to Heaven is said to have occurred. The Night of Desires (*laylat al-raghāʾib*) marks the beginning of the "holy three months" of Rajab, Shaʿban, and Ramadan.

123. *Masnavi*, book 5, lines 1537–38. See Jalal al-Din Rumi, *The Mathnawí of Jalálu'ddín Rúmí*, trans. Reynold A. Nicholson (Leiden, Netherlands: Brill, 1925), 5:93.

124. IVR RAN D191 (fol. 54b) adds a note attributing this line to Khoja Qasim Anvari (1356–1433).

125. Ḥafiẓ, *The Collected* Lyrics, 114; *Divan-i Ḥafiẓ*, 1:107.

126. Qing sources (QXMD, 65:315) refer to a Yarkand akhund by the name of Shah Abd al-Qadir, whose learning was called on in translating Persian correspondence with neighboring polities—possibly the same Shah Abd al-Qadir referred to here. One Group B manuscript gives his nisba as Balkhi (TKSawada, 3:33).

127. The Sufi doctrine of the hierarchy of saints was first articulated by the eleventh-century scholar al-Hujwiri. See *The Kashf al-Maḥjúb: The Oldest Persian Treatise on Sufism*, trans. Reynold A. Nicholson (Leiden, Netherlands: Brill, 1911), 213–14. See also I. Goldziher, "Abdāl," EI², 1:94–95.

128. On the role of the pole (*quṭb*, also translated as "axis" or "pivot") in Islamic mysticism, see F. de Jong, "al-Ḳuṭb," EI², 5:543–46.

129. Fakhr al-Din Ali b. Ḥusayn Vaʿiẓ Kashifi, *Rashaḥat-i Ayn al-Ḥayat* (Tehran: Bunyad-i Nikukari-i Nuriyani, 1356/1977), 2:485.

130. Abu Jaʿfar al-Ṭaḥawi (d. 321/933) was born into the family of a prominent disciple of al-Shafiʿi but is said to have left the school when he was around twenty years old and became a leading Ḥanafi scholar.

131. Although this excerpt purports to be a citation from Ṭaḥawi, I have been unable to locate it in any of his works. Likewise, I cannot identify the following passage from "the book entitled *Muḥiṭ*" (which most likely refers to Marghinani's *al-Muḥiṭ al-Burhani fi l-Fiqh al-Nuʿmani*, a standard work of Ḥanafi *fiqh*). It is possible that these are both false citations, fabricated to give scholarly weight to popular traditions.

132. Muḥammad Abu al-Qasim Kahi, *Divan-i Qasim Kahi* (Tehran: Talar-i Kitab, 1366), 195.

133. See Mehdi Aminrazavi, "Jurjani, Mir Sayyid Sharif," in *The Biographical Encyclopedia of Islamic Philosophy*, ed. Oliver Leaman (London: Bloomsbury Academic, 2015), 268–69.

134. See Leonard Lewisohn, "The Life and Times of Kamāl Khujandī," *Journal of Turkish Studies* 18 (1994): 163–77.

135. The text here varies in one significant way from Khujandi's published divan, where the final line of reads *maydān-i daʿvá* "the field of pretense" in place of *maydān-i maʿná* "the field of meaning," which provides a more satisfying reading. Kamal Khujandi, *Divan-i Shaykh Kamal Khujandi: Hamrah ba Sharḥ-i Ḥal u Zindagani* (Tehran: Surush, 1375/1995–96), 1:322.

136. These two men are mentioned in the anonymous *Tarikh-i Kashghar*. See Akimushkin (ed.), *Tārīkh-i Kāshgar*, 105, 147. Despite the respect he is accorded here in Kashghari's anecdote, the unfortunate Akhund Zihni was in fact executed by Abdullah Khan for insubordination.

137. The Buraq was the mysterious animal on which the Prophet Muḥammad made his nighttime ascension to Heaven, the Miʿraj. It is often described as a horselike creature with a human face and wings.

138. This is the title of a range of texts on Islamic doctrine (*al-ʿaqāʾid*). Probably what is intended here is a Persian commentary on one of these texts, such as the *Sharḥ-i Aqaʾid-i Nasafi*, or the *Sharḥ-i Aqaʾid-i Jalali*.

139. These are seventeenth-century, mostly Indian poets identified with the "Indian style" (*sabk-i Hindi*): Naṣir Ali Sirhindi (d. 1697), Muḥammad Isḥaq Shaukat Bukhari (d. 1695), Abd al-Qadir Bedil (d. 1720), and Mulla Jami Bekhud Lahuri (d. 1673).

140. The reference here is to one of the pillars of Naqshbandi Sufi doctrine, "journeying in the homeland" (*safar dar vaṭan*).

141. Cf. *Divan-i Arshi*, IPN ANRT 2277, fol. 5b.

142. Cf. Nazra Ishaq, "Critical Edition of Diwan-e-Nasir Ali Sirhindi with Introduction and Notes" (Ph.D. diss., Aligarh Muslim University, 2015), 134, which has *zamīn* "earth" for *vaṭan* "homeland."

143. A popular verse attributed to one Baba Aṣli Damavandi. Muḥammad Ali Ṣafvat, ed., *A̲sar-i Hazar u Yak Sukhanvar* (Qum, Iran: Kitabfurushi-i Tabish, 1328/1949), 14.

144. The two creations, literally "two weighty things" (*al-thaqalayn*), refers to humanity and the jinns.

145. The second line of this couplet is from Tabrizi, *Divan-i Ṣaʾib Tabrizi*, 5:2349.

146. This vague date probably refers to the seventh or eighth year of Khoja Jahan's rule in Yarkand. If we assume that he was appointed upon his father's death in 1729, then the meeting referred to here would have taken place around 1736–37.

147. Abd al-Raḥman Jami's *Nafaḥat al-Uns* and Mawlana Ṣafi's *Rashahat Ayn al-Ḥayat* are two major works of Sufi hagiography from the Timurid period. For a translation of this anecdote, see Mawlana Ali ibn Ḥusayn Ṣafī, *Beads of Dew from the Source of Life: Histories of the Khwājagān, the Masters of Wisdom*, trans. Mukhtar Holland (Fort Lauderdale, FL: Al-Baz, 2001), 133–35. It occurs in abbreviated form in the *Nafaḥat al-Uns*, 402.

148. The Preserved Tablet (*al-Lawḥ al-Maḥfūẓ*) is the tablet on which the divine decrees are written, according to Sura 85 of the Quran. See Daniel A. Madigan, "Preserved Tablet," in *Encyclopaedia of the Qurʾān* (Leiden, Netherlands: Brill, 2004), 3:261–63.

149. Khoja Muʾmin was not a direct descendant of Khoja Afaq, but of his brother Khoja Karamatullah (d. 1108/1696–97). Muʾmin was the father of Ḥusayn (Ch. E-se-yin 額色尹) and grandfather of Turdi (Ch. Tu-er-du 圖爾都), members of the Makhdumzada family who became Qing aristocrats in Beijing.

150. The term *shang* probably derives from Mo. *sang* "treasury, store house" (itself a borrowing from Ch. *cang* 倉), and is found in the compound *shangbegi*, an official responsible for taxation in the Junghar and Qing periods. Its use here for bolts of cloth may reflect the role of textiles as a unit of taxation.

151. A Tashkent manuscript (IVAN RUz 45, fols. 61b–62a) adds here that "the date of his death was 1154/1741–42."

152. NMAT, 1:35 (ghazal #10).

153. Abd al-Wahhab (Ch. A-bu-du-gua-bu 阿布都瓜布) is mentioned in Muḥammad Emin (Ṣadr) Kashghari's *Asar al-Futuḥ* (IVAN RUz 753, fol. 124a) as Niẓam al-Din Abd al-Wahhab. He was the elder brother of Khojasi Beg, who originally belonged to a family of shaykhs from Qarakhoja in the Turfan oasis. During the rule of Burhan al-Din, he was appointed to the governorship of Yarkand.

154. Group B adds: "At this time Ivaż Beg was governor of Yarkand. When he died, they brought Ghazi Beg from Khotan and made him governor. Ghazi Beg's son Umar Beg was governor of Khotan, Abd al-Wahhab Beg of Aqsu, Khojasi Beg of Ush, and Khosh Kifäk Beg of Kashgar" (TKSawada, 3:45–46).

155. Khosh Kifäk Beg (Ch. He-shi-ke 和什克) belonged to a line of aristocrats who had served the region's Chaghatayid and Junghar rulers. See J. Fletcher, "The Biography of Khwush Kipäk Beg (d. 1781) in the Wai-fan Meng-ku Hui-pu wang kung piao chuan," *Acta Orientalia Academiae Scientiarum Hungaricae* 36 (1982): 167–72.

156. Umar Mirza (Ch. E-mu-er Bi 額穆爾比) eventually fled the Tarim Basin for the Kokand khanate and returned to submit to the Qing in the spring of 1761. Soon after that, he died.

157. Khojasi (Ch. Huo-ji-si 霍集斯) is referred to in the *Asar al-Futuḥ* as Amir Sharaf al-Din Khoja Yusuf Beg. For his official Qing biography, see Qi Yunshi et al., *Waifan Menggu Huibu wanggong biaozhuan*, ed. Bao Wenhan and Qi Chaoketu (Hohhot, China: Neimenggu daxue chubanshe, 1998), juan 116. The town of Ush (Ch. Wushi 烏什) is now known as Uchturpan, reflecting a Junghar policy to relocate residents of Turfan there in the 1720s.

158. To "open Islam" is the standard term for the establishment of Islamic rule, reflecting the sense of opening new territories to Islam (cf. the Arabic *fataḥa*) and spreading the faith.

159. Daulat Bagh (Ch. Duolaitebage 多來特巴格) is a village on the southeastern outskirts of Kashgar.

160. Dabachi (r. 1753–55) was a brother of Tsewang Rabtan. In 1751 he fled to the Kazakh steppe, and in 1752 he returned to seize the Junghar throne with the support of the Khoid aristocrat Amursana.

161. Kimä (Ch. Kemai 克買) is a village in the Fayżabad oasis.

162. At this point, Group B texts add details on the civil war among the Junghars (TKSawada, 3:55–57; TKShaw, 48–49). To summarise: "Galdan-Tseren died and his son Ajan took the throne. He proved a dissolute ruler and his realm descended into chaos. His sister Ghulam Biya conspired with Nemekü Jirghal to imprison Ajan and install Nemekü Jirghal as *törä*. The plot was discovered, and they were both blinded and imprisoned. One of Galdan-Tseren's sons by a concubine, Lama Darja, then rebelled and seized the throne from Ajan. Galdan-Tseren's nephews Amursana and Dabachi then seized the position of *törä*, but fell out among themselves, and Amursana fled with five hundred Qalmaqs to Beijing. The emperor favored him and sent him back with General Saral and a thousand troops."

163. The suburb of Qaraqir (Ch. Kalakeer 喀拉克爾) is situated to the north of Kashgar, while a village of the same name lies to its south.

164. Ḥafiẓ, *The Collected* Lyrics, 97; *Divan-i Ḥafiẓ*, 1:86.

165. There is a Kalta Yaylaq (Ch. Kaleta Yayilake 喀勒塔亞依拉克) east of Kashgar near Maralbeshi. Kelpin (Ch. Keping 柯平) lies between it and Aqsu.
166. Kashghari writes *madadchi* (*madarchi* in some manuscripts) and seems to treat the word as a personal name. In fact, it represents the Mongolian word *medegeči* (Oirat *medēci*), which can be translated as "messenger, envoy." See John R. Krueger, *Materials for an Oirat-Mongolian to English Citation Dictionary* (Bloomington, IN: Mongolia Society, 1978), 596.
167. I am unable to identify who, or what, this is referring to. This phrase is missing from many manuscripts and may be a later insertion in the text.
168. On the discourse of salt and obligations to one's patron, see Hamada Masami, " 'Shio no gimu' to 'seisen' to no aida de," *Tōyōshi kenkyū* 52, no. 2 (1994): 122–48.
169. Beshkerem (Ch. Boshikeranmu 伯什克然木) and Fayżabad (Ch. Jiashi 伽師) are located in the Kashgar oasis. In 1760, shortly after the Qing conquest of the Tarim Basin, the same Muḥarram (Ch. Mai-la-mu 邁喇木) and Niyaz (Ch. Ni-ya-si 呢雅斯) mentioned here rebelled against the Qing. Some sources give Muḥarram Beg's name as Bahram Beg.
170. NMAT, 3:182 (ghazal #216).
171. *Ma<u>s</u>navi*, book 1, line 913. See *The Mathnawí of Jalálu'ddín Rúmí*, 2:51. The reference is to a ḥadith that is cited in explication of Quran 4:71: "O you who believe! Take your precautions; then go forth in companies or go forth all together."
172. The elephant that led the campaign of Abrahah, king of Yemen, on an invasion of the Ḥijaz, mentioned in Sura 105 of the Quran.
173. Khoja Afaq's son Khoja Ḥasan had been known as Ṣaḥibqiran ("the lord of the felicitous conjunction"), hence this child's nickname Qiran.
174. Cf. similar stories involving Khoja Isḥaq Vali in section 4.
175. These lines are attributed to Khoja Baha al-Din Naqshband. See Abd al-Raḥman Najim, ed., *Gulzar-i A<u>s</u>ar* (Beirut: Maṭbaʿa al-Adabiyya, 1309/1891), 24.
176. The *ushaq* (Ch. wu-sha-ke 烏沙克) were a corps of slave soldiers who served the khojas. The *A<u>s</u>ar al-Futuḥ* (fols. 134a, 152a) refers to them as the Golden Ushaq (*Altun Ushāq*), a name that calls to mind other bodyguard units such as the Altun Jilau of the Khivan khans, for which see Shir Muḥammad Mirab Munis and Muḥammad Riza Mirab Agahi, *Firdaws al-Iqbal*, trans. Yuri Bregel (Leiden, Netherlands: Brill, 1999), 584, n. 381. The term is commonly identified with Modern Uyghur *ushshaq* "small, insignificant," but given its association with the khojas, it may ultimately derive from Arabic *ʿushshāq* "lovers."
177. This refers to the relatively late conversion of Buddhist Khotan to Islam. For the legends surrounding its Islamization, see Fernand Grenard, *J.-L. Dutreuil de Rhins. Mission scientifique dans la haute Asie, 1890–1895* (Paris: E. Leroux, 1897–98), vol. 3.
178. Reading *Sögät Tagh* for *Sögä Tagh*. Sögät Mountain (Ch. Sugaite tage 苏盖特塔格) is situated close to Artush.
179. The Sharas were an *otog* of the Junghars who, along with the Makhus *otog*, resided around Qarashahr. According to a description of Junghar society, the Sharas consisted of three thousand households under two *jaisangs*, while the Makhus were five thousand households under one *jaisang*. See Christopher Atwood, "Titles, Appanages, Marriages, and Officials: A Comparison of Political Forms in the Zünghar and Thirteenth-Century Mongol Empires," in *Imperial Statecraft: Political Forms*

and Techniques of Governance in Inner Asia, Sixth-Twentieth Centuries, ed. David Sneath (Bellingham, WA: Center for East Asian Studies, Western Washington University, 2006), 241. The two groups resisted the Qing conquest and were wiped out. In the early twentieth century, the Mongolist Gustav Ramstedt recorded local traditions among the Xinjiang Mongols surrounding the disappearance of the two groups, according to which the Sharas-Makhas had settled among a friendly, far-off people and lost contact with their brethren in Jungharia. See Gustav John Ramstedt, *Seven Journeys Eastward 1898–1912*, trans. John R. Krueger (Bloomington, IN: Mongolia Society, 1978), 182.

180. Noruz marks the onset of spring, which would place these events in approximately March 1755.
181. Group B texts say that they met in Guma.
182. Strictly speaking, this is not a verse from the Quran but a line from the hadith.
183. A refence to Verse 91:3 of the Quran.
184. The only known manuscript copy of the *Divan-i Futuḥi* belongs to the collection of the Institute of Written Heritage in Dushanbe, IV ANRT 2277, fols. 67b–78a.
185. The Qushchi were among the leading groups of the "left wing" of the Kirghiz, occupying territory around Andijan at the eastern end of the Ferghana Valley. The *Tarikh-i Raḥimkhani* describes Qubad as the "head of the ranks of Kirghiz" (*sarāmad-i ṭabaqāt-i Qirqiz*) and a pillar of support to Irdana Bi of the Ming, who founded the Kokand Khanate. After a failed collaboration to capture the city of Ura Tepe (today's Istaravshan), Qubad Bi broke with Irdana Bi and shifted his sphere of activity to the Tarim Basin. See A. Z. Validov, "Nekotorye dannye po istorii Fergany XVIII-go stoletiia," *Protokoly zasedanii Turkestanskogo kruzhka liubitelei arkheologii* 20, no. 1 (1916): 106–7. The *Aṣar al-Futuḥ* (fol. 136a) says that as a child, Qubad had spent time in the service of Khoja Afaq's son Khoja Aḥmad. After the events described in *In Remembrance of the Saints*, he served as governor of Kashgar for a time, then departed for Kokand. In a letter sent to Qing officials in 1763, Irdana Bi reported that he had executed Qubad for rebellion and brigandage (QXMD, 59:233). The Qushchi "Ivaula" (Ubaydullah) whom Russian captain I. G. Andreev encountered in 1785, was therefore not Qubad but his son. For this reference, see N. Aristov, "Opyt vyiasneniia etnicheskogo sostava Kirgiz-Kazakov bol'shoi ordy," *Zhivaia starina* 3–4 (1894): 443. Qubad's two sons, Berke (Ch. Bo-er-ke 博爾克) and Ubaydullah (Ch. E-bai-du-la 額拜都拉), were both prominent Qushchi chieftains in postconquest Xinjiang, before Berke fled Qing territory for Kokand in 1783, incurring the wrath of the Qianlong emperor.
186. Ghalcha Bi is mentioned in Mir Khal al-Din Katib Yarkandi's *Hidayatnama* (IVR RAN C560, 1142/1730), fol. 138b.
187. This surviving group of Khoja Ḥasan's disciples maintained a nonhereditary master-disciple chain of transmission after Ḥasan's death in the mid-1720s. As I have argued elsewhere, this group should be considered the original Black Mountain faction, and it was only during the Qing, thanks to their alliance with those loyal to the Isḥaqiyya, that this term expanded to include the Isḥaqiyya. See David Brophy, "Confusing Black and White: Naqshbandi Sufi Affiliations and the Transition to Qing Rule in the Tarim Basin," *Late Imperial China* 39, no. 1 (2018): 29–65. A verse account of this community describes "Mavlavi Masjid" (i.e. the Akhund Mulla

Majid mentioned here) as fifth in the chain of spiritual transmission from Ḥasan. See *Silsila-i Bughrakhani-i Manẓum* (IVAN RUz 586), fol. 276b.

188. Group B texts add that his younger brothers, Mirza Murad Beg and Mirza Sherdagh Beg, were devotees of the saintly family (TKSawada, 5:30).

189. This title is not found elsewhere in Kashghari's work, but it may be a reference to Khoja Afaq.

190. The first line of this couplet is by Mawlana Ḥuzni of Isfahan, though the second line differs from the text found in reference works on him. See, for example, Muḥammad Shafiʿ Ḥusayni Amili, *Maḥafil al-Muʾminin fi Ẕayl Majalis al-Muʾminin* (Mashhad, Iran: Bunyad-i Pizhuhishha-yi Islami, 1383/2004), 182–83.

191. NMAT, 1:205.

192. Group B texts add that the party stopped in the Bughra Desert (TKSawada, 5:33).

193. NMAT, 5:237 (*Badaʾiʿ al-Wasaṭ*).

194. On the shrine of Ḥasan Fażlullah, see the note in TKSawada, 5:35.

195. Amursana's flight to Beijing took place in late 1754, and the Qing armies set out on campaign in March 1755. Dabachi was driven off by the advance guard of the Qing army in July 1755. Peter C. Perdue, *China Marches West: The Qing Conquest of Central Eurasia* (Cambridge, MA: Belknap Press of Harvard University Press, 2005), 274.

196. Upon arriving in the capital, Dabachi was given the title of *qinwang*. Group B texts add here that "until today the offspring of these Qalmaqs are in Beijing. The emperor of China accommodated him with honor and wedded his daughter to Dabachi's son," referring to Dabachi's son Lobcha (Ch. Luo-bu-zha 罗卜扎). See TKSawada, 5:37.

197. Group B texts add: "The Qalmaqs had them reside in Eren Qaburgha" (TKSawada, 5:38).

198. Textual variants here do not map directly onto group divisions. Most texts in Group A end here and skip to halfway through the following section 28, but Bodleian Library MS Ind. Inst. Turk. 10 continues and serves as my base text until that point. From Group C, Staatsbibliothek Ms. or. fol. 3292 has the same lacuna as the majority of Group A, while Bodleian Library MS Ind. Inst. Turk. 3 follows MS Ind. Inst. Turk. 10. Group B omits the rest of section 28 and jumps to the start of section 29.

199. Sura Ya Sin (Sura 36 of the Quran) is considered the heart of the Quran.

200. NMAT, 1:205.

201. Cf. Group B: "From Yarkand, Khoja Yaḥya was accompanied by Khudaberdi Shangbegi, the Qarghaliq governor Mir Ivaż Beg, and Tokhta Beg. Qubad Bi led the Kirghiz and came to Yangiḥiṣar" (TKSawada, 5:40).

202. The language here is ambiguous in Group A, but Group B clarifies that Ṣufi Khoja and Khoja Naṣrullah were two different people (TKSawada, 5:41).

203. The wording of some manuscripts make it sound as if Möngke was the name of an entire Kirghiz tribe, and some translators have interpreted the name this way. Qing archives clarify, however, that Möngke was an individual (QXMD, 24:131). Möngke's tribal affiliation is not given, but in a letter to Qing officials in 1755, Khojasi Beg informed them that he was being pressed by Kirghiz from the Buuchin, Qipchaq, and Qushchi tribes. Since the latter two are well accounted for in Kashghari's text, Möngke may have belonged to the Buuchin (Ch. *bao-qin* 包沁). The Buuchin

("musketeers") were Kirghiz within the Junghar *otog* structure who were appointed as frontier guards.

204. It is interesting that this letter is addressed to Khojasi Beg, not to Burhan al-Din, possibly giving an indication of the actual chain of command during these events.

205. Shara Muḥammad Emin Beg belonged to a line of governors of Qaynuq in the Ili Valley and served as governor of Yangiḥiṣar after Khoja Burhan al-Din's invasion. See QXMD, 149:438–46.

206. Muẓaffar Beg (Ch. Mo-zan-pa-er 漠咱帕爾) eventually joined his father Khojasi in the capital.

207. In the *Silsilat al-Ẕahab*, a nineteenth-century work reflecting a White Mountain perspective, Ali Raḥmati Ṣufi is described as one of the chief companions of Khoja Aḥmad. See Bahargül Hamut, *Silsilat az-Zahab: Kommentierung einer čagatai-uigurischen Handschrift zu den Aqtagliq Hoğilar, einer mystischen Gruppierung in Xinjiang im 16–18. Jahrhundert* (Berlin: Klaus Schwarz Verlag, 2011), 319 ff.

208. Three of these individuals can be identified in Qing sources. After the Qing deposed Burhan al-Din and Khoja Jahan, Mundi Sufi (Ch. Men-duo Suo-pi 捫多索丕), Niyaz Sufi (Ch. Ni-ya-si Suo-pi 呢雅斯索丕), and Saqal Sufi (Ch. Sa-ha-le Suo-pi 薩哈勒索丕) were detained and sent to Beijing, where the emperor spared their lives and enrolled them in the Muslim company of the Plain White Banner. See Takahiro Onuma, *250 Years History of the Turkic-Muslim Camp in Beijing* (Tokyo: NIHU Program Islamic Area Studies, 2009), 32.

209. This is a slightly corrupted verse of Saʿib Tabrizi. *Divan-i Ṣaʾib Tabrizi*, 5:2334.

210. *Tarkhan* is an ancient Central Asian title whose bearer was exempt from taxes and other imposts. Long a feature of Tarim Basin Muslim society, the title was also issued by the Junghars. See P. B. Golden, "Ṭarkhan," EI², 10:303.

211. According to Turumtai's (Ch. Tuo-lun-tai 托倫泰) report (QXMD, 20:443), this battle took place on September 28, 1755. Although Kashghari describes the forces of Yarkand and Kashgar outnumbering their enemies, Turumtai states that the army of Burhan al-Din was ten thousand strong (made up of seven thousand Muslims and three thousand Oirat), while Khoja Yaḥya and Khoja Muʾmin's numbered only seven thousand. Of these, almost four thousand were killed, two thousand switched sides, and the remaining thousand fled. The *Aṯar al-Futuḥ* (fol. 134b) gives the names of the Kirghiz defectors as Mulla Aziz Yar Bi and Raḥim Quli Bi from the Qipchaq.

212. Abd al-Raḥman b. Muljam (d. 661) was the Kharijite who assassinated Ali.

213. *Maṯnavi*, book 4, line 2877. See *The Mathnawí of Jalálu'ddín Rúmí*, 4:431.

214. Group C adds: "and the people of Kashgar have also entirely defected and gone out to greet him."

215. This passage marks the decline of the family that had been custodians of the Yaghdu shrine for the previous half-century. On the subsequent history of the shrine, see Saguchi Tōru, *Shinkyō musurimu kenkyū* (Tokyo: Yoshikawa Kōbunkan, 1995), chap. 2.

216. The peacock feather, Mo. *otagha*, was a mark of imperial favor during the Qing. Kashghari's intention here seems to be to satirize the behavior of someone who switched to the Qing side.

217. Shaw and Sawada read this as *qayt*! "turn back!" (TKShaw, 52; TKSawada, 6:75), but in a *sāqīnāma* below, the word is made to rhyme with *ʿifrīt* and must therefore be

read as *qit*. The editors of the modern Uyghur version leave it untranslated as *qit-qit* (TAUyghur, 253), and Martin Hartmann (TAHartmann, 270) interprets it as "nonsensical bellowing" (*verworrenes Gebrüll*).

218. This is a pun on the name Sherdagh: *sher* "lion", *dagh* "scar."

219. See section 6 above. The most detailed account of Ushtur Khalifa and his family is in Maḥmud Churas's *Anis al-Ṭalibin*, fols. 95a–96b, 99b–102a.

220. This man's name, Ushtur/Shutur, means "camel."

221. Ṣufi Mirza and Ḥakim Mirza were brothers. In 1760 Ḥakim Mirza (Ch. A-qi-mu 阿奇木) received the position of *sula amban*, and in 1761 he was appointed to the governorship of Tashmaliq, making him the highest-ranking Kirghiz official in the Qianlong period.

222. This is probably the same Abd al-Karim Beg whom Burhan al-Din appointed governor of Kucha and who, according to Qing sources, was responsible for the death of Kashghari's patron Us̱man's relatives in that city (Li, *Manchu*, 328).

223. The anonymous 1876 precis of *In Remembrance of the Saints* identifies Bay Döbä as "an artificial mound which still exists at a distance of half a mile from the Eastern gate of the city." "Fall of the Mussulman Dominion in Kashgharia," *The Pioneer*, March 22, 1876, 4.

224. A *mingbegi* was literarily "chief of a thousand," *yüzbegi* "chief of a hundred" (i.e., a centurion). The *mirab* was in charge of regulating water supplies, while the *parvanachi* was a scribe or secretary.

225. Group B adds a list of people present at this assembly: "From Sanju Sayyid Bashar Khoja, from Qarghaliq Ibrahim Khoja and Mir Aʿzam Khoja, from Ikki Suning Arasi Ṭalib Khoja, from the city Abd al-Raḥim Khoja and Yaʿqub Khoja, from Afur Khojam Yar Khoja, Kamal Khoja, and Mulla Yunus Qutluq, from Tagharchi Qurban Khoja, from Mishar Nabira Khoja, from Kamra Abd al-Raḥim Khoja, from Rabatchi Almas Khoja, and from Poskam Yusuf Khoja" (TKSawada, 7:37–38).

226. Saʿd al-Din Taftazani (d. 1390). See his *A Commentary on the Creed of Islam: Sa'd al-Dīn al-Taftāzānī on the Creed of Najm al-Dīn al-Nasafī*, trans. Earl Edward Eldar (New York: Columbia University Press, 1950), 115.

227. An influential work of Islamic jurisprudence in the Ḥanafi tradition by Ali ibn Abi Bakr Marghinani (1135–1197). See *al-Hidaya: Sharḥ Bidayat al-Mubtadi* (Cairo: Dar al-Salam, 2000), 4:1616.

228. Manuscripts have either *kürä* or *kürär savdāgar*, possibly deriving from Mongolian *küriy-e* "court." I take this to describe a caravan merchant in the service of the Junghars. Early Qing reports use the same word in Manchu to describe the presence of "Muslims of the court" (*kuren i Hoise*) in Junghar-held Ili (e.g., QXMD, 30:44). The *As̱ar al-Futuḥ* calls Quzghun (actual name Muḥammad Murad) one of the "elite of the *karvaniyya*," which I interpret as an alternative term for the Junghar "estate" (*otog*) of official merchantry, the Bazargan. See Kashghari, *As̱ar al-Futuḥ*, fol. 153b.

229. Tagh Boyi simply means "mountainside"; here it may refer to the flank of the Kunlun range to the south of Yarkand.

230. NMAT, 1:170 (ghazal #464).

231. IVR RAN D191 (fols. 156b–157a) attributes this couplet to Navaʾi.

232. Ṣaʾib-i Tabrizi, *Divan-i Ṣaʾib Tabrizi*, 1:409.

233. Shaykh Mushrifuddin Sa'di, *The Gulistan (Rose Garden) of Sa'di: Bilingual English and Persian Edition with Vocabulary*, trans. Wheeler M. Thackston (Bethesda, MD: Ibex, 2008), chap. 1, story 16.
234. NMAT, 2:85 (ghazal #115, substituting *ʿālam-sōz* for NMAT's *shōr-angīz*).
235. *Masnavi*, book 5, line 1707. See *The Mathnawí of Jalálu'ddín Rúmí*, 6:103.
236. The author is here providing an etymology for the river known today as the Tiznab/Tiznaf (see note 113), but referred to in some works as the Tezab. At the same time, he seems to be conflating this river with the Zarafshan (the Yarkand River). The two are distinct waterways.
237. Judging from the description that follows in section 46, this probably refers to Khoja Abdullah.
238. This is the last mention of Ghazi and Niyaz Beg. According to later Qing reports (QXMD, 45:431) both men were executed, fulfilling the prophecies made at several points in this book.
239. Bodleian Library MS Ind. Inst. Turk. 3 (fols. 115b–116a) modifies this passage to exculpate Ismaʿil Beg: "Khoja Padishah (i.e., Khoja Jahan) told him to fetch the young princes and the helpless palace staff and elderly who had been left behind. The Kirghiz Möngke came in force and caught Ismaʿil Beg by surprise, capturing him along with four of the princes and a number of palace staff."
240. The uncommon word *charāna* most likely derives from Persian *chahār-āʾina* "four mirrors," a cuirass consisting of four metal plates (Dihkhuda, *Lughatnama*, 6:8349).
241. Ḥafiẓ, *The Collected Lyrics*, 167; *Divan-i Ḥafiẓ*, 1:162.
242. A marginal note in a Saint Petersburg manuscript relates an account from a certain Wahhab Ḥaji from Aqsu, who says that on his way back from the pilgrimage to Mecca and Medina he encountered Khoja Abdullah living with his family among the Kazakhs (IVR RAN C583, fol. 381a).
243. This may refer to the Aqtam (Ch. Aketamu 阿克塔木) which lies roughly forty kilometers south of Yarkand.
244. Thomas Roebuck, *A Collection of Proverbs, and Proverbial Phrases, in the Persian and Hindoostanee Languages* (Calcutta: Hindoostanee Press, 1824), 362.
245. Ḥatim al-Ṭay was renowned for his extreme generosity.

BIBLIOGRAPHY

Manuscripts

Abd al-Shukur b. Khoja Muḥammad Yusuf. *Tazkira-i Abd al-Mannan*. IV RAN A231.
Abu l-Baqa b. Baha' al-Din b. Makhdum-i Aʿẓam, *Jamiʿ al-Maqamat*. IVAN RUz 72.
Anon. *Silsila-i Bughrakhani-i Manẓum*. IVAN RUz 586.
Arshi, Khoja Jahan. *Divan-i Arshi*. IPN ANRT 2277.
Central Asian Documents, Houghton Library MS Turk 70
Churas, Shah Maḥmud b. Mir Fażil. *Anis al-Ṭalibin*. Bodleian Library MS Ind. Inst. Pers. 45.
Ivaż, Muḥammad. *Żiya' al-Qulub*. Houghton Library MS Persian 95.
Kafshin Khoja. *Iqd al-Guhar*. Bodleian Library MS Ind. Inst. Pers. 117.
Kashghari, Muḥammad Emin (Ṣadr). *Asar al-Futuḥ*. IVAN RUz 753.
Kashghari, Muḥammad Ṣadiq. *Tazkira-i Azizan*. Bodleian Library MS Turk. d. 20.
——. *Tazkira-i Azizan*. Bodleian Library MS Ind. Inst. Turk. 3.
——. *Tazkira-i Azizan*. IVR RAN D191.
——. *Tazkira-i Azizan*. Bodleian Library MS Ind. Inst. Turk. 10.
——. *Tazkira-i Azizan*. Staatsbibliothek Ms. or. fol. 3292.
——. *Tazkira-i Azizan*. IVAN RUz 45.
——. *Tajnama* (*Tarjuma-i Tarikh-i Ṭabari*). Jarring Prov. 439.
——. *Tarjuma-i Tarikh-i Rashidi*. IVR RAN C569.
——. (?) *Tarjuma-i Tarikh-i Ṭabari*. IVAN RUz 9470.
Khoja Khamush, *Tarjuma-i Shahnama*. IVR RUz 1953.
Nadr Muḥammad Khojam. *Kashshaf al-Arifin*. IV RUz 11420.
Payravi, Shah Muḥammad ibn Ḥisam al-Din. *Jalis-i Mushtaqin*. IV RAN A232.
Qunduzi, Imam Ali. *Tavarikh-i Manẓuma*. IPN ANRT 204.
Shaykh Zinda Ali. *Ṣamarat al-Masha'ikh*. IV RUz 2619.
Yarkandi, Mir Khal al-Din Katib. *Hidayatnama*. IVR RAN C560.
Yarkandi, Muḥammad Yusuf b. Muhtashim. *Majmaʿ al-Asrar*. IVAN RUz 5468.

Published Works

Akimushkin, O. F. "Kashgarskii pokhod uzbekov pri Abdallakh-khane." In *Iranskaia filologiia. Kratkoe izlozhenie dokladov nauchnoi konferentsii, posviashchennoi 60-letiiu professora A. N. Boldyreva*, 5–9. Moscow: Izdatel'stvo Akademii nauk USSR, 1969.

——. "Khronologiia pravitelei vostochnoi chasti Chagataiskogo ulusa (liniia Tugluk-Timur-khana)." In *Vostochnyi Turkestan i Sredniaia Aziia: Istoriia, kul'tura, sviazy*, ed. B. A. Litvinskii, 156–64, 224–25. Moscow: Nauka, 1984.

——, ed. *Tārīkh-i Kāshg̣ar: anonimnaia tiurkskaia khronika vladitelei Vostochnogo Turkestana po konets XVII veka*. Saint Petersburg: Peterburgskoe vostokovedenie, 2001.

Alam, Muzaffar. "The Mughals, the Sufi Shaykhs and the Formation of the Akbari Dispensation." *Modern Asian Studies* 43, no. 1 (2009): 135–75.

Algar, Hamid. "From Kashgar to Eyüp: The Lineages and Legacy of Sheik Abdullah Nidāī." In *Naqshbandis in Western and Central Asia: Change and Continuity*, ed. Elizabeth Özdalga, 1–15. Richmond, UK: Curzon Press, 1999.

Amili, Muḥammad Shafiʿ Ḥusayni. *Maḥafil al-Muʾminin fi Ẕayl Majalis al-Muʾminin*. Mashhad, Iran: Bunyad-i Pizhuhishha-yi Islami, 1383/2004.

Aminrazavi, Mehdi. "Jurjani, Mir Sayyid Sharif." In *The Biographical Encyclopedia of Islamic Philosophy*, ed. Oliver Leaman, 268–69. London: Bloomsbury Academic, 2015.

Aristov, N. "Opyt vyiasneniia etnicheskogo sostava Kirgiz-Kazakov bol'shoi ordy." *Zhivaia starina* 3–4 (1894): 391–486.

Aṭṭar, Farid al-Din. *The Speech of the Birds: Manṭiqu'ṭ-Ṭair*. Translated by Peter Avery. Cambridge: Islamic Texts Society, 1998.

Atwood, Christopher. *Encyclopedia of Mongolia and the Mongol Empire*. New York: Facts on File, 2004.

——. "Titles, Appanages, Marriages, and Officials: A Comparison of Political Forms in the Zünghar and Thirteenth-Century Mongol Empires." In *Imperial Statecraft: Political Forms and Techniques of Governance in Inner Asia, Sixth–Twentieth Centuries*, ed. David Sneath, 207–43. Bellingham, WA: Center for East Asian Studies, Western Washington University, 2006.

Ayvażi, Rashid, ed. *Divan-i Ḥafiẓ: Bar Asas-i Hasht Nuskha-i Kamil-i Kuhan*. Tehran: Nashr-i Ṣadduq, 1376/1997.

Ärshi, Khoja Jahan. *Divani Ärshi*. Ürümchi, China: Shinjang khälq näshriyati, 1995.

Ba'izi, Mämtimin. "Kucha wanglirining näsäbnamisi." *Shinjang tarikh materiyalliri* 48 (2006): 85–105.

Babajanov, B. "Biographies of Makhdum-i A'zam al-Kasani al-Dahbidi, Shaykh of the Sixteenth-Century Naqshbandiya." *Manuscripta Orientalia* 5, no. 2 (1999): 3–8.

——. "Mawlānā Lutfullāh Chūstī—An outline of his hagiography and political activity." *Zeitschrift der Deutschen Morgenländischen Gesellschaft* 149 (1999): 245–70.

Bearman, P. J., Th. Bianquis, C. E. Bosworth, E. van Donzel, W. P. Heinrichs, et al., eds. *Encyclopaedia of Islam*, 2nd ed. Leiden, Netherlands: Brill, 1960–2005.

Bellew, Henry Walter. "History of Kashgar." In *Report of a Mission to Yarkund in 1873*, ed. Sir D. T. Forsyth, 106–213. Calcutta: Foreign Department Press, 1875.

Bergholz, Fred W. *The Partition of the Steppe: The Struggle of the Russians, Manchus, and the Zunghar Mongols for Empire in Central Asia, 1619–1758*. New York: Peter Lang, 1993.

Brophy, David. "Confusing Black and White: Naqshbandi Sufi Affiliations and the Transition to Qing Rule in the Tarim Basin." *Late Imperial China* 39, no. 1 (2018): 29–65.

Churas, Shah Maḥmud. *Khronika. Kriticheskii tekst, perevod, kommentarii, issledovanie i ukazateli O. F. Akimushkin*. Moscow: Nauka, 1976.

Colby, Frederick S. *Narrating Muḥammad's Night Journey: Tracing the Development of the Ibn ʿAbbās Ascension Discourse*. Albany: State University of New York Press, 2008.

Damrel, D. "Forgotten Grace: Khwâja Khâwand Maḥmûd Naqshbandî in Central Asia and Mughal India." Ph.D. diss., Duke University, 1991.

Dawut, Rähilä. *Uyghur mazarliri*. Ürümchi, China: Shinjang khälq näshriyati, 2001.

DeWeese, Devin. "Aḥmad Yasavī in the Work of Burhān al-Dīn Qïlïch: The Earliest Reference to a Famously Obscure Central Asian Sufi Saint." *Asiatische Studien / Études Asiatiques* 67, no. 3 (2013): 837–79.

——. "The Masha'ikh-i Turk and the Khojagan: Rethinking the Links Between the Yasavi and Naqshbandi Sufi Traditions." *Journal of Islamic Studies* 7, no. 2 (1996): 173–88.

——. "'Stuck in the Throat of Chingīz Khān': Envisioning the Mongol Conquests in Some Sufi Accounts from the Fourteenth to Seventeenth Centuries." In *History and Historiography of Post-Mongol Central Asia and the Middle East: Studies in Honor of John E. Woods*, ed. J. Pfeiffer and S. A. Quinn, 23–60. Wiesbaden, Germany: Harrassowitz, 2006.

Dihkhuda, Ali Akbar. *Lughatnama*. Tehran: Muʾassasa-i Lughatnama-i Dihkhuda, 1377/1998.

Dmitrieva, L. V., ed. *Katalog tiurkskikh rukopisei Instituta vostokovedeniia Rossiiskoi akadamii nauk*. Moscow: Vostochnaia literatura, 2002.

"Fall of the Mussulman Dominion in Kashgharia." *The Pioneer*, March 21, 1876, 3–4; March 22, 1876, 3–4.

Fleet, Kate, Gudrun Krämer, Denis Matringe, John Nawas, and Everett Rowson, eds. *Encyclopaedia of Islam, THREE* (online edition).

Fletcher, J. "The Biography of Khwush Kipäk Beg (d. 1781) in the Wai-fan Meng-ku Hui-pu wang kung piao chuan." *Acta Orientalia Academiae Scientiarum Hungaricae* 36 (1982): 167–72.

——. "Confrontations Between Muslim Missionaries and Nomad Unbelievers in the Late Sixteenth Century: Notes on Four Passages from the 'Ḍiyāʾ al-qulūb.' " In *Tractata Altaica*, ed. W. Heissig, 167–74. Wiesbaden, Germany: Harrasowitz, 1976.

——. "The Naqshbandiyya in Northwest China, Edited by Jonathan N. Lipman." In *Studies on Chinese and Islamic Inner Asia*, ed. Beatrice Forbes Manz, 1–46. Aldershot, UK: Variorum, 1995.

Gardner, Victoria R. "The Written Representations of a Central Asian Ṣūfī Shaykh: Aḥmad ibn Mawlānā Jalāl al-Dīn Khwājagī Kāsānī 'Makhdūm-i Aʿẓam' (d. 1542)." Ph.D. diss., University of Michigan, 2006.

Golombek, Lisa. "The Gardens of Timur: New Perspectives." *Muqarnas* 12 (1995): 137–47.

Grenard, Fernand. *J.-L. Dutreuil de Rhins. Mission scientifique dans la haute Asie, 1890–1895*. Paris: E. Leroux, 1897–98.

——. "La légende de Satok Boghra Khan et l'histoire." *Journal Asiatique* ser. 9, vol. 15 (1900): 5–79.

Gürsoy-Naskali, Emine, ed. *Ashābu 'l-Kähf, A Treatise in Eastern Turki*. Memoires de la Societe Finno-Ougrienne 192. Helsinki: Suomalais-Ugrilainen Seura, 1985.

Ḥafiẓ. *The Collected Lyrics of Háfiz of Shiráz*. Translated by Peter Avery. Cambridge: Archetype, 2007.

Hamada, Masami. "Le Mausolée et le culte de Satuq Bughrâ Khân." *Journal of the History of Sufism* 3 (2001): 62–87.

——. "'Shio no gimu' to 'seisen' to no aida de." *Tōyōshi kenkyū* 52, no. 2 (1994): 122–48.

Hamut, Bahargül. *Silsilat az-Zahab: Kommentierung einer čagatai-uigurischen Handschrift zu den Aqtagliq Hoğilar, einer mystischen Gruppierung in Xinjiang im 16–18. Jahrhundert*. Berlin: Klaus Schwarz Verlag, 2011.

Hartmann, Martin. "Die osttürkischen Handschriften der Sammlung Hartmann." *Mittheilungen des Seminars für orientalische Sprachen, Berlin* 1, no. 2 (1904): 1–21.

——. "Ein Heiligenstaat im Islam: Das Ende der Caghataiden und die Herrschaft der Choğas in Kašgarien." *Der Islamische Orient: Berichte und Forschungen* 1, no. 6–10 (1905): 195–374.

al-Hujwírí, 'Alí b. 'Uthmán al-Jullábí. *The Kashf al-Maḥjúb: The Oldest Persian Treatise on Sufism*. Translated by Reynold A. Nicholson. Leiden, Netherlands: Brill, 1911.

Hummel, Arthur W. *Eminent Chinese of the Ch'ing Period (1644–1912)*. Washington, DC: U.S. Government Printing Office, 1943–44.

Ishaq, Nazra. "Critical Edition of Diwan-e-Nasir Ali Sirhindi with Introduction and Notes." Ph.D. diss., Aligarh Muslim University, 2015.

Jahangir. *The Jahangirnama: Memoirs of Jahangir, Emperor of India*. Translated by Wheeler M. Thackston. New York: Oxford University Press, 1999.

Jami, Abd al-Raḥman ibn Aḥmad. *Maṣnavi-i Haft Avrang*. Tehran: Miraṣ-i Maktub, 1997–99.

——. *Nafaḥat al-Uns min Ḥażarat al-Quds*. Tehran: Kitabfurushi-i Saʿdi, 1336/1957.

Kahi, Muḥammad Abu al-Qasim. *Divan-i Qasim Kahi*. Tehran: Talar-i Kitab, 1366.

Kashghari, Muḥammad Ṣadiq. *Zubdat al-Masaʾil wa-l-Aqaʾid*. Istanbul: Shirket-i Iraniyye, 1309/1891–92.

Kashghari, Mukhammed-Sadyk. *Tazkira-yi 'Azizan*. Translated by A. Sh. Nurmanova. Almaty, Kazakhstan: Daik-Press, 2006.

Kashifi, Fakhr al-Din Ali b. Ḥusayn Vaʿiẓ. *Rashaḥat-i Ayn al-Ḥayat*. Tehran: Bunyad-i Nikukari-i Nuriyani, 1356/1977.

Ka-shi-ga-li, Mu-han-mo-de Sa-di-ke (Muḥammad Ṣadiq Kashghari). "Hezhuo zhuan." *Minzushi yiwenji* 8 (1980): 53–136.

——. "Hezhuo Zhuan." In *Zhongguo xibei wenxian congshu*, ed. Gansusheng guji wenxian zhengli bianyi zhongxin, erbian vol. 39. Beijing: Xianzhuang shuju, 2006.

Kattaev, Komilkhon. *Makhdumi A'zam va Dahbed*. Samarqand: Sug'diyon, 1994.

Khismatulin, A. A. "Khojagan." In *Islam na territorii byvshei Rossiiskoi imperii: Entsiklopedicheskii slovar'*, ed. S. M. Prozorov, 1:417–25. Moscow: Vostochnaia literatura, 2006.

Khujandi, Kamal. *Divan-i Shaykh Kamal Khujandi: Hamrah ba Sharḥ-i Ḥal u Zindagani*. Tehran: Surush, 1375/1995–96.

Kim, Ho-Dong. "The Cult of Saints in Eastern Turkistan—The Case of Alp Ata in Turfan." In *Proceedings of the Thirty-Fifth Permanent International Altaistic Conference*, 199–226. Taipei: Center for Chinese Studies Materials, 1993.

Krueger, John R. *Materials for an Oirat-Mongolian to English Citation Dictionary*. Bloomington, IN: Mongolia Society, 1978.

Kumru, Coşkun. "Muhammet Sâdık Kaşgârî'nin Tezkire-i Hâcegân Adlı Eserinin Transkripsiyonu ve Değerlendirilmesi." Yüksek Lisans Tezi, Pamukkale Üniversitesi, 2016.

Kut, Günay. *Supplementary Catalogue of Turkish Manuscripts in the Bodleian Library*. Oxford: Oxford University Press, 2003.

Lessing, Ferdinand, ed. *Mongolian-English Dictionary*. Bloomington, IN: Mongolia Society, 1980.

Levi, Scott C., and Ron Sela, eds. *Islamic Central Asia: An Anthology of Historical Sources* Bloomington: Indiana University Press, 2009.

Lewisohn, Leonard. "The Life and Times of Kamāl Khujandī." *Journal of Turkish Studies* 18 (1994): 163–77.

Lykoshin, N. S. "Kodeks prilichii na Vostoke (Adab-ul-salikhyn)." *Sbornik materialov po musul'manstvu* 2 (1900): 23–83.

Ma Dazheng, ed. *Qingdai Chahetai wen wenxian yizhu*. Ürümchi, China: Xinjiang renmin chubanshe, 2013.

Madigan, Daniel A. "Preserved Tablet." In *Encyclopaedia of the Qurʾān*, 3:261–63. Leiden, Netherlands: Brill, 2004.

Marghinani, Ali ibn Abi Bakr. *al-Hidaya: Sharḥ Bidayat al-Mubtadi*. Cairo: Dar al-Salam, 2000.

Mäshhuri, Ibrahim. *Divani Mäshhuri*. Kashgar, China: Qäshqär Uyghur näshriyati, 1985.

"Mazar khodzha Iskhaka Vali bin Makhdum-i-Azama." *Spravochnaia kniga Samarkandskoi oblasti* 6 (1898): 197.

Miyawaki, Junko. "Did a Dzungar Khanate Really Exist?" *Journal of the Anglo-Mongolian Society* 10, no. 1 (1987): 1–5.

Muginov, A. M. *Opisanie Uigurskikh rukopisei Instituta Narodov Azii*. Moscow: INA AN SSSR, 1962.

Mukhlisov, Iusupbek. *Uyghur klassik ädäbiyati qolyazmilirining katalogi*. Ürümchi, China: Shinjang yärlik muziyigha täyyarliq körüsh bashqarmisi, 1957.

Munis, Shir Muḥammad Mirab, and Muḥammad Riza Mirab Agahi. *Firdaws al-Iqbal*. Translated by Yuri Bregel. Leiden, Netherlands: Brill, 1999.

Munshi, Muḥammad Yusuf. *Taẕkira-i Muqimkhani*. Tehran: Miraṡ-i Maktub, 2001.

Najim, Abd al-Raḥman, ed. *Gulzar-i Aṡar*. Beirut: Maṭbaʿa al-Adabiyya, 1309/1891.

Nasr, Seyyed Hossein, Caner K. Dagli, Maria Massi Dakake, and Joseph E. B. Lumbard, eds. *The Study Quran*. New York: HarperOne, 2015.

Navoiy, Alisher. *Mukammal asarlar to'plami*. 20 vols. Tashkent, Uzbekistan: Fan, 1987–2003.

Newby, Laura. *The Empire and the Khanate: A Political History of Qing Relations with Khoqand c. 1700–1860*. Leiden, Netherlands: Brill, 2005.

Nurmanova, A. Sh. "Mukhammed-Sadyq Qashghariding "Tazkira-yi 'Azizan" shygharmasy: derektanulyq zertteu." *Izvestiia NAN Respubliki Kazakhstan* 3 (2007): 8–14.

Onuma, Takahiro. *250 Years History of the Turkic-Muslim Camp in Beijing*. Tokyo: NIHU Program Islamic Area Studies, 2009.

——. *Shin to chūō Ajia sōgen: yūbokumin no sekai kara teikoku no henkyō e*. Tokyo: Tōkyō daigaku shuppankai, 2014.

Osman, Gayretcan. "Muhemmed Sadik Kaşgari Üzerindeki Araştırmalar." In *T. C. Ordu Üniversitesi Uluslararası Klasik Türk Edebiyatı Sempozyumu*, ed. Muhammet Kuzubaş, Salih Okumuş, and Nuh Doğan, 287–92. Ordu: Ordu Üniversitesi Yayınları, 2013.

Papas, Alexandre. "Khojas of Kashgar." In *Oxford Research Encyclopedia of Asian History*, 2017.

——. *Soufisme et politique entre Chine, Tibet et Turkestan: Étude sur les Khwajas Naqshbandis du Turkestan oriental*. Paris: Librarie d'Amérique et d'Orient, Jean Maisonneuve successeur, 2005.

——. "Un manuscrit inconnu à propos des soufis de Kashgarie conservé à la Bibliothèque Nationale Firdawsi (Tadjikistan)." *Studia Iranica* 35, no. 1 (2006): 97–108.

Paul, Jürgen. *Doctrine and Organization: The Khwājagān/Naqshbandīya in the First Generation After Bahā'uddīn*. Berlin: Das Arabische Buch, 1998.

——, ed. *Katalog sufischer Handschriften aus der Bibliothek des Instituts für Orientalistik der Akademie der Wissenschaften, Republik Usbekistan*. Stuttgart, Germany: Franz Weiner Verlag, 2002.

Perdue, Peter C. *China Marches West: The Qing Conquest of Central Eurasia*. Cambridge, MA: Belknap Press of Harvard University Press, 2005.

Qäshqäri, Muhämmäd Sadiq. *Äshabul kähf täzkirisi*. Ürümchi, China: Shinjang Uyghur Aptonom Rayon az sanliq millät qädimki äsärlär ishkhanisi, 1994.

——. *Täzkirä'i Äzizan*, ed. Nijat Mukhlis and Shämsidin Ämät. Kashgar, China: Qäshqär Uyghur näshriyati, 1988.

Qing shilu. Beijing: Zhonghua shuju, 1985–1987.

Qi-shi-yi. *Xiyu wenjian lu*. Edo: Senshōbō, Kansei 13/1800–1801.

Qi Yunshi et al. *Waifan Menggu Huibu wanggong biaozhuan*, ed. Bao Wenhan and Qi Chaoketu. Hohhot, China: Neimenggu daxue chubanshe, 1998.

Qoshghariy, Muhmmad Sodiq. *Yakhshi kishilar odobi (Odob-as-solihin)*. Tashkent, Uzbekistan: Yangi asr avlodi, 2002.

Qutluqov, M. *Muhammad Sodiq Koshghariy*. Tashkent, Uzbekistan: Özbekiston KP Markaziy komitetining birlashgan nashriyoti, 1968.

Ramstedt, Gustav John. *Seven Journeys Eastward 1898–1912*. Translated by John R. Krueger. Bloomington, IN: Mongolia Society, 1978.

Roebuck, Thomas. *A Collection of Proverbs, and Proverbial Phrases, in the Persian and Hindoostanee Languages*. Calcutta: The Hindoostanee Press, 1824.

Roth Li, Gertraude. *Manchu: A Textbook for Reading Documents*. Honolulu: University of Hawai'i Press, 2000.

Rumi, Jalal al-Din. *The Mathnawí of Jalálu'ddín Rúmí*. Translated by Reynold A. Nicholson. Leiden, Netherlands: Brill, 1925.

Sa'di, Shaykh Mushrifuddin. *The Gulistan (Rose Garden) of Sa'di: Bilingual English and Persian Edition with Vocabulary*. Translated by Wheeler M. Thackston. Bethesda, MD: Ibex, 2008.

Ṣafi, Mawlana Ali ibn Ḥusayn. *Beads of Dew from the Source of Life: Histories of the Khwājagān, the Masters of Wisdom*. Translated by Mukhtar Holland. Fort Lauderdale, FL: Al-Baz, 2001.

Ṣafvat, Muḥammad Ali, ed. *A̱sar-i Hazar u Yak Sukhanvar*. Qum, Iran: Kitabfurushi-i Tabish, 1328/1949.

Saguchi, Tōru. "The Revival of the White Mountain Khwājas, 1760–1820 (from Sarimsāq to Jihāngīr)." *Acta Asiatica* 14 (1968): 7–20.

——. *Shinkyō musurimu kenkyū*. Tokyo: Yoshikawa Kōbunkan, 1995.

Saidakhmedov, I. A., M. Iu. Iunuskhodzhaeva, and G. Iu. Astanova. "Agiograficheskie sochineniia kak istochnik dlia izucheniia dukhovnoi i politicheskoi zhizni Vostochnogo Turkestana." In *Iz istorii Srednei Azii i Vostochnogo Turkestana XV–XIX vv*, ed. B. A. Akhmedov, 149–62. Tashkent, Uzbekistan: Fan, 1987.

Saidullaev, I. "Istoriko-literaturnoe proizvedenie 'Tazkirai Khodzhagan' Mukhammeda Sadyka Kashgari." *Izvestiia Akademii nauk KazSSR* 1 (1979): 41–45.

Salakhetdinova, M. A. "Sochinenie Mukhammed-Sadyka Kashgari 'Tazkira-i Khodzhagan' kak istochnik po istorii Kirgizov." *Izvestiia Akademii nauk KirgSSR* 1 (Istoriia) (1959): 93–125.

——. "Soobshcheniia o kirgizakh v 'Khidaiat-name' Mir Khal' ad-Dina." *Izvestiia Akademiia nauk Kirgizskoi SSR*. Seriia obshchestvennykh nauk 3, no. 2 (1961): 133–40.

Sartori, Paolo. "Between Kazan and Kashghar: On the Vernacularization of Islamic Jurisprudence in Central Eurasia." Forthcoming.

Sawada Minoru. " 'Tazukira i hōjagān' Nihongo yakushi (1)." *Toyama Daigaku Jinbun Gakubu kiyō* 61 (2014): 59–86; 62 (2015): 89–118; 63 (2015): 33–57; 64 (2016): 81–106; 65 (2016): 21–44; 66 (2017): 55–82; 67 (2017): 31–60; 68 (2018): 27–43; 69 (2018): 33–50.

——. "Three Groups of *Tadhkira-i khwājagān*: Viewed from the Chapter on Khwāja Āfāq." In *Studies on Xinjiang Historical Sources in Seventeenth-Twentieth Centuries*, ed. James A. Millward, Shinmen Yasushi, and Sugawara Jun, 9–30. Tokyo: Toyō Bunko, 2010.

Sayrami, Mulla Musa. *Tarikhi Hämidi*, ed. Änvär Baytur. Beijing: Millätlär näshriyati, 1986.

Schwarz, Florian. *"Unser Weg schließt tausend Wege ein": Derwische und Gesellschaft im islamischen Mittelasien im 16. Jahrhundert*. Berlin: Klaus Schwarz Verlag, 2000.

Schwarz, Henry G. "The Khwājas of Eastern Turkestan." *Central Asiatic Journal* 20, no. 4 (1976): 266–96.

Semenov A. A., et al., eds. *Sobranie vostochnykh rukopisei Akademii nauk Uzbekskoi SSR*. Tashkent, Uzbekistan: Izdatel'stvo Akademii nauk UzSSR, 1952–1987.

Shaw, Robert B. "The History of the Khōjas of Eastern-Turkistān Summarised from the Tazkira-i-Khwājagān of Muḥammad Ṣādiq Kāshgharī." Supplement to *The Journal of the Asiatic Society of Bengal* 66, part 1 (1897).

Shinmen, Yasushi. "The History of the Mausoleum Aṣḥāb al-Kahf in Turfan." *Memoirs of the Research Department of the Toyo Bunko* 61 (2003): 83–104.

Shipton, Eric. *Mountains of Tartary: Mountaineering and Exploration in Northern and Central Asia in the 1950s*. London: Hodder & Stoughton, 1950.

Steingass, Francis Joseph. *A Comprehensive Persian-English Dictionary*. London: Routledge & Kegan Paul, 1963.

Sugawara Jun. "Sōshutsu sareru 'Uiguru minzoku bunka': 'Uiguru koten bungaku' no hukkō to bobyō no 'hakken.' " *Ajia yūgaku* 1 (1999): 74–86.

Tabrizi, Ṣa'ib-i. *Divan-i Ṣa'ib Tabrizi*, ed. Muḥammad Qahraman. Tehran: Shirkat-i Intisharat-i Ilmi va Farhangi, 1985–1991.

al-Taftazani, Saʿd al-Din. *A Commentary on the Creed of Islam: Sa'd al-Dīn al-Taftāzānī on the Creed of Najm al-Dīn al-Nasafī*. Translated by Earl Edward Eldar. New York: Columbia University Press, 1950.

Thum, Rian. *The Sacred Routes of Uyghur History*. Cambridge, MA: Harvard University Press, 2014.

Trippner, Joseph. "Islamische Gruppen und Gräberkult in Nordwest-China." *Die Welt des Islams, New Series* 7, no. 1 (1961): 142–71.

Valad, Sulṭan. *Valadnama*. Tehran: Mu'assasa-i Nashr-i Huma, 1376/1997–98.

Validov, A. Z. "Nekotorye dannye po istorii Fergany XVIII-go stoletiia." *Protokoly zasedanii Turkestanskogo kruzhka liubitelei arkheologii* 20, no. 1 (1916): 68–118.

Valikhanov, Ch. Ch. "O sostoianii Altyshara ili shesti vostochnykh gorodov Kitaiskoi provintsii Nan-Lu (Maloi Bukharii) v 1858–59 gg." In *Sobranie sochinenii v piati tomakh*, 3:97–218. Alma-Ata, Kazakhstan: Glavnaia redaktsiia kazakhskoi sovetskoi entsiklopedii, 1985.

Waite, Edmund. "From Holy Man to Villain: Popular Historical Narratives About Apaq Khoja Amongst Uyghurs in Contemporary Xinjiang." *Inner Asia* 8, no. 1 (2006): 5–28.

Wang Dongping. *Ming Qing Xiyushi yu Huizushi lungao*. Beijing: Shangwu yinshuguan, 2014.

Wang, Jianping. "Islam in Uighur Society as Recorded by Chinese Gazetteers in the Late Qing Dynasty." In *Central Asia on Display: Proceedings of the VII Conference of the European Society for Central Asian Studies*, ed. Gabriele Rasuly-Paleczek and Julia Katschnig, 309–24. Münster, Germany: Lit, 2004.

Welsford, Thomas. *Four Types of Loyalty in Early Modern Central Asia: The Tūqāy-Tīmūrid Takeover of Greater Ma wara al-nahr, 1598–1605*. Leiden, Netherlands: Brill, 2013.

——. "Rethinking the Ḥamzahids of Ḥiṣār." *Asiatische Studien* 65, no. 3 (2011): 797–823.

Wu Mu and Zhang Fengfeng, "Lun Qian-Jia nianjian Xibuchake Bulute." *Zhongguo bianjiang shidi yanjiu* 26, no. 3 (2016): 42–52.

Xu Fulu. *Xiyu wangshi: Xinjiang zuihou yige wanggong 200 nian de jiazu jiyi*. Beijing: Huawen chubanshe, 2006.

Zhongguo diyi lishi dang'anguan and Nei Menggu daxue Mengguxue xueyuan, eds. *Dayičing gürün-ü dotuɣadu yamun-u Mongɣol bičig-ün ger-ün dangse*. Hohhot, China: Nei Menggu renmin chubanshe, 2005.

Zhongguo diyi lishi dang'anguan and Zhongguo bianjiang shidi yanjiu zhongxin, eds. *Qingdai Xinjiang Manwen dang'an huibian*. Guilin, China: Guangxi shifan daxue chubanshe, 2012.

Zlatkin, I. Ia. *Istoriia Dzhungarskogo khanstva (1635–1758)*. Moscow: Nauka, 1964.

INDEX

Abd al-Aziz Khalifa b. Ushtur, 31
Abd al-Karim, 173
Abd al-Karim Khan, 24–26, 235n41
Abd al-Khaliq Beg b. Abd al-Wahhab, 146, 178
Abd al-Laṭif Sulṭan, 24
Abd al Raḥim Beg, 146, 178
Abd al-Raḥim (relative of Khudayar Beg), 100–1
Abd al-Raḥman b. Muljam, 156
Abd al-Raḥman Beg (Zarqi) b. Shara Muḥammad Emin, 146, 178, 209
Abd al-Raḥman Jami, xv, 60
Abd al-Raḥman Khalifa, 179
Abd al-Sattar, 178
Abd al-Sattar (of Artush), 97–98, 102–3
Abd al-Sattar Beg b. Abd al-Wahhab, 146, 173, 178
Abd al-Wahhab Beg, 87, 96–97, 103–4, 129, 135, 144–46, 155, 162, 173, 178, 209, 244n153
Abdullah Afżal, 57
Abdullah Beg the Kirghiz, 146, 178
Abdullah ibn Masʿud, 66
Abdullah Iʿraj, 57
Abdullah Khan (Chaghatayid), 29, 73
Abdullah Khan (Shaybanid), 27–28
Abu Bakr, 11, 14, 58, 126, 219–20
Abu l-Fażl Bukhari, 70
Adam, 1–2, 40, 66, 82, 201
Afaqiyya, xi
Aḥmad (Moghul), 12
Ahriman, 175
Aʾisha Beg, 177, 191, 210
Aʾisha (wife of the Prophet), 5, 132
Akhund Haji Abdullah, 73, 75, 94, 179
Akhund Haji Ubaydullah, 179
Akhund Khoja Isḥaq, 55,
Akhund Mir Abid al-Din, 72, 75–76
Akhund Mirza Barat, 41–42
Akhund Mulla Abd al-Qahir, 179
Akhund Mulla Khurd, 21–22
Akhund Mulla Kifäk, 187
Akhund Mulla Maḥmud, 121, 139, 143, 156, 161
Akhund Mulla Majid, 128, 155, 246n187
Akhund Mulla Mashhuri (Mulla Ibrahim), 40, 49
Akhund Mulla Niyaz Kalan, 187
Akhund Mulla Noruz, 128, 155
Akhund Mulla Saʿid, 20–21
Akhund Mulla Taqi, 42–43, 99,
Akhund Mulla Umar Baqi, 125, 163, 179, 204, 206
Akhund Shah Abd al-Qadir, 63, 66, 179, 242n126
Akhund Yaʾsi, 73–75
Akhund Zihni, 73–75
aʿlam akhund, 143, 156, 163, 179, 187, 204, 239n81
Alexander (the Great), 174, 210
Ali, xi, 31, 57, 68, 126, 156, 197; Arabic verse attributed to 39, 113
Ali Beg, 178
Alim Shah Beg, 44–45
Alisher Navaʾi, xix, 127, 137, 174; quotations from 49, 87, 108, 131–32, 137, 199, 205, 218
Allah Quli Beg, 146, 178, 189

Alp Ata, 26
Amir Nur al-Din, 10
Amir Sayyid Ali, 7
Amir Sayyid Kulal, 59–61
Amu Darya, 21
Amursana, xiii, 96, 104, 133–34, 136, 147–48, 178, 180, 188, 190, 192, 201, 209
Andijan, 127–28, 155, 159, 183
angels, 11, 15, 22, 49, 78, 139
Aqa'id, 75
Aqbash Khan, 38, 43
Aq Burut, 179
Aq Saray, 36
Aqtam, 220
Aq Yar, 36
Aqsay, 143
Aqsu, xxi, 26, 29, 36, 51, 54, 85–87, 94–96, 99, 103, 105, 129, 135–36, 144, 146–47, 162, 168, 172, 179
Aqyol Bahadur, 179
Aristotle, 75, 90, 174
Arshi: *see* Khoja Yaʿqub
Artush, xv, 97–99, 102–3, 122
Arzu Muḥammad, 139, 158
Ashur Quzi, 191–96
Asif b. Barkhiya, 174
Azhdar Niyaz Ṣufi, 147, 178
Aẓim Shah b. Khosh Kifäk, 160
Azrael, 85

Babaq Sulṭan, 32, 34
Babur, 18–19
Baburiyya, 19
Bagh-i Buland, 28–29, 39
Baḥram, 75, 88
Barlas (tribe), 102–3
battles: of Panipat 18; of Kashgar 27, 47; of Ush 150–51; of Yarkand 34, 45, 172–76, 202–3; battle cries 166, 170, 173, 175
Balkh, 21–22, 40
Baqiʿ Cemetary, 28
Barchuq, 120
Barmas, 75, 88
Bay, 202
Bayan Aghacha, 100, 141
Bayazid Bistami, 59
Bay Döbä, 175
Bay Polad, 192–94, 196
Bedil (poet), 76
Bekhud (poet), 76
Beshkerem, 106, 143–44, 178
Bibicha Kashghari, 19
Bibi Malika Kasani, 19

Black Mountaineers (*Qarataghlïq*), 161; conflict with White Mountaineers xxi–xxi
Brahman, 33–34
Bukhara, 23, 27, 40, 59–60
Bulghar, 25
Buraq, 74
Buzurjmihr, 174

Chaghatayid Dynasty, ix, xi
charity: almsgiving 86, 130, 138, 197, 222; endowment 86. See also *waqf*
China, 33, 133–34, 180; capital of 136, 147; emperor of 97, 104, 134, 147, 163, 176, 188, 192
Chinese, 33, 146, 159, 170, 178, 184, 186; army 134–36, 147, 149, 162, 180–81, 183, 202; envoy 161, 178
Chongbaghish (Kirghiz), 145, 172, 202
Commentary on Nasafi's Aqa'id, 186
court merchant (*bāzargān* etc.), 48, 188, 191

Dabachi, 95, 133–34, 136, 147, 180
Dahbid, 28, 39
Dajjal, 175
Danjin Jaisang, 147, 178
Darvish Bakavul, 99–100, 105, 127–28, 155, 179, 183
Darvish Muḥammad Quzi, 18–19
Daulat Bagh, 95
Daulat Khoja, 146
deputies (*khulafā*), xi, xvii, 17, 21, 28–32, 35–37, 59–60, 219
dervish: *see* Sufi
Dolan, 146, 178, 202
dream visions, 9, 11, 15–16, 20, 24–27, 32, 39, 60, 63–65, 107
Dughlat tribe, xxi

Egypt, 113
Erke Khan, 50, 87, 240n98

Faridun, 90
Farman Quli Beg, 146, 178
Faṭima Zahra, 57, 138
fatwá, 61, 83, 187
Fayżabad, 36, 95–96, 106, 151, 178
Ferghana, 14
firmly grounded scholars, 56
friends of God (*avliyāʿ*), xiv, 58, 60, 62. *See also* saints

Gabriel, 66, 219
Galdan-Tseren, 52, 244n162

Ganzhou, 25
Ghalcha Bi, 128
Ghazi Beg, 104, 108–12, 115–19, 122–25, 140, 163, 165–66, 176–77, 179, 188–89, 195, 198–206, 209–10, 216
Ghiyas̱ Khoja, 188–89, 198
Giyumars, 201
Golden Gate, 44
Golden Palace, 99–100, 160
Golden Shrine (Altunluq), xxi, 29, 32, 35–36, 39, 54, 87, 138, 197

hadith, 2, 3, 39, 46, 55–58, 67, 71, 74, 81–82, 86, 106–7, 110, 142, 145, 150, 187 198–99, 216
Ḥafiẓ: quotations from 26, 56, 66, 101, 163
Ḥafiẓ Niẓam, 21, 23
Haftyak, 7
hajj pilgrimage, 72, 75–76, 163–64, 184–85
Ḥakim Mirza, 172, 178, 202
Halima Banu, 99
Hamdam Bakavul, 179
Ḥasan Fażlullah Khoja, 133
Ḥasan of Basra, 81
Hashim Sulṭan (Kazakh), 44–46
Ḥatim (al-Ṭay), 75, 88, 222
Ḥażrat Mazar, 41, 161
heaven: as arbiter of fate 149, 163, 183–84, 191, 197, 209; depicted as cupbearer, 82, 146; dome of 53, 81, 121; injustice of of 99, 153–54; shoes of those destined for 20, 114
Hell, 81, 116, 131, 150, 185, 193, 223, 225; shoes of those destined for 20, 114
Herat, 174
Hidaya, 187
Hidayatullah: *see* Khoja Afaq
Ḥiṣar, 23
Holy Law (*sharīʿa*): on holy war and collaboration with infidels 123, 146, 164, 166, 185–87, 195, 201; observance and promotion of 4, 26, 31–32, 37, 41, 51, 53–54, 61, 83, 85, 94, 96, 120, 126, 164, 174, 222; saints and 69; sayyids and 71; schools of 69; sciences of the 56–58;
holy war, 116, 128, 183, 185, 196; merit of 91–92, 110, 121, 128, 145, 164, 166, 182, 185, 201; obligation to 120, 185–87; unfulfilled desire for 89, 121, 167–68
houris, 49, 133

Ibrahim (prophet), 12, 66
Ilyas Mir Akhur, 147, 178
Ilyas (prophet), 68
imam, 54, 61, 118; of the age 110, 142; as prayer leader 86, 138. *See also* individual imams
Imam Ali Riża, 57
Imam Ḥasan, 78, 82, 126
Imam Ḥusayn, 57, 78, 82, 126, 148, 166, 169–70, 173, 197
Imam-i Aʿẓam (Hanafi), 69–70
Imam Jaʿfar Ṣadiq, 57–58
Imam Muḥammad Baqir, 57
Imam Musa Kaẓim, 57
Imam Shafiʿi, 69
Imam Ṭaḥawi, 69–70
Imam Zayn al-Abidin, 57
Invisible Beings (*rijāl al-ghayb*), 12–13
India (Hindustan), 18–19, 43, 51, 215
infidels (unbelievers): conversion of 25, 121, 123; of Ju 33–34; submission to 53, 92, 110, 120–21, 127, 142, 144–45, 163–64, 185–86, 193
In Remembrance of the Saints: reception and study of xxiv–xxvi, manuscripts of xxvi–xxviii
Iran, 4, 19
Iraq, 18, 159
Iṣam Qarani, 68
Isfiduk, 21, 28
Ishan-i Kalan, 19, 21, 23–24, 29, 62
Isḥaqiyya, 147
Ismaʿil Beg b. Adil Shah Darkhan, 211
Ismaʿil Khan, 30, 32–35
Israfil, 66–67
Ivaż Khalifa, 179

Jamila Aghacha, 129
Jamshid, 90, 201
Jan Baqi Beg, 139
Jarub Beg [*or* Jarub Mirza], 44–46
jarghuchi, 50, 89
jaisang, 147, 209
Jirjis, 12
Ju, 33, 237n63
Judgment Day: as end of time 6, 11 ,14, 16–17, 24, 32, 38, 86, 110, 118, 174, 181, 193, 221, 225; as metaphor for cataclysmic event 30, 41, 53, 78, 114, 123, 156; portents of 73; trials of 48, 53, 80, 82, 87, 131, 142, 145, 148, 169, 207
Junghars, ix, xvi, 46. *See also* Qalmaqs

Kaaba, 38, 62, 67
Kalta Yaylaq, 103, 151
Karbala, 78, 82, 126, 148, 154, 164, 216, 225
Kasan, 8, 12, 19

Kashgar: author's patrons in 3–5; Khoja Isḥaq Vali in 24–26; Shaybanid attack on 27; Afaqiyya in 29–30, 32, 34, 41–44; Junghar campaign against 47; Khoja Yusuf ruling in 94–95, 120–21; Qalmaq envoy to 105–8; Khoja Abdullah's coronation in 139–42; capture by Khoja Burhan al-Din 156–62; army of 165–66, 171–72
Kashgaris, 47, 150, 158, 166, 171, 173
Kashmir, 33, 35
Kazakhs, 24, 44, 46, 159
Kelpin, 103
Kendir Pass, 8
Khalifa Ṣabir, 117
Khalifa Ubaydullah, 49
Khanim Padishah, 35, 41–43
Khan Khoja, 34
Khanqah Gate, 44
Khiżr, 59, 68, 70
Khoja Abd al-Khaliq b. Makhdum-i Aʿẓam, 19
Khoja Abd al-Khaliq Ghijduvani, 10, 40, 59–60
Khoja Abd al-Majid b. Akhund Mulla Taqi, 99, 102, 156–61
Khoja Abdullah b. Shadi, 57, 62
Khoja Abdullah b. Yusuf, 86, 90, 93–95, 99–100, 120, 131, 139–43, 151, 155–62, 165–66, 168, 175–76, 179, 183, 195, 198, 203, 206, 210–19
Khoja Abid b. Ubaydullah, 87, 194
Khoja Afaq (Hidayatullah), xi, xvi, xxii, 29–30, 32–35, 37–38, 40–41, 43, 46, 51, 62, 86, 135, 163
Khoja Aḥmad b. Ubaydullah, 87
Khoja Aḥmad b. Yaḥya, 43–44, 47, 135
Khoja Aḥmad Ṣiddiq, 59–60
Khoja Aḥmad Yasavi, 59
Khoja Ala al-Din, 10
Khoja Ali Ramitani, 59–60
Khoja Arif Rivgari, 59–60
Khoja Avliya-yi Kalan, 59–60
Khoja Ayyub b. Danyal, 54
Khoja Baha al-Din b. Makhdum-i Aʿẓam, 19
Khoja Baha al-Din Naqshband, xi, 10, 56, 59–62, 68
Khoja Burhan al-Din b. Aḥmad, xi, xxii–xxiv; release from Junghar captivity 135; advance on Ush 143; descriptions of court and retinue 146–48, 177–78; capture of Kashgar 154–55, 158, 161–62; capture of Yarkand 165–66, 202–3
Khoja Burhan al-Din (Erke Khoja) b. Yusuf, 91, 131, 179, 213–14
Khoja Danyal b. Abdullah, 33, 35, 37–40, 43–54, 57, 63
Khoja Dost b. Makhdum-i Aʿẓam, 19
Khoja Ḥasan b. Afaq (Ṣaḥibqiran), xxii, 41, 128, 155, 186
Khoja Ḥasan (Qiran Khoja), 114
Khoja Hashim b. Baha al-Din Dahbidi, 62
Khoja Inayat, 166, 196–97
Khoja Inayatullah, 179
Khoja Iṣam al-Din, 84
Khoja Isḥaq Vali b. Makhdum-i Aʿẓam, xi, xvi, 5, 19–29, 36, 39, 53, 62, 86, 119
Khoja Jahan b. Aḥmad, xi
Khoja Kamal Khujandi, 72–73
Khoja Laq Khalifa, 179
Khoja Mahdi b. Afaq, 41, 43
Khoja Maḥmud Faghnavi, 59–60
Khoja Maʿṣum, 192, 196
Khojam Naẓar Dorgha [*or* Khojam Naẓar Khoja], 179, 213–14, 219
Khoja Muḥammad Amin b. Makhdum-i Aʿẓam (Ishan-i Kalan), 19, 21, 23–24, 29, 62
Khoja Muḥammad b. Makhdum-i Aʿẓam, 19
Khoja Muḥammad Baba Sammasi, 59–60
Khoja Muḥammad Islam (Khoja Juybari), 23
Khoja Muḥammad Parsa, 61
Khoja Muḥammad Qasim, 20
Khoja Muḥammad Yusuf, xi, 29–32
Khoja Muʾmin, 86
Khoja Muʾmin b. Yusuf, 90, 92, 99–100, 131, 141–44, 148, 150–52, 154–55, 162, 165, 179, 183
Khojam Yar, 171, 203
Khoja Naṣir Ali (Sirhindi), 76–77
Khoja Naṣrullah, 140, 143, 179
Khoja Niẓam al-Din (Khamush) b. Danyal, 54, 83, 85–87, 94
Khoja Qasim Khalifa, 29, 237n54
Khoja Quṭb al-Din b. Isḥaq Vali, 29
Khoja Quṭb al-Din b. Yusuf, 90, 131, 179, 194
Khoja Sarimsaq b. Burhan al-Din, xxiii–xiv
Khoja Shadi b. Isḥaq Vali, 29–31, 57, 62
Khoja Shahbaz b. Isḥaq Vali, 29, 86
Khojash Khoja, 179
Khoja Shams al-Din b. Ubaydullah, 87–88, 116, 125, 127
Khoja Shuʿayb b. Abdullah, 33, 35, 37–38
Khojasi Beg, xxiii, 94–95, 97, 144–46, 244n157; capture of Dabachi 134; conspiracy to release Afaqiyya khojas 135
Khoja Ṣiddiq b. Yaʿqub (Futuḥi), 75–76, 78, 108, 115–19, 123–25, 129, 132, 179
Khoja Sulṭan Ibrahim b. Makhdum-i Aʿẓam, 19
Khoja Ubaydullah Aḥrar, 8–9, 18, 62, 84–85
Khoja Ubaydullah b. Danyal, 54, 57

Khoja Ubaydullah b. Shadi, 30, 33, 87
Khoja Umar, 124, 179
Khoja Yaḥya b. Afaq (Khan Khoja), 29, 34, 41–43, 135
Khoja Yaḥya b. Ubaydullah, 87–88, 108, 115, 137, 139–40, 142–44, 148, 150–52, 154, 165, 167, 176, 179, 218
Khoja Yaᶜqub (Khoja Jahan "Arshi") b. Danyal: childhood 40; virtues of 54–56, 71–75; genealogy 57, status as pole 63–66; poetry by 9, 76, 79–81, 171, as ruler of Yarkand 109–11, 122–24, 127, 165–66, 176–77, 179, 193–96; capture by enemies 115; resolve to go on hajj 163–64; surrender to Khoja Burhan al-Din 215–18
Khoja Yusuf b. Danyal, 5, 83, 85–86, 97–108, 115, 117–18, 123–24, 135–36, 142, 148–49, 154–57, 160, 168, 175, 179, 183, 213; childhood among the Junghars 48–51; appointed to Kashgar 54; escape from Ili 88–96; sons 90; declares Islamic rule in Kashgar 120–22; calls for support 127–28; illness 129–33; death 136–39
Khoja Yusuf (companion of Naqshband), 61
Khojagan, xv–xvi, 6, 10–11, 17–20, 31, 40, 52, 130. *See also* Naqshbandiyya, Path
Khosh Kifäk Beg, xxiii, 91–92, 95, 98, 102, 104, 106, 118, 143, 157, 244n155; flight from Kashgar 159–60
Khotan, xv, xxiii, 26, 29, 36, 51, 54, 87–88, 103–4, 116–20, 123–25, 127, 136, 139, 145, 179, 215
Khotanese, 118–19, 124–25, 127
Khudaberdi (governor of Kucha), 178
Khudayar Beg, 96–103
Khujand, 39–40, 43
Khung-Taiji, 49, 51–52, 240n96
Kimä, 96
Kirghiz, xi, xiv; 42, 91–93, 100–2, 104, 106, 116 –20, 121, 124–25, 127–28, 136–37, 139–40, 144–46, 148, 151–55, 157–60, 162, 171–73, 178, 181, 183–84, 198, 200, 202–3, 206–7, 209, 213, 219, 221; author's negative view of 151, 153, 157, 159; Isḥaq Vali's conversion of 24–25, 236n43; in Qing Xinjiang xxiii–xiv; raid on Yarkand 44–46
Kuhak River, 28

Laṭif Bakavul, 42

madrasa, 55, 75–76; Royal (in Kashgar) 72; White (in Yarkand) 87
Maḥmud's elephant, 113, 168
Makhdum-i Aᶜẓam, xi, xvi, xxvii, 6–21, 23–24, 28, 45, 57, 62, 157, 233n7
Makhdumzada, xi, 30–39
martyrdom, 34–35, 38, 42–43, 126, 150, 159, 175, 225; premonition of 77–78; rank of 78, 81–82, 92, 121, 126, 164, 166–67, 170, 183, 186, 201, 213; tradition of 148, 64, 182, 216. *See also* Imam Ḥasan, Imam Ḥusayn, Karbala
Maskhara Gate (Yarkand), 206
Ma<u>s</u>navi xix; quotations from 64, 109, 157, 206
Mawlana Ḥafiẓ al-Din, 59
Mawlana Luṭfullah Chusti, xxvii, 21, 23, 62
Mawlana Muḥammad Amin, 10
Mawlana Muḥammad Qanuni, 10
Mawlana Muḥammad Qażi, 8, 10–12, 14, 23
Mawlana Niẓam al-Din Khamush, 83–85
Mawlana (Mavlavi, i.e. Rumi), 41, 109
Mawlana Yaᶜqub Charkhi, 9, 62
Mecca, 17, 60, 183, 185, 219
medechi, 105, 139, 147, 245n166
Medina, 14–15, 17, 219
Michael, 66
mingbegi, 179
Mir Ivaż Beg, 146
Mir Noruz Khazinachi, 147, 178
Mir Sayyid Sharif Jurjani, 71
Mir Yusuf Sayyid, 19
mirab, 179
miracles, 13, 14, 24, 33, 30, 114, 154; capacity for 55–56; inflicting death 84–85; intervention in military affairs 18, 27; restoring dead to life 24
Mirza Abd al-Laṭif, 85
Mirza Abd al-Manaf, 179
Mirza Abd al-Wahhab, 170, 179, 215
Mirza Danyal (Barlas), xix, 103
Mirza Hadi Beg, xix, xxi, 85, 232n3
Mirza Ḥaydar, b. Mirza Danyal xix, 103
Mirza Ḥaydar Khan b. Shihab al-Din, 219
Mirza Murad Beg, 168, 179
Mirza Niyaz Beg, 179
Mirza Niyaz Beg (governor of Qarghaliq), 146
Mirza Qasim Beg, 129, 169, 179
Mirza Shah Murad Beg, 179
Mirza Sherdagh Beg, 170, 179
Mirza Ulugh Beg (Timurid), 84–85
Mirza U<u>s</u>man Beg, xvi, xix, xxi–xxiv, 3, 169, 232n2
Mirza Zulfiqar Beg, 179
Moghulistan, 4, 29, 51, 127, 176
Moghuls, 12
Möngke Bi, 139, 247n203

Moses, 66, 208
Mount Qaf, 133, 175
mountain men (*taghlïq*), 173, 188, 202, 213, 215, 217
Mubarak Shah, 98–99
Muḥammad Abdullah Bakavul, 112, 115, 124, 179, 215
Muḥammad Emin Beg b. Khudayar, 146, 178
Muḥammad Emin Beg b. Qalandar, 43
Muḥammad Emin Khan, 35, 43, 46–47
Muḥammadi Mir Akhur, 115, 117–18, 179
Muḥammad Khan [*or* Muḥammad Sulṭan], 25–28
Muḥammad (prophet), xi, 55, 57, 82; exemplary qualities of 16, 55–56, 67–68, 75, 81, 185; death 138; flight from Mecca to Medina 219–220; initiator of holy law 4, 26, 32, 41, 69, 94, 126, 182; praise for 2, 125, 142; shrine of 13, 28; visions and signs of 23–24, 26, 64. *See also* hadith, sayyid
Muḥammad Ṣadiq Kashghari, xiii; biography and other works xviii–xxi
Muḥammad Vali Dorgha, 179
Muḥammad Yar Beg, 146, 189
Muḥarram Beg, 106–7, 144, 148, 178
Muḥiṭ, 71
Mulla Baqi Sartarash, 178
Mulla Barat Akhund, 147, 178
Mulla Ivaż Akhund, 147, 178
Mulla Maḥmud, 121, 139, 143, 156, 161
Mulla Muḥammad Kerek-yaragh, 179
Mulla Muḥammad Saḥaf, 21
Mulla Niyaz Akhund, 147
Mulla Qalam, 178
Mulla Qutlugh Akhund, 147
Mulla Sangin Khalifa, 25–26
Mulla Ṣiddiq, 192
Mulla Yoldash (companion of Khoja Abdullah), 213
Mulla Yoldash (companion of Khoja Burhan al-Din), 209
Mundi Ṣufi, 147, 173, 178
Musa Beg, 146, 178
Muṣliḥ al-Din Khujandi, 16, 40
Muẓaffar Beg b. Khojasi, 146
Muzart Pass, 94–95

Nafaḥat al-Uns, 60, 84
Naqshbandiyya, xi, xv, 10. *See also* Khojagan
Nayman (Kirghiz), 145
New Year's Day (Noruz), 111, 123
Nishtar Niyaz Ṣufi, 147, 178
Niyaz Beg, 179
Niyaz Beg (deputy governor of Yarkand), 104, 111, 176–77, 179, 189–91
Niyaz Beg (governor of Artush), 97
Niyaz Beg (governor of Fayżabad), 106–7, 178–79
Niyaz Ṣufi, 173
Noah, 3, 141
Nur al-Din Sulṭan, 29
Nushirvan, 4, 75, 88, 90, 174, 222

Ottuz Oghul (Kirghiz), 145
Özgand, 14, 16

Padishah Khoja (title), 43, 142, 151
Paradise: bird of 18, 63; entry into 28, 82, 142; for infidels 82, 216; rewards of 82; tree of (Lote Tree) 63, 213. *See also* houris
parvanachi, 179
Path, xv, 6, 29, 33, 41, 55–62, 126, 173, 223–224; of the Khojagan 10–11, 17, 19, 31; Straight Path 142
Pharaoh, 81, 208–9
Pir Muḥammad Khan, 22–23
Plato, 75, 90
Polad Quzi Khalifa, 179
pole (*quṭb*), xvi, 5, 19, 29, 41, 59, 63, 90; appointment of Khoja Yaʿqub as 63–65; doctrine of 66–68; Makhdumzada claim to position 16–17; of the poles 17–18, 68, 79. *See also* saints

Qabaq Atqu Gate, 117, 198, 203
Qalandar Beg, 43
Qalmaqs: civil war among 133–34; court in Ili 50; dress 91, 119; as enemy of Muslims 42, 159, 186, 222; language 118; merchants 111, 121; Muslims loyal to 97, 101, 103, 111, 139, 192, 194; rule in Tarim Basin 46–47, 51, 53, 89, 98, 122, 186; support for Khoja Afaq 34–35, 41; support for Khoja Burhan al-Din 147–50, 161–62, 173–76, 180–81, 183–84, 202, 209, 213
Qaraqir, 100, 117, 124
qarakhan (Junghar garrison), 44, 98, 111, 122 147, 239n90
Qarazangi Beg, 44–45
Qarghaliq, 146, 206
Qasim b. Muḥammad b. Abu Bakr, 58
Qipchaq (Kirghiz), 92, 100, 104, 116, 145, 172, 178, 202
Qubad Mirza [*or* Qubad Bi] (Bahadur Bi), 128, 145, 155–58, 162, 172, 175, 178, 183, 202, 246n185

Quran, 7, 21, 57–58, 123; recitation of 5, 54, 81, 83, 88, 130, 139–40, 156, 160, 221; opening verse (*fātiḥa*) 25, 30, 121, 132, 219; Sura Ya Sin 137; use in oath-taking 119, 122, 153, 164, 177, 198–99, 204–5, 215
Quranic verses, 1, 2, 6, 12, 15, 17, 30, 32, 35, 38, 41, 53, 56–57, 67, 70, 78, 81–82, 86–87, 110, 112, 115, 120, 125–26, 137, 140–41, 175, 185, 202, 213, 217, 220
Qushchi (Kirghiz), 128, 172, 178, 202
Quzghun, 188–89

Raḥima Aghacha, xix, 5, 169
Raḥman Quli Beg (Taghliq), 146, 162, 173, 178, 209, 215, 217
Raḥmati Ṣufi, 147, 178
Rashahat Ayn al-Ḥayat, 84
River Gate (Kashgar), 99, 106, 160
Rustam, 80, 90, 113, 167–70, 183, 197, 210–11
Rustam Sulṭan (Shaybanid), 27

Saᶜadat Beg, 146, 178
Ṣabir Kerek-yaragh, 179, 219
Saᶜd al-Din Taftazani, 186
Ṣaʾib Tabrizi: quotations from 58, 83, 147, 204
saints: hierarchy of in Sufism 66–67; as intercessors 82, 105, 191; Muḥammad as chief of 2, 24, 219; in reference to Makhdumzadas xv, 5–6, 197, 208, 225; signs of sainthood 68–70. *See also* friends of God, pole (*quṭb*)
Ṣaliḥ Khalifa, 179, 184, 189
Salman Fars, 58
salt (as metaphor for patronage), 106, 158, 176–77, 193
Sam, 90, 113, 167, 183
samāᶜ (mystical dance), 38, 115
Samarqand, xi, 10, 18, 26–28, 39–40, 84
Sanju, 37
Saqal Akhund [*or* Saqal Ṣufi], 147, 178
sāqīnāma, xvii, 168–70, 173–75, 207–9
Sariq Beg Yasavul, 147, 173, 178, 209, 215, 217
Sariq Qalpaq (Kirghiz), 120, 145
Sarts, 46
Sart Beg, 146
Satan, 98, 151, 156
Sayram, 146, 178, 202
sayyid descent: of the khojas xi, 57; proof of 69–71; honor of 148, 187, 215, 219
Sayyid Aḥmad, 57
Sayyid Beg, 43
Sayyid Burhan al-Din, 57
Sayyid Burhan al-Din (Qilich), 15–17, 57
Sayyid Jalal al-Din, 57
Sayyid Kamal al-Din Majnun, 14–15, 57
Sayyid Khoja, 57
Sayyid Muḥammad, 57
sayyids of Kasan, 19
Sayyid Ṭalib, 57
Sengge, 34
Seven Sultans, 14, 234n20
Seven Cities (Yettishahr), 51, 86, 110
shadiyana (drumbeat), 46, 151, 161, 190, 209, 240n92
Shah Beg, 98–99
Shah Ḥasan, 57
Shah Ḥusayn, 57
Shah Jaᶜfar Beg, 44–45
Shah Maḥmud Sulṭan b. Pir Muḥammad, 22
Shah Yaᶜqub Beg, 179
Shahyar, 202
Shah Żiya al-Din Khalifa, 179
Shara Muḥammad Emin Beg, 146, 178, 189, 209
Sharas (Qalmaqs), 121, 245n179
Sharifa Aghacha, 210
Shawkat (poet), 76
Shaykh Abu Bakr Qaffal Shashi, 62
Shaykh Abu l-Ḥasan Kharaqani, 59
Shaykh Abu l-Qasim Gurgani, 59
Shaykh Abu Yusuf Hamadani, 59
Shaykh Sarmadi Khoja Ali Farmadi, 59
Shaykhs of the Turks, 56
Shihab al-Din Bakavul, 115–16, 124, 170, 179, 206, 215, 219
shrines: of Alp Ata 26; of Bukhara 60; of Ḥasan Fażlullah Khoja 133; of Isḥaq Vali 28, 39; Makhdum-i Aᶜzam 28–29, 39; of Muṣliḥ al-Din Khujandi 40; of the Prophet 14; of Shahbaz in Aqsu 29, 86. *See also* Golden Shrine, Ḥażrat Mazar, Yaghdu
Six Cities (Altishahr), 200
Sögät Mountain, 121
spiritual lineage (*nisbat*), 14, 21, 23, 55–63
spiritual poverty, 16, 80–81
spiritual retreat, 10–11, 20, 210
states of being (*ḥāl*), 11, 17, 54, 59
Ṣufi Khoja, 140–41, 179
Sufi lodge (*khānqāh*), xxi, 36
Ṣufi Mirza, 172, 178, 183, 202
Sufis: categories of 67; dervishes 13, 15, 18, 21, 31, 55, 61, 109, 154; fanatics, ecstatics (*dīvāna*) 35, 38–39, 42–43, 147, in retinue of Khoja Burhan al-Din 147, 161–62, 178
Sufism, xiv–xv
Sulayman (prophet), 72, 154, 174
Sulṭan Beg, 179

Sulṭan Ḥusayn Mirza (Timurid), 55, 174
Sulṭan Ibrahim (b. Adham), 16
Sulṭan Ibrahim (Lodi), 18
Sulṭan Ilek Mażi, 14–16
Sulṭan Khoja, 192–93, 196
Sulṭan Satuq Bughra Khan (Qarakhanid), xv, 19, 234n29
Syria, 159

Tagh Boyi, 191
Tahamtan, 168
Tahmuras, 168
tangga, 27, 35, 51
tarkhan, 150, 189
Tarkhan Niyaz, 139
Tashkent, 8–9, 12
Tashmaliq, xxiv
tavakkul (trust in God), xvii, 109, 115, 154, 165, 196, 199
taxation: *baj* and *kharaj* 53, 103–4, 180; poll tax (*jizya*) 51, 134, 180,
tazkira, xiv–xv, 6
Taz Qipchaq (Kirghiz), 202
Temür Khan, 50, 86, 121
Tiläk Bahadur, 179
Tiznab River, 38–39
Tokhta Beg, 144, 148
Tokhta Khoja, 179, 219
Torghut (Qalmaqs), 51
Turkistan, 4
Twenty-Four Risalas (of Makhdum-i Aᶜẓam), 19
Toqquz Qipchaq (Kirghiz), 145, 202
Toqquzkent, 36
Tuman River, 158, 160
Tuqal Mirza, 101, 171, 179, 203
Turan, 4, 19
Turfan, xx–xxi, 35, 172
Tursun Qashqa, 179
Turumtai Hiya, 147, 178
Tüshük Tagh, 43, 239n83

Ubaydullah b. Abdullah Afżal, 57
Ufal Niyaz Beg, 179
Ulugh Aylam, 85
Ulugh Azizim, 132–33
Umar Beg, 146, 178
Umar (caliph), 126
Umar Mirza [*or* Umar Bi] (Qipchaq), 92, 116, 124–25, 127, 139, 144, 152, 172, 178, 183, 202, 244n156
Urus Mirza, 171, 179, 203
Ush (Uchturfan), 94, 105, 129, 134–36, 139, 143–44, 146–47, 150–52, 154, 157–58, 162, 165, 172, 176, 183, 202
ushaq, 117, 245n176
Ushtur Khalifa, 26, 29–30, 170
U̱sman, 173
U̱sman (caliph), 28, 126
Uways Qarani, 68

vizier, 127, 145, 173–74, 188, 192

waqf (pious endowments), xi, xvii, xxi, 28, 36, 87
Wanya, 106
White Turbans, 49–50, 135

Yaghdu, 32, 41. *See also* Ḥażrat Mazar
Yangiḥiṣar, 29, 32, 139, 145, 172, 202, 209, 215
Yarkand: Khoja Afaq's rule in 34–36, 39–41; Aqbash Khan's capture of 43; Hashim Sultan in 44–46; Junghar campaign against 46–47; Khoja Jahan ruling in 56, 122–24; Qalmaq envoy to 109–15; Kirghiz surrounding 152–53; siege and capture of 172–76, 202–3; Khoja Ḥasan's raid on 186
Yarkandis, 150, 152, 179
Yazid (Umayyad caliph), 82
Yolbars Khan, 29–30
Yopurgha, 131
Yusuf Beg, 146, 178
Yusuf Qadir Khan (Qarakhanid), 118

Zakariya, 12
Zarafshan (Yarkand) River, 116, 181, 207, 211
ẕikr (meditation, remembrance), 41, 59–60
Zubayda Begim (Qarghabash Khoja), 133
Zuhra Begim (Sariq Babaqim), 133

TRANSLATIONS FROM THE ASIAN CLASSICS

Major Plays of Chikamatsu, tr. Donald Keene 1961

Four Major Plays of Chikamatsu, tr. Donald Keene. Paperback ed. only. 1961; rev. ed. 1997

Records of the Grand Historian of China, translated from the Shih chi of Ssu-ma Ch'ien, tr. Burton Watson, 2 vols. 1961

Instructions for Practical Living and Other Neo-Confucian Writings by Wang Yang-ming, tr. Wing-tsit Chan 1963

Hsün Tzu: Basic Writings, tr. Burton Watson, paperback ed. only. 1963; rev. ed. 1996

Chuang Tzu: Basic Writings, tr. Burton Watson, paperback ed. only. 1964; rev. ed. 1996

The Mahābhārata, tr. Chakravarthi V. Narasimhan. Also in paperback ed. 1965; rev. ed. 1997

The Manyōshū, Nippon Gakujutsu Shinkōkai edition 1965

Su Tung-p'o: Selections from a Sung Dynasty Poet, tr. Burton Watson. Also in paperback ed. 1965

Bhartrihari: Poems, tr. Barbara Stoler Miller. Also in paperback ed. 1967

Basic Writings of Mo Tzu, Hsün Tzu, and Han Fei Tzu, tr. Burton Watson. Also in separate paperback eds. 1967

The Awakening of Faith, Attributed to Aśvaghosha, tr. Yoshito S. Hakeda. Also in paperback ed. 1967

Reflections on Things at Hand: The Neo-Confucian Anthology, comp. Chu Hsi and Lü Tsu-ch'ien, tr. Wing-tsit Chan 1967

The Platform Sutra of the Sixth Patriarch, tr. Philip B. Yampolsky. Also in paperback ed. 1967

Essays in Idleness: The Tsurezuregusa of Kenkō, tr. Donald Keene. Also in paperback ed. 1967

The Pillow Book of Sei Shōnagon, tr. Ivan Morris, 2 vols. 1967

Two Plays of Ancient India: The Little Clay Cart and the Minister's Seal, tr. J. A. B. van Buitenen 1968

The Complete Works of Chuang Tzu, tr. Burton Watson 1968

The Romance of the Western Chamber (Hsi Hsiang Chi), tr. S. I. Hsiung. Also in paperback ed. 1968

The Manyōshū, Nippon Gakujutsu Shinkōkai edition. Paperback ed. only. 1969

Records of the Historian: Chapters from the Shih chi of Ssu-ma Ch'ien, tr. Burton Watson. Paperback ed. only. 1969

Cold Mountain: 100 Poems by the T'ang Poet Han-shan, tr. Burton Watson. Also in paperback ed. 1970

Twenty Plays of the Nō Theatre, ed. Donald Keene. Also in paperback ed. 1970

Chūshingura: The Treasury of Loyal Retainers, tr. Donald Keene. Also in paperback ed. 1971; rev. ed. 1997

The Zen Master Hakuin: Selected Writings, tr. Philip B. Yampolsky 1971

Chinese Rhyme-Prose: Poems in the Fu Form from the Han and Six Dynasties Periods, tr. Burton Watson. Also in paperback ed. 1971

Kūkai: Major Works, tr. Yoshito S. Hakeda. Also in paperback ed. 1972

The Old Man Who Does as He Pleases: Selections from the Poetry and Prose of Lu Yu, tr. Burton Watson 1973

The Lion's Roar of Queen Śrīmālā, tr. Alex and Hideko Wayman 1974

Courtier and Commoner in Ancient China: Selections from the History of the Former Han by Pan Ku, tr. Burton Watson. Also in paperback ed. 1974

Japanese Literature in Chinese, vol. 1: *Poetry and Prose in Chinese by Japanese Writers of the Early Period*, tr. Burton Watson 1975

Japanese Literature in Chinese, vol. 2: *Poetry and Prose in Chinese by Japanese Writers of the Later Period*, tr. Burton Watson 1976

Love Song of the Dark Lord: Jayadeva's Gītagovinda, tr. Barbara Stoler Miller. Also in paperback ed. Cloth ed. includes critical text of the Sanskrit. 1977; rev. ed. 1997

Ryōkan: Zen Monk-Poet of Japan, tr. Burton Watson 1977

Calming the Mind and Discerning the Real: From the Lam rim chen mo of Tsoṇ-kha-pa, tr. Alex Wayman 1978

The Hermit and the Love-Thief: Sanskrit Poems of Bhartrihari and Bilhaṇa, tr. Barbara Stoler Miller 1978

The Lute: Kao Ming's P'i-p'a chi, tr. Jean Mulligan. Also in paperback ed. 1980

A Chronicle of Gods and Sovereigns: Jinnō Shōtōki of Kitabatake Chikafusa, tr. H. Paul Varley 1980

Among the Flowers: The Hua-chien chi, tr. Lois Fusek 1982

Grass Hill: Poems and Prose by the Japanese Monk Gensei, tr. Burton Watson 1983

Doctors, Diviners, and Magicians of Ancient China: Biographies of Fang-shih, tr. Kenneth J. DeWoskin. Also in paperback ed. 1983

Theater of Memory: The Plays of Kālidāsa, ed. Barbara Stoler Miller. Also in paperback ed. 1984

The Columbia Book of Chinese Poetry: From Early Times to the Thirteenth Century, ed. and tr. Burton Watson. Also in paperback ed. 1984

Poems of Love and War: From the Eight Anthologies and the Ten Long Poems of Classical Tamil, tr. A. K. Ramanujan. Also in paperback ed. 1985

The Bhagavad Gita: Krishna's Counsel in Time of War, tr. Barbara Stoler Miller 1986

The Columbia Book of Later Chinese Poetry, ed. and tr. Jonathan Chaves. Also in paperback ed. 1986

The Tso Chuan: Selections from China's Oldest Narrative History, tr. Burton Watson 1989

Waiting for the Wind: Thirty-Six Poets of Japan's Late Medieval Age, tr. Steven Carter 1989

Selected Writings of Nichiren, ed. Philip B. Yampolsky 1990

Saigyō, Poems of a Mountain Home, tr. Burton Watson 1990

The Book of Lieh Tzu: A Classic of the Tao, tr. A. C. Graham. Morningside ed. 1990

The Tale of an Anklet: An Epic of South India—The Cilappatikāram of Iḷaṅkō Aṭikaḷ, tr. R. Parthasarathy 1993

Waiting for the Dawn: A Plan for the Prince, tr. with introduction by Wm. Theodore de Bary 1993

Yoshitsune and the Thousand Cherry Trees: A Masterpiece of the Eighteenth-Century Japanese Puppet Theater, tr., annotated, and with introduction by Stanleigh H. Jones Jr. 1993

The Lotus Sutra, tr. Burton Watson. Also in paperback ed. 1993

The Classic of Changes: A New Translation of the I Ching as Interpreted by Wang Bi, tr. Richard John Lynn 1994

Beyond Spring: Tz'u Poems of the Sung Dynasty, tr. Julie Landau 1994

The Columbia Anthology of Traditional Chinese Literature, ed. Victor H. Mair 1994

Scenes for Mandarins: The Elite Theater of the Ming, tr. Cyril Birch 1995

Letters of Nichiren, ed. Philip B. Yampolsky; tr. Burton Watson et al. 1996

Unforgotten Dreams: Poems by the Zen Monk Shōtetsu, tr. Steven D. Carter 1997

The Vimalakirti Sutra, tr. Burton Watson 1997

Japanese and Chinese Poems to Sing: The Wakan rōei shū, tr. J. Thomas Rimer and Jonathan Chaves 1997

Breeze Through Bamboo: Kanshi of Ema Saikō, tr. Hiroaki Sato 1998

A Tower for the Summer Heat, by Li Yu, tr. Patrick Hanan 1998

Traditional Japanese Theater: An Anthology of Plays, by Karen Brazell 1998

The Original Analects: Sayings of Confucius and His Successors (0479–0249), by E. Bruce Brooks and A. Taeko Brooks 1998

The Classic of the Way and Virtue: A New Translation of the Tao-te ching of Laozi as Interpreted by Wang Bi, tr. Richard John Lynn 1999

The Four Hundred Songs of War and Wisdom: An Anthology of Poems from Classical Tamil, The Puṟanāṉūṟu, ed. and tr. George L. Hart and Hank Heifetz 1999

Original Tao: Inward Training (Nei-yeh) *and the Foundations of Taoist Mysticism*, by Harold D. Roth 1999

Po Chü-i: Selected Poems, tr. Burton Watson 2000

Lao Tzu's Tao Te Ching: *A Translation of the Startling New Documents Found at Guodian*, by Robert G. Henricks 2000

The Shorter Columbia Anthology of Traditional Chinese Literature, ed. Victor H. Mair 2000

Mistress and Maid (Jiaohongji), by Meng Chengshun, tr. Cyril Birch 2001

Chikamatsu: Five Late Plays, tr. and ed. C. Andrew Gerstle 2001

The Essential Lotus: Selections from the Lotus Sutra, tr. Burton Watson 2002

Early Modern Japanese Literature: An Anthology, 1600–1900, ed. Haruo Shirane 2002; abridged 2008

The Columbia Anthology of Traditional Korean Poetry, ed. Peter H. Lee 2002

The Sound of the Kiss, or The Story That Must Never Be Told: Pingali Suranna's Kalapurnodayamu, tr. Vecheru Narayana Rao and David Shulman 2003

The Selected Poems of Du Fu, tr. Burton Watson 2003

Far Beyond the Field: Haiku by Japanese Women, tr. Makoto Ueda 2003

Just Living: Poems and Prose by the Japanese Monk Tonna, ed. and tr. Steven D. Carter 2003

Han Feizi: Basic Writings, tr. Burton Watson 2003

Mozi: Basic Writings, tr. Burton Watson 2003

Xunzi: Basic Writings, tr. Burton Watson 2003

Zhuangzi: Basic Writings, tr. Burton Watson 2003

The Awakening of Faith, Attributed to Aśvaghosha, tr. Yoshito S. Hakeda, introduction by Ryūichi Abé 2005

The Tales of the Heike, tr. Burton Watson, ed. Haruo Shirane 2006

Tales of Moonlight and Rain, by Ueda Akinari, tr. with introduction by Anthony H. Chambers 2007

Traditional Japanese Literature: An Anthology, Beginnings to 1600, ed. Haruo Shirane 2007

The Philosophy of Qi, by Kaibara Ekken, tr. Mary Evelyn Tucker 2007

The Analects of Confucius, tr. Burton Watson 2007

The Art of War: Sun Zi's Military Methods, tr. Victor Mair 2007

One Hundred Poets, One Poem Each: A Translation of the Ogura Hyakunin Isshu, tr. Peter McMillan 2008

Zeami: Performance Notes, tr. Tom Hare 2008*Zongmi on Chan*, tr. Jeffrey Lyle Broughton 2009

Scripture of the Lotus Blossom of the Fine Dharma, rev. ed., tr. Leon Hurvitz, preface and introduction by Stephen R. Teiser 2009

Mencius, tr. Irene Bloom, ed. with an introduction by Philip J. Ivanhoe 2009

Clouds Thick, Whereabouts Unknown: Poems by Zen Monks of China, Charles Egan 2010

The Mozi: A Complete Translation, tr. Ian Johnston 2010

The Huainanzi: A Guide to the Theory and Practice of Government in Early Han China, by Liu An, tr. and ed. John S. Major, Sarah A. Queen, Andrew Seth Meyer, and Harold D. Roth, with Michael Puett and Judson Murray 2010

The Demon at Agi Bridge and Other Japanese Tales, tr. Burton Watson, ed. with introduction by Haruo Shirane 2011

Haiku Before Haiku: From the Renga Masters to Bashō, tr. with introduction by Steven D. Carter 2011

The Columbia Anthology of Chinese Folk and Popular Literature, ed. Victor H. Mair and Mark Bender 2011

Tamil Love Poetry: The Five Hundred Short Poems of the Aiṅkuṟunūṟu, tr. and ed. Martha Ann Selby 2011

The Teachings of Master Wuzhu: Zen and Religion of No-Religion, by Wendi L. Adamek 2011

The Essential Huainanzi, by Liu An, tr. and ed. John S. Major, Sarah A. Queen, Andrew Seth Meyer, and Harold D. Roth 2012

The Dao of the Military: Liu An's Art of War, tr. Andrew Seth Meyer 2012

Unearthing the Changes: Recently Discovered Manuscripts of the Yi Jing (I Ching) *and Related Texts*, Edward L. Shaughnessy 2013

Record of Miraculous Events in Japan: The Nihon ryōiki, tr. Burton Watson 2013

The Complete Works of Zhuangzi, tr. Burton Watson 2013

Lust, Commerce, and Corruption: An Account of What I Have Seen and Heard, *by an Edo Samurai*, tr. and ed. Mark Teeuwen and Kate Wildman Nakai with Miyazaki Fumiko, Anne Walthall, and John Breen 2014; abridged 2017

Exemplary Women of Early China: The Lienü zhuan *of Liu Xiang*, tr. Anne Behnke Kinney 2014

The Columbia Anthology of Yuan Drama, ed. C. T. Hsia, Wai-yee Li, and George Kao 2014*The Resurrected Skeleton: From Zhuangzi to Lu Xun*, by Wilt L. Idema 2014

The Sarashina Diary: *A Woman's Life in Eleventh-Century Japan*, by Sugawara no Takasue no Musume, tr. with introduction by Sonja Arntzen and Itō Moriyuki 2014; reader's edition 2018

The Kojiki*: An Account of Ancient Matters*, by Ō no Yasumaro, tr. Gustav Heldt 2014

The Orphan of Zhao *and Other Yuan Plays: The Earliest Known Versions*, tr. and introduced by Stephen H. West and Wilt L. Idema 2014

Luxuriant Gems of the Spring and Autumn, attributed to Dong Zhongshu, ed. and tr. Sarah A. Queen and John S. Major 2016

A Book to Burn and a Book to Keep (Hidden): Selected Writings, by Li Zhi, ed. and tr. Rivi Handler-Spitz, Pauline Lee, and Haun Saussy 2016

The Shenzi Fragments*: A Philosophical Analysis and Translation*, Eirik Lang Harris 2016

Record of Daily Knowledge *and* Poems and Essays*: Selections*, by Gu Yanwu, tr. and ed. Ian Johnston 2017

The Book of Lord Shang: Apologetics of State Power in Early China, by Shang Yang, ed. and tr. Yuri Pines 2017; abridged edition 2019

The Songs of Chu: An Ancient Anthology of Works by Qu Yuan and Others, ed. and tr. Gopal Sukhu 2017

Ghalib: Selected Poems and Letters, by Mirza Asadullah Khan Ghalib, tr. Frances W. Pritchett and Owen T. A. Cornwall 2017

Quelling the Demons' Revolt: A Novel from Ming China, attributed to Luo Guanzhong, tr. Patrick Hanan 2017

Erotic Poems from the Sanskrit: A New Translation, R. Parthasarathy 2017

The Book of Swindles: Selections from a Late Ming Collection, by Zhang Yingyu, tr. Christopher G. Rea and Bruce Rusk 2017

Monsters, Animals, and Other Worlds: A Collection of Short Medieval Japanese Tales, ed. R. Keller Kimbrough and Haruo Shirane 2018

Hidden and Visible Realms: Early Medieval Chinese Tales of the Supernatural and the Fantastic, compiled by Liu Yiqing, ed. and tr. Zhenjun Zhang 2018

A Couple of Soles: A Comic Play from Seventeenth-Century China, by Li Yu, tr. Jing Shen and Robert E. Hegel 2019

The Original Meaning of the Yijing*: Commentary on the* Scripture of Change, by Zhu Xi, tr. and ed. Joseph A. Adler 2019

Plum Shadows and Plank Bridge: Two Memoirs About Courtesans, Mao Xiang and Yu Huai, tr. and ed. Wai-yee Li 2020

The Diary of 1636: The Second Manchu Invasion of Korea, Na Man'gap, tr. with introduction by George Kallander 2020

Top Graduate Zhang Xie: The Earliest Extant Chinese Southern Play, tr. and introduced by Regina S. Llamas 2020

GPSR Authorized Representative: Easy Access System Europe, Mustamäe tee 50, 10621 Tallinn, Estonia, gpsr.requests@easproject.com

www.ingramcontent.com/pod-product-compliance
Lightning Source LLC
Chambersburg PA
CBHW021107110726
47900CB00007B/2078

* 9 7 8 0 2 3 1 1 9 8 1 9 6 *